Verbal Hygiene

In this book, Deborah Cameron takes a serious look at popular attitudes towards language and examines the practices by which people attempt to regulate its use. Instead of dismissing the practice of 'verbal hygiene' as a misguided and pernicious exercise, however, she argues that popular discourse about language and values serves an important purpose for those engaged in it.

A series of case studies deals with specific examples of verbal hygiene: the regulation of 'style' by editors, the teaching of English grammar in schools, the movements for and against so-called 'politically correct' language and the recent explosion of advice to women on how to speak more effectively. In each case she argues that verbal hygiene provides a way of making sense of linguistic phenomena, and that it represents a symbolic attempt to impose order on the social world.

Addressed to linguists, professional language-users of all kinds and to anyone interested in language and culture, *Verbal Hygiene* calls for legitimate concerns about language and value to be discussed, by experts and lay-speakers alike, in a rational and critical spirit.

Deborah Cameron teaches in the Programme in Literary Linguistics at Strathclyde University. She is the author of *Feminism and Linguistic Theory* (1985) and co-authored *Researching Language* (1992).

THE POLITICS OF LANGUAGE

Series editors: Tony Crowley, University of Manchester,
Talbot J. Taylor, College of William and Mary, Williamsburg,
Virginia

'In the lives of individuals and societies, language is a factor of greater importance than any other. For the study of language to remain solely the business of a handful of specialists would be a quite unacceptable state of affairs.'

Saussure

The Politics of Language Series covers the field of language and cultural theory and will publish radical and innovative texts in this area. In recent years the developments and advances in the study of language and cultural criticism have brought to the fore a new set of questions. The shift from purely formal, analytical approaches has created an interest in the role of language in the social, political and ideological realms and the series will seek to address these problems with a clear and informed approach. The intention is to gain recognition for the central role of language in individual and public life.

Verbal Hygiene

Deborah Cameron

London and New York

First published 1995
by Routledge
11 New Fetter Lane, London EC4P 4EE

Simultaneously published in the USA and Canada
by Routledge
29 West 35th Street, New York, NY 10001

Reprinted 1996

Routledge is an International Thomson Publishing company

Typeset in Baskerville by
J&L Composition Ltd, Filey, North Yorkshire
Printed and bound in Great Britain by
TJ Press (Padstow) Ltd, Padstow, Cornwall.

British Library Cataloguing in Publication Data
A catalogue record for this book is available from the British Library

Library of Congress Cataloguing in Publication Data
A catalogue record for this book is available from the Library of Congress

ISBN   0–415–10354–1 (hbk)
ISBN   0–415–10355–X (pbk)

Contents

Preface

'Traditional British pastimes are under threat', a Sunday newspaper warned recently.[1] It was not talking about the morris dancing or village cricket so beloved of the heritage industry, nor about such unremarkable suburban pursuits as gardening or home improvement. Rather it was alluding to the strange leisure activities of those who in Britain are disparagingly labelled 'anoraks' (the term refers to an unfashionable style of wind-proof jacket): hobbies such as trainspotting, matchstick model building, collecting old bricks and hoarding memorabilia from long-defunct television programmes.[2] The report did not in fact make much of a case for such pastimes being 'under threat'. On the contrary, it suggested that new and ever more esoteric pursuits are springing up all the time. The Muzzle Loaders Association is dead; long live the Street Lamp Interference Data Exchange!

How is all this relevant to a book entitled *Verbal Hygiene*? One rough definition of the phrase 'verbal hygiene' might be 'the urge to meddle in matters of language'.[3] Expressing that urge in a variety of ways is a traditional and perennially popular pastime – though it is not confined to either Britons or 'anoraks'. Language is, notoriously, something which engenders strong feelings: in Britain and the US we may not have academies to refine and regulate our language, but there is no shortage of enthusiasts who take a proprietary interest in it, dedicating some portion of their leisure time to the collection of unusual linguistic specimens, the tracking down of new or 'misused' expressions and the promotion of various language improvement schemes.

In the US, participants in these activities have a name. They are known as 'language mavens', as in 'Language mavens will have been keeping a close watch on such-and-such an expression', the formulaic opening of a thousand columns by William Safire in the *New York Times*. Even where the term *maven* is uncommon (as in Britain), the 'language maven' is a recognizable species. Recently I heard it lampooned in a BBC radio skit on 'the British Association of Pedants'. I heard a trailer for this item and made a note to tune in, assuming it would be a report on a real organization.

What do language mavens do? Stereotypically, they write letters to newspapers deploring various solecisms and warning of linguistic decline. The press is an important forum for language mavenry in general: it is striking how many newspapers run regular language columns and how much feature space they devote to linguistic topics. During a single week in May 1992, for example, *The Times* carried a long feature about authority and style, a leader about split infinitives and a sharp exchange of letters debating the use of lower-case type on motorway signs.

Newspapers are not, however, the only reading matter available to people who count language among their recreational interests. Railway station bookstalls and public libraries offer a rich variety of popular literature about language: books with titles like *The Joy of Lex*, *The Gentle Art of Verbal Self-Defense* and *Parliamo Glasgow* can stay in print for years. There is also a surprisingly large market for more serious (and expensive) works: when the travel writer Bill Bryson published a book on American English in 1994, he remarked that the idea had come from his publishers, who had noticed that while his travel books did poorly in the US, an earlier book on language had 'sold rather well'.[4] A profitable subgenre of publishing caters to the demand for linguistic arcana, ephemera and trivia with dictionaries of this and glossaries of that. As Roy Harris commented in 1983 when reviewing a clutch of these publications in the *London Review of Books*, 'modern lexicography is the last refuge of that mania for amassing curiosities and odd tit-bits of information which for so many centuries in Europe passed for "polite" learning' (1983:13).

The same interest in linguistic 'curiosities' is observable in broadcast media, especially the radio. Over the years, BBC radio has broadcast innumerable features and panel games whose basic premise is that ordinary people are fascinated by new, exotic or otherwise interesting words, and are always ready to hear about such perennial subjects as slang, swearing, dialects, etymology and linguistic change. I recently listened to a radio request show in which a listener asked for a repeat broadcast of the dramatic tie-breaker from the first British national dictation contest (apparently set to become an annual fixture) in which contestants had to spell *orectic*, *nescience* and *objicient*. The prize was a facsimile edition of Johnson's Dictionary.

Dedicated language mavens also have their own specialist outlets. Just as there are journals and fanzines for people whose interest is guns or comic books or *Star Trek*, so there are publications for readers whose interest is the English language – titles such as *English Today* and *Verbatim*, which (like gun magazines) may include contributions from professional experts, but are not read primarily by experts and cannot be classed as scholarly journals; they are more like the newsletters of hobbyist organizations. Recently, too, a forum has opened up where language mavens can communicate on a global scale. Anyone who has ever wandered through the electronic parallel universe of discussion groups and bulletin boards accessed through the Internet will know that many users regard cyberspace as an ideal arena for swapping linguistic trivia and debating matters of usage.[5]

Some people take their interest in language even further, by joining or forming a society. In Britain, national associations exist to promote plain English, the Queen's English, simplified spelling, the Scots language and Esperanto. Such organizations run the gamut from the ultra respectable mainstream to the esoteric fringe. In the latter category, for instance, there is a California-based group – the International Society for General Semantics – one of whose objectives is to abolish the English verb *to be* on the grounds that it encourages sloppy thinking. This sort of thing is the linguistic equivalent of associations devoted to the mysteries of UFOs and crop circles.

It should not be forgotten that some of the great linguistic projects of the past, whose fruits we now treat as monuments of scholarship, have owed their genesis or their execution to amateurs. *Roget's Thesaurus*, for example, was essentially the product of one man's utopian desire to bring order to the chaotic realm of meanings; Roget, a physician, turned to it after his retirement. Even that most respected and respectable reference work, *The New* (later *The Oxford*) *English Dictionary*, was much indebted to the labour of volunteers; its present-day editors are still bombarded with correspondence drawing attention to mistakes and omissions.

What these examples show (and they could be multiplied) is that there exists a whole popular culture of language, in which many people participate to some degree. Some are occasional and fairly passive consumers, a few are fanatical crusaders, and there is a continuum of interest and commitment between these two extremes. What is clear, however, is that a great many people care deeply about linguistic matters; they do not merely speak their language, they also speak copiously and passionately *about* it. This book is an attempt both to listen to what such people have to say, and to understand *why* they say the sorts of things they do.

Such a project may puzzle at least two groups of people (both, I hope, among the readers of *Verbal Hygiene*): on one hand those educated language-users who take much of the discourse I will be examining as obvious common sense; and on the other hand professional linguists, who find the same discourse obscure, deluded or simply uninteresting.[6] In taking up the subject of verbal hygiene I am, among other things, intervening in an ancient debate between experts and laypeople on the nature of language – what it is, what it should be, why it matters. Furthermore, I am making my intervention from a position that is to some extent critical of both camps.

The story of this book begins with an actual encounter between an 'expert' (me) and a layperson of strong opinions. One day in the mid-1980s, I happened to see a hand-lettered sign tied to a street lamp in London, announcing an exhibition about 'the use and abuse of language' at the Conway Hall. My curiosity aroused, I made my way there and found myself in a room full of newspaper cuttings stuck up on display boards with handwritten commentary. This exhibit, it turned out, had been mounted by a group of concerned citizens who had formed a society to combat the abuse of language. After a few minutes, one of these people approached me and engaged me in conversation. In the course of our talk, I mentioned I was a linguist. At this revelation he became visibly excited. 'A linguist!' he said. 'How marvellous! Do tell me what linguists are doing to combat the abuse of language.' Embarrassed, I made my excuses and left.

Anyone who knows anything about linguistics will understand why I was embarrassed. Linguists typically regard people like the man in the Conway Hall in much the same way that Aristotle regarded the sophist Prodicus, whose obsession with the 'correctness of names' he dismissed with the comment: 'this is the sort of thing said by men who love to lay down trivial laws, but have no care to say anything sensible.'[7] Whether or not we go along with Aristotle's opinion, there is clearly a vast gulf between what interests linguists about language and what seems to interest everyone else about it.

The linguistic questions laypeople care most about are questions of right and wrong, good and bad, 'the use and abuse of language'. In fact, it would not be overstating the case to say that most everyday discourse on language is above all evaluative discourse (even the language maven who simply collects unusual words has made a judgement that some words are more interesting than others). This overriding concern with value is the most significant characteristic that separates lay discourse on language from the expert discourse of linguists. As scientists, professional linguists aspire to objectivity and not to moral or aesthetic judgement. So when the man in the Conway Hall asked me what linguists were doing to combat the abuse of language, I did not know what to say. I could hardly give the textbook answer: 'Nothing. That isn't what linguistics is about. Linguistics is descriptive, not prescriptive.' I could not say this, or anything like it, not only because it would have been intolerably rude, but also because my interlocutor would not have understood it.

The incomprehension, it should be said, is mutual. Linguists not only disapprove of the forms that popular interest in language typically take; they find the whole phenomenon somewhat bewildering – much as a chemist might be puzzled by laypeople forming an association devoted to the merits of the inert gases. Reviewing Marina Yaguello's book *Les fous du langage* (translated as *Lunatic Lovers of Language* (1991)) in the Linguistic Society of America's journal *Language*, Robbins Burling can only marvel at the scale of the futile and unnecessary activity Yaguello's study of linguistic obsession reveals: 'it remains' he concludes, 'a striking fact that a wonderful amount of human effort has been invested in attempts to improve on the languages we already have' (Burling 1993:170). A striking fact, but clearly not one on which Burling feels he can shed much light. On the contrary, he seems to feel it would be better left in decent obscurity – a sentiment in the grand old tradition of experts berating laypeople for their ignorant and silly ideas.

But are the ideas in question uniformly silly, and even if they are, is it enough merely to wonder at them, and then move on to more serious matters? I am certainly not going to argue that popular concerns should dictate the scholar's agenda, or that linguists should jettison their principles for the sake of the man in the Conway Hall. But two things do concern me about the gulf between linguists and lay language-users.

One concern is that when linguists dismiss certain phenomena as unworthy of investigation they are failing to live up to their own descriptive ideals. Silly or not, value judgements on language form part of every competent speaker's linguistic repertoire. One of the things that people know how to do with words is to evaluate them, and I can see no principled justification for neglecting or deriding this metalinguistic ability. There is something paradoxical (as opposed to merely patronizing) about labelling ideas irrelevant and meaningless, when the people who hold the ideas patently regard them as relevant and meaningful. The beliefs about language that inform people's use of it arguably fall within the scope of what descriptive linguists ought to be able to give an account of.

The second thing that concerns me is the cultural and political effect of the polarization of the two perspectives, a polarization so extreme they seem unable to engage with one another at any level that is satisfactory to both. On those occasions where something to do with language becomes a matter of widespread public concern (as in the case of the English National School Curriculum, or the debate on 'political correctness'), the result is an exchange carried on very much at cross-purposes, if indeed there is any exchange at all.

On 5 July 1993 I tuned into BBC Radio 4's regular Monday morning cultural discussion programme *Start The Week* to hear my profession being denounced by Michael Dummett, Emeritus Professor of Logic at Oxford University. The topic of the day was the decline of English usage, and Professor Dummett was explaining that he attributed the current parlous state of the language to the widespread influence of ridiculous ideas peddled by professional linguists. Linguistics, he said, had proclaimed to the world that Language Does Not Matter and may therefore be abused with impunity.

The alleged decline of language was a commonplace of educated discourse centuries before the emergence of linguistic science, and holding linguists responsible for it is no longer very original either. What made me sit up and take notice on this occasion was the messenger rather than the message – not just because Professor Dummett is a distinguished academic, but because he is also noted as a liberal supporter of humanitarian causes. And yet on the subject of language, he found himself in agreement with the most philistine and reactionary anti-intellectuals.

The state of the language is among very few concerns capable of producing such improbable alliances between right and left, the inhabitants of the ivory tower and the denizens of the backwoods. It is a subject on which even people of undoubted intelligence, impeccable scholarly credentials and otherwise liberal opinions do not hesitate to talk illiberal and reactionary nonsense. It produces discourse in which opinions – not to say prejudices – do not merely substitute for facts, but are triumphantly paraded as somehow superior to facts; discourse in which it seems that what linguists *know* about language can simply be dismissed, because linguists do not *care* about language.

A linguist might justifiably retort that non-linguists have some funny ways of showing how much they care. Take, for example, a memorandum once issued by William Rees-Mogg when he was editor of *The Times*, which informed editorial staff that '"consensus" is an odious word. It is never to be used, and when it is used it should be spelt correctly'. There is, perhaps, an element of self-mockery about this, but it is nevertheless intended seriously, as an instruction to writers and sub-editors that the word *consensus* is to be avoided in *The Times* in future. And the remarkable thing is that where language is concerned, we see nothing odd in such whimsical injunctions.

Imagine, by contrast, the managing director of a large company issuing a memo informing staff that 'green is an odious colour. It is never to be worn, and when it is worn it should be of the correct shade'. This would surely be considered very odd indeed (just as, when the US presidential candidate Ross Perot pronounced an anathema on men wearing blue shirts, this was cited continually as proof of his eccentricity).

Of course, many organizations do operate dress codes for their staff – I am not claiming there is anything outlandish about prescription *per se* – but the rules are generally expected to be reasonable. Ross Perot is laughed at not for making rules, but for making what most people regard as downright silly rules. People may differ on whether it is right to insist, say, on men wearing ties or women wearing skirts, but normally the issues involved will at least be capable of being discussed. Even those who disagree with a policy will probably be able to imagine a rationale for it (e.g. 'clients expect it'), and will concentrate any resistance on demolishing that rationale. How, by contrast, does one begin to argue with the proposition that such-and-such a word is 'odious'? Why do we routinely allow discussions of language to proceed along these lines, treating pronouncements such as Rees-Mogg's as somehow endearing rather than preposterous?

One might say that at least linguists care enough about language to approach it in a spirit of rational enquiry, eschewing the cant, cliché and whimsy that passes for serious discussion among the Dummetts and Rees-Moggs. But one might also wonder whether linguists have thrown the baby out with the bathwater, by criticizing not just silly rules, but the entire evaluative discourse to which those rules belong. The typical response of a linguist faced with somebody like Dummett or Rees-Mogg is not merely to take issue with the specific (and, let us grant, often eccentric) value judgements he is proposing, but to deny that there could be *any* legitimate interest in questions of linguistic value. Rather than insist that discussions about the ethics and aesthetics of language use should be held to the same standard of rational argument that prevails on other subjects, linguists often appear to be suggesting it is a vulgar error to discuss such things at all.

I do not believe that a concern with language and value is by definition irrational and silly. I do believe, however, that the standard of public discourse on linguistic topics is lamentably low. Linguistic debates have a tendency to lapse sooner rather than later into irrationality and mystification, becoming ritual exchanges of received ideas that can only end in stalemate. What is needed to change this unproductive situation is direct critical engagement with the practices and ways of thinking that have produced it. But this requires some understanding of, and perhaps even some sympathy with, the concerns that lie behind it.

As a student, I learned that what lay behind misguided folklinguistic beliefs was simple ignorance and prejudice. Now, although I agree ignorance and prejudice play a part, I take people's continued allegiance to their beliefs (some misguided, some not, and very few of them 'simple') above all as a measure of their commitment to the discourse of value: a discourse with a moral dimension that goes far beyond its overt subject to touch on deep desires and fears. It is important for linguists to acknowledge that there is more to people's beliefs than the ignorance and prejudice that meet the eye; for in order to displace the most powerful ideology there is, namely common sense, it is necessary to grasp its hidden principles and to understand the reasons for its enduring popular appeal.

From Aristotle's day to ours, the 'wonderful amount of human effort . . . invested in attempts to improve on the languages we already have' has persistently been deemed unworthy of serious intellectual consideration. This book, by contrast, is dedicated to the proposition that before we either accept certain ideas about what makes language 'good' as profound and indisputable truths, or dismiss them out of hand as merely trivial and nonsensical, we should make some attempt to elucidate their logic.

Undertaken critically – as it should be, and in these pages, I hope, will be – this enterprise is not incompatible either with a concern about the way language is used or with a linguist's commitment to analyse how it works. If evaluative discourse is an important resource through which people make linguistic phenomena make sense, then there is every reason for linguists to concern ourselves with the beliefs and practices of Michael Dummett, William Rees-Mogg and the man in the Conway Hall: not in order that we may come to share their outlook on language (though I will argue that at some level we all do share it) but in order to understand it better.

Acknowledgements

I would like to express gratitude to the many people who offered me their assistance, co-operation and constructive criticism while I was researching and writing *Verbal Hygiene*. Some have asked to remain anonymous, but the fact that I cannot name them does not make me any less in their debt.

Among those I can name, I particularly want to thank the friends and colleagues on whom I have imposed most, and from whom I have learned most: Meryl Altman, Simon Frith, Keith Nightenhelser, Helen Reid-Thomas and the other members of the research group I have belonged to since 1986: Elizabeth Frazer, Penelope Harvey, Ben Rampton and Kay Richardson.

I am also grateful to those who have given me more specific assistance with some part of this project, by suggesting references, sharing their own work, passing on contacts, providing or granting access to otherwise inaccessible information, answering questions, participating in interviews or commenting on drafts. For their various contributions I thank Melanie Aspey, Jill Bourne, Janet Brand, Rebecca Bunting, Mary Crawford, Mary Dearborn, Lucinda DeWitt, Eamon Dyas, Christine Forde, Liz Hampson, Roy Harris, Linda Jackson, Simon Jenkins, Colleen Kennedy, Ruth King, Cheris Kramarae, Clare Lees, London Association for the Teaching of English, London Linguistics and Politics group, Dominic Lutyens, Jennifer MacKay, Marilyn Martin-Jones, Pete May, Mitch Merback, Sharon Millar, Sarah Pearsall, Euan Reid, Janine Scancarelli, Beverley Skeggs, Ken Turner and Anne Turvey. I also thank the audiences in Canada, England, Scotland and the US who heard me present work in progress and whose responses invariably helped me to improve it.

This book would not exist without the support of commissioning editors Claire L'Enfant and Julia Hall and series editors Tony Crowley and Talbot Taylor. Nor could I have met my deadlines without the help of my colleagues in the Programme in Literary Linguistics at Strathclyde University, who generously allowed me a leave of absence to write. Finally, and despite all textual indications to the contrary, I am pleased to acknowledge the contribution of those readers and editors who practised verbal hygiene on the manuscript of *Verbal Hygiene*, especially the copy editor Ann Grindrod. In a book on this subject it is especially appropriate to call attention to their work; but I will not depart from the time-honoured custom of reminding the reader that any errors which remain should be blamed entirely on me.

The author and publishers are grateful to News International plc for permission to quote from unpublished material relating to the style policy of *The Times* which is held in the company archive, and extracts from which appear on pages 57–63.

A much abbreviated version of Chapter 4 previously appeared as 'Words, words, words' in *The War of the Words: The Political Correctness Debate*, edited by Sarah Dunant (1994); and some parts of Chapter 5 were first published in *Applied Linguistics* (Cameron, 1994) as 'Verbal hygiene for women: linguistics misapplied?'. Thanks to Virago Press and Oxford University Press respectively for permission to reprint extracts from previously published material.

1 On verbal hygiene[1]

SINCE THE DAWN OF TIME . . .

In the 1983 edition of their popular introductory linguistics textbook, Victoria Fromkin and Robert Rodman reproduce a cartoon in which two disgruntled cavemen are attempting to converse. One says to the other: 'f w wnt t tlk rlly gd, w'll hv t nvnt vwls' (p. 47). For Fromkin and Rodman's purposes, this is a joke about phonetics. For my purposes it contains a deeper insight into language-using as a human activity: that humans do not just use language, they comment on the language they use. Frequently they find it wanting and, like the cavemen, propose to improve it.

Caveman jokes are of course jokes about us, the cavepeople's descendants; their underlying thesis is that some things just don't change. These two cavemen grumbling about the difficulty of speaking 'rlly gd' without vowels might well remind us of more contemporary archetypes: the stock figure the British call 'Disgusted of Tunbridge Wells', for instance, who writes letters to newspapers deploring this or that usage; or 'Mr Crank', a mild-mannered man who has devoted his leisure hours for twenty years to perfecting a new spelling system or arguing for the abolition of the verb *to be*.[2] The cavemen's own usage would incense at least one real-life linguistic busybody, Edward Koch, who as mayor of New York City once compiled a list of vulgar New Yorkisms he wanted city teachers to eliminate from children's speech, including the use of 'really good' as an adverbial. Practices like these, born of an urge to improve or 'clean up' language, exemplify the phenomenon I call *verbal hygiene*.

Of course, the humour of the caveman cartoon derives partly from the absurdity of supposing that anyone 'invented vowels'. I am not going to suggest that all characteristics of languages are produced by verbal hygiene, nor that all are equally amenable to being modified by it. I am interested, though, in the possibility that verbal hygiene in the abstract is as basic to the use of language as vowels are to its phonetic structure, and as deserving of serious study.

That is not to say that the particular verbal hygiene practices of Disgusted, Mr Crank and Mr Koch are somehow natural or inevitable, for clearly they are culturally constructed and specific. Yet I do believe that the essential precondition for these practices – normativity – *is* fundamental. It is part of what language-using is about, and not just something perversely 'grafted on'.

Perhaps it is significant that philosophers pondering the nature of human communication have so often produced their own versions of the caveman joke: the myth of the 'Ur language', the original Word, speech before the Fall or at the dawn of time. Wittgenstein, for example, in his *Philosophical Investigations* (1953), imagines a communication system used by builders in their construction work. The language consists of a few terse utterances such as 'Block!', or 'Slab!'. This is a 'language game' that serves the immediate purposes of the builders, but Wittgenstein points to its essential incompleteness. For one thing, it lacks the quality of creativity that linguists identify as a crucial 'design feature' of natural languages. Its repertoire of utterances is finite and extremely restricted. Another striking defect is the absence of any metalinguistic resources. There is no way for one builder to say to another, 'What do you mean "Block!" It's the slab you need', or 'Don't talk to me in that tone of voice'. This lack of reflexivity is both disabling and implausible. When one speaker's utterance invites another's response – and this too is presumably a design feature of human languages – the possibility must always be open that the response will focus on the norms for linguistic performance itself. As Mikhail Bakhtin noted in his own riff on the 'Ur-language' myth, no single speaker ever broke the prehistoric silence. There must have been at least two, in dialogue. Perhaps one of them criticized the other's choice of words.

Because language-using is paradigmatically a social, public act, talking (and writing and signing) must be carried on with reference to norms, which may themselves become the subject of overt comment and debate. In our everyday interactions we take this for granted; and necessarily so, for without recourse to such ordinary metalinguistic practices as correcting slips of the tongue, asking what someone meant by something and disputing their usage of particular words, the enterprise of communicating would be even more fraught with difficulty than it already is. The elaborate, institutionalized forms of verbal hygiene investigated in this book may seem peripheral, remote from ordinary metalinguistic practices; but they are built on the same foundation.

I am making a claim, then, for the significance of verbal hygiene as a general phenomenon. But of course, it does not exist as a general phenomenon: it only exists concretely in specific practices, and these are always socially situated, embedded in history. Mythic scenarios from an imagined 'dawn of time' may prompt us to abstract philosophical speculation about verbal hygiene, but they cannot do justice to its actual manifestations. Most of this book will therefore be devoted to examining verbal hygiene as it is practised in a particular time and place: my own.

Fortunately there is no shortage of material. Living in an advanced stratified society at the end of the twentieth century, I am surrounded by a complex array of practices regulating language use, many of them highly codified and institutionalized, accompanied by passionate debate and exploited by profitable industries. Verbal hygiene is a going concern in my culture. It is also a neglected one in my discipline, linguistics.

This last assertion will puzzle many readers. Surely, when I use the term 'verbal hygiene', I am referring to what linguists know as 'prescriptivism', a topic extensively commented on and with a growing scholarly literature of its own (e.g. Baron 1980; Crowley 1989; Joseph 1987; Milroy and Milroy 1985; Trahern 1988). Let me make clear, then, that despite some overlap in meaning, 'verbal hygiene' is not intended as a synonym for 'prescriptivism'. Although they are probably not obvious, my reasons for rejecting the latter term and preferring to coin an alternative are crucial to my argument, and I will therefore discuss them in some detail.

PROBLEMS OF 'PRESCRIPTIVISM'

In the discourse of linguistics (a phrase I use advisedly, acknowledging that some linguists dissent from the received views of their discipline) the term 'prescriptivism' has a particular value attached to it, a negative connotation that is almost impossible to avoid. This is problematic for me because it tends to pre-empt certain questions I particularly want to ask.

Prescriptivism is negative for linguists in two senses. First, it is negative in the everyday sense of being a bad or wrong thing. The typical attitude to it among linguists runs the gamut from despair at prescribers' ignorance to outrage at their bigotry, and is aptly if apocalyptically summed up in the title of a 1950 book by Robert Hall, *Leave Your Language Alone*. Apart from its sternly negative tone, which is obvious enough, this title also implies a separation of language from its users: rather like those shop assistants and bank clerks who complain that if only the customers would stop bothering them they would be able to get on with some work, the phrase 'leave your language alone' suggests that language would be better off without the constant unwelcome attentions of its speakers.

This is an attitude that I would want to question. When I suggested earlier that making value judgements on language is an integral part of using it and not an alien practice 'perversely grafted on', I was implicitly taking issue with the assumptions made in this finger-wagging tradition, where the evaluative concerns of speakers (embodied in their 'prescriptivism') are by implication seen as both alien and perverse.

One important point to make about the anti-prescriptivist 'leave your language alone' tradition within linguistics is that in a certain sense it mirrors the very same value-laden attitudes it seems to be criticizing.

All attitudes to language and linguistic change are fundamentally ideological, and the relationship between popular and expert ideologies, though it is complex and conflictual, is closer than one might think.

As an illustration of this, let us consider the following observation on popular folklinguistic attitudes made by the sociolinguist James Milroy (1992: 31–2):

> The belief that language change is dysfunctional is most clearly expressed in popular attitudes to language. These commonly conceive of languages as ideal and perfect structures, and of speakers as awkward creatures who violate these perfect structures by misusing and corrupting 'language'. . . . These attitudes are strongly expressed and highly resistant to rational examination.

A striking thing about this observation is that, with only a few modifications, it could equally stand as an account of prevailing attitudes to prescriptivism among linguists (the changes are marked here by the use of italics):

> The belief that *prescriptivism* is dysfunctional is most clearly expressed in *expert* attitudes to language. These commonly conceive of languages as *naturally variable and changing* structures, and of speakers as awkward creatures who violate these *natural* structures by misusing and corrupting 'language'. . . . These attitudes are strongly expressed and highly resistant to rational examination.

Clearly, there are significant differences between these two versions. The 'folk' version valorizes some unspecified quality of 'perfection', and advocates active intervention to protect it, while the 'expert' version valorizes what linguists regard as 'natural' – variability – and therefore advocates leaving languages alone. But we can surely agree that there are also similarities: neither the folk nor the expert view is neutral with respect to what is 'good' linguistically speaking, and both views distinguish between language (perfect/natural) and speakers (corrupters of perfection/naturalness). Linguists and non-linguists each defend what they consider to be the natural order of things. The result is that the folk view of all language change is displaced in linguistics on to one particular sort of change: that which results from prescriptive 'interference'.

An excellent example of this attitude (and one which I will discuss in more detail later on) can be found in a recent popular book by the linguist Robin Lakoff, *Talking Power* (1990). Lakoff asserts (p. 298):

> For change that comes spontaneously from below, or within, our policy should be, Let your language alone, and leave its speakers alone! But other forms of language manipulation have other origins, other motives, other effects, and are far more dangerous.

For Lakoff there is a difference between 'spontaneous' changes, which should be 'let alone', and 'other forms of language manipulation' which do not arise spontaneously but are engineered deliberately, and are 'far more dangerous'. In other words, language change is healthy only when it comes 'from below, or within' – that is, without the conscious agency of language-users.

The idea of language as a natural phenomenon existing apart from its users is associated historically with the nineteenth-century precursor of modern linguistics, comparative philology. It has 'expert' rather than 'folk' roots, though by now it is part of folk wisdom as well. James Milroy cites it precisely in order to challenge it: as he says (1992: 23), 'it is not true that language is a living thing (any more than swimming, or bird-song, is a living thing): it is a vehicle for communication *between* living things, namely human beings.' His own approach places emphasis on the activities of speakers and stresses that 'the language' is always an abstraction or idealization.

On the other hand, Milroy does appear to share the expert view of prescription as unnatural interference that sets arbitrary limits on the inherent variability of languages (cf. Milroy and Milroy 1985). While he castigates earlier historians of language for their own unnoticed, pro-standard prejudices, he seems less acutely aware of the value judgement implied by the conventional use of such terms as 'natural' in relation to variation and change. If 'natural' here means something like 'observed to occur in all speech communities to a greater or lesser extent', then the kind of norm-making and tinkering linguists label 'prescriptive' is 'natural' too: not all languages and varieties undergo the institutional processes of standardization, but all are subject to some normative regulation. If we accept Milroy's point that language is not a living thing but a social practice of living things, then the processes affecting it are social processes.[3]

The linguist's (often extreme) distaste for prescriptivism is, I have been arguing, an ideologically non-neutral one dependent on value judgements that are 'highly resistant to rational examination'. But there is more to this anti-prescriptive stance than moral indignation. Prescriptivism is also a negative term for linguists in a more technical sense. It is the disfavoured half of a binary opposition, 'descriptive/ prescriptive'; and this binarism sets the parameters of linguistics as a discipline. The very first thing any student of linguistics learns is that 'linguistics is descriptive not prescriptive' – concerned, in the way of all science, with objective facts and not subjective value judgements. Prescriptivism thus represents the threatening Other, the forbidden; it is a spectre that haunts linguistics and a difference that defines linguistics.

Again, this absolute binary distinction is something I prefer not to take for granted. I have already tried to show that anti-prescriptive discourse makes value judgements about language, just as prescriptive discourse does; but there are additional reasons to be sceptical of the claims of linguistics to be 'descriptive not prescriptive'. Those claims have been criticized as incoherent by a number of linguists and philosophers. To put in a nutshell what is argued at length in their various critiques (e.g. Baker and Hacker 1984; Harris 1980, 1981; Taylor 1990), the standard notion of linguistic rules as 'descriptive' – crudely, 'natural' rather than normative – is either disingenuous or it is a category mistake.

'Descriptive rules' are formulae which capture the patterned regularities in language. That such regularities exist is not in doubt, nor is the fact that many are below the level of speakers' consciousness. Yet this is hardly a warrant for claiming that the same rules the linguist formulates are either 'in the language' (as a structural linguist might assume) or 'in the speaker' (as a post-Chomskyan mentalist might claim). Language-using is a social practice: the human capacity for acquiring and using language is necessarily actualized within social relationships. Thus the sort of behavioural regularity captured in a rule must arguably arise in the first place from speakers' apprehending and following certain norms.

One of the issues at stake in this argument is the nature and scope of authority in language. Both in traditional grammar and in modern linguistics, the conventional way of expressing a rule is in a simple declarative statement, such as 'a verb agrees with its subject in number' – a convention suggesting naturalness rather than normativity. But as Talbot Taylor (1990) observes, we are not fooled when other injunctions are phrased in this way into thinking they embody some kind of natural law instead of mere temporal authority. 'There is no smoking anywhere on the London Underground', for example, means not that lighting up has been rendered impossible by a convenient act of God, nor that a scientist has ascertained the empirical validity of the generalization, but that smoking has been forbidden by the relevant authority, London Transport. In more general matters of social behaviour it is not always so easy to identify the relevant authority, or to know whence it derives its legitimacy. But to deny that authority could be at work (by saying, for instance, that such-and-such a usage is 'just a fact about the grammar of x') is a mystification.

Mystification on this point occurs in various forms and to varying degrees. For example, the psychologist Michael Billig identifies one form when he notes a general tendency for social scientists to take the efficacy of rules for granted and to neglect questions about their origins and the reasons for their hold on us:

> Psychologists and sociologists often tend to assume that the essential aspect of rules lies in the fact that rules are followed. Yet there is an equally important, but sometimes neglected aspect to rules: namely that rules arise from and themselves give rise to arguments.
>
> (Billig 1991: 50)

Billig exemplifies the point with reference to the Talmud, surely one of the world's most exhaustive attempts to regulate every aspect of existence by means of rules – its catalogue of prescriptions for pious Jews runs to more than sixty volumes. But as Billig points out, a huge proportion of the Talmud is taken up not with the rules themselves but with interminable rabbinical arguments about them. This 'argument – rules – argument' sequence is endlessly self-perpetuating, since every rule generates further argument, which in turn necessitates laying down more rules, which themselves become the focus for new arguments, and so on.

Mainstream linguistics exemplifies a rather different and perhaps stronger form of mystification. Linguists are even less interested in the arguments surrounding rules than the psychologists and sociologists Billig mentions, for the dominant concept of a rule in linguistics is one that brooks no argument at all. Such rules are not injunctions that we can follow or flout. They are as definitive as '$E = mc^2$'. The types of rules that do give rise to arguments – in other words, prescriptions – are often not seen as proper linguistic rules at all.

This attitude marginalizes questions of authority, making its workings difficult to perceive, let alone to challenge. It also has the effect of concealing the authority of linguistic science itself. Most linguists would repudiate the charge of authoritarianism, for they claim to have abjured all prescription on principle. Yet if 'leave your language alone' is not a prescription, what is it?

James Milroy (1992) addresses the confusion that exists around the question of normativity when he asserts that 'all language descriptions, no matter how objective they are, must be *normative* . . . because to be accurate they have to coincide with the consensus norms of the community concerned' (pp. 8–9).[4] He goes on to criticize the way linguists often equate 'normative' with 'prescriptive', claiming there is a distinction between observing norms (which is what linguists are doing whether they admit it or not) and enforcing them (as precriptivists try to do).

Milroy notes that descriptive (norm-observing) statements are often treated by language users as if they were prescriptive (norm-enforcing) – for example, people often use a work like the *English Pronouncing Dictionary*, which records the norms of Received Pronunciation (RP), as a guide to 'correct' pronunciation – but he dismisses this as 'irrelevant', a question of social attitudes to RP and not of the kinds of statements being made about it in the dictionary. (No one, he drily informs us, has used his own account of Belfast pronunciation in this way.) I think he is right up to a point, in that attitudes to the phenomenon being described do affect the way a description is taken. But I also think Milroy fails to follow his own argument to its logical conclusion.

I do not find it irrelevant for our understanding of language and linguistic change that norm-observing is so often interpreted as, or turned into, norm-enforcement. Indeed, it is striking that among present-day users of English the most revered authorities are those that claim most unequivocally to be 'descriptive', and therefore disinterested (the most obvious example is *The Oxford English Dictionary*, which is usually taken to settle any argument about the existence, meaning and spelling of English words). Because science itself has authority in modern society, while at the same time the discourse of value remains a highly salient one for everyday talk about language, the absolute distinction between observing norms and enforcing them cannot be maintained in practice.

Nor, it must be said, has this distinction been rigorously maintained by professional linguists, some of whose activities are overtly norm-enforcing. An obvious instance is the field of 'language planning', where linguists either advise, or work directly for, governmental agencies concerned with solving language problems in a given society (the Hebrew Language Academy in Israel, which oversees the development for modern purposes of a language that was once 'dead', is a well-known example of the language-planning enterprise). Presumably this kind of normative endeavour is considered acceptable among linguists because of its basis in expert scientific knowledge. However, there is a double standard here: apparently it is other people's 'prescriptivism' that linguists find deplorable; their own expert prescriptions should be accorded a different status.[5] The very fact that 'language planning' is distinguished from 'prescriptivism' in the scholarly literature[6] underlines the point made earlier, that 'prescriptivism' is less a neutral description of certain activities than a value judgement on them.

These observations on the instability of the descriptive/prescriptive opposition in theory and practice do not imply that linguists must stop investigating language use, nor even that they should necessarily refrain from engaging in norm-enforcing activities like language planning. But perhaps the arguments put forward above should make linguists think twice about denying the normative character either of what they study or of their own activity in studying it. For what these arguments imply is that the overt anti-prescriptive stance of linguists is in some respects not unlike the prescriptivism they criticize. The point is that *both* prescriptivism *and* anti-prescriptivism invoke certain norms and circulate particular notions about how language ought to work. Of course, the norms are different (and in the case of linguistics, they are often covert). But both sets feed into the more general arguments that influence everyday ideas about language. On that level, 'description' and 'prescription' turn out to be aspects of a single (and normative) activity: a struggle to control language by defining its nature. My use of the term 'verbal hygiene' is intended to capture this idea, whereas to use the term 'prescriptivism' would just recycle the opposition I am trying to deconstruct.

Not only is 'prescriptivism' too negative a term for my purposes, and too dependent for its meaning on the problematic 'descriptive/prescriptive' opposition; it is also too narrow to capture the full range of my concerns. In theory, 'prescriptivism' could refer to any form of linguistic regulation, but in practice it is strongly associated with those forms that are most conservative, elitist and authoritarian. Attempts to promote an elite standard variety, to retard linguistic change or to purge a language of 'foreign' elements are the instances most readily evoked by the epithet 'prescriptive', for linguists and non-linguists alike.

Yet it is crucial to see that this narrowly conceived 'prescriptivism' – elitist, conservative and purist – is only one kind of verbal hygiene among many, only one manifestation of the much more general impulse to regulate language, control it, make it 'better'. This impulse takes innumerable forms, not all of which are conservative, authoritarian or (arguably) deplorable. A random list of verbal hygiene practices in which present-day speakers of English are engaged might include, for example, campaigning for the use of plain language on official forms; belonging to a spelling reform society, a dialect preservation society or an artificial language society; taking courses in 'communication arts' or 'group discussion', going for elocution lessons, sending for correspondence courses on 'good English' or reading self-improvement literature on how to be a better conversationalist; editing prose to conform to a house style; producing guidelines on non-sexist language, or opposing such guidelines. And these are only the institutional cases: the group of schoolchildren cruelly mimicking a classmate's 'posh' accent are also practising verbal hygiene, as are the workers who institute a 'swear box' and fine one another for using 'bad language'.

Few of these practices feature in the literature on 'prescriptivism', and collectively they cannot be made to illustrate any single coherent political ideology or perspective on language. What unites them is their defiant refusal to 'leave your language alone' – a refusal that is grounded in a strong concern with *value*.

Verbal hygiene comes into being whenever people reflect on language in a critical (in the sense of 'evaluative') way. The potential for it is latent in every communicative act, and the impulse behind it pervades our habits of thought and behaviour. I have never met anyone who did not subscribe, in one way or another, to the belief that language can be 'right' or 'wrong', 'good' or 'bad', more or less 'elegant' or 'effective' or 'appropriate'. Of course, there is massive disagreement about what values to espouse, and how to define them. Yet however people may pick and choose, it is rare to find anyone rejecting altogether the idea that there is *some* legitimate authority in language. We are all of us closet prescriptivists – or, as I prefer to put it, verbal hygienists.

I hope it will be clear already that in saying this I am not suggesting that we are all closet elitists and authoritarians. Our norms and values differ: what remains constant is only that we *have* norms and values. There are, for example, many people who disapprove strongly of what they call 'prescriptivism', meaning the pedantry of traditional gram-marians, while at the same time accepting the equally normative arguments of George Orwell's 'Politics and the English language' (1946), and taking all due care to ensure their own usage is free from any taint of 'bias'. There are scholars who have spent their careers championing the cause of linguistic tolerance, yet who nevertheless, as editors and contributors to scholarly journals, impose on themselves the obligation not merely to write in standard English, but to conform to every arbitrary convention laid down in the *Chicago Manual of Style*. I am not accusing such people of hypocrisy and bad faith. I am arguing that in a crucial sense things could not be otherwise; there is no escape from normativity.

It follows that if we find some particular verbal hygiene practice objectionable, the solution is not simply to denounce all prescription. If normativity is an inalienable part of using language, to abandon prescription in the broad sense is to abandon language itself. Let us be clear, though, that this is not an apologia for every kind of linguistic authoritarianism. On the contrary, it might pave the way for more effective intervention in politically important linguistic debates. Anti-prescriptivists have too often fought the battle against authoritarianism on the wrong terrain, and in consequence their challenge has been too easily brushed aside.

Later in this book, for example, I consider the acrimonious debate on English in the National School Curriculum that took place in England and Wales during the 1980s and early 1990s. The agenda was set by right-wing conservatives who wanted to restore traditional grammar and mastery of standard English to their central place in the curriculum. Liberal linguists countered by arguing that grammar, while a valid and even valuable thing to study, should be 'descriptive and not prescriptive'. In 1987, the right-wing commentator John Marenbon enlivened an otherwise predictable pamphlet on the teaching of English with a ringing denunciation of the linguists' argument. According to Marenbon, the linguists had missed the point, which was that 'grammar prescribes by describing' (1987: 20). The point of doing a 'descriptive' grammatical analysis is precisely to establish what the norms of grammar are, so they can be prescribed with confidence to users of the language.

This, no doubt, is a faithful account of what most western grammarians since the Greeks have believed themselves to be doing. In its emphasis on the normative character of language descriptions it is not unlike the argument advanced by James Milroy. I am disinclined to respond by asking Marenbon if he believes that Einstein formulated the theory of relativity in order to prescribe to the universe, for language is not gravity and the rules under discussion are not laws of nature. In short, I find myself in agreement with Marenbon's critique of descriptivism.

Yet this in itself does not make us allies. What is important politically is that Marenbon and I draw quite different conclusions from our rejection of the over-simple descriptive/prescriptive opposition. In fact, I think his conclusion – that it is dangerous and misguided to question the received norms of traditional grammar – is a *non sequitur*. It does not follow from the inevitability of normativity in language-using that any particular set of norms must be accepted uncritically and forever. On the contrary, to speak of norms – as opposed to 'descriptive rules' – is to place language use firmly in the sphere of the social; it is to acknowledge Michael Billig's point that 'rules arise from, and themselves give rise to arguments' (1991: 50). It is not Marenbon's rejection of descriptivism but his unquestioning acceptance of particular prescriptions that marks him out as a linguistic authoritarian.

In order to challenge verbal hygiene practices we find objectionable, to defend those we see value in and to decide which are which, we must be willing to engage in arguments about rules. We must shift the terrain for debates like the one on the National Curriculum so that instead of asking 'should we prescribe?' (a question Marenbon quite reasonably counters with another – 'what is the alternative?'), we pose searching questions about who prescribes for whom, what they prescribe, how, and for what purposes.

THE LINGUISTICS AND POLITICS OF VERBAL HYGIENE: AUTHORITY, IDENTITY AND AGENCY

I suggested earlier that verbal hygiene is deserving of serious study because, like vowels, it is 'there'. But in the light of these observations on the National Curriculum debate, it might also be argued that verbal hygiene deserves attention because of the peculiar cultural and political significance it assumes in many contexts. Verbal hygiene is a double discourse, one that needs to be read in two frameworks simultaneously. To say that verbal hygiene debates just play out 'deeper' social conflicts in the arena of language is to overlook those features of verbal hygiene that are grounded in specifically linguistic attitudes and beliefs; it is also to gloss over the crucial question why *language*, rather than something else, becomes the arena where certain social conflicts find symbolic expression. Conversely, to deny that ideas about language are recruited very often to non-linguistic concerns is to miss most of what gives meaning to any particular verbal hygiene debate.

The peculiar resonance possessed by apparently trivial issues (e.g. pronouns, spelling or swearing) derives from a combination of linguistic and non-linguistic concerns. To understand this complex interaction, it is necessary to examine verbal hygiene practices closely, exposing their unspoken assumptions to critical scrutiny. The word 'critical' is important here. It does not amaze me, nor in itself does it worry me, that we have verbal hygiene practices; but I find it both remarkable and worrying that so many otherwise reasonable people are so slow to question their content and their functions.

Authority

Linguistic conventions are quite possibly the last repository of unquestioned authority for educated people in secular society. Tell such people
that they must dress in a certain way to be admitted to a public building,
and some at least will demand to know why; they may even reject the
purported explanation as absurd and campaign for a change in the rules.
Tell them, on the other hand, that the comma goes outside the quotation
marks rather than inside (or for that matter vice versa as is conventional
in North America) and they will meekly obey, though the rule is patently
as arbitrary as any dress code.

Moreover, the social function of the rule is not arbitrary. Like other
superficially innocuous 'customs', 'conventions' and 'traditions' (dress
codes included), rules of language use often contribute to a circle of
exclusion and intimidation, as those who have mastered a particular
practice use it in turn to intimidate others. Within the privileged space of
the academy, for example, where it is normally a sign of intellectual
competence to broach the question 'why?', questioning the minutiae of
linguistic conventions is a sign of incomplete or faulty socialization. A
first year student may ask why the comma goes here and not there, but
her teacher would never put the same question to the editor of a
scholarly journal. It might also be noted here that linguistic bigotry is
among the last publicly expressible prejudices left to members of the
western intelligentsia. Intellectuals who would find it unthinkable to
sneer at a beggar or someone in a wheelchair will sneer without
compunction at linguistic 'solecisms'.

One of the many things that need to be explained about verbal
hygiene is why so many forms of it work so well: why the question
'why?' is so persistently unasked, even (or perhaps especially) by people
who otherwise pride themselves on their critical faculties. How is it that
people can combine a strong concern for value in language with a
near-total lack of scepticism about the criteria normally used to
measure it?

Among the answers that could be given (and often are) is the seductively
simple one that questions of usage are too trivial for people to waste
breath disputing. This is not on the face of things a very satisfactory
answer, since in fàct a great deal of breath, acres of paper and hours
of teaching and editorial time are expended on these questions daily. But
it has recently been suggested that perhaps such practices are just
lingering anachronisms, legacies of an age when questions about
language possessed a kind of significance they have since lost.

In *The State of the Language* (Ricks and Michaels 1990), a collection of
articles intended for a non-specialist readership, the American usage
commentator Geoffrey Nunberg develops this argument at some
length. Only when grammatical conventions signify something other

than themselves, Nunberg asserts, will their content be a matter of controversy. This was the case in the eighteenth and nineteenth centuries, when 'grammar provided a metaphysics for criticism, and its rules were the schemas for all the rules that regimented the conduct of public discourse' (1990: 474–5). But today the symbolic significance of grammar has been eroded, not least by the success of linguistic science. And when grammar ceases to be a metaphysics of anything, norms that were once the subject of impassioned debate become 'ossified in a body of traditional lore': there is 'no larger issue at stake' in usage questions, and 'precisely because they are unimportant, we submit to arbitrary precedent' (p. 475).

This is an interesting argument, but in one important respect I think it is wrong: grammar has *not* lost its old symbolic status. Again, the debate on the National Curriculum illustrates the point. The capacity of grammar to signify 'all the rules that regiment the conduct of public discourse' was mobilized very effectively by the Right in this debate, and was taken up enthusiastically – from which we may infer that it remains a common-sense idea. Nor, incidentally, is this kind of symbolism a monopoly of conservatives harking back to the nineteenth century. There is surely no more striking example of grammar functioning as 'a metaphysics of criticism' than the debate on so-called 'politically-correct' language that began with feminist critiques of conventional usage in the 1970s and is still raging as I write. In this debate, which I discuss in detail in Chapter 4, it is precisely the substance of linguistic rules, their non-triviality and non-arbitrariness, that is at issue.

What these cases seem to show is that defenders of 'arbitrary precedent' are not, *pace* Nunberg, *indifferent* to the rules (if they were, why not just accept someone else's equally arbitrary reform?). Rather, the defenders of precedent in these instances have actively invested in a certain kind of authority. Exactly what kind is a complicated question for students of verbal hygiene.

No doubt one component of the kind of authority we are dealing with is the respect people have for custom and practice, for traditional ways of doing things. You can accept that traditional rules are arbitrary and still defend them on the 'if it ain't broke, don't fix it' principle that, other things being equal, there is some intrinsic value in continuity. Yet this cannot be the whole story of verbal hygiene, for two reasons. First, as I have just suggested, the uncritical acceptance of custom and practice seems more widespread and more marked in relation to language-using than it does in relation to many other social practices. If this observation is accurate, it requires some explanation. Second, many verbal hygiene debates arise precisely because there is dispute about whether some aspect of traditional usage needs fixing. That the appeal to what is customary is so often maintained in the face of an argument to the effect that traditional ways are glaringly *imperfect*, suggests there might be more to linguistic conservatism than the principle of continuity *per se*.

In the case of language use, it might be argued that investment in traditional authority manifests not just a general preference for continuity over change, but also an attachment to values and practices that were impressed on people in the formative stages of their personal linguistic histories. One of the most important factors producing language conservatism (often among people whose other views are the reverse of conservative) must surely be the long apprenticeship served by speakers, and more especially by writers. As I noted earlier in passing when I alluded to a 'circle of intimidation', mastering any complex and difficult craft gives you an inbuilt incentive to defend its practices. If I have invested time and effort learning how to write according to a particular set of prescriptions, I will take some convincing that those prescriptions are not necessary and desirable; to admit that the rules are both arbitrary and pointless is to devalue my own accomplishment in mastering them.

Furthermore, by the end of my apprenticeship I will probably have internalized certain norms to such an extent that I am no longer capable of experiencing them as arbitrary, even if intellectually I know perfectly well that they are. When academics and other professional language-users wince at 'solecisms' – split infinitives, dangling modifiers, misplaced apostrophes, whatever – I am prepared to believe that the pain they feel is genuine, and not just a snobbish affectation.

This has a bearing on a question I am frequently asked: 'if the conventions are arbitrary and pointless, why do you conform to them so meticulously yourself?' The answer is that particular practices of verbal hygiene are ingrained in me as they are in everyone who has been schooled in using language – the more schooling, the more ingrained the response. My own case is of interest only because I am a linguist: I have undergone a process of professional socialization designed among other things to get rid of 'inappropriate' value judgements. It has worked, up to a point. I am much less sensitive than I once was, and if old sensitivities intrude, at least I know enough to put terms like 'solecism' in scare-quotes. But I still find there are things that leap to my eye as if emblazoned in neon. I can choose to suppress the irritation I feel when I see, for example, a sign that reads 'Potatoe's'; I cannot choose not to feel it.

If we seek to understand the pervasiveness and the effectiveness of verbal hygiene, it is crucial to acknowledge that linguistic conventions are routinely felt to be of a different order from many other social rules and norms. Their authority is not just an external imposition, but is experienced as coming from deep inside.

This raises the question of how norms 'get into' or are 'taken up by' language-users: processes little studied in sociolinguistics, though their outcome – people's demonstrable sensitivity to linguistic norms, their fine-tuned awareness of prestige and stigma – is taken for granted by sociolinguists. The problem is how we get from large-scale historical developments such as standardization on one hand to the actual behaviour of individual speakers on the other. What are the mechanisms through which people who have never heard of Caxton or Swift come to subscribe to what Milroy and Milroy (1985) label the 'ideology of standardization'? This is a gap in our understanding that sociolinguistics has not really filled. It is often assumed, for instance, that speakers become sensitive to prestige norms of language through the interventions of their parents and, more decisively, their teachers; yet we have very few investigations of how this happens in practice.

Identity

The gaps that exist in sociolinguistic accounts of people's behaviour are understandable if we consider that sociolinguistics sees itself as a branch of *linguistics*. It is called 'socio' linguistics because in order to explain the phenomena that are its special province, namely linguistic variation and change, it must make reference to social divisions and categories. But it is linguistic rather than social patterning that defines the field for most of its practitioners (cf. Trudgill 1978). Social phenomena provide the explanatory means, not the end. That is why so many sociolinguists have been content to work with simple, commonsensical ideas about the social.

In sociolinguistics, the reasons why speakers produce certain patterns of variation are most often understood with reference to the truism that 'language reflects society'. People's use of linguistic variables can be correlated with their demographic characteristics: their belonging to particular classes, races, genders, generations, local communities. The linguistic behaviour is taken to 'reflect' the speaker's social location. Alternatively, some linguists argue for a more active conception of speakers' behaviour: that language is used to 'mark' social identity. Consciously or unconsciously, speakers use speech to signal their sense of themselves as belonging to group A and being different from group B. In both accounts, it is implicitly assumed that the relevant categories and identities exist prior to language, and are simply 'marked' or 'reflected' when people come to use it.

But any encounter with recent social and critical theory will cast doubt on such an approach. The categories that sociolinguistics treats as fixed givens, such as 'class', 'gender' and even 'identity', are treated in critical approaches as relatively unstable *constructs* which are therefore in need of explanation themselves. Furthermore, in critical theory language is treated as part of the explanation. Whereas sociolinguistics would say that the way I use language reflects or marks my identity as a particular kind of social subject – I talk like a white middle-class woman because I am (already) a white middle-class woman – the critical account suggests language is one of the things that *constitutes* my identity as a particular kind of subject. Sociolinguistics says that how you act depends on who you are; critical theory says that who you are (and are taken to be) depends on how you act.

The philosopher Judith Butler offers a particularly thoroughgoing version of this argument in her book *Gender Trouble* (Butler 1990). Because so many people believe that even if gender is a social construct it is constructed on a 'natural' foundation, namely sex, gender identity is usually taken as one of the most fixed and stable components of personal identity. Butler, however, suggests that this is an illusion: 'Gender is the repeated stylization of the body, a set of repeated acts within a highly rigid regulatory frame that congeal over time to produce the appearance of substance, of a natural sort of being' (1990: 33).

For 'gender' here, I take it we could substitute any apparently fixed and substantive social identity label. And what Butler is saying is that such social identities do not simply exist (they only have 'the appearance of substance'); rather they are brought into being when social actors repeatedly *perform* them.[7] The reason we perceive ourselves, and are perceived by others, as particular kinds of people is that we repeat the actions that define those kinds of people until in time they come to seem like a fixed and integral part of our nature.

This does of course raise the question why people endlessly perform the 'appropriate' acts, constructing recognizable, stable and solid-looking identities. Why can we not perform just any old identity, or a multiplicity of identities? One answer to this is that up to a point we can and do. In societies where individuals are positioned within a complex variety of social relations, it is part of being socially competent to perform identity differently in different situations (e.g. in 'public' and 'private' settings, or with different groups of people). Conversely, there are plenty of cases where people deviate from their society's notions of competent behaviour. There are people who fail to produce a single or stable identity (some of those we define as mentally ill fall into this category); there are people who produce 'deviant' or unexpected identities (e.g. those who pass for the opposite sex), and there are people whose identities are ambiguous, undecidable or unintelligible.

As these examples imply, however, there are penalties, ranging from being judged 'eccentric' to being ostracized or persecuted to being locked up and stripped of your rights, for constructing an identity in defiance of cultural prescriptions, or for failing to construct a proper identity at all. Butler's account, in other words, makes use of the idea of normativity – the 'highly rigid regulatory frame' she mentions in relation to gender. There are codes which define what is intelligible, acceptable and normal: individuals transgress those codes at their peril.

Butler defines what the codes prescribe as 'repeated stylizations of the body', a formulation that most obviously evokes such characteristics as appearance, dress, demeanour, gesture and gait. But I assume her argument could also apply to language-using, and especially to speech: that there are 'stylizations' of the voice (its pitch, tone and accent), of lexical, grammatical and interactional choices, the repetition of which contributes to the construction of a 'congealed' social and personal identity for the speaker. Speaking is a classic example of an act that is constantly repeated over time; it is also a classic example of an activity done within a 'rigid regulatory frame'.

The standard sociolinguistic account does not exactly deny these observations, but in supposing that speakers' acts of identity simply reflect something that exists prior to and irrespective of those acts it leaves certain things unexplained. If identity pre-exists language, if it is given, fixed and taken for granted, then why do language-users have to mark it so assiduously and repetitively? In Butler's account, the repetition is necessary to sustain the identity, precisely because it does not exist outside the acts that constitute it. Then again, if people's behaviour automatically reflects an identity which is a combination of 'inherent' attributes (e.g. race, gender) and social location (e.g. having grown up in a certain community), how do we explain the exceptional cases of 'deviant', unpredictable or radically changeable behaviour? In Butler's account, the culture's 'regulatory frame' constrains but does not totally determine what it is possible for social actors to do. This frame defines what acts are required to produce an intelligible, acceptable or normal identity; its definitions cannot simply be ignored, but they can be negotiated, resisted and in some circumstances deliberately modified.

From a critical perspective, then, the norms that regulate linguistic performance are not simply reflections of an existing structure but elements in the creation and recreation of that structure. It therefore becomes necessary to ask where the norms 'come from' and how – that is, through what actual practices – they are apprehended and internalized, negotiated or resisted.

In my view, studying verbal hygiene practices is a useful way to carry forward the investigation of these questions. Debates on verbal hygiene are of particular interest: conflict renders visible the processes of norm-making and norm-breaking, bringing into the open the arguments that surround rules. Verbal hygiene practices that are not the subject of debate are also illuminating: examined closely, they show how norms become naturalized and how unquestioned ('conventional') ways of behaving are implicitly understood by social actors. Overall, then, the investigation of normative practices, whether contested or taken for granted, has the potential to cast light on the relations between language, society and identity.

Agency and 'the natural'

The view of language and identity that I have just proposed raises the vexed question of agency: of how much control speakers have over language. The tendency in contemporary theories of language – in poststructuralist/postmodernist accounts as well as in linguistic science – has been to posit speaking subjects acted on by language and largely unable to act upon it themselves. I would certainly agree that speakers do not have total control over their own discourse, for a historically embedded normative practice does not permit the untrammelled exercise of individual free will. But verbal hygiene is an interesting case of people acting as if they did in fact have total control. It is difficult to imagine a more triumphant assertion of agency than a proposal to invent a new language (e.g. Esperanto); even more modest initiatives like traditional prescriptive grammar bespeak a touching faith in our ability to maintain standards and reverse 'degenerative' changes by enforcing rules more assiduously. The impulse behind verbal hygiene, then, is quite strikingly an impulse to mastery over language.

Here it might be objected that many or most verbal hygiene schemes come to nothing: neither Esperanto nor traditional grammar has been an unqualified success, and from this we may infer that verbal hygienists are in the grip of a delusion about the extent of their agency. That, indeed, is one of the arguments deployed in 'leave your language alone' diatribes: people are urged to desist from their meddling on the grounds that it is futile and will have no effect whatever.

Yet is there not something paradoxical about this? We do not usually try to forbid acts we believe are incapable of succeeding. Endlessly insisting that verbal hygiene cannot work implies a belief – and indeed a fear – that it might work all too well. And history suggests this fear is not wholly unjustified. There is scope, albeit not unlimited scope, for effective intervention in language; if we deny this in principle or erase specific instances of it from the record, we are guilty of mystification.

We can see how commonplace such mystification is if we examine, for example, the responses of linguists to one recent and quite effective example of verbal hygiene: the change that has taken place during the past twenty years in the conventions for marking gender in English. Generic and non-specific reference in English is clearly in a state of flux, as commentators acknowledge (cf. Quirk *et al.* 1985), because of verbal hygiene pressure exerted by feminists. But linguists have frequently responded to the shift in two ways, both equally mystifying.

The first response is to treat feminist demands for non-sexist language as yet another deplorable example of misguided prescriptive interference. This was the position of the Harvard linguistics faculty, when in 1971 it went to the trouble of writing to the college newspaper to assure feminists that masculine generics were just a neutral fact of English grammar (see Miller and Swift 1976). More recently, the Linguistics Association of Great Britain produced a slightly different version of the same argument. In 1984, the LAGB sponsored a panel on language and gender at which proposals were made to amend the association's own constitution, removing generic masculine pronouns and renaming the office of chairman. This was opposed from the floor on the grounds that 'whatever the merits of the [feminist] case', an organization of professional linguists would lose all credibility if it were seen to endorse prescription (for an abbreviated record of this discussion, see Coates 1985). Unlike the Harvard faculty, the LAGB remained agnostic on the 'merits of the case', but nevertheless expressed unwillingness to promote any change through prescriptive intervention.

The second response is the reverse of the first: it is to present the move away from masculine generics and other sexist conventions as an instance of linguistic evolution, as if the specific campaigns mounted by feminists against sexist language had nothing to do with it. Thus for instance Jenny Cheshire (1984: 33–4), in an article summarizing the relationship between language and gender in English, attributes recent changes in linguistic usage not to the agency of feminists engaging in specific verbal hygiene practices (such as producing institutional non-sexist language guidelines), but to a general change in the social position of women which language eventually 'reflected'.

These responses to a recent and ongoing linguistic change demonstrate once again how confused linguists become when faced with deliberate attempts to intervene in the course of a language's history. The first response is bewildering because it fails to acknowledge that the *status quo* – the use of the generic masculine – is only the reflex of an earlier prescription (see Bodine 1990 for copious documentation). Those LAGB members who opposed amending the constitution were therefore in the position of asserting that while today's prescription is prescriptive, yesterday's is not: at some point it has mysteriously become 'a fact about English grammar' (this of course begs the question why the feminist alternative could not, given time, do likewise).

The second response is no less bewildering, because it seems to deny – contrary to the known facts – that anyone could ever have prescribed anything. According to this argument, the *status quo* at any point must result from a process of natural selection, as language evolves to meet its speakers' changing needs. Presumably, then, those of us who were involved on either side of the argument at the LAGB panel might as well have saved our breath; such questions can only be decided by the language itself in the fullness of time.[8]

These responses underline the importance attached to the category of the 'natural' in discussions of linguistic change. The pairing 'natural/unnatural' is parallel to 'descriptive/prescriptive', and its terms have similar values attached to them: 'natural' change is good, while 'unnatural' change is bad. Thus linguists who approve of non-sexist language are likely to present it as a case of natural evolutionary development ('language reflects society'), whereas those who disapprove will present it as unnatural and unnecessary tinkering ('leave your language alone').

We can see how this strategy works, and where it leads, by returning to the passage from Robin Lakoff's book *Talking Power* which I quoted earlier in the chapter:

> For change that comes spontaneously from below, or within, our policy should be, Let your language alone, and leave its speakers alone! But other forms of language manipulation have other origins, other motives, other effects, and are far more dangerous.
>
> (Lakoff 1990: 298)

The context in which Lakoff makes these remarks is a discussion of prescriptive grammar that sets out the orthodox professional view of prescriptivists as petty tyrants trying vainly to turn back the unstoppable tide of linguistic change. Lakoff's debt to Robert Hall is evident in her rhetoric; but it is also evident that she wants to apply the 'leave your language alone' principle *selectively*. Tolerance for what people do with words is not, it seems, without limits. This raises the question, how can limits be set?

Lakoff's answer is to distinguish between 'spontaneous' change (which comes from 'below', that is, from the unselfconscious behaviour of ordinary speakers; or from 'within', which I take to mean from inherent tendencies in language itself) and deliberate 'manipulation' practised, the context makes clear, by powerful groups with vested interests. One should be 'let alone', the other resisted. Although she does not use the terms 'natural' and 'unnatural', the distinction Lakoff wants to draw is similar, and it raises similar problems.

One difficulty is *how* to draw the line, since in practice many contentious linguistic changes come partly from 'above' and partly from 'below' or 'within' – they have both a planned and a spontaneous element (a point I will discuss in more detail in Chapter 4). But the most pressing problem is not how one distinguishes spontaneous from orchestrated changes in practice so much as *why* one's attitude to a change should depend above all on whether or not it is 'spontaneous'. Is Lakoff suggesting that all willed changes, irrespective of their substance, are equally to be condemned, while conversely all 'spontaneous' changes are equally to be applauded? If she is, then her audience could be forgiven for finding this a lame and unconvincing argument. 'If you are going to make value judgements at all', they might say, 'then surely there are more important values than spontaneity. How about truth, beauty, logic, utility?'.

In fact I would argue that Lakoff's value judgements are not based on the spontaneous/deliberate criterion, but are covertly ideological: really, she is judging changes by their agents, and specifically by the degree of power and the intention to abuse that power which she attributes to those agents. The section from which the quoted passage comes is entitled 'Governmental euphemism'; the 'manipulations' we are invited to condemn are attributed to politicians, military spokespersons and media 'spin doctors'. With the best of liberal intentions, Lakoff is defending the linguistic rights of the 'little guy', on one hand against the prescriptivists who rap him over the knuckles for spontaneously changing his usage, and on the other against the powerful interest groups who tamper with language deliberately to manipulate him, because they have 'political axes to grind' (1990: 298).

I am not without sympathy for Lakoff's concerns, but I have reservations about the way she presents her case, as if it were not a notable piece of political axe-grinding in its own right. The distinction between spontaneous change (good) and deliberate manipulation (bad) does not work even at the pragmatic level of identifying all and only those linguistic practices Lakoff regards as abuses of power: 'change from above' (that is, deliberate or conscious change) cannot always be identified with the agency of powerful groups. If we took Lakoff at her word we would logically have to condemn, for example, not only the deliberately evasive language she castigates politicians and spin-doctors for using, but also, and for exactly the same reason, the plain language campaigns which citizens have just as deliberately set up to combat manipulation by the powers that be.

The problem, then, is Lakoff's failure or refusal to make explicit what really lies behind her judgement that some kinds of change are legitimate while others are not. Identifying the good with the natural (and the bad with the unnatural) is an effective device for circumventing arguments about the validity of certain judgements; for, according to popular wisdom as well as science, 'you can't argue with nature'.

Lakoff, like many other linguists, evidently regards 'spontaneous change from below or within' as the norm, and deliberate intervention in language as a special case. This can lead, as I have noted already in the case of non-sexist language, to a certain rewriting of linguistic history: 'successful' changes are assimilated retrospectively to the 'natural selection' model, and the conflicts that surrounded certain changes are not fully acknowledged. The preference for evolutionary accounts is also in effect a preference for apolitical explanations of change; the history of a language becomes a narrative made up of seamless transitions from one consensus to another. While the role of deliberate agency in language change should not be overstated (for just as no one invented vowels, so no one ever organized to bring about a vowel shift), denying it can be a factor, or treating it as somehow aberrant is equally unenlightening. The study of verbal hygiene provides a useful corrective to naturalizing tendencies that obscure how some changes occur.

I do not want to suggest that linguistics is the only place where these tendencies are found, for on the contrary they are also rife in almost every kind of verbal hygiene. The enthusiasm of so many verbal hygienists for linguistic Darwinism may seem strange: from a perspective that valorizes the natural, verbal hygiene itself is damned as an unnatural practice. In fact, though, the idea of language as a natural organism with its own evolutionary dynamic has important rhetorical functions in the discourse of verbal hygiene.

In May 1992, I took part in a public debate with the then editor of *The Times*, Simon Jenkins, which focused on a new style guide he had just launched and was planning to publish (both the event and the guide are discussed in detail in Chapter 2). The report of the debate that appeared in *The Times* contains the following remarks:

> Every freshman today knows, as Dr Johnson ruefully recognized 200 years ago, that it is futile in principle to set rules to stop the incessant and inexorable flow of that great natural force, the English language. Previous attempts to subdue it have regularly been frustrated as the spontaneous drive to communicate has broken up prescriptions and precedents, just as the root filaments of a germinating plant shatter blocks of concrete. Who was the editor of *The Times* to stand in the way of that irresistible force?
>
> (*The Times*, 20 May 1992)

This is an exemplary piece of 'natural' rhetoric, building on a series of images in which language is compared to phenomena of nature (rivers or waterfalls, germinating plants) while prescription is compared to that most unnatural substance, concrete. The editor of *The Times* appears as a lone, humble figure in this magnificent natural landscape. In his modest way, and always (like Johnson) acknowledging the inherent limitations of the enterprise, he must attempt to subdue 'that great natural force, the English language'.

This kind of rhetoric achieves two important things. First, it distances some prescribers – those who know the limits of their authority – from others, the 'real' prescriptivists, who are lunatics and megalomaniacs. The point of setting up these straw prescriptivists is to make your own prescriptivism look ultra-mild and reasonable. Second, and more significantly, the clichéd invocation of irresistible natural forces dramatizes verbal hygiene as one form of the archetypal struggle between man and nature. Although nature will always triumph, we can understand and indeed admire man's heroic determination to tame her unruly ways.

Yet as we contemplate this unfolding drama, there is a fundamental point from which our attention is being diverted. Arguments about language use are not between man and nature, they are between groups of people with differing opinions and interests. It is not 'the English language' that verbal hygiene attempts to subdue, it is particular users of that language. The passage I have quoted eloquently minimizes the authority of its subject: 'who [is] the editor of *The Times* to stand in the way of that irresistible force?'. The implied answer is: no one very much. The language will crush him like an ant if he fails to accord it proper deference. But if we were to ask instead, 'who is the editor of *The Times* to stand in the way of people who want to write in Scots or in patois, of feminists, gay militants, spelling reformers and enthusiasts of American slang?', the answer would be rather different. The struggle waged in *The Times* style guide may be more comic than epic, but at least the editor is in a position to win it. The rhetoric of man versus nature obscures what is really at stake in verbal hygiene battles, while glossing over the unequal positioning of the combatants.

It also, of course, begs the crucial question: why have verbal hygienists from Samuel Johnson to Simon Jenkins bothered to make rules at all, if they believe it is 'futile in principle' to do so? What higher value or sacred duty impels them to battle with great natural forces?

There is a clue in *The Times*'s reference to 'the spontaneous drive to communicate'. (Note the reappearance here of the word *spontaneous*, on which the linguist Robin Lakoff also placed such emphasis.) Only two days earlier, in fact, the paper had run a leader on the subject of the split infinitive, in which it defended this stigmatized construction in cases where the alternative would be ambiguous or unclear. The editorial ended with the following pronouncement: 'Rules are created to aid the communication of meaning. In the cause of meaning they can sometimes be broken' (*The Times*, 18 May 1992). The same paradoxical advice appears in all kinds of style guides, and tempers even George Orwell's recommendations in 'Politics and the English language'. The higher purpose that justifies verbal hygiene – or renders it pointless – is *communication*.

COMMUNICATION: VERBAL HYGIENE AND THE FEAR OF FRAGMENTATION

That the true function of language is to serve as 'a means of communication' is a theme harped on by verbal hygienists across the cultural and political spectrum. It is the cliché trotted out by the Queen's English Society whenever its members meet to extol the virtues of standard English: if we didn't abide by a single standard communication would break down. It is the major argument of the racist and xenophobic US English movement, which campaigns to outlaw languages other than English in public domains: we need a common language or the nation will fragment. Conversely, it is the theme of Orwell's 'Politics and the English language', according to which totalitarianism succeeds by preventing us from communicating our thoughts clearly, so that in time we cease to have any clear thoughts at all. It is the justification used by some supporters of feminist language reforms, who claim that gender-neutral terms make English clearer and less ambiguous; and by their opponents, who have called non-sexist guidelines 'an attack on the means and the hope of communication' (Kanfer 1972: 79). 'Communication' is ritually invoked as the goal of verbal hygiene schemes from the grandiose (e.g. Esperanto) to the petty (e.g. *The Times* style guide), and from the ultra-conservative (e.g. US English) to the radical fringe (e.g. advocates of so-called 'politically correct' language). It is worth enquiring more closely into what these various parties might mean by 'communication'.

In a series of important works, Roy Harris (1980; 1981; 1987) traces the persistence in western linguistic thought of the view that communication is ideally 'telementation'; that is, a process which transfers ideas intact from one mind to another. Since humans are not telepathic, they must perform telementation by way of language; this leads in turn to the assumption that languages are what Harris calls 'fixed codes'. For if speakers did not share a common code, one speaker's message could not be decoded by another to produce an exact transfer of ideas.

Although it is anachronistic (for the idea predates current communication technologies), the obvious analogy is with what goes on when two machines 'communicate'. If you produce a text on your computer and then send me the file, I need the right software to make it readable on my machine. Given a shared program, the message on my screen will reproduce exactly what was on yours; without such a program the message will be unreadable.

The way many verbal hygienists talk about communication is very much in this 'all-or-nothing' tradition. We must agree to go by the rules, they say, because otherwise we will soon be unable to decode each other's messages. Any message that deliberately flouts the conventions we have agreed to, or that is constructed according to novel conventions, risks precipitating total communicational breakdown.

As Roy Harris points out, however, this argument depends on the telementation/fixed code model being a plausible account of how human beings communicate. And in his view it is not plausible. The greatest strength of language − its flexibility, which enables us to use it in novel situations to mean an infinite number of things − also entails its greatest weakness, which is indeterminacy: the impossibility of ever definitively pinning down what a particular utterance means. This is not to say we 'cannot communicate', but rather to redefine what communication is, abandoning the notion of an exact transfer of ideas from mind to mind.

From this point of view, the anxieties expressed in so much verbal hygiene discourse are misplaced and even absurd. Take, for example, an argument put forward against wanton neologizing on the part of feminists: that faced with a word like *herstory*, speakers outside the magic circle of initiates will search their code-books in vain and so be unable to assign the word a meaning. This is to put humans on a par with spellcheck programs. We are constantly using our creative abilities to make sense of words we have never met before, as well as to make new interpretations of old words. If this were not possible, vast swathes of discourse – for instance advertisements, or literature from Dr Seuss to *Finnegan's Wake* – would all be quite unintelligible. (*Herstory* is surely more transparent than *supercalifragilisticexpialidocious*, a word that is meaningful to millions of 5-year-olds.) Or take the idea that a non-standard construction such as the English double negative cannot be decoded by speakers of the standard language because, in the superior logic of their code, 'two negatives make a positive'. I have yet to meet any speaker of any variety of English who on hearing Mick Jagger sing 'I can't get no satisfaction' has entertained for one moment the belief he means the opposite.

Non-standard and unconventional uses of language can only be seen as a threat to communication if communication itself is conceived in a way that negates our whole experience of it. The speciousness of the arguments put forward to justify particular verbal hygiene practices might lead us to suspect that the fetish of communication is really just a cover for some other obsession. We are back once again to the way verbal hygiene is not just about ordering language itself, but also exploits the powerful symbolism in which language stands for other kinds of order – moral, social and political.

The social analogue of a 'breakdown in communication' is a break-down in cultural and political consensus, the eruption into public discourse of irreconcilable differences and incommensurable values. Thus the anxiety that gets expressed as 'if we don't obey the rules we won't be able to communicate' might equally be defined as an anxiety about moral relativism or social fragmentation. Just as 'we speak the same language' is a metaphor for sharing interests and values, so the idea that meaning is contested and relative is metaphorically a recognition of the inevitability of difference and conflict. There are forms of verbal hygiene for whose proponents this recognition holds no terrors (their activities will be discussed in Chapter 4). But most forms of verbal hygiene are practised in order to ward off the threat, by making language a fixed and certain reference point.

The anxieties that lie behind the rhetoric of 'communication' are not, of course, novel. But in the conditions of the late twentieth-century West, one might argue that the old anxieties are likely to become intensified. Geoffrey Nunberg notes, for example, that there has been a change in the main project of verbal hygiene from the eighteenth to the twentieth century:

> The line of language criticism that stretches from Addison to Fowler was part of the larger critical enterprise of articulating a body of cultural values within

a relatively homogeneous public sphere. . . . But the modern view of the importance of language owes more to writers like Orwell, whose language criticism was concerned with maintaining a coherent political discourse in a culturally and ideologically fragmented community.

(Nunberg 1990: 475–6)

This cultural and ideological fragmentation is more openly on display now than it was in Orwell's time, let alone 200 years ago. The relative homogeneity of the public sphere in the past was a function of its small size and its social exclusivity. As the sphere of public discourse has grown and its exclusivity has been challenged, new problems have inevitably emerged around its language.

In the nineteenth century, verbal hygiene movements on behalf of disempowered groups tended to be about getting access to public discourse. Thus women at the Seneca Falls conference in 1848, a landmark of organized feminism in the US, passed a resolution condemning the taboo on female public speakers; Chartists in England battled for the right to speak and present petitions to parliament; access to literacy was an important issue for enslaved and colonized peoples. In the twentieth century, however, radical forms of verbal hygiene practised by citizens of western democracies are more concerned with contesting the terms of discourse in the public sphere. It is no longer enough that the descendants of slaves, Chartists and suffragettes should be permitted to speak: they are not content to speak in their masters' voices, according to conventions laid down within traditions that excluded them. Indeed, the new advocates of what has come to be called 'political correctness' are putting pressure on the masters to change their own tune.

This kind of pressure has undoubtedly had effects on the rhetoric of verbal hygiene. When, for example, *The Times* tells us its style guide is 'not prescriptive', 'not an attempt to establish some kind of cultural dictatorship', what this signifies is a wish to disclaim forms of authority that are no longer acceptable, or indeed sustainable, today. But that does not mean the traditional arbiters of usage are willing to relinquish all authority to an unfettered democratic pluralism. What commentators say about the new pluralism and its linguistic reflex in so-called 'permissiveness' reveals that this is still an area of considerable conflict. The very term 'permissive' is paradoxical, for it implies the existence of an authority with the power to grant or withhold its permission.

Geoffrey Nunberg is once again an illuminating source. Waxing lyrical about 'pluralism', he remarks apropros of terms like *gay* and *native American*:

Over the past twenty years, it has become an accepted principle of usage that every political or social group has the right to name itself and its own, unless the changes have collateral linguistic effects.

(1990: 476)

This remark might suggest that the triumph of pluralism has been overstated. Not only is Nunberg proclaiming a 'right', the right to

name oneself, that in a pluralist society would hardly be worthy of
remark; he is also suggesting that in some circumstances (if the changes
have 'collateral linguistic effects') that right could actually be denied.
The question begged here is, of course, by whom? Who has the authority
to rule on such matters, conferring or withholding approval of other
people's names? Among whom, exactly, has the right to choose your own
name become 'an accepted principle of usage'? Not, we may speculate,
among gay activists or native Americans themselves: presumably they
took it as axiomatic. It is just that their opinions were (and are) of no
importance.

Covertly, Nunberg is still discussing a public institution – 'usage' –
under the control of a homogeneous group (male, straight, Anglo-Saxon
and from a dominant social class). As other groups exert pressure from
below, these gatekeepers of usage may toss them a few scraps (so long as
there are no 'collateral linguistic effects'). That is an accommodation,
but it hardly qualifies as pluralism.

Although I believe Geoffrey Nunberg sometimes misrepresents current
tendencies in verbal hygiene, he is certainly right to point out that verbal
hygiene priorities are subject to historical change; and this is clearly a
matter of some significance for any serious investigation of verbal hygiene
practices at a particular point in time. The practices investigated in this
book are a heterogeneous set, and in later chapters I will try to resist any
temptation to flatten out the specificity of each particular case. In this
introduction, however, it is proper to ask whether there is a set of general
characteristics or tendencies which distinguish the verbal hygiene
practices of contemporary English-speaking societies. In the following
section, therefore, I will attempt to place current hygienic preoccupations in a longer historical perspective, and to consider the issues of
continuity and change.

HYGIENE IN HISTORY

In a keynote address on language planning which he delivered to an
international conference of applied linguists in 1993, the distinguished
scholar J.V. Neustupný began by asserting that 'language management' –
a broader term than 'language planning', and one whose range of
reference is comparable in many respects with my own 'verbal
hygiene' – was an activity as old as human history.[9] He also suggested
that one of its most important motivations was to adjust linguistic norms
to prevailing socioeconomic conditions. In societies where these conditions are similar, therefore, it should be possible to identify common
concerns in language management; on the other hand it is likely that any
society at different stages of its socioeconomic development will have
differing linguistic priorities. Neustupný distinguished, for example,
'pre-modern', 'early modern', 'modern' and 'postmodern' types of

language management, and suggested that the present situation in many or most places is one of transition between the 'modern' and the 'postmodern' types.

Postmodern societies are characterized economically by post-industrialism, consumerism and globalization. The reflexes of these characteristics in language management, according to Neustupný, are on one hand a desire for rationalization (regulating language use to make production more efficient), but on the other hand a move towards diversity and democratization (maximizing markets by catering to various consumer reference groups with varying needs and tastes).

Geoffrey Nunberg's point about the new 'permissiveness' or 'pluralism' represents one side of the postmodern coin, the diversifying and demo-cratizing side. Postmodern societies are often linguistically diverse, migration being one consequence of a globally organized economy, and linguistic diversity has long been felt to require management. Currently, however, there is a shift towards evaluating diversity more positively, and seeking to preserve rather than eliminate it – what Neustupný labels 'the variation ideology'. This finds expression in many contemporary verbal hygiene movements and practices: policies or campaigns promoting minority language rights, the maintenance of heritage languages and the preservation or revival of 'endangered' languages and dialects. Conversely, there are movements of resistance to diversity, of which 'US English'-style campaigns are the most visible examples.

Democratization, the principle of equal access to and participation in important linguistic practices, can also be seen at work in contemporary verbal hygiene movements. Apart from the 'variation ideology' which valorizes linguistic (and ethnic) diversity as a social good in itself, a further argument for accommodating diversity is that it enables minority participation in public discourse. But democratic ideals have other verbal hygiene reflexes too, many of them falling under the heading of anti-elitism. For example, Neustupný referred to 'plain language' move-ments whose aim is to force arcane professional registers to converge towards lay vernaculars. He also spoke in less specific terms of a general weakening of norms and a postmodern preference for innovation over conservatism (which in language will often entail a preference for vernacular over historically cultivated elite varieties).

Again, there are verbal hygiene movements of resistance to this development (e.g. the Queen's English Society); the tendency itself is more often observable in the weakening or abandonment of traditional practices such as the rigid policing of accent that used to be routine in broadcasting, or the lexicographical principle of illustrating usage only from the 'best writers'.

If we flip the postmodern coin to reveal its other, rationalizing side, we find that postmodern forms of language management are having significant effects in the shape of what Norman Fairclough (1992) has called the 'technologization of language'. Fairclough argues that as advanced capitalist economies increasingly shift from manufacturing to service industries, and as manufacturing itself is reorganized in line with new global imperatives, large numbers of workers who would once have been treated simply as 'hands' are being redefined as linguistic actors needing specific training in 'communication skills'. Thus 'links are being set up between research into existing language practices, redesign of language practices to improve their "effectiveness", and training of personnel in new language practices' (Fairclough 1992: 5).

This verbal hygiene of the corporation represents a new kind of linguistic authority and social control. Nor is communication training confined to the workplace: many of its techniques and theoretical under-pinnings are drawn from discourses of therapy and applied social science, and it is also prominent in 'self-help' activities designed to enhance 'personal effectiveness' in all areas of life. The delivery of a presidential address to the nation on television and the conduct of a family dinner-table conversation can equally be made accountable to notions of 'communication skills' and subjected to verbal hygiene intervention.

It does need to be said that developmental accounts like Neustupný's are always idealized, imposing upon historical time neat boundaries that do not, in reality, exist. Contemporary tendencies towards diversity and democratization are certainly worth remarking upon, but in the real world they clearly coexist with much older tendencies towards uniformity and elitism. The ultra-traditional 'Disgusted of Tunbridge Wells' remains a vocal and influential figure; so for that matter does 'Mr Crank', the modern (as opposed to postmodern) rationalist who is animated by a desire to perfect linguistic systems. (If the postmodern response to global linguistic diversity is a minority language rights charter, Mr Crank's answer is more likely to be Esperanto.) A great deal of discourse on language in the late twentieth century is an inglorious muddle of many different, and contradictory, impulses.

We may also be sceptical about whether any of the specific linguistic developments Neustupný and Fairclough point to as 'postmodern' are actually new. Arguments for plain language, for example, recur through-out the history of western linguistic thought (see Chapter 2 for illustra-tions); the impulse to preserve the rich diversity of human speech against the tide of rationalization was one of the main underpinnings of the nineteenth-century project of dialectology; and there is no great novelty about training people to communicate more effectively or persuasively, which was after all the project of classical rhetoric. Even developments that may with justice be called unprecedented very often serve predict-able and well-established ends: the computer technology that heralds a supposed communicational revolution has also brought us, among other things, a new obsession with checking our grammar, spelling and style.

There is, then, continuity as well as change in verbal hygiene; the most important changes concern not so much the ideas behind it as the kinds of discourses (and media) in which those ideas now circulate, and the extension of certain practices from a small elite to a much larger population. To be sure, these are significant developments, but they do not constitute a complete break with the past. It should also be acknowledged that verbal hygiene practices have their own histories, which intersect with other, more general historical developments, but cannot necessarily be reduced to them. Bearing that point in mind, we must now turn to the specific practices which will form the subject matter of this study.

EXPLORING VERBAL HYGIENE

In this introductory chapter I have tried to construct a framework for investigating the workings of verbal hygiene by spelling out what it is, why it is of interest and what general principles and concerns underlie it. But the project of discussing verbal hygiene in general can only be taken so far; for as I have tried to emphasize, the practices in which it lives are extremely diverse in their forms, goals and effects. Except at the abstract level of being concerned with *value*, verbal hygiene is not a unified and coherent discourse. It is not even a series of enterprises that can be neatly divided along such axes as right/left, conservative/innovative, modern/postmodern. Verbal hygiene practices are interesting and significant in their complex particularity, their fine detail. It is time, then, to get specific.

In this study I have chosen to focus on a small number of specific verbal hygiene practices and debates. I analyse their texts – the manuals, guidebooks and rule books in which practices are codified, and the polemical literature in which they are contested – and where appropriate I trace their history, observe and interview their practitioners. I have two concerns: to document what particular verbal hygiene practices involve, and to understand what they mean, both for those who engage in them and for the wider culture in which they arise.

The instances I have chosen are obviously only a small subset of those I could have studied. My selection reflects my own interests, taking in both issues that concern me politically and practices that simply make me curious. I have also been constrained, needless to say, by limitations on what material I could gain access to. Some organizations practising verbal hygiene are very secretive; commercial enterprises are often unwilling to divulge trade secrets on terms an academic researcher can accept. Individual privacy can also be be an issue: some kinds of verbal hygiene are stigmatized and people do not want to talk about being involved in them.

The first two case studies deal with practices which play a part in the maintenance of what Milroy and Milroy (1985) dub 'the ideology of standardization'. Chapter 2 examines the relatively neglected area of 'style', focusing in particular on the activities of editors in making and enforcing rules for writing that are not only about correct usage, but about wider considerations such as 'clarity' and 'elegance'. Chapter 3 returns us to the more familiar terrain of grammar, and specifically the teaching of English grammar in schools. It examines a recent and passionate debate on the National Curriculum for England and Wales, paying particular attention to the symbolic and moral meanings that were attached to the notion of 'grammar'.

Chapter 4 discusses the contemporary verbal hygiene debate which is likely to be most familiar – and most controversial – to readers of this book, namely the debate which addresses questions of so-called 'political correctness'. If any current linguistic contest deserves the epithet 'post-modern' this one does, and in my discussion of it I will try to show both how it departs from more traditional verbal hygiene models and why it is so politically explosive.

Finally, I turn to a practice exemplifying a type of verbal hygiene that is not exactly new, but whose distinctively contemporary forms are becoming increasingly widespread: linguistic training and self-help. Chapter 5 is concerned with the recent development of advice for women on effective communication. Here I want to emphasize that verbal hygiene is not only a practice of institutions or political movements; it is also very often an activity of individuals who are less interested in changing the world than in improving themselves and their prospects. In these cases there is a great deal of fascinating detail to document. Who seeks advice from an image consultant, and what do they get for their money? What actually goes on in an assertiveness training course?

One thing that should not be underestimated, and which I will try to probe in every case, is the strength of passion with which people engage in verbal hygiene, and the pleasure they often derive from their activities. As I suggested in the preface, verbal hygiene could in some senses be thought of as the popular culture of language; as with all popular culture studies, the study of verbal hygiene must enquire into the sources of interest and pleasure that make something 'popular'. It is after all pleasure as much as political interest that keeps so many people moving in the tracks of the cartoon cavemen.

In the dialogue on *The Times* style guide I have already mentioned, Simon Jenkins told a story that underlined this point. Having decided (by his own account very reluctantly) to overhaul the style guide he inherited when he took the editor's job, Mr Jenkins hit on an idea for getting the groundwork done: he would go out to dinner with Bernard Levin and Philip Howard, two *Times* writers with sharply differing views on language, and in the course of the meal they would thrash out 'all the really knotty problems of English usage from A to Z'. By the end of the evening, they had only reached C.

Simon Jenkins told this story to convey just how knotty are the problems of English usage, when you come to consider them in detail. But what struck me was that he and his dinner companions, all distinguished members of the journalistic establishment, had obviously enjoyed arguing at length about abbreviations, appellations, and so on. As leading British opinion-formers they could have been discussing pressing affairs of state; as senior employees of a major communications company they could have turned their attention to matters of business; but they chose to spend several hours debating questions of language. This is a sign both of the importance they attributed to language and of the pleasure they found in the activity. The issues at stake in codifying English usage for *The Times* engaged these men's intellects and roused their emotions.

It is not easy for linguists to fathom why this should be so – why so many people care so deeply about talking (and writing) 'really good', and why they hold the views they do on what counts as 'good'. Although linguistics offers its own compensations, enabling its practitioners to find a different sort of pleasure in the workings of language, the professional socialization that linguists undergo tends, as I have already pointed out, to distance them from the passions which inspire verbal hygiene and to cut them off from the gratifications it affords. Perhaps, indeed, this lack of empathy is one reason why metalinguistic practices have been more sneered at than studied: they have been relegated to the margins and separated from issues considered more central to the study of language, even language 'in use'.

Yet as I have tried to indicate, the two things – how people understand and evaluate language, and what they actually do with it – may not be so easily separated. Studying the discourse in which people reflect on language, and the practices whereby they attempt to intervene in language, is not only of sociological interest; it may also add something to our understanding of the infinitely complex phenomenon that human language is.

2 Restrictive practices
The politics of style[1]

STYLE AS VERBAL HYGIENE: CLEANING UP THE PRINTED WORD

This chapter is about 'style', and the verbal hygiene practices in which it is institutionalized. The idea of style as institutional may at first seem counter-intuitive, for we think of style as personal, as the linguistic hallmark of a particular individual ('Hemingway's style' or 'Jane Austen's style'). Yet outside the realms of great literature it is evident that style means something rather different, something less about individuality than conformity to rules. As Simon Jenkins, formerly editor of *The Times* newspaper, reminded his staff in 1992, 'Great writing may break rules, but good writing does well to observe them' (*The Times* 1992: 5).[2] But what are the rules for 'good writing', and who makes them? What is the source of their authority and influence?

There is no mystery about the authority of *The Times* style guide for *Times* writers. If Simon Jenkins disliked a particular usage he had the power to ban it outright. Idle or bloody-minded reporters who ignored the instructions in the guide could expect, at least in theory, to have the offending expressions removed from their copy by a vigilant sub-editor.

What is more mysterious, however, is where people like Simon Jenkins come by the particular notions about good and bad writing which their subordinates 'do well to observe'. Although his authority to make rules for *Times* writers is in principle absolute, neither Mr Jenkins nor those in receipt of his prescriptions are likely to regard them as a capricious display of power: few of the rules, if any, are of his own invention, and he is quick to defer to higher authorities himself – to Fowler (of *Modern English Usage* fame), Gowers (*Plain Words*) and *The Oxford Dictionary for Writers and Editors* (*ODWE*). Nor is it likely that these authorities plucked their own recommendations out of thin air. The precepts of style form a body of received ideas, receding endlessly into the past without ever appearing to reach any ultimate source.[3]

This does not prevent them from being pervasive and powerful. On the contrary, their status as conventional wisdom means they can be repeated *ad nauseam* by people who, by their own admission, can neither pinpoint their origins nor justify their content. It takes a real effort of will to recognize that commonplace observations on what makes writing good or bad are not self-evident, and some indeed are quite bizarre.

For example, *The Times* style guide sees nothing odd in holding up entire word classes for disparagement or commendation. 'Death to all qualifiers!' it proclaims on page 6, and then tells us in the same section that 'the verb is the engine of a sentence' (with the exception, presumably, of that one). These self-contradictory assertions can be recycled to sage nods all round, without anyone feeling the need for a supporting argument.

Pronouncements of this type circulate widely in literate society, but there is one place where received ideas about style are particularly elaborate, systematic and influential; that is, among the craft professionals whose job it is to regulate the language of published printed text. Despite the frequency with which people cite named authorities, whether canonical writers from Dryden to Orwell or authors of reference works such as Fowler and Gowers, the stylistic dicta of individuals remain of minor importance unless and until they are taken up by institutions as professional norms. The institutions that matter most here are journalism and publishing; the key actors in reproducing particular notions of 'style' are not authors and academics, nor even teachers of composition, though they play a significant supporting role, but copy editors.[4]

For most readers, the labour of copy editors in producing the taken-for-granted appearance of published printed text – books, newspapers and periodicals, advertisements and public notices of all kinds – is all but invisible. Our tendency is if possible to identify a text with its author, and to suppose, without giving the matter much thought, that what we see on the page is neither more nor less than what the author wrote. We acknowledge the person who wielded the pen, but not the one who wielded the blue pencil (or its hi-tech equivalent, given that much copy today is edited on computer). And yet the marks of editing are all over published writing. Authors writing for publication not only anticipate that their work will be edited, they participate in editing it even as they write.

Consider the text you are reading now. From the moment I began to compose it, it was shaped by all kinds of rules and norms: the rules of standard English grammar and spelling, the norms of appropriate diction and tone, as well as ideas about style that go beyond correctness or appropriateness to a more aesthetic sphere of 'elegance' (e.g. be brief, be specific, avoid jargon and cliché). I cannot claim I always observe all the relevant prescriptions, and sometimes indeed I deliberately flout them (for instance, as this paragraph shows, I have little time for the traditional rule 'avoid the first person singular'). But when I make this sort of choice I am aware I may be called to account for it. Thus long before an editor ever sees my text, I am influenced by my knowledge of editorial practices and preferences.

At a certain stage of composition this book was contracted to a particular publisher, a development that typically brings with it further editorial considerations. Many publishers issue their authors with a booklet setting out key features of the 'house style'. The purpose of this document is to clarify points of usage on which it is thought educated writers may reasonably disagree. The booklet tells you, for instance, whether to write *-ise* or *-ize*, *August 4 1914* or *4 August 1914*; it explains the house policy on such 'sensitive' issues as the gender of pronouns and the naming of ethnic groups; it guides you through a maze of fine distinctions about single versus double quotation marks, dashes and parentheses, bold and italic type.

Its recommendations on all these points contain an element of arbitrariness. Rival houses may well favour different usages. But on the assumption that the products of a single house should be homogeneous, authors are expected to amend their own usage where it diverges from the preferences of the publisher. Once again, then, before a text is actually scrutinized by an editor it will most likely have been written to comply with a number of specific editorial rules.

Eventually, a text like this one goes to the publishing house, where it is passed to a copy editor. The editor checks once again that it conforms to house style, and also to a much larger body of rules contained in the publisher's preferred 'style bible' – a general and comprehensive reference work (in Britain usually the *ODWE*, in the US commonly *The Chicago Manual of Style*). The application of these authorities together with the editor's own judgement produce a long list of queries and amendments which must be settled before the book can go to press.

The practice of editing in accordance with house style attracts surprisingly little criticism from those whose writing is on the receiving end. Authors do object to 'bad' editing, and resist what they regard as obtuse or unnecessary changes. The novelist Nicholson Baker, for instance, reviewing a scholarly history of punctuation, recalls occasions when he has argued with an editor about, say, whether to write *pantyhose* or *pantyhose*; he alludes to the 'power-crazed policy-makers at Merriam-Webster' and regrets that 'according to the *Chicago Manual of Style* . . . dash-hybrids are currently illegal in the US' (Baker 1993). But the comparison of dictionaries and style manuals with government policy documents and penal codes is apt and amusing precisely because writers do routinely submit to editorial authority – Chicago's ruling on the 'dash-hybrid' is, in its own sphere, as compelling as a decision made by the US Supreme Court. I did once hear an author denounce house style rules as a form of censorship. Her remarks, made at a conference on censorship where most speakers had concerned themselves with politics or sex, were received with some incredulity. It seemed self-important, pretentious and petty for anyone to make such a fuss about low-level stylistic tinkering.

Yet there is a certain incoherence about this response. If the question 'why make a fuss?' can be used to convict an author of pettiness, can it not with even greater justice be addressed to the publishers? They, after all, care enough about trivial style points to spend money producing house style guides and employing copy editors, not to mention bearing the hidden cost of lengthening books' production time. Since publishing is a commercial enterprise, one imagines there must be a very good reason for this expensive concern about style. But what could it be? Would the heavens really fall if authors were allowed to make their own choice between -*ise* and -*ize*, or indeed to alternate at random between the two?

It should be acknowledged that copy editors do more than just tinker with stylistic minutiae. On one hand they look out for serious problems, such as missing or garbled sections of text; on the other they provide technical instructions to the typesetter. In recent years, some publishers have encouraged editors to pay more attention to these major matters and less to minor stylistic infringements. Routledge, for instance, no longer has an extensive list of house style requirements: its policy is to follow the author's own preferences as far as possible.[5] This shift occurred partly because senior editors felt the strict style rules of the past were difficult to justify; but there were also economic reasons for it. Publishers have gone over to new technology to cut the cost of book production, and in order to maximize the savings this makes possible, it is desirable to minimize editing changes. This does not mean that Routledge authors can do exactly as they please: editors remain necessary because authors remain fallible. It does mean, however, that 'acceptable' usage will not be amended simply to make it conform to the prescriptions of some overarching authority, or to ensure that every book in the catalogue observes exactly the same conventions.

Interestingly enough, my informant at Routledge told me that while most of the freelance copy editors to whom she regularly gave work had adjusted to the new minimalism, some had not. There were editors who felt that the absence of strict guidelines made the job more difficult; there were also those who clung to the traditional stylistic norms of their craft and were therefore more pernickety than the publisher wished (or had budgeted for). This did not surprise me. My discussions with individual editors and my reading of literature addressed to those learning the craft suggested that copy editors generally do take pride in their knowledge of arcane rules, and they do regard minor stylistic tinkering as a crucial part of their function.

The American expert Elsie Myers Stainton, author of a number of books for professional and aspiring editors, has no compunction about making a fuss. She says in her guide to *The Fine Art of Copyediting* that 'the good copyeditor, above all, is a fusspot – one who cares' (Stainton 1991: 5).[6] Editors whom I interviewed agreed that it was their job to care about the minutiae, and felt strongly that giving this responsibility to authors, especially if the result were alternation between stylistic variants, would be a recipe for disaster. (I was surprised how often the belief was expressed that a lot of writers, and particularly journalists, could not write decent prose unaided; they might have good ideas and good contacts, but they lacked the editor's skills in the use of English.) My informants conceded that in some cases – not all – one variant might have no intrinsic superiority over another. Their cardinal principle, however, was that text must be *consistent*.

Invited to explain why consistency was so crucial, they reacted with surprise: its virtues seemed to them self-evident. (The index to *The Fine Art of Copyediting* has no fewer than eleven entries under the heading of 'consistency', and not one of them comments even in passing on the reasons for its importance.) Pressed to justify it, however, my informants came up with two arguments.

The first argument is that editorial practice is determined by market preferences: it is readers who demand consistency in published text on points like *-ise* versus *-ize* or the form of historical dates. Random alternation would bring immediate complaints. *The Times English Style and Usage Guide* subscribes to this view, remarking that 'inconsistency in style . . . irritates readers' (*The Times* 1992: 5). I asked Simon Jenkins if he had any evidence for this belief in the form of, say, readers' letters of complaint about inconsistencies in *The Times*. He was unable to cite any specific examples, but nevertheless stood by the belief.[7]

The second argument elaborates on the first by suggesting a reason why readers would naturally be irritated by inconsistency, and in the process linking consistency with that most uncontentious of all stylistic virtues, 'clarity'. According to this argument, if a reader's attention is captured by some formal detail, like an inconsistency of spelling, usage or typography, it is thereby inevitably diverted from the proper contemplation of the author's meaning. Inconsistency foregrounds the medium and so detracts from the clear communication of the message. Editors who advanced this view allowed that foregrounding the medium might be exploited as a literary device, but we were discussing the editing of non-literary and non-fictional texts. In such cases, more than one of my informants maintained that even where readers are not conscious of an inconsistency, it affects them subliminally.

The same points are made about that other great editorial fetish, 'correctness'. In *The Complete Plain Words* Gowers explains that norms of correctness must be observed, even though some of them make writing *unclear*, because lapses 'irritate the educated reader and distract his attention' (1954: 2). C.E.M. Joad, in a book ambitiously entitled *How To Write, Think and Speak Correctly* asserts that 'if we habitually use "incorrect" forms . . . we tend to distract the attention of our hearers and readers from the thought behind what we say to the form in which we say it; and this . . . badly impairs the efficiency of our expression' (Joad, n.d.: 10).[8]

The conviction that published text must be made consistent and correct was expressed by every professional I talked to, from the most pedantic traditionalist to the most permissive minimalist ('minimalism' here might be defined as the belief that, *pace* Elsie Myers Stainton, consistency and correctness are the only things that really matter). Here we have a striking illustration of two particularly widespread and powerful beliefs about good writing in English: the belief that it should be *uniform* and the belief that it should be *transparent* (as Orwell put it, 'like a window pane').

This preference for uniformity and transparency is, of course, a value judgement, and in due course I will return to examine its ideological roots and implications more closely. Meanwhile, however, I will pursue the editors' first claim – that they are only giving readers what they want – a little further. For I wish to argue that on the contrary, uniformity and transparency of style, especially the former, are essentially products of the craft tradition itself. To the extent that readers demand them, it is because they have been trained to demand them by consuming the products of the craft professionals. Among the interests being served by the production of uniform text are some rather specific professional interests.

STYLE AS CRAFT: FROM UNIFORMITY TO HYPERSTANDARDIZATION

The belief that language should ideally be used in a consistent or uniform manner is a central tenet of what Milroy and Milroy (1985: 26) call the 'ideology of standardization'. In the classic formulation of Einar Haugen (1972), language standardization has two main goals which, taken together, serve the overall objective of enhancing communication: maximal elaboration of function (a standard language should be usable for every purpose) and minimal variation in form (a standard language is codified to ensure uniformity in grammar, spelling, pronunciation, etc). For the Milroys, the most salient aspect of the process is the pursuit of uniformity at all levels of language use through 'suppression of optional variability' (1985: 36). In other words, if there are two (or more) ways of expressing the same thing – two spellings, two word forms, two past tense markers, two syntactic structures – just one will be selected as the norm or 'standard'. Those who aspire to use standard English cannot be content to alternate, as their ancestors did and as many non-standard users still do, between *lie* and *lay*, *himself* and *hisself*, *I saw her* and *I seen her*, *haven't you got any* and *aint you got none*. They need to be told which of these possibilities is 'correct'.

In English, the process of standardization has been going on for centuries. Today's copy editors are involved in it, but in what would seem on the face of things to be rather peripheral ways. Dealing almost always with text that is already in standard English, they concern themselves with those marginal areas of usage where a degree of optional variability still exists. Much of what we call 'style' refers, in fact, to this domain of residual variation. And the great puzzle about it, seen from this point of view, is that it seems to be exorbitant, beyond what is needed for efficient communication, carrying the principles of linguistic standardization to excessive and apparently pointless lengths.

Yet this is to underestimate the symbolic importance of editors' contribution. To see why, we must return to Milroy and Milroy's phrase 'the ideology of standardization'. Why call it an *ideology*, rather than simply a historical fact? In theory, the English language is highly standardized: within the core grammar of the standard dialect there is little variation, and in some parts of the system – for example, spelling – there is virtually none. Although the inherent variability and mutability of languages ensures that standardization can never be 'finished', it might well seem that present-day standard English comes as close as is humanly possible to meeting the goal of 'minimal variation of form'.

Yet as the Milroys point out, this is something of an illusion. English speakers' belief in uniformity (both in its existence and in its desirability) far exceeds their ability to produce it in their actual speech and writing. There is actually far more residual variation than most discussions of 'standard English' allow for. Thus however trivial and peripheral they may appear, the activities of copy editors are crucial, because they help to sustain the *illusion* of a uniform standard language. The fact that published printed text is more nearly uniform than any other kind of language underpins the 'ideology of standardization' by persuading English speakers, against all evidence to the contrary, that uniformity is the normal condition whereas variation is deviant; and that any residual variation in standard English must therefore be the contingent and deplorable result of some users' carelessness, idleness or incompetence.

In November 1992 the *Guardian* newspaper reported the results of a survey carried out by the Gallup organization for the Adult Literacy and Basic Skills Unit (*Guardian*, 12 November 1992). One thousand adults had been asked to spell six common words: *accommodation*, *business*, *height*, *necessary*, *separate* and *sincerely*. The results showed that only one in six of those surveyed got all of them right, while one in ten got all of them wrong. The word that caused least trouble, *height*, was still misspelled by 16 per cent of the sample; the most troublesome word, *accommodation*, defeated 73 per cent. Within the limits of its methodology, this survey appears to be good evidence for the proposition that most people do not spell with 100 per cent accuracy. There is variation in even this most thoroughly standardized and highly codified area of English usage.

The survey results were described as surprising and even shocking. The director of the Adult Literacy Unit was quoted as saying, 'it may be a sad state of affairs, but millions of people do have problems with spelling'. Predictably, suggestions were also made that this 'sad state of affairs' must reflect a decline in standards of literacy. This, in fact, is a perverse interpretation. No earlier study was cited and, broken down by age cohort, the 1992 survey findings are inconclusive: more of the very oldest informants got all six words right, but more of the youngest got five out of six. The most parsimonious reading of the statistics is that standards of accuracy in spelling have remained fairly constant at a figure considerably less than 100 per cent.[9]

The myth of 'falling standards' is resorted to in cases like this one in order to save the ingrained but unwarranted belief that accurate spelling is the norm, while spelling mistakes are an aberration. The source of this delusion is our constant exposure to published printed text, a form of language from which errors have been removed by editing – that is, by the addition of an extra stage of production during which trained specialist professionals explicitly check every word. The demand for absolute linguistic uniformity which professionals claim they are responding to may indeed exist, but it would never have arisen without the example of their own products; and only those products can be relied upon to satisfy it.

It is not difficult to see that this situation has certain advantages for the professionals. It ensures that their skills will continue to be valued in the trade, but at the same time it creates new opportunities for that trade. When professional standards become everyone's standards, whether in the realm of home-cooking, interior decoration or writing, a market opens up for products packaging craft skills for amateurs. This, in fact, turned out to be the real message of the press release on the spelling survey. According to the report in the *Guardian*, 'the literacy unit is backing commercial educational videos . . . [that] could reach people too embarrassed to attend basic skills classes'. A helpful note at the foot of the report informs readers that a videotape entitled 'Spell well at any age' can be theirs for £12.99 (about US $20).

How long this professional advantage will continue in relation to spelling is unclear; the report does not mention the existence of new technology in the form of spellcheck programs for personal computers, widespread use of which would render 'Spell well at any age' obsolete. The development of software for checking spelling, grammar and even 'style' does not diminish the authority of verbal hygiene norms – on the contrary – but it does alter the role of professional verbal hygienists. Even now, with conformity to house style a matter of a few keystrokes courtesy of a word processor's 'search and replace' function, authors are doing more of their own editing than was the case ten years ago. Perhaps copy editors will follow the scribes, printers and compositors of the past, deskilled and finally made redundant by technological advances.[10] On the other hand, it is noticeable that the 'authentic' ability to spell, not just without the aid of spellcheck programs but even without the aid of a dictionary, continues to be valued. There are, perhaps, reasons for this that have less to do with utility than morality; we will return to them later in this chapter.

Meanwhile, this discussion has drawn attention to the very important fact that for some people at least, writing has always been a business or a job of work. The implications of this are given little consideration in standard histories of the English language; here, however, I will consider them more explicitly, and raise questions about the role played by commercial interest in the production and reproduction of a uniform standard English.

Uniformity: selling standards

We can distinguish two main approaches to writing the history of standard English: one 'traditional' (stressing social consensus) and the other 'revisionist' (stressing social conflict). In the traditional account, the impetus for the standardizing of English is located in the dialectal diversity that followed the period of Anglo-Norman rule in England. The Conquest of 1066 had disrupted Anglo-Saxon traditions by imposing French as the language of 'high' domains such as law and administration. Writing in English did not cease, but it was curtailed and made marginal, and when English re-emerged in domains that French had occupied there was concern that the language was too variable to serve the communicative needs of a more centralized state. One dialect had therefore to be selected as a standard for written communication across different English regions and its norms codified to ensure it would be used with enough consistency to make it functional as a lingua franca.

The dialect chosen for this purpose was the south-eastern Midland variety used by the Court and mercantile class around London. In consequence, whereas in Chaucer's time writers had used the dialect of their region (hence the very noticeable differences between, say, *The Canterbury Tales* and *Sir Gawain and the Green Knight*), by Shakespeare's time this kind and degree of variation had disappeared from written English. As time went on and codification proceeded, the internal variability of written English (exemplified by Shakespeare's notoriously inconsistent spelling, for instance) was also reduced – at least, as the Milroys remind us, in theory.

Revisionist historians do not dispute the sequence of events in the traditional account, but they emphasize that standardization served a particular set of class interests: those of the economically and politically dominant south-easterners whose dialect was, not coincidentally, selected to be the standard, while other people's dialects were reduced to the level of patois. Standardization was not simply a response of the whole society to some common, objective 'communicational need'. It was the authoritarian creation of a small and self-serving elite. Historians such as Dick Leith (1983) and Tony Crowley (1989) stress that the process has continued, through the agency of educational institutions and mass media, to maintain oppressive class relations in Britain.

It seems then that there are two answers to the question, 'whose interests did standardization serve?'. Traditional histories say it served the interests of society as a whole, by enhancing communicative efficiency and promoting national unity, whereas revisionist histories say it served the interests of a dominant class by reinforcing their cultural, economic and political privilege. One or other of these accounts will explain most things about standardization in English, but arguably not all. There are aspects of the process that do not seem to have much to do with either the overt (communicational) goals of standardization, or its covert (social) goals, and which are more convincingly explained in relation to the more specific interests of people who made a living from linguistic production: craft professionals.

All commentators acknowledge the importance of *written* language in the standardizing process. Written language is standardized earlier and more comprehensively than speech; indeed, any codification of speech norms is usually dependent on a standard for writing (think of Johnson's dictum that we ought to pronounce as we spell, or the way non-standard pronunciation is stigmatized as 'dropping letters', which rather absurdly implies that speakers are 'really' reading from an invisible teleprompter). But this line of argument can be taken a stage further: for in private writing there was, and still is, variation. The existence of a standard for writing is dependent on the existence of a standard for *professionally produced* writing. Today this means published, printed text; before the advent of printing, it meant text produced by professional scribes. In other words, as I have already noted, to the degree that there is uniformity of usage, it is maintained in particular by the activities of trained craft professionals. It is these people's labour that produces the uniform spelling and consistent style of published materials, which in turn set the standard against which all written language (and eventually spoken language too) will come to be evaluated. In most cases, however, the professionals on whose activities standardization has depended have not been concerned only with the greater good of the language, the interests of the nation, or even those of the ruling class. They have had interests of their own.

Among the most famous documents bearing on the 'need' for standardization in the late medieval period and much quoted in histories of the language, is Caxton's preface to *Eneydos*, one of the earliest printed English texts. Caxton's preface laments the diversity of usage in England, and while the theme was not new, as Harris and Taylor (1989) point out, Caxton's stake in the question was both novel and material. As a printer, a proprietor of a new technology for mass-producing texts, Caxton faced a choice of some commercial moment. What form of language would appeal to the largest market? It was already clear that he must print in the vernacular, not Latin or French, but the existence of several varieties of that vernacular, minimally codified, presented a problem. Obviously Caxton had every reason to favour standardization, and to try if he could to hasten the acceptance of one variety as the norm; for this would make England a single market for linguistic products. The preface to *Eneydos*, with its classic verbal hygiene rhetoric of (to put it in modern terms) improving communication, should be read, as Harris and Taylor suggest, at least partly as economic self-interest.

Printed text would eventually become the most pervasive source of standard English norms, setting a *de facto* standard for all written texts. The influence of this professionally maintained standard would in turn create a demand for textbooks and manuals through which individuals might be helped to achieve the same standards in their own writing: dictionaries of hard words and later of all words, grammars and style guides, and eventually products such as 'Spell well at any age'. Today, the professionals themselves turn to the same authorities for guidance as they formulate and reformulate the conventions of published printed text. The reference compilers for their part, aided by new technology, amass vast corpora of published printed text with which to update their reference works at increasingly short intervals. It is an endless circle, turned by commercial interest – and today it revolves at an ever-increasing speed.

The contemporary publisher has an economic investment in linguistic expertise and its acceptance as such by the widest possible public. This would seem to favour the project of making language use ever more uniform: the existence of too many competing authorities touting different 'standards' might raise the suspicion that the whole enterprise was arbitrary and thus self-defeating. Yet in practice the conditions of the marketplace may encourage a proliferation of standards, causing imagined or idealized uniformity to coexist with actual diversity. This complicates the traditional picture, in which the course of a (standard) language's history is determined by its speakers' common interest in communicational efficiency and their desire for consistency.

Diversity: 'style' as a commodity

In his history of English spelling, D.G. Scragg (1974) gives an early example of market forces promoting diversity instead of uniformity. It has often been assumed, he notes, that the advent of printing was crucial to the standardization of English spelling, for in a mass production process the vagaries of individual scribal error can be eliminated. Yet Scragg maintains that the immediate effect of printing in England was exactly the reverse: spelling became more variable than it had been immediately prior to the change.

Among the reasons he gives for this paradox are the employment of foreign labour in the printing trade, with no uniform training and sometimes no competence in the English language; and the practice of charging by the inch, which encouraged printers to put in extraneous letters. If these factors were indeed relevant, they illustrate how professional practice may serve purely professional interests. Presumably the printers' practices were undesirable both in the eyes of their customers and from the point of view of the developing 'ideology of standardization'. But those practices nevertheless persisted until conditions in the trade changed (Scragg tells us the situation settled down as former scribes began to enter printing and to reassert their own craft traditions).

Attempts to regulate and standardize written language had in fact begun with the efforts of scribes. In some cases these efforts were codified: Elizabeth Eisenstein remarks in her detailed historical survey of the shift from manuscript to print culture, *The Printing Press as an Agent of Change*, that 'writing manuals . . . were not unknown in the age of scribes'. She adds, however, that such manuals, 'like the manuscript grammar books and primers used by different teachers in different regions in fifteenth-century England . . . were variegated rather than uniform' (Eisenstein 1979: 82-3).

'Variegation' is presented here as a limiting effect of the pre-print era; yet it would be wrong to suppose that our modern, printed analogues of the writing manual and the grammar are not also, though doubtless to a lesser extent, variegated rather than totally uniform. There is an obvious parallel between the 'variegated' manuals in existence during the scribal era – each one presumably devised for a specific group of scribes working in one scriptorium or locality – and the contemporary institution of publishers' or newspapers' house styles. The very concept of house style is a departure from the overt goal of standardization, i.e. maximal uniformity of usage. Although the differences that define house styles are very minor, they nevertheless lead to a proliferation of slightly varying 'standards' – as if every manufacturer of electrical goods offered a slightly different design of plug.

There is, however, a difference between plugs and house styles. Whereas minor variations in plug design would be seriously dysfunctional from the consumer's point of view – a plug has no intrinsic value and is useless if it cannot be connected with the consumer's electricity supply – small variations in style may add value to linguistic products. This has nothing to do with communicational 'need', but it is certainly related to the social differentiation function of language. 'Style' in the modern marketplace is itself a commodity, and can be packaged like other commodities for a variety of potential customers.

The clearest illustration of this principle is provided by newspapers and periodicals. I do not know of any book publisher that uses its house style as a selling point, and besides, as I noted earlier, there is a growing trend towards favouring the authorial over the institutional voice, mainly because of the drive to cut production costs. Newspapers and periodicals, however, are different: they too have engaged in drastic cost-cutting, but they do not have a single author, and more importantly their position in the market depends, as a book publisher's arguably does not, on their possessing a recognizable and consistent identity. Their way of using language is as much a part of this identity as the more obvious features of their format – size, typeface, page layout, etc. Some have attempted to sell themselves on the basis of their style, and even to sell their stylistic secrets directly to the public.

In fact it was a popular tabloid, the *Daily Mirror*, that first got in on this particular act by publishing a book called *Daily Mirror Style* (Waterhouse 1981). Subsequently however, the use of style as a selling point became associated with the high-class end of the market, where excellence in the use of English began to be touted as one of the characteristics which gives the quality press its quality. The point of this strategy was not only to add value to existing products, namely the newspapers themselves, but also to create a niche for additional products.

The most notable example of this approach to marketing was that of *The Economist*, which ran an advertising campaign in the mid-1980s proclaiming its allegiance to Orwellian principles of plain English. It was also the first quality publication to package its in-house style guidelines for wider public consumption, which it did in a volume entitled *The Economist Pocket Style Book* (1986). By way of justification, the blurb informs us that '*The Economist* newspaper has a tradition of clarity, style and precision in the use of English that stretches back nearly a century and a half'.

This is a good example of the two-pronged strategy noted above: first, *The Economist* urged people to buy the paper for its stylistic excellence, drawing attention to an 'added value' its target audience might not otherwise have considered; second, having prepared the ground, it tried to sell them a spin-off product, the *Pocket Style Book*. It is also a good example of the 'quality' theme: the appeal to 'a tradition . . . that stretches back a century and a half' has no relevance to the actual contents of the book, which was compiled in 1985 and focuses, as one would expect, on contemporary stylistic issues, citing only the standard modern authorities: Fowler, Gowers, Orwell and *ODWE*.

In 1992, a similar strategy was adopted by *The Times. The Times English Style and Usage Guide* already mentioned in this chapter was written primarily as an in-house document for *Times* journalists, but at the time of its adoption for that purpose there were also plans to publish it.[11] That may be why News International so actively sought to publicize the guide's existence: a lecture/debate (sponsored by *The Times*) was organized at Oxford to coincide with the paper's adoption of the new document, and invitations were sent out to other representatives of the media; Simon Jenkins spoke beforehand on BBC radio and the entire occasion was reported at length in *The Times* the following day.

One result of all this was that Mr Jenkins found himself making some copies of the in-house version available for purchase, in response to popular demand. His public utterances caused a stampede of enquirers wanting to know how they could get hold of the guide. The obvious enthusiasm of so many people for a text telling them how to write in the style of *The Times* seemed to vindicate what had struck me until then as the rather curious public relations exercise of having a high-profile launch for a book that was not yet for sale.

This response casts doubt on an idea which is very prominent in the *Times* guide itself: the idea that a newspaper's house style simply mirrors the usage of its readers. '*The Times*' we are told, 'should use the language of its readers, but that language at its best, clearest and most concise' (1992: 5). It might be more accurate to say that the stylistic choices made by a newspaper are intended to reflect not the way its readers really use language, but a way of using language with which readers – and just as importantly, advertisers – can identify. This entails paying particular attention to linguistic details that, while trivial enough in themselves, carry important and recognizable social or political contrasts.

The status and discernment of a *Times* reader is conveyed by the newspaper's style guide through small but symbolic restrictions. The usages that are 'banned' tend to be either slang and cliché (strongly associated in the British context with tabloid journalism), or Americanisms (not impossible in a liberal broadsheet, but out of keeping with the traditional, conservative British establishment image of *The Times*). At the more down-market newspaper *Today*, by contrast, banned words are those that smack of the class milieu that the newspaper's readers, though upwardly mobile by aspiration, most likely inhabit themselves: they include *mum*, *dad*, *kids/kiddies*, *lady* (described, tellingly, as 'a coy genteelism') and *toilet* (*Today* 1985).

The social and political outlook of a newspaper also tends to be signalled in its rules about nomenclature or appellations – *spokesman* versus *spokesperson*, *Mr Major* as opposed to just *Major* (or, to use Simon Jenkins's own self-mocking example, *Elvis* versus *Mr Presley*: even now, *The Times* recommends the latter in news stories, with a firm 'even if it looks odd' (1992: 16)), *Princess Anne* or *The Princess Royal*. Such nuances help to create the newspaper's 'brand image', but it should be noted that they are susceptible to pressure from the market. If it turns out that house rules are seriously out of step with the values of readers and advertisers, the rules may be modified. Thus for example the *New York Times*, which had for years refused to print the title *Ms* under any circumstances, was forced to begin doing so by this sort of explicit pressure.

Hyperstandardization and competing 'authorities'

Overall, the practices of craft professionals in regulating published printed text promote a curious mixture of uniformity and diversity that would not be predicted – or condoned – by common-sense wisdom about the goals of standardization. On one hand, uniformity is taken to an extreme that might well be called 'hyperstandardization': the mania for imposing a rule on any conceivable point of usage, in a way that goes beyond any ordinary understanding of what is needed to ensure efficient communication. When Caxton complained in his preface to *Eneydos* that he did not know whether to use the word 'egges' or the word 'eyren' and that either would meet with blank incomprehension from people familiar with the other, he was noticing a substantial impediment to linguistic exchange among English speakers. The kind of variation copy editors deal with today – *-ise* or *-ize* and the like – could hardly be said to present a comparable problem.

Nor does hyperstandardization usually serve the other, covert purpose of codification, that of distinguishing polite from vulgar usage. Despite the occasional intrusion of social shibboleths such as *Today*'s ban on the word 'toilet', style rules do not usually police the standard/non-standard boundary (*toilet* is not non-standard but merely 'common'): rather they regulate the nuances of an already standard and formal register among the small elite that has occasion to use it. The triumph of *-ise* over *-ize* (or *lavatory* over *toilet*) is hardly to be compared, in sociopolitical terms, with the defeat of Kentish by the south-east Midland dialect.

On the other hand, there is competition between slightly different 'standards'. This goes on, not only at the level of newspapers' and publishers' house style rules, where differentiation is motivated by the desire to convey certain social and political attitudes through linguistic choices, but more surprisingly, even among the stylistic authorities to which editors defer.

The politician and writer Roy Hattersley, smarting from a lengthy bout of proof-correcting in January 1993, wrote a newspaper column in which he rather waspishly pointed this out (*Guardian*, 11 January 1993). Irritated by his editor's blue-pencilling, he went to his reference shelf and conducted a comparative analysis, from which he drew this conclusion:

> Anyone who searches through a whole shelf of dictionaries will find virtually every possible variation on what is supposed to be standard English. Indeed,

on some basic questions of style and grammar, the works of reference exhibit
a unanimity which is reminiscent of the Labour Party in the early 1980s. . . .
You buy your textbook and take your pick.

Hattersley takes as an example the question of how the item *between*
should be used. The traditional dispute here concerns whether you can
use it in relation to more than two objects, or whether in that case
amongst is to be preferred. According to Hattersley, the Collins dictionary
says *amongst* is mandatory, the Shorter Oxford equivocates and Fowler
recommends *between*. He then goes on to consider the matter of *-ise* and
-ize, where he finds the *ODWE* favours *-ize* while Chambers prefers *-ise*.
Confronted with this diversity of 'authoritative' opinion, Hattersley's
editor predictably responds that consistency is all. Hattersley himself,
however, takes refuge in a different platitude: 'One of the many glories of
the English language is its inconsistency.'

For all that this is a commonplace sentiment, in this context it is surely
a very odd one. To rejoice in linguistic inconsistency (or to put it less
pejoratively, variation) is one thing, to rejoice in the inconsistency of
reference works quite another. If, as Roy Hattersley suggests, 'you buy
your textbook and take your pick', then why bother buying the textbook
at all? Why not simply make the choice unaided, without recourse to any
authority?

The puzzle, in essence, is to decide what kind of authority it is that the
publishers of dictionaries and other modern linguistic reference works
are selling. One might have thought that their defining function, in virtue
of which they are treated as possessing authority, would be to provide
language-users with a higher degree of certainty about what counts as
'correct' English than those users could get from their own heads. But at
this point we encounter the complications produced by the ideology of
linguistic descriptivism.

Contemporary linguistic authorities typically claim to be 'descriptive':
they tell us they are simply recording the facts of usage, not prescribing
them. This immediately begs the question of why anyone would seek
guidance from a text that did nothing more than describe their own
behaviour. On the assumption that this would be an absurdity, we could
hypothesize that the superiority of a reference work's judgements to the
judgements of any individual language-user must lie in the fact that the
reference compilers have based their recommendations on a much larger
sample of 'the facts of usage' than any one individual could compass.
This would explain why the individual does not just give up on reference
works, but it still leaves the question of why there should be any variation
between (or amongst) authorities: for if there is a set of 'facts of usage',
they should be the same facts regardless of who records them. Indeed, if
we followed this argument to its logical conclusion there would be no
obvious reason for the existence of more than one work of reference in

each category (e.g. scholarly dictionary, foreign learners' dictionary, pocket dictionary, etc.).

The fact that we have many linguistic authorities, and that they do differ, can be explained in two ways. First, that despite their rhetoric they are really prescriptive, not descriptive; and second, that the differences in what they prescribe have nothing to do with the so-called 'facts of English usage', but are more like the contrasts noted earlier between the styles of different newspapers; that is, they are motivated by considerations of marketing and 'brand image'. Variation is kept within reasonable bounds only because commercial rivals share a common interest in maintaining the belief that there is some uniform standard for correctness in language: Roy Harris (1983) compares dictionary publishers with rival toothpaste manufacturers who must ultimately subordinate their differences to the common pursuit of a perfect smile, remarking that 'if the public ceased to believe in lexical perfection . . . the financial consequences would be dire'.

The argument that dictionaries and so forth are prescriptive rather than descriptive has been made many times and I will not repeat it here, except to say that my own view – set out in more detail in Chapter 1 – is that one cannot in principle make an absolute distinction between describing and prescribing, and this argument does not apply only to lexicography. Dictionaries, however, do particularly invite questions about the nature of their authority, because that authority is so visible and so fetishized. Dictionaries are big business in a way that linguistics monographs and even grammar books are not; one consequence of this is competition between them, and advertising which foregrounds their status as commodities. On the other hand, dictionaries enjoy a strange and privileged status as cultural monuments. For example, the publication of a new edition of the *Shorter Oxford Dictionary* in September 1993 was a media event: the dictionary was reviewed in every quality newspaper, in several cases by someone ostentatiously distinguished, for all the world as if the *Shorter Oxford* had been a work of literature in its own right; or as though it was the English language itself that the reviewer had been asked to assess.

Such treatment makes it obvious that the *Shorter Oxford* is not just the linguistic equivalent of the Ford Escort manual (which no one would dream of reviewing, however brilliantly a new version of it encapsulated the workings of a Ford Escort). But nor is the *Shorter Oxford* just any dictionary. It is an *Oxford* dictionary, and the point is not irrelevant: this product's major selling point is precisely its status as a national monument. The 'big' *OED* is treated to all intents and purposes as if it were synonymous with the English language: so weighty is its authority that recently a Canadian lawyer who had come across a typographical error in it ('dept' for 'debt') was moved to enquire anxiously of the Oxford lexicographers: 'do you consider there is any risk that "in dept" will now become acceptable usage, apparently being sanctioned by the most respected authority on our language?'. The co-editor of the *OED* replied that while on balance he considered this unlikely, since *debt* is spelt correctly 1,917 times in the dictionary, nevertheless it was not impossible: 'it must be touch and go!' (correspondence quoted in Cochrane 1993: 20).

If dictionaries really were like car manuals, it would be difficult to interpret the claims rival publishers are apt to make for their products as 'authoritative' or even 'the most authoritative'. In the descriptivist paradigm of grammar or lexicography, the meaning of 'authority' undergoes a certain shift. The personal authority of, say, Dr Johnson, whose judgements one trusts to the extent that one trusts him as a model of learning, taste and correct form, is transformed by descriptivism into a 'scientific' authority, to be respected for its ability to collect, synthesize and adequately present 'the facts of usage'. Yet there is, at the very least, an ambiguity between these notions of 'authority' in a dictionary's claim to be 'more authoritative' than its competitors. For how can one set of facts have more authority than another? It seems very unlikely that Oxford University Press, say, would accuse its rivals of presenting a mere catalogue of errors or deliberate lies. Covertly, then, a claim to (greater) authority must rest on values rather than facts. Oxford is, in essence, presenting itself as Coke to other dictionaries' Pepsi ('the Real Thing') – a matter of image, not substance. Even where it does actually differ from rival products, the meaning of the difference depends less on what it is than on the qualities consumers attribute to the 'brand'.

Where linguistic authorities are in conflict, it often seems that the last thing to be considered in choosing between them is the linguistic merits of the alternatives they propose. To illustrate the point, let us consider a case where the editorial decision-making process produced a result in flagrant defiance of that cardinal principle, consistency.

Restrictive practices

A friend of mine once worked as a copy editor for a major publisher in New York. The project she worked on was a large encyclopedia, and her job was to edit a large number of contributions from all over the world in accordance with the rules laid down in the *Chicago Manual of Style*.

Among these rules is one that concerns the use of *that* or *which* in relative clauses. *That* is prescribed in those cases where the clause is 'restrictive', e.g. 'the book that Nigel gave me was no good', while *which* is used in 'non-restrictive' clauses, e.g. 'the book, which Nigel gave me, was no good'.

The difference between the two sentences above is one of those subtleties beloved of language mavens everywhere. In the first sentence, the relative clause *that Nigel gave me* 'restricts' the reference of *the book*, making clear that I am talking specifically about the particular book that Nigel gave me, as distinct from all the other books I possess. In the second sentence the information that Nigel gave me the book in question is still present, but it simply adds incidental information rather than being necessary for the identification of one out of a whole class of possible referents.

English speakers normally put *which* in non-restrictive clauses, but they quite often fail to observe the part of the rule that prescribes *that* in restrictive clauses: many native speakers find it equally acceptable to use either 'the book that Nigel gave me' or 'the book which Nigel gave me' (as well as a version with no relative pronoun, 'the book Nigel gave me'). It is not that such people perceive no difference between restrictive and non-restrictive relative clauses; it is rather that, for them, the distinction is carried by the commas that mark off the non-restrictive clause (or the prosody, in the unlikely event of someone uttering this sentence), and not by the choice of pronoun. Nevertheless, the *Chicago Manual of Style* insists on *that* rather than *which* in restrictive relative clauses. Copy editors therefore spend a good deal of time correcting *which* to *that* in writers' copy.

British readers unacquainted with the *Chicago Manual of Style* may well have followed this discussion with a degree of bewilderment. The rule about *that* and *which* is not insisted on in Britain as it is in the US; though some authorities (such as Fowler and *The Times* guide) do recommend it, it is not an absolute prescription. Bewilderment mixed with irritation was certainly the reaction of many British contributors to the encyclopedia my friend was editing. She sent them proofs with the *whiches* changed to *thats*; they promptly returned them with the *thats* changed back to *whiches*. My friend referred the matter to her boss, the 'copy chief', for an authoritative ruling on the entire pronoun question. After due deliberation he handed down his decision. Britons could write *which* if they wanted, but Americans must go by the book and write *that*.

This incident is absurd, and it was recounted to me as an absurdity. Nevertheless, it reveals a number of interesting things. First, it reveals that editorial practices need have nothing to do with communicational efficiency. Although the use of *which* in restrictive clauses may strike educated Americans as inelegant, one can scarcely imagine it interfering with their comprehension of the text. Second, it is notable that the copy chief did not try to resolve the *that* versus *which* problem by an appeal to rational principles. His solution implicitly acknowledged that no principled argument could be advanced in support of either alternative. Third, the outcome reveals that the much-vaunted principle of consistency can be ignored in certain circumstances. The copy chief did not say, as one might have expected, that while the rule might be arbitrary, it must be observed by all. On the contrary, he ended up allowing the encyclopedia as a whole to exhibit the very inconsistency the rule was supposed to eliminate.

The chief did not however go so far as to give individual authors freedom of choice on the relative pronoun issue. The overall inconsistency of usage had to be structured by national affiliation – one rule for British writers, another for US writers (inevitably disputes arose later about how to categorize Australian and Canadian contributors). The underlying concern, then, was not that the text should be either clear or consistent: it was that people should follow rules. Indeed we might read the whole affair as a kind of demarcation dispute in which members of one 'guild', the American copy editors, agreed to respect the differing craft practices of their colleagues across the Atlantic, while continuing to uphold the authority of such practices in themselves.

Arguably, however, it was not only the need to preserve editorial authority that led to the bizarre outcome of the relative pronoun controversy; it is also relevant to consider the working culture of the copy editors. Editors are not just automata, mindlessly applying the rules. What looks like excessive zeal on their part may in fact be a mixture of self-interest and subversion, as practised by alienated workers everywhere.

My friend and most of her fellow toilers on the encyclopedia fell short of Elsie Myers Stainton's ideal: they were not caring fusspots but graduate students working for doctoral degrees. Casual editorial work suited their need for flexibility at reasonable rates of pay, and they suited the publisher's need for a smart and highly literate workforce which would nevertheless be relatively cheap and disposable. They were hired to work on a specific project, and liable to be laid off when it was finished. While they worked they were paid by the hour. This particular group may well have represented an extreme of casualization and at times disaffection, but freelance arrangements of a roughly comparable kind are common in the editing trade, and these conditions affect the way the job is done.

For example, it was in the encyclopedia editors' interests to prolong work rather than hurrying to finish it. They lost money – and ultimately their jobs – if they worked too quickly. On the other hand, as casual workers they were easy to fire if they were thought to be shirking or 'padding their hours'. The best way to cope with these conditions was to edit copy with extreme thoroughness, both to display conscientiousness and to maximize the hours for which they would be paid. In their attempts to meet these criteria, they adopted the maxim of 'not just passing copy'. Whatever could be queried would be. This group of editors took particular pleasure in generating an obscure query that would need referring up to the copy chief. This was at once a good delaying tactic, proof of keenness and an outlet for underused creativity.

From an editor's perspective, then, hyperstandardization has its advantages: it makes a thorough editing job a relatively long job, a source of financial as well as professional satisfaction. I am not, in fact, the only linguist to have harboured this sort of suspicion. A review of a (British) monograph in the (US) scholarly journal *Language* ends with the following remark:

> [The author] and presumably the [publisher's] copy editor make no attempt to observe the infamous that/which distinction in restrictive relative clauses. For this relief, much thanks, and why can't American publishers give up on this device, whose sole virtue (speaking as the husband of a copy editor) is to give copy editors more billable hours?
>
> (Aronoff 1992: 610)

That billable hours are not the sole reason for editorial practices is strikingly borne out by the fact I noted earlier: that some copy editors continue to enact the role of 'fusspot' even when their employers are begging them not to (the employer who told me this did pay by the hour, but there was a limit beyond which editors had to fuss at their own expense). Even among the encyclopedia casuals, for whom editing was a pin-money job and not a lifetime vocation, it was obvious there was professional pride at stake as well as dollars and cents. The working conditions and culture of editors are defined by a combination of economic and professional considerations, and these are both factors in explaining, if not the phenomenon of hyperstandardization itself, then at least how and why it is enacted so zealously in everyday working practice.

Similar points could be made about the culture of sub-editors on newspapers and periodicals. They too are often freelance, working a certain number of hours each week on each of several different titles. Those I interviewed prided themselves on their mastery of – and ability to switch effortlessly between – the very different conventions of, say, a traditional weekly women's magazine, a London listings publication and a left-wing national daily newspaper. The subbing they did in the course of a typical week made them conscious of differences (especially in such matters as the preferred length of sentences, which usually reflects the presumed educational level of the readership), and they were also aware that there was a certain arbitrariness about house style rules; but at the same time their freelance status made them feel they had little stake in any particular set of rules. Professionalism, for them, meant being able to get straight on with it, whatever 'it' happened to be. As one freelancer told me, you would be more inclined to argue a point if you were actually a member of staff. Another took some pleasure in changing usages he disliked (in his case ones he considered sexist and racist) unobtrusively, without making an issue of it and trying to get the rules changed.

Copy and sub-editors are the foot-soldiers of hyperstandardization, and their chiefs (perhaps) are the junior officers. I have argued that it is these people's activities which are crucial in reproducing 'style', and therefore up to this point I have concentrated on trying to show what those activities consist of, in what conditions they occur and what overt and covert purposes they might serve. But this leaves certain questions unanswered. What about the generals, the people who decide on the actual substance of the rules to be used in professional practice? If we are interested not just in the everyday practice of editing but also in the 'theory' behind it, it is necessary to examine how rules are made as well as how they are routinely enforced.

FROM PRACTICE TO THEORY: THE CONSTRUCTION OF 'COMMON USAGE'

Tracing a stylistic norm to its source and discovering an underlying motivation for it is not easy; for as I noted when I first raised the question, 'who makes the rules?', even those who have unambiguous authority, such as Simon Jenkins at *The Times*, do not regard themselves as rule-makers; they see themselves as restating traditional wisdom or common sense, and therefore they typically say little or nothing about the reasons behind the rules. Stylistic authority is thus presented as a seamless consensus, maintained over decades or even centuries, and its precise character is felt to need little elaboration.

The Fine Art of Copyediting, for example, is replete with vague references to what 'stylists' have recommended (Stainton 1991). Certain canonical figures do regularly appear in contemporary style documents (Aristotle, the Augustans, Orwell, Fowler, Strunk and White), but the purpose of citing such figures is invariably to support a point the writer is asserting as indisputable common sense (a quote from a canonical source encapsulates 'what oft was thought but ne'er so well expressed', if I may make use of the same strategy by way of illustration). Arguably, however, this presentation of stylistic authority as a matter of tradition and consensus is a mystification – for in fact, the decisions of specific individuals working in present-day institutions have considerably more influence than it implies.

This point takes us back to what I alluded to earlier as the 'endless circle' – or perhaps a better image would be a 'feedback loop', whereby there is constant interaction between the established body of lore and the decisions made by specific individuals. On one hand decision makers in journalism and publishing consult existing authorities to find out what they regard as acceptable usage; but on the other hand, the examples that will 'authoritatively' illustrate acceptable usage tomorrow come overwhelmingly from the published printed text of today. So when a dictionary or other reference work claims to be describing 'the facts of usage', much of the usage it describes will itself have been shaped by prescriptions like the ones in, for instance, the house style booklets of major publishers and *The Times* style guide.

This last is an apt example, in fact, because as a newspaper of record

The Times is particularly likely to be a source for lexicographers and grammarians. Thus when a *Times* editor or writer of the future goes to the dictionary for guidance, he or she may well be looking at a description of acceptable usage that is based on the usage of *The Times*. And the crucial point here is that the usage of *The Times* is not just, as the dictionary would have us believe, representative of educated English usage in general: it is the outcome of some very specific decisions and stylistic choices, made by identifiable individuals.

One consequence of this concentration of decision-making power in the hands of senior craft professionals is that what gets described as 'common usage' may in certain cases distort the facts about most people's usage (even taking 'most people' here to have the narrow sense of 'most educated users of the standard language'). For example, any reference work purporting to describe the 'facts of usage' in the US would be bound to include the that/which rule, since the distinction is observable in just about every American print source. Yet this reflects, not *common* usage, but specifically the usage of the *Chicago Manual of Style*, the absolute dominance of that text as a style bible for American publishers and the zeal with which copy editors enforce its prescriptions.

If the that/which rule becomes obsolete, it will not be simply because ordinary English-speakers have ceased to observe it (for frankly it is doubtful whether most of them ever routinely observed it), but because someone compiling a style book, or more likely a new edition of an influential style book, decides to break ranks, and others decide to follow. (Another, in this case unlikely, possibility is a sustained verbal hygiene campaign against the that/which rule, like the campaign against generic masculine pronouns.) Of course, perceptions of what really is 'common usage' are not wholly irrelevant, for once again the continual interaction between reference works and print sources will lend momentum to a change of this kind. As fewer and fewer print sources manifest the distinction, reference sources that continue to insist on it will appear more and more old-fashioned, and those responsible for compiling them will feel pressure to reconsider. Conversely, when the reference works relax the rule, even the most conservative editor may feel compelled to do likewise. The point is, though, that it is in published printed text rather than 'common usage' that standards are maintained or modified.

The process described here is illustrated, as it happens, in Elsie Myers Stainton's note on *that* and *which* in the 'concise manual of style for copyeditors' that appears in *The Fine Art of Copyediting*. Having first outlined the traditional distinction, Stainton goes on:

> Many stylists now disregard this time-honored rule. The editor who tries to preserve the distinction is being conservative, and although following the rule might make the author's sentences easier to read and the exposition clearer, if your author thinks the distinction useless and passé and does not wish to observe it, you had better not try. . . . If frustrated, you might, just here and there, show the value of changing a *which* to *that* and vice versa.
>
> (1991: 52)

It is clear that Stainton herself is a devotee of the that/which rule (though predictably she does not explain *why* it should make text 'clearer' and 'easier to read'). Yet apparently she senses that a time has arrived when she must in fairness acknowledge that her preference is 'conservative', no longer shared by 'many stylists' (she does not tell us who these stylists are) and considered by many authors to be 'useless and passé'. In other words, we may infer from this passage (and especially from the choice of such a term as *passé*) that there are fashions in linguistic style as in styles of dress or home decor.

The question of the rule's *utility*, asserted but not justified by Stainton (and denied, also without justification, by Aronoff in the review I quoted on page 53), is something of a red herring: nothing about the English relative clause *per se* has changed, and therefore it would be logical to suppose that if the rule was ever useful it must in principle remain useful, while conversely if it is useless now, it must equally have been so before. What has changed is perception, or linguistic taste.

The question is, though, where do such changes in perception, fashion, taste and so forth arise? Again this is something that tends to get obscured or taken for granted in most discussion. Like their scholarly descriptive counterparts, even obviously prescriptive texts such as *The Times*'s style guide make much of the need to adjust to 'natural' linguistic changes. The very first sentences of the guide read, 'English is not a language fixed for all time. Speech changes and its written form should change too' (p. 5). These observations locate the source of change elsewhere, in speech. They also imply two rather contradictory propositions about the relation of speech to writing. On one hand, writing is described as simply parasitic on speech ('its written form'), and therefore presumably liable to change as speech changes. On the other hand, the notion that writing '*should* change' in line with the spoken language suggests that it will not 'naturally' change of its own accord: someone has to sanction change by altering the rules that guide writers. It is at this point, the point where sanction is given to, or withheld from, a development occurring elsewhere, that an individual like the author of *The Times*'s style guide wields significant influence.

This influence is all the more significant because writing is not, in fact, merely parasitic on speech (nor is speech necessarily the source of all innovation). Written language – especially in its published printed form – is both more permanent and more prestigious than the spoken word. It is the written form most users will take as defining what counts as 'the language'. In declaring that a certain form, which may or may not be genuinely novel – a new word, a different relative pronoun rule, a title such as *Ms* or a group label like *Native American*[12] – will be adopted in future by a publication such as *The Times*, the originator of a style guide performs an important gatekeeping function, moving the form thus adopted from the margin to the mainstream, and conversely ensuring that other forms which are *not* adopted remain marginal.

Announcing such decisions, style guides may refer to 'common usage', but even a cursory examination will show that this criterion has been (and indeed has to be) selectively interpreted. To take only one example, the 1992 *Times* guide informs us that the word *chairman* is 'still common usage referring to men and women' (p. 31). It is difficult to know exactly what 'common' means in this context. Statistically common (i.e. not rare), or the common (shared) practice of all speakers of English? The second, stronger definition is clearly untrue in this case, and even the first depends on what range of sources you sample. The question whether *chairman* should be used for men and women is precisely a controversial one which has produced conflicting norms among speakers of present-day English. Although they rarely invent new usages, to the extent that they are making choices about which of the norms in circulation are to be used in the most influential linguistic products, gatekeepers like Mr Jenkins may be said to set trends rather than just follow them.

It is therefore of the greatest interest to examine the decision-making processes of gatekeepers and the ideas and value judgements about language that influence their decisions. I now propose to look at the stylistic decisions made over a period of years on *The Times*. This is arguably a more revealing case study than the decision making of grammarians and lexicographers, for the latter group of codifiers are more circumscribed by the requirement of scholarly objectivity; that is, they are less likely to make their value judgements explicit. Newspaper style guides may not always explain or justify their judgements, but they can more easily be read symptomatically, as a digest of prevailing common-sense ideas about 'good writing'. And in the case of *The Times*, which updates its style guides regularly, it is also of interest to consider whether and how these ideas have changed.

MOVING WITH *THE TIMES*: 80 YEARS OF A NEWSPAPER'S STYLE[13]

My historical investigation of *Times* style was made possible by the fact that the newspaper has an archive, in which are kept not only copies of past style guides beginning with the first edition of 1913, but also, for the period following the Second World War, selections of internal correspondence relating to the periodic amendment and revision of whatever guide was in force at the time. There are memos in which staff members or committees preparing new editions of the guide solicited and received advice and comments from their colleagues; there are interim memos on usage issued by the editor of the day; in some cases the letters of complaint from readers that prompted the editor to send out a memo have also been preserved.

The Times is unusual in the amount of attention it has paid to forging and documenting its house style. Many newspapers do not have formal style books for their writers: reporters and sub-editors simply rely on general authorities such as *ODWE*, backed up with occasional *ad hoc* pronouncements on particular usages. Even where some kind of style book exists, regular and systematic revision as practised by *The Times* is surprisingly uncommon. One informant who had worked on a national daily newspaper's magazine supplement recalled its style sheet as a dog-eared palimpsest which was hard for writers to use even if they wanted to, and I was also told that an attempt in 1985 to create a style book for the new title *Today* had not been a great success because the writers, already in the habit of turning to other sources, paid little attention to it.

Establishing and maintaining a style book's authority would seem to require time and effort, demanding a strong commitment on the part of department heads, chief sub-editors and the editor of the paper to monitor what appears in print and to take swift action to enforce the rules where necessary. The correspondence files show that at *The Times* this kind of monitoring and enforcement had been developed over a long period.

The Times is therefore an excellent case study for the investigator of verbal hygiene. For one thing, the documentation available is exceptionally full; but in addition, there are interesting ideological reasons why this newspaper has traditionally had such a strong style policy: it has practised verbal hygiene in a highly deliberate way because it has seen itself, and been seen by others, as occupying a special position in British journalism and society. *The Times* is an institution, and has been conscious of its obligations to that other cherished institution, the English language.

The earliest versions of the style book are brief and impersonal. The 1913 edition is a simple alphabetical listing of problematic spellings and doubtful forms, followed by detailed instructions on the correct setting of classified advertisements. It states its purpose in the following terms:

> The Editor will be glad of suggestions from time to time for incorporation in this list, by way of correction or addition. Any words and expressions should be suggested as to which the spelling or style is in doubt.
>
> (*The Times* 1913)

The editions of 1928, 1936 and 1939 follow the same format and are very little different in content – though the booklet gradually becomes larger as more and more 'corrections and additions' are incorporated into it.

By 1939 staff were also being issued with a pamphlet entitled *English in The Times* (an amended edition was produced in 1945), which announces its purpose thus:

> The Editor is circulating to those who work inside Printing House Square, and to all his regular contributors outside it, the following list of misused or

overworked words and expressions which he wishes to find in THE TIMES as seldom as possible.

What the editor of 1939 wishes to find in his newspaper as seldom as possible is strikingly similar to what Orwell was to excoriate some years later in 'Politics and the English Language' (1946): a style marked by abstraction, over-complexity and verbosity. Here are some sample entries:

> *Accommodation* – A dull word (p. 1).
> *Bureaucratic language* is the source of a great deal of dull English. When the plain meaning can be discerned, there is no reason why we should not give it, unless we are quoting in full (p. 2).
> *Deal with* – perhaps the dreariest verb in the language (p. 4).
> *Interesting* – a feeble adjective (p. 6).
> *Shopkeepers' language* is often bad; e.g. 'quotation' should be 'price' (p. 10).
> *Very* – There was a time when 'very' was not allowed in *The Times* and it would be a good rule to restore (p. 11).

The pamphlet concludes with example sentences parodying (as, once again, Orwell was later to do) the kind of language that should be avoided, such as:

> With regard to the discussion which took place at yesterday's meeting, in reference to the position arising out of the present situation, the result, so far as the practical point of view is concerned, was of a purely negative character.

This, readers are told, should be expressed in *The Times* by the sentence 'Nothing came of yesterday's discussion' (1939: p. 12).

From 1953 on, the content of *English in The Times* was incorporated into the style book proper, and the convention was introduced of having an editor's foreword in which a certain general philosophy of *Times* style was summarized. The 1953 foreword, written by Sir William Haley, drew attention to *The Times*'s status as a '"newspaper of record" – perhaps even . . . "a national institution"', and noted that because of this status, '*The Times* has a special responsibility to maintain the standards of a philologically correct, unslovenly and accurate English'. Five years later, in an internal memo soliciting comments on the revised draft that would become the 1960 edition of the guide, Haley reiterated this view: '*The Times* should strive to maintain the purity of the language and a sense of style . . . it is very desirable that *The Times* should continue to be regarded as a model (and when it lapses as an awful warning)' (memo from the Editor, 13 October 1958).

When the new edition was issued in 1960, Haley contributed a new foreword. It addresses the same concerns about maintaining high standards while avoiding 'dull' prose, but there is also a slight change of emphasis from 1953:

> Language is a living thing; this revised edition of the Style Book is an effort to keep *The Times* written in correct and accurate English, without being pedantic. . . . every member of staff should write with the ease,

interest and understanding of his readers in mind. *The Times* must be both lively and lucid.

(The Times 1960)

The main innovations here are that the word 'pedantic' appears as a pejorative term, while language is proclaimed to be 'a living thing' – an assertion destined to be repeated by subsequent editors right up to the present day. These changes, though slight, seem to indicate a shift away from the traditional authoritarian concept of *The Times* as a guardian of linguistic 'purity', defined by philological criteria, towards a more modern view which stresses the need for responsiveness to 'natural' linguistic change; though the bulk of the guidance in the style book is the same as it ever was.

William Rees-Mogg, who took over as editor in 1967, makes no bones in his foreword to the 1970 revised style book about the status of many norms (though not all) as 'choices' or 'preferences'. Having acknowledged that style rules are not written on tablets of stone, this editor is obliged to say something about the criteria they are based on; what he does in fact say is worth quoting at some length.

> The revised *Times Style Book* is intended to help the paper to be both correct and consistent. Many of the entries are simple matters of correctness in which mistakes are often made. Others are matters of choice in which *The Times* chooses to use one of several correct variants.
>
> The English language changes continuously and the *Style Book* has to be revised periodically in order to take account of new forms and to change preferences that have come to seem obsolete. The style in which *The Times* itself should be written is based on the traditional plain style of English prose. It should be simple and clear. It should not sound affected, and should be neither archaic nor exaggeratedly contemporary in tone.
>
> . . . The tone of *The Times* has always been calm and judicious. It is this professional tone – clear, to the point, impartial and sensible – which is one of the essential virtues of the prose style of this newspaper.

(The Times 1970)

Here we have a much fuller exposition of the general stylistic values and the prose tradition *Times* writing is meant to represent. Apart from correctness, what the newspaper is striving for is a set of qualities associated with the 'plain style of English prose' (clear, simple, timeless, matter-of-fact), which express what Rees-Mogg would like to define as *The Times*'s personality: 'calm and judicious' in tone, 'impartial and sensible' in outlook. Like the shibboleths discussed earlier in relation to the current *Times* guide, these qualities of language are part of a newspaper's brand image, giving it a distinctive institutional voice. Rees-Mogg's is a particularly clear statement of the image he wants *Times* writers to project; later on in this chapter we must look more closely at *why* the 'plain style of English prose' has acquired its significance as a mark of judiciousness, impartiality and good sense.

To talk about language being a 'living thing' is to acknowledge that any style guide will stand in need of constant amendment as new problems of usage become visible to its users. *The Times* has tended to produce revised guides at roughly ten-year intervals since the Second World War, but it is clear from the internal correspondence file that every guide was felt to be in need of revision almost as soon as it came into force, and there were constant amendments between revisions. Indeed, since it could take years to produce a new version – the 1960 edition was put in hand as early as January 1957 – and each revision entailed a great deal of consultation, questions of style were under discussion at Printing House Square almost continuously.

The most common procedure for making interim amendments was for the editor to send out a memorandum on style to his staff, which then became part of the rules. Sometimes the memo was occasioned by a query from a staff member, or a complaint from a reader; sometimes it arose from the editor's taking exception to something he saw in the newspaper.

Between June 1968 and May 1970, for example, William Rees-Mogg issued ten *ex cathedra* pronouncements headed *Memorandum on Style*. The first is an excellent example both of the sort of thing editors were moved to comment on and of the peremptory tone they typically adopted in doing so: '"Consensus" is an odious word. It is never to be used and when it is used it should be spelt correctly' (Memorandum on Style no. 1, 21 June 1968). The second (25 July 1968) objected in similar terms to *prestigious* ('makes almost any sentence sound like an estate agents' advertisement'). Others concerned the use of *invite* as a noun, the misuse of *minuscule* (which according to the memorandum means 'a small cursive script developed in the dark ages'), the fact that *liaise with* is 'not a Times usage' and that the phrase *very real*, like *very unique*, has no meaning. The last two cited were direct responses to readers' complaints.

Harold Evans, who took over with the Murdoch regime in 1981, continued the tradition whereby the editor would pronounce on stylistic questions in brisk memos to the staff. In March 1981 he sent out a note headed *Usage* which read: '*The Times* will never inflict on the population "lose out" as *The Guardian* did this morning but twice I have seen in *The Times* the phrase "not less than 283 . . . "' (12 March 1981). This may have made writers more punctilious about the correct use of *less* and *fewer*, but only a few weeks later Evans was compelled to issue a further memo: 'We had a headline recently saying somebody "Lost out". The Americanism "out" is unnecessary. Honesty pays, it does not pay off' (1 July 1981). An intervening memo is on a topic that, perhaps surprisingly, had not previously arisen in the archived correspondence: 'Could you please make certain that no obscene four-letter word gets into the paper without the express permission either of myself or the Deputy Editor' (23 March 1981).[14]

Apart from their intrinsic interest, these examples show how much power over the specifics of usage was wielded directly by individuals, especially successive editors of *The Times*. In some respects the style of this newspaper of record is a steady accretion of personal idiosyncrasies, turned into rules by editorial fiat and then into custom and practice by the passing of time. *The Times* was and is conservative: once something got into the style book it tended to persist, being carried over in each revision unless and until someone happened to query it. Every edition, including even the unusually radical revision undertaken by Simon Jenkins, contains recognizable traces of its predecessors; and this sedimentary process leads to mystification, the automatic restatement of rules whose origins and rationale no one can remember or reconstruct. We see here a scaled-down version of the same process that results in such long-lived fetishes as the 'that/which' rule or the 'will/shall' distinction: conventions which for all anyone knows may once have been enforced at the whim of a single individual, but which nevertheless continue to be revered as Holy Writ.

Arguably however it requires a strong institutional culture to sustain this kind of authority. It is striking that in many of the memoranda in which editors make rules without offering reasons, there is a rhetorical appeal to a particular notion of *The Times*'s style which is assumed to be shared by all staff members, since it is embedded in the newpaper's history and its ethos. The memo's recipient gets a sense of eternal verities being invoked – even or especially when the judgement in question is by definition either a deliberate *change* in practice or a ruling on something for which no rule had previously existed. When, for example, William Rees-Mogg pronounced that *liaise with* was 'not a *Times* usage', he seemed to imply that the point was self-evident; but since no such rule actually appeared in the style book, how was anyone supposed to have divined it in advance? What exactly *is* a '*Times* usage'? The criteria, or non-criteria, call to mind the slogan that used to advertise a brand of sherry: 'one instinctively knows when something is right'.

In the 1990s version of the guide, a reader still has the sense that a great deal depends on instinct and on *ex cathedra* pronouncements by the editor, but the precise things that 'one instinctively knows' have changed considerably over time. For example, one is no longer instinctively a classicist, apt to decide disputed spellings (including the vexed question of *-ise* versus *-ize*) on grounds of etymology, and to complain that there are too few staff members equipped to check Greek quotations in proof. One is no longer the kind of xenophobe who writes that 'owing to the Arabs' unfortunate vagueness about names it is difficult to know how to describe them' (*The Times* 1953: 14) and insists on spelling the name of the Anglo-French supersonic aircraft 'Concord' (memo, 26 June 1963) – though one is still given to a rather unreflective prejudice against 'Americanisms'.[15] And thankfully, one no longer sees the need for a whole section in the style book devoted to 'nautical solecisms', though in a good example of the sedimentary process described above, 'naval nomenclature' still takes up two-and-a-half pages.

Another thing that has changed is the secrecy with which *The Times* used to surround its style book. A recurring theme in the correspondence I examined was the need to keep the style guide 'in-house', rebuffing even those enquirers who might be thought to have legitimate grounds for requesting it. A stiff editor's memo of 9 September 1965 – which is by no means the first or the last on this subject – reminds staff that 'as you know, these books are strictly private and confidential and should not be allowed outside the building'. William Rees-Mogg acknowledged in a personal letter to someone who had enquired about it that '[the style book] has in the past been treated as a document of the highest secrecy' (9 February 1967).

Twenty-five years later, the decision to publish the style book no doubt reflects changes in the institutional culture of *The Times*[16] and a trend towards greater openness in many spheres of life, but it also underlines what I drew attention to earlier in this chapter: the sense that linguistic style is no longer a hallowed mystery but a marketable commodity (though in this case the mystique is also the selling point). Other changes in *Times* style policy may reflect a recognition that *The Times* is no longer a national institution in the old sense, nor even the natural reading matter of every English gentleman and member of the British establishment. The current style guide is at pains to acknowledge that no newspaper can now pretend to the kind of authority over English usage that was assumed by, say, Sir William Haley. The preface to the published version stresses that 'this guide is not a work of stylistic dictatorship' (Jenkins 1992: 5); it is 'for enlightenment and pleasure' (p. 6). Earlier guides and editors took a very different view of their function.

What does remain, however, is the general commitment spelt out by William Rees-Mogg in his foreword to the 1970 style book to 'the traditional plain style of English prose' with its 'clear and simple' diction, its 'calm and judicious tone' and its connotations of impartiality, matter-of-factness and plain good sense. This is still the institutional voice of *The Times*, and indeed the voice of many institutions that promote 'good writing' in the late twentieth century. In the final section of this chapter I will look more closely at the development and symbolic meaning of this particular voice as the dominant stylistic ideal.

STYLE AS IDEOLOGY: TRANSPARENCY AND 'PLAIN LANGUAGE'

Earlier I mentioned two ingrained beliefs about good writing in English: the belief that it should be uniform and the belief that it should be transparent. The 'traditional plain style of English prose' to which William Rees-Mogg alluded in his foreword to *The Times* style guide of

1970 is a combination of both, stressing on one hand 'correct and consistent' usage (uniformity), and on the other 'simple and clear' prose (transparency). These are interdependent rather than separate but equal ideals, and uniformity is essentially conceived as subservient to transparency. Thus the most common reason editors give for their insistence on correct and consistent usage is that it makes the writer's meaning more directly accessible to the reader, without distracting attention from the content to the form.

Uniformity may be a necessary condition for transparency, but it is not a sufficient one. In addition to rules about the minutiae of grammar, spelling and punctuation, good writing requires a set of global stylistic maxims, too general to be formulated as specific rules of usage: injunctions to be clear, precise, definite, simple and brief, while avoiding obscurity, ambiguity, vagueness, abstraction, complication, prolixity, jargon and cliché. And whereas authorities acknowledge, however reluctantly, the natural mutability of grammar and vocabulary, they typically present clarity *et al.* as if they belonged to some pure and timeless realm of self-evidently desirable qualities. In fact these norms are neither universal nor neutral. They have a history and a politics.

The way of using language that I am calling 'transparent', after Orwell's memorable image of writing as a pane of glass, is more often referred to as Rees-Mogg refers to it, using the term *plain*: plain style, plain language or plain English. Anyone familiar with the history of English will know that the merits of plainness have been much debated in the past five hundred years. Plainness was a key term, for example, in the so-called 'inkhorn controversy' of the sixteenth and seventeenth centuries, when the question at issue was whether to enrich English vocabulary by importing Latin loan-words or by coining alternatives. In this case the supporters of Latin 'eloquence' won. But only a little later the Enlightenment brought renewed emphasis on plainness, and a correspondingly strong distrust of rhetoric – criticized by Locke in *An Essay Concerning Human Understanding* (III:x, section 34) as 'that powerful instrument of error and deceit'.

In literary discourse there have been various moves to and from plain English (e.g. the rejection of the 'euphuistic' for the 'plain' style by prose writers in the seventeenth century, or the Romantics' reaction against 'polite' poetic diction at the end of the eighteenth); while in the sphere of religion, attitudes towards plain versus elevated language have been, and continue to be, a source of dispute among believers. During the last fifty years, the question of plain English has become particularly salient in the domain of 'official' communications addressed by the state to its citizens. Sir Ernest Gowers's classic *Plain Words* was written for British civil servants just after the Second World War as part of a deliberate effort to 'improve official English' (Gowers 1973: iii). A number of US states have 'plain language amendments' serving a similar purpose.

Examples such as these show that plainness is, if not timeless then at least a very old ideal (among those whom Gowers cites in support of it are Aristotle, St Paul, Roger Ascham, Cervantes, Defoe and Macaulay). Historically it has also however been a contested ideal, whose defenders have often felt the need to counter criticisms that plain language is flat, dull, commonplace, unrefined or vulgar. Today, though, the notion that anyone could reasonably be against plainness runs counter to common sense. In recent times it seems there has been less and less need to defend plain language *per se*.

It is striking that the virtues of plainness are no longer presented as merely functional, but also as aesthetic. To judge from Gowers's disclaimers in *Plain Words*, where he emphasizes that he is not promoting 'fine writing' in the civil service, but only intelligible prose, he would be surprised to find himself cited by *The Times* style guide forty years later as one of 'the masters on style' (*The Times* 1992: 8). But the sentiment is endorsed by all kinds of contemporary commentators, in academe and even literary circles as well as in journalism and administration.

The dominance of the plain language ideal is particularly noticeable in guidance aimed at relatively unskilled writers, such as the handbooks used by American college students taking composition classes, or the style-checking software which has recently become available to users of personal computers. The compilers of such guidance ground their prescriptions in a set of general assumptions about good and bad writing, and overall these exhibit a remarkable unanimity.

A good illustration of the stylistic values that pervade guidance on how to write is provided by the manual that accompanies a piece of software entitled *Editor*, which is published and recommended for use with students by the US Modern Language Association (Thiesmeyer and Thiesmeyer 1990). *Editor* works by going through a text that the user has written and flagging usages that the program's authors have included in a large dictionary of problems and errors. The user must then consider how to eliminate the problem or correct the error.

Some of the problems *Editor* flags up are superficial errors of typography, spelling and punctuation, or else more serious cases of ungrammaticality. These will come to light when the user runs a dictionary called FIX; as the name implies, they are problems that require fixing if the finished product is to be in correct standard English. There are, however, three further dictionaries: TIGHTEN, POLISH and CONSIDER. These embody assumptions about good style rather than just correct usage. In the manual, *Editor*'s authors explain what markers of poor style they have programmed the system to draw attention to.

TIGHTEN, for example, is 'based on a common stylistic assumption: shorter is better' (p. 38). It 'flags three kinds of phrases – redundant, wordy and tautological – to promote concise, forceful writing' (p. 38).

The authors claim that 'repeated use of this dictionary and thoughtful attention to its messages constitute a tutorial in concise, vigorous style' (p. 38). POLISH embodies the stylistic assumption that 'fresher is better', and therefore checks for 'pretentious diction, clichés, trite expressions, and vague terms' (p. 38). 'This dictionary', the authors comment, 'has the goal of educating your taste' (p. 38). CONSIDER is somewhat less prescriptive than TIGHTEN or POLISH: it picks up such features as archaisms, jargon, colloquialisms and slang, sexist language and 'empty modifiers', and asks the user to consider whether he or she really wants to keep them.

Editor belongs to a well-established tradition of twentieth-century commentary on style; many readers will have noticed its very obvious debt to the rules for plain English formulated by George Orwell in 'Politics and the English language', a canonical text which will be discussed in more detail below. *Editor* is also typical of its genre in offering only the vaguest of justifications for its stylistic norms: reflecting 'common assumptions' (p. 38) and 'widely accepted principles of usage' (p. 12), they are presented as matters of consensus, not controversy. The program's authors are conscientious in spelling out exactly what assumptions and principles are embodied by its various dictionaries – 'shorter is better', 'fresher is better', good writing is 'concise', 'vigorous' and 'forceful', whereas bad writing is 'trite', 'pretentious' and 'wordy' – but they apparently consider these judgements so obvious as to require no further comment. Nor do they feel impelled to explain what they mean by asserting that 'x is *better*'. Better for what, and according to what criteria?

Better here is probably intended as both a functional and an aesthetic judgement: better for making your meaning clear, but also better in the sense of being more pleasing to read. *Editor* wants, among other things, to educate the developing writer's *taste*. This might suggest one reason why plainness has come to be so highly valued. Like many aesthetic norms, this one has a social dimension. The aesthetic of plainness is a class aesthetic, an affirmation of aristocratic and educated middle-class good taste, whereas 'pretentious' diction is the mark of the socially pretentious. It is notable for example how many of A.S.C. Ross's infamous distinctions between 'U' (upper class) and 'non-U' vocabulary are in effect distinctions between the plain and the more elaborate and/or 'refined' term (thus *wealthy* is 'non-U' for *rich*, *ill* in the sense of 'nauseated' is 'non-U' for *sick*, *home* is the 'non-U' for *house* (see Ross 1954)).

The supposed vulgarity of elaborate diction has also attracted correspondence in the letters column of *The Times*. In 1939, for instance, a Mr G.H. Palmer wrote enquiring why a railway menu promised diners 'a supplementary portion' instead of 'second helpings'. A.P. Herbert replied the next day by referring Mr Palmer to the railway's official reply, which asserted that 'for the few who do not understand the meaning of "supplementary" there would be many who would accuse us of un-educated crudity if we quoted the phrase in such plain verbiage as you suggest' (Gregory 1989: 193). Long and fancy words are preferred by the class of people who fear they might otherwise be suspected of 'un-educated crudity'; but as the use of such words becomes the mark of that class, the class above distances itself by deriding them as 'non-U' — or, in the more contemporary vocabulary of *Today* newspaper, as 'coy genteelisms'.

In order to understand fully the rise and rise of plainness, however, it is also necessary to consider the fact that arguments about plain versus more elaborate language have typically arisen in the context of broader moral, ideological and political debates. The inkhorn controversy was partly about national identity; other controversies have been about the proper relationship of humankind to God, or of citizens to the state. There is thus much more at stake than simply getting a message across intelligibly, or even tastefully. Obviously, the question whether to address the deity in everyday vernacular, in a special archaic or poetic register or in a sacred liturgical language is not a question about what God will have least difficulty understanding; rather it is a question about the symbolic representation of the believer's relation to God. Similarly, a decree that civil servants should write 'thank you for your letter' instead of 'your communication of the 5th *inst.* is hereby acknowledged' does more than just make the message clearer and save government stationery. It sends a message about the functionary's role in relation to the public, marking it as less distant, less formal and less hierarchical than the alternative. (Gowers's golden rule, tellingly, was 'be short, be simple, be human'.) In these cases, using a certain style of language becomes a *moral* matter, to do with recognizing obligations to others and representing them in the form as well as the content of the language you use.

The idea that style norms have a strong moral element is developed by the philosopher Berel Lang in a thought-provoking collection of essays, *Writing and the Moral Self* (Lang 1991). In an essay called 'Strunk, White and grammar as morality' (Strunk and White are the authors of a classic writing handbook, *The Elements of Style* (1979)), Lang detects a 'structural analogy' between discourse about good writing and discourse on ethical conduct. One striking similarity can be found in the canonical syntax of stylistic prescriptions, which tend to the bald imperative (e.g. Strunk and White's famous 'omit needless words') and the axiomatic statement (e.g. 'brevity is always a virtue'). Like moral precepts expressed in similar form ('thou shalt not kill'; 'eating people is wrong'), these prescriptions discourage the question 'why?'. As Lang remarks (1991: 15), 'the reader [of Strunk and White] is constantly ordered about, and if the orders do not persuade by their own force they will not persuade at all.'

The core of the analogy for Lang, however, is the strong connection we make between the stylistic qualities of writing and the moral qualities of the writer. Consider for example the commonplace argument that even the most trivial spelling mistakes are to be deplored because they show that the writer is 'careless' and 'sloppy' – they are, in other words, outward signs of a deeper flaw in character. In handbooks such as *The Elements of Style*, readers are shown how to construct an acceptable moral self by conforming to certain stylistic norms: 'to summarize the ideals of written style for Strunk and White . . . is to compose a model of human character: honest, plain, forthright, patient, simple' (Lang 1991: 17). As Lang points out, this is not the only conceivable model either for good writing or good character. If Strunk and White's prescriptions do 'persuade by their own force' it is not only because people share their conviction that style *is* character, but also because they admire the same virtues (and deplore the same vices) as Strunk and White do.

It is in this light that we must consider the consensus that currently seems to exist on the virtues of a plain and transparent style. The way of writing recommended by modern authorities has come to signify not merely the aristocratic good taste championed by A.S.C. Ross or the old-fashioned Yankee virtues Berel Lang detects in Strunk and White, but the values we cherish as essential to democracy, and conversely opposition to values we regard as inimical to democracy. For example, in spite of its aristocratic associations, plainness often stands symbolically against elitism. It is not acceptable in modern society for class or professional elites to address people in a way they find unintelligible, pretentious or suggestive of very distant and authoritarian social relations. But in addition, plainness has acquired another, even more morally compelling symbolic function. It has become a symbol of the struggle against totalitarianism.

Plain language and the defence of democracy

Since the rise of fascism in Europe in the 1930s a powerful verbal hygiene discourse has developed connecting the manipulation of language with the totalitarian policing of thought. Transparency and plainness in language have been invested with a particular capacity to resist such manipulation, and therefore they have acquired not just functional and aesthetic value, but the moral value associated with political freedom itself. Once again, William Rees-Mogg's foreword to the 1970 *Times* style guide is a good example of this line of thought: among the words he uses to describe the 'traditional plain style of English prose' prescribed for *The Times* are *calm, judicious, impartial* and *sensible*. These are the ideals of a responsible free press in a democratic society, whereas their opposites evoke the shrillness of extremist hate literature and the hysteria of a Nuremberg rally.

The best-known, though not the only elaborator of the verbal hygiene discourse in which these connections are made was George Orwell, who wrote about linguistic corruption as a key tool of totalitarian states at a time when much intellectual effort was being devoted to understanding the apparently unprecedented phenomenon represented by Nazism and then Stalinism. In his novel *Nineteen Eighty-Four* (1949), Orwell invented a language, Newspeak, that prevented dissent by destroying the link between words and meanings, and therefore the logical relations among propositions on which rational argument depends. In Newspeak, antonyms became synonyms ('war is peace') and in consequence contradictions became analytic truths. This rendered Party dogma at once meaningless and indisputable.

In the best-known of his essays on language, 'Politics and the English language' (1946), Orwell identified tendencies of the same kind, though not the same degree, in the actual public discourse of the period. In English as distinct from Newspeak, 'war is peace' would still be a contradiction in terms; but Orwell argued that if you replaced the transparent terms 'war' and 'peace' with euphemisms, vague circumlocutions and impenetrable technical jargon, the recipient of your message might not spot the contradiction.

Such clouding of meaning, Orwell felt, was an increasingly salient characteristic of English prose – less because of any totalitarian conspiracy than because of muddled thinking and careless writing, any fashion for which was easily spread through mass communications media. Bad habits, however, are curable: Orwell therefore applied himself to formulating maxims that would make writing more transparent.

The overarching principle in 'Politics and the English language' is 'let the meaning choose the word, and not the other way about' (p. 168). In other words, think about what meaning you want to convey and then choose the exact words that convey it. More specific recommendations to aid writers in making their choices include using fewer words rather than more, preferring short and simple words over long and complex ones, choosing native rather than foreign expressions, concrete rather than abstract terms and freshly invented rather than familiar or clichéd combinations.

This is not original advice. Most of the points made in 'Politics and the English language', as well as some of its most striking rhetorical strategies, were ubiquitous in writing about writing well before Orwell's essay appeared. For example, a much quoted passage of the essay rewrites a verse of Ecclesiastes in hideously prolix modern jargon. The same technique is used in the 1939 pamphlet *English in The Times*, and in A.P. Herbert's letter to that newspaper about the railway menu's 'supplementary portions', where Herbert suggests that if Nelson had lived in the mid-twentieth century his 'England expects that every man will do his duty' would have been 'England anticipates that as regards the current emergency, personnel will face up to the issues and exercise appropriately the functions allocated to their respective occupation-groups' (Gregory 1989: 194). Orwell's argument about the corruption of language, and his identification of particular linguistic features (such as verbosity, abstraction and jargon) as carriers of that corruption, had already become conventional wisdom before the war.

Yet where many others saying similar things have been forgotten, Orwell has had extraordinary influence. References to his work turn up everywhere: skimming through the newspaper just before I sat down to write this, I immediately came across an article that began, 'Orwell, thou should'st be living at this hour', and went on to complain about 'the linguistic perversions that nowadays characterize the debate about British broadcasting' (Naughton 1993). This allusion (which incidentally flouts almost every one of Orwell's own linguistic maxims, being complex and Latinate in vocabulary as well as adorned with a thumping cliché in the opening misquotation) neatly demonstrates both the status of the argument as received truth and the nature of Orwell's (limited) originality.

Earlier advocates of plainness had rather different grounds for criticizing the alternatives. Opponents of 'inkhorn terms' dwelt on their wilful obscurity and foolish affectation; *English in The Times* was apt to dismiss the usages it disapproved of as 'dull', 'feeble', 'flabby' and 'dreary', while A.P. Herbert implied that they reflected the vulgar pretentiousness of the semi-educated petty bourgeoisie. The Orwellian by contrast views bad writing as a 'perversion' – what before the war was merely tasteless and tiresome becomes in post-war rhetoric pathological and dangerous. Orwell's contribution was to take stylistic preferences that were already well-established, and offer those who subscribed to them a more significant and morally compelling justification than simple snobbery.

Time has made 'Politics and the English language' into a cliché in its own right, and it is worth taking seriously Orwell's own objection to clichés – that their familiarity stops us from thinking about what they mean and whether they make sense. The theory of communication underlying Orwell's work is rarely subjected to critical scrutiny; but on closer examination it turns out to be based on simplistic and questionable assumptions.

Orwell's notion of what communication is can be seen in his injunction to 'let the meaning choose the word', which suggests there is a prior and independent realm of meanings, each of which can be expressed in a linguistic form that corresponds to it exactly. If a writer gets the 'right' form, the word that properly names the object or idea he or she wishes to indicate, the result will be completely transparent communication. The reader will be able to look right through the language to its object, just as one can see through a clear pane of glass an undistorted image of whatever is behind it. Conversely, if the writer gets the 'wrong' word, whether deliberately or by inadvertence, the effect will be equivalent to a flaw or tint in the glass. The image will be distorted, or cloudy, or in extreme cases impossible to make out at all.

This account depends on a notion of communication as *telementation* (transfer of ideas from mind to mind) accomplished by way of a fixed code relating words and meanings in a one-to-one correspondence. (Sir Ernest Gowers similarly defined good writing as 'the choice and arrangement of words in such a way as to get an idea as exactly as possible out of one mind into another', while *The Oxford Miniguide to English Usage* (Weiner 1983) quotes the axiom that 'the perfect use of language is that in which every word carries the meaning that it is intended to, no less and no more'.) Orwell's argument for plain language assumes that the more simply writers express themselves the more likely it is that telementation will succeed. Conversely, where writers do not express themselves in the plainest words available, their meaning will remain hidden or vague.

If, however, the telementation-by-fixed-code account of communication is wrong, then we cannot assume either that plain language will be automatically transparent or that the alternative will be automatically misleading. And as I argued in Chapter 1, communication cannot be telementation. Interpreting utterances involves the creative deployment of speakers' inferential capacities; it is not limited to automatic word-by-word decoding. In consequence, there can never be any guarantee that a hearer's interpretation will perfectly match the intentions of the speaker, however plain and simple the words that pass between them. Hearers may arrive at interpretations that contradict or go beyond the literal reading of an utterance (if this were not so, it would be impossible to make sense of metaphor and irony); they may attribute meanings to speakers which those speakers did not intend or foresee, and even infer propositions that speakers had specifically sought to conceal.

The creative inferential powers of competent language-users are seldom acknowledged by those who write style books. On the contrary, such texts assume a world full of people whose literal-minded obtuseness borders on the ridiculous. For example, a much-cited illustration of the perils of ambiguity, quoted in Gowers, is 'if the baby does not thrive on raw milk, boil it'. Now, this sentence invites editing on the grounds that the ambiguity makes it risible, but to say it requires editing to make the meaning clear strains credulity. What degree of idiocy would be needed to ponder the ambiguity and conclude, either that it was undecidable or that the writer recommended boiling the baby? Here the charge of unclarity is no more than a pretext for the critic to parade his or her superior linguistic sensibilities.

Orwell, to be fair, was not this kind of pedantic snob. Nevertheless, his anxieties about the politically motivated abuse of language beg similar questions about the behaviour of language users. If Orwell himself can cut through the verbiage of 'elimination of undesirable elements' and explain to us that what it really means is 'imprisoning or murdering your political opponents', why should other people be unable to do the same? Does the particular value of short, simple words for conveying meaning clearly depend on the notion that most people are stupider than Orwell, and/or have a smaller vocabulary?

That would be one argument, and for certain advocates of plain language – for instance, the Plain English Campaign – it is a prominent one. The campaign does not say that people are stupid, but it is not ashamed to say that many people's level of education makes certain kinds of language inaccessible to them, while some specialized kinds of language are inaccessible to almost everyone (for example, the fourteen-page, single sentence document that sets out my rights and obligations as a leaseholder, and which I have never succeeded in parsing). Actually it seems that Orwell himself was well aware of this anti-elitist argument and supported it, though he makes little of it in 'Politics and the English language'. In March 1947 one of his columns in *Tribune* noted that a mass observation report on people's responses to a government White Paper on the economy

> found, as usual, that the abstract words and phrases which are flung to and fro in official announcements mean nothing to countless ordinary citizens. Many people are even flummoxed by the word 'assets', which is thought to have something to do with 'assist'!
>
> (Orwell 1968: 357)

It would be hard to deny the force of this argument in relation to official writing addressed to the mass of 'ordinary citizens' – which is presumably why plain language in this context has been official policy in Britain since Gowers's early efforts in 1948. But it is surely not the same argument that makes plainness normative in, say, academic writing, or persuades such establishment organs as *The Times* and *The Economist* to adopt plain English as a matter of policy. For these advocates plainness is an ideological symbol, and what it symbolizes above all is the possibility of a neutral or value-free language. A transparent way of writing supposedly reveals its object as it is, warts and all, whereas the style Orwell criticized, and took to its extreme in his imaginary language Newspeak, can only conceal or obfuscate the truth.

'Collateral damage' and the politics of discourse

In order to pursue this argument, let us consider a recent example of language that has been criticized for being obfuscatory: the allied forces' use, during the 1991 Gulf War, of the phrase 'collateral damage' to describe the killing of civilians in attacks on military targets. The classic Orwellian argument for finding this usage objectionable would be that (a) it is jargon, and to the extent that people cannot decode it, it conceals what is actually going on; and (b) it is a euphemism, abstract, agentless and affectless, so that even if people succeed in associating it with a real act or event they will be insulated from any feeling of repulsion and moral outrage.

This sounds plausible enough, but once again it reduces the process of interpreting to something more like machine decoding. It implies that when faced with the unfamiliar phrase 'collateral damage', speakers of English will come up either with no meaning or with a simple aggregate of the meanings of *collateral* and *damage*, which does not convey the reality the compound term is supposed to describe. Then, the argument goes on, the bland connotations of 'damage' coupled with the implicit denial of intention or responsibility in 'collateral' will be taken at face value, enabling the politicians and military to manipulate public opinion.

This is not a very convincing account. To begin with, real speakers are very unlikely to rest content with 'does not compute' as a reaction to a novel expression. If they cannot decode a meaning they will infer one, and this will involve identifying some real-world event to which the new term must relate. They may end up inferring something at odds with the coiner's intentions (though repeated exposure to a term will refine initial hypotheses about its meaning), but the point is that they will make something of it rather than nothing.

Furthermore, it is impossible to prevent speakers from engaging in metalinguistic speculation on the reasons why one term was chosen over other possibilities; that is, evaluating as well as simply interpreting phrases like 'collateral damage'. One possible inference here is precisely that the allies, in describing a certain state of affairs as 'collateral damage', are trying to minimize what is happening and their own responsibility for it. And the moment such an inference is made, any attempt at concealment and disinformation has failed; the allies have merely added duplicity to murder on the list of their offences.

An Orwellian might reply that even if 'collateral damage' obscured neither the fact of civilian deaths nor the intention to minimize their impact, it still enabled people to keep a certain emotional distance from those deaths, thus contributing to the *de facto* acceptance of mass murder. This is the 'euphemism' argument, and since it is often accepted without question it will bear closer examination.

A euphemism is a term used deliberately to avoid or soften the negative associations of words that deal directly with taboo subjects: the classic example might be *pass away* for *die*. Conversely, a dysphemism is brutally negative, flaunting and intensifying negative connotations: *kick the bucket* and *croak* do this job with regard to death. The two concepts, euphemism and dysphemism, imply the existence, somewhere in the middle, of neutral terms that merely *describe* reality without positive or negative colouring. In the case I have been outlining, the obvious candidate is the word *die* itself. Everyone knows that if I say, 'she passed away', this is merely a polite form of words for 'she died'. It is a form of superstitious word magic whereby I can convey the meaning without ambiguity, but without actually allowing the taboo word to pass my lips.

Not all purported cases of euphemism are as simple as this one, however. No doubt one virtue of 'collateral damage' from the viewpoint of those who coined it is indeed that it does not allude directly to killing or dying. But in other respects it is a more complicated case than 'she passed away': it does not permit the same immediate, totally conventional and unambiguous 'translation'. To put the point in its most basic terms, if 'collateral damage' is a euphemism, what exactly is it a euphemism for? What would be the neutral, transparent description?

In the last few paragraphs I have defined the term 'collateral damage' in several different ways, including 'the killing of civilians', 'civilian deaths', 'murder' and 'mass murder'. For all that they use plainer words, these are no more neutral descriptions than 'collateral damage' itself. To choose any one of them, and to object to any one of them, is in essence to state a position on the morality of the allies' action. If you find the allies' strategy unjustifiable you will probably regard the nominalization 'civilian deaths' as a euphemistic denial of agency which implicitly devalues Iraqi lives; if you believe that the strategy is regrettable but necessary you will probably find 'murder' and 'mass murder' overly emotive and biased against the allies. It is impossible to come up with a description which could not be interpreted as in some way taking sides.

There is always a point of view in language, but we are apt to notice it only when it is not one we share. The politics of discourse are about getting others to believe that the point of view embodied in this or that verbal representation is not really a point of view but just the plain truth of the matter, whereas alternative representations are biased and perverse. Certainly, those who talk about 'collateral damage' and 'the elimination of undesirable elements' are engaged in this kind of politics. But so too are those who tell us that what should have been said in both cases is 'murder', and that referring to murder as 'collateral damage' is a perversion of the English language.

The plain style favoured by Orwell, and by many others before and since, has particular advantages in the contest over what (or whose) representations are more transparent, natural and 'true'. A plain representation is still a representation, but it aspires to make itself invisible, like the proverbial pane of glass. In consequence its ideological presuppositions may also become invisible.

In journalism particularly, the ideal of a fit between language and the external world so close you cannot see the join has important ideological functions. As William Rees-Mogg says in his foreword to the 1970 *Times* style guide, the plain style is the outward sign of a cluster of qualities such as judiciousness, matter-of-factness, impartiality and good sense. It is a code, not unlike the code of realism in fiction. Realist texts seem to give their readers unmediated access to the world, but the effect is achieved by deploying particular conventions of language that signify the real without actually corresponding to it. For example, it is a well-known paradox that actual speech transcribed on the page looks artificial compared to the conventional dialogue we find in novels, remote though that dialogue is from real spoken language. Nor do practised readers find anything odd in the 'omniscient narrator' who introduces the characters and regulates their interactions, though no such entity exists in the real world. In a somewhat similar way, the journalistic use of a terse, simple, concrete language conventionally signifies unmediated access to the objective facts of the story. It is a language uniquely suited to the prevailing ideology of news reporting.

In the summer of 1993 I was mystified for days by a billboard in New York City advertising *Life* magazine, which bore the legend '*Life*. For people who appreciate the difference between a view and an opinion'. To me this seemed like a distinction without a difference. What *was* the difference, I asked myself, and which of the two was meant to be the positive term? The mystery was solved when I saw another advertisement on the side of a bus which read, 'The last thing New Yorkers need is another opinion'. At the same time, someone explained to me that 'view' in the first advertisement was a play on words, an allusion to *Life*'s reputation for the quantity and quality of its photographs. The magazine was selling 'views without opinions', the prototypical 'view' being the one you get through a camera lens. The use of plain language in a newspaper also signifies 'views without opinions': it is the closest linguistic analogue of the camera that never lies, and should be treated with similar suspicion.

STYLE, COMMUNICATION AND AGENCY IN LANGUAGE

The uniform and transparent style that constitutes 'good writing' in present-day English is a complicated construct with many functions. Depending on the circumstances and purposes for which it is being recommended, it can be a populist or anti-elitist gesture or a mark of the writer's good taste, a proof of 'authentic' moral virtues such as honesty and sincerity or a sign of the painstakingly acquired craft skills in which professional writers and editors take pride. Such is our uncritical attitude to it, it can be all these things at once.

Perhaps the most striking thing about verbal hygiene practices connected with style is that they betray a deep desire to believe in the perfectibility of communication, and to deny that it is inherently imperfect because of the variability of language, the indeterminacy of meaning, the irreducible distance between words and things. As Berel Lang suggests (1991: 2):

The imagination, reacting against the partisan networks of history, understandably dreams of a neutral instrument – a medium at once transparent and subservient that would not speak for itself but would only do as it was told. Among human artefacts, writing has not been the only competitor for this role, but it has been the strongest and most persistent one, more so even than thought – since, unlike thinking, writing has the *appearance* of intractability.

But in their attempts to make language 'do as it is told', to prevent it from drawing attention to itself and to the values it embodies, verbal hygienists mystify both the workings of language and the agency of its users.

It is this mystification, and not any particular style of writing in itself, that I have been trying to criticize in this chapter. That writing may be good, bad or indifferent I do not deny; nor would I necessarily want to say that the particular qualities that present-day users of English have learned to take as virtues – for instance, clarity, consistency, precision and plainness – have no merit. My criticisms are directed instead to the metalinguistic discourse in which their merits have been canvassed, and the metalinguistic practices in which they have been enforced. I have tried to show that the arguments used to justify particular ideas about style are historically variable and contingent, and that they have frequently served vested interests – class, professional and ideological.

We could discard those arguments without necessarily discarding the way of writing they are meant to be arguments for; in my own opinion we could discard some of the restrictive practices described here (e.g. those that make a fetish of consistency, or discover non-existent ambiguities for the pleasure of feeling superior) without losing those stylistic values for which a more convincing case could be made. But we would first need to make such a case, which would also entail noticing that statements about 'good writing' are not self-evident truths about language but value judgements upon it.

In the preface to this book I imagined someone sending out a memo informing the employees of a large company that 'green is an odious colour. It is never to be worn, and when it is worn it is to be of the correct shade'. Even if the recipients of such a memo were in no position to do anything but comply with the arbitrary colour preferences of their superiors, they would surely regard the injunction as absurd; in their private conversations they would treat the memo and its originator with scorn rather than respect. Yet the attitude of highly literate people to similarly arbitrary and dogmatic statements about language use is more akin to reverence. It sometimes seems that the more such people pride themselves on their love of language and their skill in using it, the less inclined they are to engage in rational or critical discourse about it.

It could be argued that no great harm is done by this: there are worse things in the world than the fussing of an Elsie Myers Stainton, the pomposity of a William Rees-Mogg or the imperiousness of Strunk and White. Yet it could also be said that all of these contribute to a kind of discourse on language, characterized by authoritarianism, mystification, irrationality and lack of critical engagement, that ought to worry anyone who professes to care about language or about the wider culture of which it is part.

In this chapter I have tried to show that stylistic values are symbolic of moral, social, ideological and political values. When we write, as Berel Lang points out, we are constructing not only a representation of the world but also a representation of ourselves as social and moral agents. (The word *style* comes from *stylus*, denoting a writing implement whose marks bear the visible imprint – the 'hand' – of the individual who wielded it.) I am not suggesting that individuals should, or indeed *could* invent their own style of writing out of nothing, without reference to tradition or convention. I am suggesting rather that we need not take linguistic traditions and conventions so much at face value as we usually do: we can ask ourselves what they mean, and in the light of the answer, decide how far we wish to perpetuate them in our own use of language.

3 Dr Syntax and Mrs Grundy

The great grammar crusade[1]

STIRRING THE POLITICAL JUICES: DR SYNTAX MEETS MRS GRUNDY

In Britain towards the end of the 1980s there was an extraordinary outbreak of public concern about the teaching of English, especially English grammar. At the height of the hysteria, almost every day seemed to bring forth some new and more intemperate manifestation: among those who favoured the public with their views were academics, politicians, columnists and leader writers, novelists, denizens of obscure right-wing think-tanks, union leaders, peers of the realm and – inevitably – Prince Charles, whose remarks in praise of grammar confirmed its new status at the centre of a national crusade. Passions ran high and were slow to subside; between 1987 and 1994 Secretaries of State for Education came and went, Margaret Thatcher's administration gave way to that of John Major, but grammar remained stubbornly on the political agenda.

A few heads were shaken in regret or disbelief. The critic Colin MacCabe (1990: 7) suggested the affair had 'some claim to be the most ignorant and the most viciously stupid public debate of the past 20 years'; Simon Jenkins, in a column written for the right-wing *Sunday Times*, marvelled at the strength of feeling the issue engendered, observing sardonically (under the headline 'Dr Syntax To Wed Mrs Grundy Shock'[2]): 'grammar is the fastest-rising topic in the Tory firmament, now almost on a par with hanging and dole fraud. No matter that most constituency chairmen hated the subject. The nation's grammar stirs the political juices' (*Sunday Times*, 20 November 1988).

I began by calling this extraordinary: was it really so extraordinary? The deplorable state of the nation's English is after all a longstanding obsession, well-documented in any number of surveys (see Crystal 1984; Milroy and Milroy 1985; Crowley 1991). In this case, however, it was something more than routine pedantry. Somehow the perennial question of grammar became emblematic and all-pervading. Why this happened, and what it was emblematic of, are the questions I want to address in this chapter.

In order to understand the furore about grammar, it is necessary to know something about the immediate context for it. Ostensibly it arose as part of a wide-ranging debate about education, precipitated by the planning and subsequent implementation of a piece of legislation in England and Wales, the Education Reform Act of 1988. The Act's most dramatic and contentious reform was to introduce a 'National Curriculum' in all state schools.[3] Many aspects of this curriculum caused public controversy; none, however, was more controversial than the question of what place in it English grammar should occupy.

If it seems parochial to devote so much attention to this local controversy, I want to emphasize from the outset that the issues raised by it are of more than merely local interest. Analogous debates on education have occurred in other contexts too; the discourse on language that will be examined here is equally available, and just as powerful, elsewhere.

To mention only one example: in the last ten years the issue of the curriculum has been an ideological battleground, not only in Britain but strikingly also in the US. By 1988 both countries were embarking on a third term of radical right-wing government. In the sphere of education, the radical Right focused on two related problems: an alleged decline in standards, and an alleged drift away from the values education had traditionally sought to transmit. Influential conservatives on both sides of the Atlantic proposed to address this crisis of standards and values by instituting a 'core curriculum' – a set of skills, competencies, ideas and canonical texts, exposure to and mastery of which would form the common inheritance of all educated people.[4] In each case this proposal encountered resistance from opponents who found it over-prescriptive, elitist and ethnocentric. And in each case, questions of language played a key role in what American commentators dubbed the 'curriculum wars'.

To point out these similarities is not to deny the differences between the two countries. The most salient linguistic and educational issues are not the same in Britain and the US; nor are the institutional frameworks within which those issues must be addressed.[5] Although American and British conservatives had certain ideological and political goals in common, different local conditions were bound to produce different outcomes. Thus Britain, like the US, had its 'curriculum wars'; but unlike the US, Britain – or, to be more exact, England and Wales – ended up with a national school curriculum. It is useful at this point to give a brief account of how and why this came to pass.

The 1988 Education Reform Act is widely regarded as the most radical shift in policy and practice enacted by a British government since the Second World War. The Act accomplished significant change by way of two sets of provisions. First, it introduced a new framework for the management of state schools, weakening or, if a school so wished, even bypassing the control of local education authorities. Second, the Act provided for a National Curriculum which all state school pupils aged from 5 to 16 were required to follow. Official bodies set up under the new law specified what subjects were to be studied and laid down detailed programmes of study for every subject. Schools' adherence to these was to be checked by compulsory testing of children at four 'key stages': at ages 7, 11, 14 and 16.

The overall effect of this legislation was to concentrate power in the hands of the Secretary of State for Education, or statutory bodies that were answerable to him, where previously that power had resided with agencies that were notionally independent of the government. This was partly a shift from local to central control, but to say only that would be an over-simplification. Schooling in England and Wales had traditionally been overseen by local education authorities, but a significant degree of centralization had been ensured by two other factors: the national public examination system which effectively dictated much of the secondary school curriculum, and the existence of a national inspection system (Her Majesty's Inspectorate of Schools, known as 'HMI'), which monitored standards in schools across the country. The 1988 Act, therefore, was not a simple replacement of a locally controlled system by a centrally controlled one; rather it altered the balance between local and central administration, and shifted the locus of central control from autonomous institutions to bodies which the government directly appointed and regulated. The aim of this move was to put schooling in the service of a particular conservative ideology, and to lessen the influence of bodies with differing ideologies, such as left-wing local authorities and the liberal 'educational establishment' that supposedly dominated the Inspectorate.

Conservatives in the US could not have contemplated such an extension of central (that is, federal) control, for the division of powers between central and local agencies is historically a much more sensitive matter. Right-wingers in the US have been more apt to campaign for the removal of all federal influence than for its intensification. Even William Bennett, who served as Education Secretary in the Reagan administration, felt compelled in his own reports proposing a school core curriculum (Bennett 1987 and 1988) to reaffirm the absolute prohibition on federal interference with decisions about what to teach in schools.[6]

Despite working in a culture less hostile to centralization, the British government did not find it easy to implement its reforms, and the saga did not end with the passage of legislation through Parliament. The introduction of the new curriculum, and especially of the new tests, attracted opposition from parents and teachers, to which the government at times responded with straightforwardly coercive measures, at other times with a climb-down.[7] Inevitably, too, the long drawn-out process of reform was affected by changes in the government's political fortunes: there were several different Secretaries of State for Education during the period of transition, and there were times when, because of such pressing issues as a threatened rebellion over European union by right-wing conservatives in Parliament, educational matters were either put on the back burner or used (it was rumoured) in political man-oeuvres designed less to carry forward a coherent policy than to placate the rebels. These changing circumstances and conflicting pressures meant that the course of reform was neither smooth nor straight.

On certain points, however, the conservatives did appear to carry both party sentiment and public opinion with them. The most notable such instance was their call for a return to traditional standards, values and methods in the teaching of the English language. That call was couched in a powerful verbal hygiene discourse whose key term was *grammar.*

Below, I propose to examine the workings of this discourse and the reasons for its appeal. I will argue that it drew much of its power from the contrast people perceived between its explicit, unabashed norma-tivity and the apparent anti-normativity or relativism of the arguments with which its opponents tried to counter it. The call for a return to traditional grammar was wrapped up in a moral discourse on good and bad, right and wrong; so much so, in fact, that its moral element often obscured the linguistic and educational questions that were supposedly being addressed. The effect was to surround the subject of grammar in a fog of mystification, using arguments about language that must be judged as weak and incoherent even by the unexacting standards of the verbal hygiene genre they belong to. And yet *because it acknowledged the salience that questions of value possess for language-users, this discourse had an impact unmatched by competing discourses which dismissed or played down evaluative concerns.*

The great grammar crusade illustrates a paradox to which this book repeatedly draws attention. It is a classic case where a bad argument, put forward by people who know little or nothing about language, never-theless succeeds, because although much of its substance is nonsensical it engages with the underlying assumptions of its audience and therefore makes a kind of sense; whereas the opposing argument put forward by experts fails, because it is at odds with the audience's underlying assumptions and is therefore apprehended as nonsensical.

Linguists should consider this paradox very carefully. There is no common-sense belief that linguistic scientists so urgently wish to displace as the fetish of prescriptive grammar, and there is no common-sense belief that has been so resistant to their efforts at displacement. One of my aims in this discussion is to show *why* popular beliefs about grammar are so difficult to shift; another is to suggest that a resolutely anti-normative discourse is highly unlikely to shift them.

That is not to say that there is no alternative to weak and incoherent arguments; what has to be acknowledged is rather the evaluative impulse that makes certain arguments appealing. By this I do not mean only that we have to acknowledge people's deep-rooted *belief* that it is possible and indeed proper to make value judgements on language. More radically, we have to entertain the possibility that this belief is justified: not mistaken, not illogical, not unwarranted by the observable facts of everyday experience and behaviour. Accordingly I will argue that while the grammar debate *was* irrational and reactionary, this was not simply because it was about 'values' and 'standards'. It was irrational and reactionary because of the particular values and standards the idea of grammar was made to symbolize. The real challenge is to persuade people that there are other values and other standards that might underpin the use and the teaching of language.

MORAL PANIC

I am going to suggest that the grammar furore bears more than a passing resemblance to the sort of periodic hysteria cultural historians have labelled 'moral panic' (Cohen 1987). Although there are differences as well as similarities, I believe the parallel is an illuminating one if we wish to understand why, in Simon Jenkins's words, 'the nation's grammar stir[red] the political juices'. Before we consider the grammar debate itself, it is therefore worth looking more generally at the phenomenon of moral panic.

A moral panic can be said to occur when some social phenomenon or problem is suddenly foregrounded in public discourse and discussed in an obsessive, moralistic and alarmist manner, as if it betokened some imminent catastrophe. In the past hundred years in Europe and America we have had outbreaks of this kind centring on prostitution and 'white slavery', drugs, the 'Jewish problem', juvenile delinquency, venereal disease, immigration, communism, overpopulation, pornography, rock music and pit bull terriers.

These are not claimed as cases of moral panic simply because they inspired public anxiety: some degree of concern about many of them would be perfectly reasonable. But there are times when concern goes far beyond what is reasonable. In the words of the criminologist Jock Young, 'moral panic' describes 'cases where public reaction [is] completely disproportionate to the actual problem faced' (*Guardian*, Letters, 8 July 1994). In a moral panic the scale of the problem is exaggerated, its causes are analysed in simplistic terms, anxiety about it climbs to intolerable levels, and the measures proposed to alleviate it are usually extreme and punitive. Analysts have suggested there are underlying sociological reasons why public concern gets 'out of hand' in this way; and that vested interests are often at work encouraging it to do so.

Moral panic works by channelling, at least temporarily, the diffuse anxieties and hostilities that exist in any society towards a single, simple problem, such as 'drugs', 'Jews' or 'communism'. The discovery of this 'problem' entails the creation of a scapegoat – the junkie, the fifth columnist, the Zionist conspirator. This generic 'folk devil' is usually identified with a real social group, whose members then bear the brunt of hostility and blame. Moral panic thus has the potential to lead to such extreme forms of repression as witch-hunts and pogroms, and in some cases may even be orchestrated for that purpose.

Scholars have suggested that moral panic in the form we know it is a product of the modern mass media. This is not only (though it is partly) because newspapers, say, have an interest in promoting certain ideological or political positions. More generally, the mass media depend on presenting their audience with a steady supply of problems and crises, and it may be in their interest to exaggerate a problem, fostering the impression that there really is a crisis and not just business as usual.

Because of the role they play in the modern public sphere as privileged sources of information and arbiters of opinion, the media have considerable agenda-setting power. The most commonplace incident or pedestrian report can be turned into an issue by media attention, whereas without that attention the same incident would go unnoticed and the report would gather dust. Having thus established something as an issue, the media can return to it under the guise of 'responding to public concern' – even though most of the concern is of their own making. These are effective strategies for manufacturing or dramatically intensifying public concern about an issue, to the degree where others, politicians for example, will find it very hard to ignore.

The analysis of moral panic as the outcome of a certain cultural process – it does not simply 'erupt' but gets *constructed* in a particular way, primarily by the media – is aptly illustrated by a panic that took place a few years ago about dangerous dogs savaging Britain's children. Without denying that attacks on children by dogs give cause for concern, it is difficult to believe that the incidence of this problem has increased exponentially in recent years, or that it has ever been more than a minor footnote in the statistics on child injury and death. Yet in the late 1980s there was an upsurge of concern sufficient to pressure Parliament into passing legislation to control certain breeds.

Concern about savage dogs may have been set off by the coincidental occurrence of more than one serious (and therefore newsworthy) incident in a relatively short space of time, but it gained momentum because the media made an issue of it. Not only the most serious incidents but all known incidents, including minor injuries and narrow escapes, began to be faithfully reported, and this made it seem as though dangerous dogs were suddenly everywhere. In truth they were no more ubiquitous than they had been before; but where previously they had not been considered worth reporting, now journalists were actively digging for cases to publicize.

Oddly enough, the problem of savage dogs has now virtually disappeared from public view. Either the law that was made in the wake of the panic is the most effective regulatory measure in history, and has totally eradicated what was presented only yesterday as an epidemic of canine lawlessness, or else the dogs are behaving much as they did before, and it is the media who have reverted to their previous sporadic interest.

The media's power to manufacture concern should not be exaggerated however; full-scale panic cannot be generated around just anything. In 'successful' panics there are obvious recurring themes. For example, sex, drugs and crime do not fade away, they are simply recycled in new forms: syphilis becomes Aids, opium becomes heroin or crack. This is not, however, or at any rate not only, because certain social problems have proved intractable over time. If that were the only consideration there would be perpetual panic, whereas in fact it goes in cycles. To understand cycles of panic, it is necessary to acknowledge that the apparent problem is not always the real one. Behind the facade of legitimate concern about, say, drug abuse, there are usually deeper and less socially acceptable anxieties being expressed in coded terms.

In their study *Policing the Crisis*, for example, Hall *et al.* (1978) analysed a panic about 'mugging' which seized Britain during the 1970s. After more than 300 years of persistent urban street crime, why was this epidemic suddenly discovered? A clue was found in the scenario presented by media reports of the 'problem'. Muggers were depicted as young black men, their victims as respectable white people. What looked on the surface like a panic about crime was at a deeper level a panic about race. The media scenario resonated with racist anxieties about the changing ethnic composition of British inner cities, and what could not legitimately be said about black people *per se* found expression in the coded discourse of 'mugging'. Even the dangerous dog panic had an analogous social subtext. The keeping of certain kinds of dogs was persistently associated in news reports with a male working-class subculture characterized by irresponsibility, criminality and mindless violence. The savagery of the dogs symbolized the savagery of their owners, and a call for more control over the animals was a coded expression of 'respectable' people's fear of what was portrayed as an emerging 'underclass'.

These cases exemplify a classic pattern. Whatever the specific event or phenomenon that triggers a panic, it will only get going if it mobilizes more general anxieties, and these tend to be about perceived social changes by which important sections of the community feel threatened. Typically the changes are too far advanced to be reversed; but panic legitimizes repressive measures aimed at containing them (in the mugging example these included more aggressive policing of black communities – an important precipitating factor in the civil disturbances that occurred some years later).

Moral panics do not occur randomly, then, but cluster around the obvious points of social conflict: around relations of race, class, gender, generation, sexual practice and political dissent. And they are fundamentally conservative responses to conflict. Harking back to a mythical golden age when all streets were safe, all families happy, all workers industrious and all values consensual, they address symptoms rather than causes, aim at containment not amelioration and locate the threat almost always in a subordinated group.

In the light of all this, it might be thought that grammar is a very unpromising candidate for triggering moral panic, remote as it is from the staple themes of sex and drugs and rock and roll. And yet the fact is that in the case we are concerned with here, grammar *did* bring forth an extraordinary surge of passion – almost, as Simon Jenkins noted, on a par with hanging. And if we keep in mind that moral panics are highly coded affairs, this becomes less surprising: for questions of language can readily become a code for issues of race, class and culture. In what follows I will examine how this coded discourse worked; but first I will consider how far the actual events of the controversy conformed to the pattern of a moral panic.

THE GRAMMAR 'PANIC': A BRIEF HISTORY

The first stage in a panic is the discovery of a 'problem'. In this case, the problem can be stated as follows: because of English teachers' wilful neglect of grammar, children were leaving school illiterate and undisciplined. The 'permissive' teachers became the main scapegoats, along with the linguistic and educational theorists who had brainwashed them with half-baked theories and trendy left-wing nonsense.

This theme appeared in the media as early as 1982. In a piece written for the *Observer* newspaper entitled 'The decline and fall of English grammar', former public school headmaster John Rae sounded an elegiac note, arguing that grammar, like so many other indices of a civilized society, had fallen victim to the permissive ethos of the 1960s. Self-expression had been valued over conformity to rules, and grammar-teaching had been abandoned in favour of 'creative writing' in the classroom. So far, so familiar: the same observation had been brought out sporadically by individual conservatives ever since the 1960s. The novel move Rae made, however, was to argue that the decline of grammar might actually have *caused*, rather than being a consequence of, or simply going along with, other kinds of decline. Twenty years on, a generation that had not learned to respect 'nice points of grammar' no longer seemed to care about standards in any sphere. It was time, Rae suggested, to halt the rush toward anarchy and barbarism by reintroducing grammar to the nation's schools.

The identification of this 'problem' and the scapegoating of 1960s classroom liberals were in time revealed as deliberate manoeuvres in a planned campaign. In this case, however, the primary responsibility for whipping up anxiety cannot be laid at the door of the media. The main instigators were right-wing ideologues (hereafter referred to as the 'pro-grammar conservatives'); and though they showed considerable sophistication in using the media, their real object was to influence the educational reforms on which the Thatcher government was poised to embark.

The existence of such a lobby was a political sign of the times. The dominance of the Right in British politics from 1979 had allowed a flowering of debate and dissent within the Conservative party itself; radical right-wing think-tanks and pressure groups had proliferated, and within a fairly short time had become well-organized, influential and respectable. Later on, some of their members and associates would be appointed to participate in the official deliberations of government bodies, and their literature would be considered by those bodies as 'evidence'.

In the case of grammar, the radical Right had begun by conducting a guerilla-style campaign. Apart from occasional opinion pieces like John Rae's in newspapers, they worked mainly through polemical pamphlets, limited circulation journals and small press publications. Crucially however, these were not just left to gather dust. Although they were read by few people in their original form, those who did read them were often politically well placed. Furthermore, they were soon taken up by the media.

An early sign of media interest in right-wing ideas about language was the respectful attention accorded to John Honey's volume about English teaching, *The Language Trap*, when it appeared in 1983. Honey took issue with orthodox educational opinion, represented by what was then the most recent major policy document on English teaching, the Bullock report entitled *A Language For Life* (DES 1975). Bullock had held that the language children brought from home should be accorded value in school. Honey argued that on the contrary, schools were failing working-class and ethnic minority children if they did not insist on the exclusive use of standard English. In 1983 this argument was considered daring and iconoclastic, and it attracted a good deal of media interest. The interest was not sustained, because at the time there was no 'peg' on which to hang an extended discussion; but that was soon to change.

In 1987 the Thatcher government initiated the planning of a National Curriculum. The procedure used throughout the planning process was to set up working groups to make recommendations for each subject area; there would be an English working group to draft the curriculum for this crucial 'core' subject. But before this group set to work, the then Secretary of State for Education, Kenneth Baker, had already taken the unusual step of announcing the formation of a separate committee under Sir John Kingman, whose brief was specifically to enquire into the teaching of the English language in schools. In a press notice announcing the committee's terms of reference (16 January 1987), Baker said:

> I am working towards national agreement on the aims and objectives of English teaching in schools in order to improve standards. But I have been struck by a particular gap. Pupils need to know about the workings of the English language if they are to use it effectively. Most schools no longer teach old-fashioned grammar. But little has been put in its place. There is no common ground on teaching about the structure and workings of language . . . . We need to equip teachers with a proper model of the language to help improve their teaching.

Despite Baker's remark about the need for 'common ground' and his reference to traditional grammar teaching as 'old-fashioned', the setting up of a committee to produce a 'proper model of the language' suggested that the government might be responding directly to pressure exerted by the pro-grammar conservatives: perhaps the minister had been 'struck' by this 'gap' because a lobby had been at pains to draw his attention to it, and perhaps he was hoping the Kingman committee would present a future working group on the English curriculum with a *fait accompli*.

This, however, was not what happened. The Kingman committee's report was published in 1988 (DES 1988a). The report's conclusions were not to pro-grammar conservatives' liking, and the Secretary of State himself was also conspicuously unenthusiastic about them. Nevertheless, the planning process continued along the lines that had been established at the outset. The English working party (which would deal with literature and drama as well as language) was duly convened under the chairmanship of Brian Cox, and its report appeared not long afterwards (DES 1989). The Cox Report was even less satisfactory to right-wingers than the Kingman Report; and their dissatisfaction (the reasons for which will be explained below) ensured that what should have been the end of the controversy – the official publication of the working party's conclusions – was actually only the beginning of a protracted and bitter struggle.

Before we turn to what happened next, it is necessary to summarize the main causes of contention. I will go on to argue that language *per se* was not the ultimate object of right-wing concern; but to the extent that the argument was conducted on linguistic terrain, what issues about language teaching were at stake in it? For although Kingman and Cox had been given broad terms of reference, it was clear there was an implicit, more specific agenda.

Essentially there were three connected points of controversy. One was whether grammar should be formally taught at all. As John Rae and Kenneth Baker had noted, most schools in Britain had abandoned traditional grammar lessons based on rote-learning and drilling as they adopted more 'progressive' and 'pupil-centred' teaching methods, partly (as Rae alleged) for ideological reasons, but mainly because of research findings suggesting traditional methods were not effective, and that grammar-teaching itself was of questionable value. At the time, these conclusions and the associated changes in practice had been endorsed by governmental committees of inquiry; conservatives in the 1980s, however, wanted traditional grammar and traditional methods restored.

The second point of controversy was what kind of grammatical model to adopt – a prescriptive one based on Latin paradigms and expressed as a set of commandments, or a descriptive one based on linguists' analyses of how people actually use English? Whereas linguists and the so-called 'educational establishment' favoured the latter alternative, conservatives favoured the former, which was more in line with their views on the third and most controversial point, namely, the purpose for which grammar was to be taught. For conservatives, the object of the exercise was to ensure that pupils would learn to use standard English correctly. In framing this objective they were motivated not only by positive attitudes to the national language, but also by prejudice against non-standard English; and they took it as obvious common sense that if you wish to eradicate non-standard English and replace it with standard English, the way to do this is to teach standard grammatical rules explicitly. (Conversely, they assumed that ignorance of standard English was rife *because* schools had ceased to teach grammar formally.) Expert opinion, while not disputing that everyone should be able to use the standard language, maintained that formal grammar teaching had little effect on actual language use; it further maintained that teaching standard English and/or grammar need not, and should not, entail intolerance for other varieties.

With expert and pro-grammar conservative opinion so polarized on these crucial issues, it is not surprising that the Kingman and Cox committees were unable to satisfy both sides; but as appointees of a radical right-wing government they might have been expected to be more sympathetic to the pro-grammar faction. Their recommendations showed, however, that they had been influenced significantly by expert evidence. Although both committees made a point of endorsing the importance of standard English and the usefulness of teaching language structure explicitly (thus challenging the views of many education professionals, particularly those at the 'progressive' end of the spectrum), neither report endorsed a return to traditional models and methods of grammar teaching or condoned intolerance of dialect variation.

Brian Cox has described, in tones of some indignation, the effect his committee's report had on those responsible for commissioning it. When he presented it to the Secretary of State, Cox tells us, Mr Baker 'very much disliked it. He had wanted a short Report, with strong emphasis on grammar, spelling and punctuation, which would please the Prime Minister and be easy for parents to read' (Cox 1990: 1). This strongly negative initial reaction to the working group's proposals was presumably delivered in private; but it was soon echoed, or more exactly amplified, in public. For it was at this point that the media began to play an important role in the grammar affair, joining with pro-grammar conservatives in their efforts to discredit the committees from which the Right had expected so much and received, as they saw it, so little. The upshot was an outbreak of the sort of press coverage – massive in quantity, hysterical and alarmist in quality – which is found in cases of moral panic.

The unfolding debate about English teaching was presented to the public liberally garnished with scare stories about falling standards among pupils and ideological subversion among teachers. In some cases these stories were deliberately fed to the media by right-wing organizations; as with the dangerous dog panic mentioned earlier, however, it is clear that once the topic was established as an issue, journalists went digging for such stories on their own initiative. For example, they sought access to teacher education institutions and wrote scathing reports on the 'permissive' methods of English teaching being advocated to trainee teachers; they also became conscientious readers of professional journals for English teachers, and selectively reproduced pieces in which the 'experts' appeared to be claiming that spelling and grammar did not matter, while the children whose work was under discussion seemed unable to spell the simplest word or to write a grammatical sentence.

When other interested parties entered the debate, they did so on terms which had already been established: anyone who dissented from pro-grammar conservatism was forced on to the defensive. The most significant group of dissenters, not surprisingly, were English teachers themselves. But because of the form media coverage of the issue had taken, namely a barrage of scare stories in which the ludicrous notions of these professionals were held responsible for widespread near illiteracy, contributions from anyone with either specialist knowledge or direct experience had effectively been discredited before they were even made.

So effective were the media and the pro-grammar conservatives in keeping up the steady flow of horror stories and complaints that the years between 1988 and 1992 were virtually a state of linguistic emergency. The issue of grammar was not laid to rest by the passing of the

Education Reform Act, but continued to be a rallying point for attempts to whip up anxiety about language, literacy and educational standards. And in time these attempts began to have the desired effect.

In 1991, when the National Curriculum was already in the process of being introduced in schools, conflict broke out over teacher training materials produced by a body which the government had itself set up to disseminate the Kingman report's model of language to practising teachers, LINC (Language in the National Curriculum). When LINC sought to publish its materials under the imprint of Her Majesty's Stationery Office the government refused its agreement; it also refused to release the copyright so a commercial publisher could bring out the materials. This refusal appears to have been ideologically motivated: the materials contained too many references to issues of class, race and gender and took too 'permissive' a line on grammar.

Then in September 1992 the Secretary of State for Education, acting with the National Curriculum Council, announced a further review of English teaching, in effect overturning the statutory orders made only a few years before. The results of this review seemed to have been predetermined: before the panel had even met it was reported that its recommendations would place more emphasis on spelling, grammar and the speaking of standard English.

When new draft orders were issued for consultation (DFE 1993[8]) it seemed that the pro-grammar conservatives had finally got what they had wanted all along, for on the key issues of grammar teaching and the use of standard English these revised orders did exactly what the review announcement had suggested they would, and they bore virtually no trace of the more moderate recommendations made by Kingman and Cox. Cox himself repudiated the new document as pandering to extremism. A teacher who had been appointed to the review body reinforced this view when she resigned before its work was finished. Among the main reasons she cited for her resignation was the dominance throughout the discussion of papers produced by a right-wing think-tank, the Centre for Policy Studies. She alleged that no evidence from any other source had been considered.

Revelations such as this gave fresh ammunition to critics of the English curriculum, and by this time there was also widespread discontent with the management of the National Curriculum in general. But the grammar/standard English issue marked the line where most criticism stopped. The revised orders' restoration of traditional concepts of grammar, and their insistence on standard English as the only acceptable dialect in school, were popularly hailed as a victory for common sense. Articles appeared in newspapers in which teachers recanted their earlier neglect of grammar, or criticized other teachers for neglecting it; leaders in the quality press regretted the bureaucracy of the National Curriculum tests, the arrogance of those in charge and the narrowness of the new literature curriculum, but they strikingly did not regret the emphasis on grammar and standard English.

The 1993 review was not the last word on the English curriculum. Its proposals became caught up in a more general overhaul of the statutory orders for all subjects, which was necessitated by widespread boycotting of national tests by teachers' unions on the grounds that they were too complex and time-consuming. The overhaul was intended to streamline and simplify, but in the case of English it also provided an occasion for conflict over grammar and standard English to break out again in public. What followed demonstrated the disproportionate political significance this issue had by now assumed.

Right from the start, the National Curriculum was continually subject to revision – a lengthy process in which advisory panels sat, draft documents were issued for consultation, the results were (in theory) considered and incorporated, and the final result was a new set of statutory orders issued by the Secretary of State. This cumbersome procedure inevitably gave rise to rumours and leaks which were picked over in the press long before the process was officially completed. By 1994 a third version of the English orders was in the pipeline, and there were reports in the press that it would be very different from the previous year's effort. The new orders were rumoured to contain what one newspaper called 'notable concessions to the liberal English teachers' (*Independent on Sunday*, 13 March 1994).

The actual substance of the rumours reported in this article suggested these 'notable concessions' were nothing more radical than a partial return to the original recommendations made by the Cox Committee. Nevertheless, reporting of the new document highlighted the outrage of pro-grammar conservatives who felt earlier gains were being eroded. Even in the *Independent*, not a right-wing paper, it is striking that the reporter interprets the changes as intended to placate 'the liberal English teachers' – and that English teachers are by now being described axiomatically as 'liberal', though in truth they represent a wide spectrum of political opinion, like any other profession to which thousands of people belong.

But the sting in the tail of this particular story is that when the 1994 document was issued for consultation, it did not bear out earlier press speculation on its contents. Far from making notable concessions, it appeared even more obsessed with standard English than the previous document. It soon emerged that the discrepancy between prediction and reality was not because the press had got hold of inaccurate rumours; the panel advising the government had indeed made 'concessions', but at the last minute these had been removed or watered down by ministers. References to bilingualism and dialect diversity were deleted; references to standard English were strengthened and placed more prominently throughout the document; the Secretary of State himself had intervened to reinstate the demand that all teachers at all times must correct children's non-standard speech.

The panel members responded by issuing a press statement asking why and by whom their recommendations had been 'ignored or changed beyond recognition since our last meeting'. One panellist remarked that 'politically, Standard English still remains an area where prejudice and opinion are elevated over knowledge', and charged that it had by now become a 'ministerial obsession' (quoted in *TES*, 13 May 1994). This extremely public row, centring on allegations of political interference which appeared to be well-founded, suggested that the entire grammar/ standard English issue had become so important for conservatives, and their position on the issue so entrenched, that government ministers acting in its defence apparently did not care if the processes of consultation and advice-seeking were publicly exposed as a sham.

Statutory orders for English were issued in 1995, a full eight years after Kenneth Baker first announced the formation of the Kingman Committee. It would be wrong, however, to treat the policy-making process from 1987 to 1994 as merely chaotic; its many false starts and abrupt changes of direction in part reflected the persistence of the pro-grammar conservatives and their ability to mobilize support at crucial moments, not only in the corridors of power but also through the media and their influence on public opinion.

The grammar debate did not take place in isolation. To talk about a 'grammar debate' is to abstract a single thread from what became a very complex and confusing web of discourse on education. Over time the controversy about grammar became linked with other controversial issues, notably pedagogy ('child-centred' versus 'chalk and talk'), reading ('phonics' versus 'real books') and literature ('the classics' versus 'relevant texts'). I compare the resulting discourse to a web, because just as a web is a structure whose intertwined threads give the whole a resilience no single strand possesses, so in the debate on education each freshly-mooted 'problem' reinforced all the others.

Grammar, however, was not just one concern among many: it occupied a privileged place at the centre of the web. Controversy about it emerged early, and persisted after other controversies had died down. The media, especially the print media, were far more interested in grammar than in, say, the science and technology curriculum. Newspaper columns and editorials were haunted by the spectre of a language and culture under threat: a nation disunited, illiterate, populated by school leavers unable to fill in a simple job application form or make themselves understood at an interview – not because they were intrinsically stupid but because no one cared enough to teach them proper English. The malign and destructive ideologies that gripped these young people's teachers would have their full flowering in the later careers of the young people themselves: ignorant, inarticulate and unemployable, they would turn to anti-social and criminal behaviour. These images were powerful, and they resonated across the social and political spectrum.

What the pro-grammar Right, assisted by the media, accomplished with these ideas and images over a period of several years was a steady movement towards more and more authoritarian views of what English teaching should be, sustained by increasingly authoritarian decision-making procedures, which in turn were legitimated by increasingly vitriolic attacks on the English teaching profession. And this movement was propelled throughout by regular surges of anxiety, comparable in intensity to the anxiety that is usually provoked by such staples of moral panic as crime and drugs.

So far, then, I have argued that the grammar debate followed the pattern of moral panic in a number of ways. Although the events just outlined are more complex and more long drawn-out than most classic moral panics, because of the interaction between the activities of policy makers, organized interest groups and the media, many of the important features of a panic were present. There was the initial discovery of a 'problem', the prompt identification of scapegoats, the uncovering of more and more scare stories which fostered a disproportionate sense of crisis, and the inexorable shift towards more and more authoritarian 'solutions' in the light of widespread public anxiety.

But if the debate on grammar was a case of moral panic, one crucial question remains to be asked: what was the panic really about? What buried anxieties, what threatening social changes could have caused English grammar to inspire such strong emotions?

These are complex questions, perhaps more complex than they appear. Some of the answers must be sought in the immediate political context; but others lie in the cultural significance of grammar itself, in meanings which existed long before the events just described. Only when we understand what grammar symbolizes at the deepest level can we hope to understand how its meaning is deployed at particular times for particular purposes.

It is frequently assumed that grammar, at least in Britain, is essentially a symbol of *class*. That is not untrue, but it is not the whole truth either. No doubt the yoking together of Dr Syntax and Mrs Grundy serves particular class interests; but their union also stands for a cluster of values whose appeal for many people cuts across class divisions. Unless we pay attention to this subterranean symbolism, we will be unable to make sense of the capacity that grammar has to inspire moral panic. We will be left, like Colin MacCabe, to shake our heads in bafflement at the pointless, vicious stupidity of public arguments about it.

GRAMMAR AS MORAL METAPHOR: THE ROOTS OF PANIC

The rhetoric of pro-grammar conservatives, as exemplified by any random sample of their public utterances, *is* baffling in certain respects. To the outside observer it may well seem both pointless and stupid, if only because it so often says little or nothing about the subject it claims to be addressing. Typically, a cursory mention of grammar will be followed by what looks like an irrelevant moral homily. Here are a few symptomatic examples, produced in different contexts by different individuals at different stages of the debate:

> The overthrow of grammar coincided with the acceptance of the equivalent of creative writing in social behaviour. As nice points of grammar were mockingly dismissed as pedantic and irrelevant, so was punctiliousness in such matters as honesty, responsibility, property, gratitude, apology and so on.
>
> (John Rae, *Observer*, 7 February 1982)

> If you allow standards to slip to the stage where good English is no better than bad English, where people turn up filthy at school . . . all these things tend to cause people to have no standards at all, and once you lose standards then there's no imperative to stay out of crime.
>
> (Norman Tebbit MP, Radio 4, 1985)

> All the letters sent from my office I have to correct myself, and that is because English is taught so bloody badly. . . . We must educate for character. That's the trouble with schools. They don't educate for character. This matters a great deal. The whole way schools are operating is not right. I do not believe English is being taught properly. You cannot educate people properly unless you do it on a basic framework and drilling system.
>
> (Prince Charles, 1989)

> I would always be wary of anything [i.e. any way of teaching English] that took away from discipline. Children should be taught in a very formal way, otherwise the sloppiness goes on throughout their lives.
>
> (Jeffrey Archer, quoted in *Independent on Sunday,* 13 March 1994)

In each of these utterances there is a characteristic slippage between linguistic and moral terms. (In the last case, there is not even 'slippage': without additional information a reader cannot know that Jeffrey Archer is talking about grammar or language at all.) Ignorance or defiance of grammatical rules is equated with anti-social or criminal behaviour. Grammar needs to be taught, we gather, less to inculcate the norms of polite usage than to encourage respect for persons and property, to keep people clean and law-abiding, to build their 'character' and discourage indiscipline or 'sloppiness'.

It is especially baffling that these moral arguments for the teaching of grammar are antithetical to the instrumental arguments that Thatcherites in the 1980s routinely advanced for the teaching of everything else. The debate on other core curriculum subjects was dominated by such considerations as 'the needs of industry' and the future employability of young people. Grammar could be given a perfectly plausible justification along the same lines, for after all, employers claim to want a literate workforce with good 'communication skills'. It is suprising, then, to find such acolytes of Mrs Thatcher as Norman Tebbit and Jeffrey Archer eschewing this sort of argument and preferring to plunge into the treacherous waters of 'standards' and 'discipline'. It suggests that for pro-grammar conservatives, grammar is a 'sacred' subject, to be pursued for quasi-mystical reasons transcending mere utility. As the Battle of Waterloo was won on the playing fields of Eton, so the challenges facing the nation today will require the moral fibre that comes by way of spelling tests and parsing drills.

Yet here is a further source of bafflement: for the connections being made here are obscure to say the least. One can almost see how public school sports might be a relevant preparation for a military campaign. But how exactly would knowing the parts of speech translate into a compulsion to launder your school uniform, or prevent you from going out and vandalizing someone's car? Our commentators treat this chain of cause and effect as if it were self-evident – with one small but significant exception. Just before the passage I have quoted from his *Observer* piece, John Rae says that the parallel he is going to make between respect for grammatical rules and respect for social niceties is not 'an intellectual conceit'. That, of course, is exactly what it is: a conceit, a metaphor. And in this metaphor lies the key to grammar's deep symbolic meaning.

The otherwise baffling observations of pro-grammar conservatives become intelligible if we hypothesize a systematic analogy between the structure of language and the structure of society. More specifically, as Jill Bourne and I have argued elsewhere (Cameron and Bourne 1989), conservatives use 'grammar' as the metaphorical correlate for a cluster of related political and moral terms: *order, tradition, authority, hierarchy* and *rules*. In the ideological world that conservatives inhabit, these terms are not only positive, they define the conditions for any civil society, while their opposites – *disorder, change, fragmentation, anarchy* and *lawlessness* – signify the breakdown of social relations. A panic about grammar is therefore interpretable as the metaphorical expression of persistent conservative fears that we are losing the values that underpin civilization and sliding into chaos.

This metaphor supplies the missing link between bad grammar and bad behaviour. If conformity to the rules of orderly speech signifies conformity to the laws of society, acquiescence in its traditional hierarchies and acceptance of legitimate authority, it becomes easier to see why disregard for 'nice points of grammar' should be construed as leading inexorably to disrespect for persons, property, institutions ('turning up filthy at school') and finally the law itself. It also becomes easier to make sense of the discursive web I mentioned earlier, in which grammar comes to be paralleled with various terms that on the face of things have nothing in common with it: with Shakespeare, for instance (not Jamaican dub poetry), with 'chalk and talk' teaching methods (not child-centred active learning), with phonics (not real books). What unites these terms with each other and with grammar is not any obvious surface similarity but a shared symbolic meaning: 'Shakespeare' symbolizes tradition and the hierarchy of literary value, 'chalk and talk' signifies an orderly, as opposed to a chaotic classroom, and 'phonics' is based on fixed rules rather than idiosyncratic experience.

Grammar is the critical anchoring point in this web, since it brings together all the terms that constitute the metaphorical code. At some level, conservatives understood that it was the perfect overarching symbol of their goals in reforming education – essentially, the reimposition of authority and discipline. A demand for more grammar-teaching boils down to the traditional Tory crusade for law and order carried on by other means. This, in fact, has been a recurring theme in official reports on English teaching since the beginnings of mass education in Britain. Nearly seventy years before the 1988 Education Reform Act, the Newbolt report had observed:

> The great difficulty of teachers in Elementary schools in many districts is that they have to fight against the powerful influences of evil habits of speech contracted in home and street. The teachers' struggle is thus not with ignorance but with a perverted power.
>
> (Newbolt 1921, quoted in Crowley 1989: 243)

The teaching of correct English is persistently depicted as part of a more general 'struggle' against dark social forces, and specifically as a means to counter the anarchy of the (working-class) 'home and street'.

That this way of thinking about grammar continues to flourish is underlined by Marilyn Butler, a professor of English literature at Cambridge University, in her account of an occasion in 1993 when she addressed an audience of Tory grassroots activists. She found them much less concerned about the other strands of the ongoing debate on English teaching than about grammar, which they conceived in strikingly metaphorical terms. Butler writes (1993: 11):

> The schools they wanted would remedy social anarchy on the housing estates, joy-riders on the streets, and child murderers at shopping centres. Mr Clarke [the Home Secretary] might not have got far with his recent assault on crime, but they had not lost faith in his subliminal alternative, classroom discipline for an unruly remedial group. No one seemed at all concerned whether or not the young knew *Daffodils* by heart. They wanted them to learn grammar and spelling, and correct spoken English from the time of entry. They wanted them taught rules. . . . They cared only for correctness, which they understood symbolically as law. What I was hearing

had nothing essentially to do with teaching a modern discipline in a modern classroom. They voiced deep anxieties about society, fear of those sections they thought of as lawless, and an angry demand that their government assert control.

What appears to Butler and to other outsiders so peculiar in this sort of rhetoric – its effortless elision of the literal and the figurative, so that notions of linguistic correctness and grammatical rules collapse instantly into a moral discourse with fear of anarchy and lawlessness at its heart – seems to ordinary conservatives (and probably to many people with no strong party allegiance) the most natural and obvious thing in the world. Moreover, it should be acknowledged that the metaphor, as metaphor, is in many ways an apt one: grammar is a *traditional* practice imposing *order* on languages by describing their structure in terms of *hierarchical rules* which have *authority* for speakers. The association between grammar and authority or discipline is particularly ancient. Classical and neoclassical representations of the seven liberal arts that comprised education for the ancient Greeks (grammar, dialectic, rhetoric, arithmetic, astronomy, geometry and music) typically personify Grammar as a stern figure holding a book in one hand and a birch rod or whip in the other.[9]

During the twentieth century, however, some elements of the ancient metaphorical code have been challenged by a powerful competing discourse. The 'enemy within' is linguistic science, which preserves a notion of grammar as ordered, hierarchical and rule-governed, but dispenses with tradition and authority as necessary components of its meaning. Linguistics has introduced a new definition of grammar as 'descriptive not prescriptive', in which the rules are underwritten not by traditional authority but by internalized native speaker competence.

For conservatives this is a major blow. Tradition and authority are crucial to their concept of social order, and if the language/society analogy is to hold (which of course it does not for linguists), they must also remain central in the definition of grammar. Because of this consideration, pro-grammar conservatives in the 1980s debate were obliged to fight on two fronts simultaneously. Not only were they forced to defend grammar itself, they were also compelled to defend a particular concept of grammar – traditional prescriptive grammar – against the dangerous 'new orthodoxy' of descriptive linguistics. This explains what might otherwise seem a puzzling feature of the debate: its tendency to wander away from the central terrain of education into the more arcane byways of sociolinguistics. The battle against the 'new orthodoxy' was one that pro-grammar conservatives needed to fight; but it was also the one they found hardest to win.

CONSERVATIVES VERSUS LINGUISTS: THE ATTACK ON THE 'NEW ORTHODOXY'

The notion of descriptive grammar is anathema to conservatives because it destroys the link between grammar and authority. Not only does this challenge the general preference for authority among conservatives, it also leads down the slippery slope of linguistic (and by analogy, moral) relativism. If the rules of grammar are located 'inside' native speakers and not in some external authority, it is obviously much more difficult to apply uniform standards of correctne̒ss. Provided it conforms to some-one's internalized structural rules, any old usage will be accepted. Instead of being able to condemn usages as 'bad grammar', at worst we will be able to censure them as 'inappropriate in a particular context'.

The suggestion that there are no absolute values and standards of correctness, either in language or elsewhere, is repugnant to conservative thinking, and those linguists who proclaimed this 'new orthodoxy' were specifically targeted for attack. Charging, correctly, that the new orthodoxy had pervaded educational thinking since the Bullock Report, the pro-grammar conservatives set out to ensure that it would not taint the thinking of the Kingman and Cox committees.

John Honey's early salvo *The Language Trap* (1983) had argued that in adopting the new orthodoxy, schools were hurting the very pupils they most earnestly desired to help, namely, working-class children speaking non-standard vernaculars. It was all very well proposing the linguist's axiom that 'all varieties are equal', but since no one else in society believed this, to act on it was to perpetuate social disadvantage. Standard English remained the mark of intelligent, educated speak-ers, and working-class children would suffer unless they were taught it and made to use it in school.

Honey himself does not believe that 'all varieties are equal', and his views go beyond his emphasis on the point (which no linguist doubts) that varieties are differently *evaluated* because of social prejudice. A much-quoted comment from his book noted that a variety like Black English, 'adequate to the needs of its speakers' in Brixton, would not necessarily be adequate to the more sophisticated needs which black Brixtonians might develop if only they were better educated.

Honey's argument rests on the undoubted fact that there is widespread bias against non-standard Englishes, and it plays on fears that children will be used as pawns in a futile game of social engineering. What remains unquestioned, though, is the idea that linguistic prejudice must be accepted rather than challenged. In other spheres this would not be so readily accepted. There is, after all, a lot of colour prejudice in Britain, but that fact is never invoked to suggest that black children in Brixton schools should be taught the proper use of skin lightening cosmetics. Language is a different case not just because speech is considered more amenable to alteration than skin colour but because people do generally agree with Honey: they believe non-standard varieties are inferior to standard ones, and ultimately just *wrong*.

Some right-wing polemicists were willing to make this argument more directly. By 1987 a more ambitious theoretical challenge than Honey's was being mounted by John Marenbon in a pamphlet sponsored by the Centre for Policy Studies entitled *English Our English: The New Orthodoxy Examined*. Marenbon, a Cambridge University academic who would go on to become involved in the National Curriculum Council's revision of the statutory orders for English (though he later resigned in a disagreement over testing), devotes his pamphlet to a point-by-point examination of the tenets of the 'new orthodoxy', including the key claims that 'grammar should be descriptive not prescriptive' and 'all varieties are equal'.

On the first point, as I noted in Chapter 1, he argues that grammar is by definition prescriptive: it 'prescribes by describing' (p. 20). On the issue of the equality of varieties, he extends Honey's implicit argument that standard English is not merely accorded more prestige than other dialects; it is actually superior on conceptual and linguistic grounds because of its long history of continuous development for the highest purposes of thought, argument and aesthetic expression.

On both these points Marenbon shows facility in presenting arguments with just enough substance to make readers ignore the gaps and shifts that enable him to draw tendentious conclusions. For instance, as I said in Chapter 1, I believe he is correct in characterizing grammatical rules of the kind that differentiate standard from non-standard English as essentially normative; but his conclusion that we must therefore revere the particular norms that have come down to us is based on the value he accords tradition in and for itself, and does not follow directly from his deconstruction of the descriptive/prescriptive opposition.

A similar point can be made about his argument for the superiority of standard English. It is true that the historical development of this dialect gives it resources (mainly lexical and stylistic rather than grammatical) which non-standardized dialects lack (though they are capable of developing them, just as standard English had to do when it took over certain functions from Latin). This suggests that in current circumstances there really might be things you cannot easily do with a non-standard dialect, and for which it is necessary to resort to the standard. But most critiques of non-standard Englishes dwell not on what is allegedly ineffable in them, but precisely on those areas where they provide direct grammatical equivalents for the standard form – multiple instead of single negation, for example. These direct equivalents are then labelled errors or illogicalities. The claim that non-standard English is 'restricted' because of what is absent from it slides inexorably into the quite different, and wholly untenable, claim that it is restricted because of features actually present in it.

Once again, Marenbon's argument can only rest on tradition: on his conviction that standard English embodies 'the best that has been thought and said'. For all that he dresses this up in the clothing of rational argument, he is using exactly the same trick that right-wing critics have accused the liberal sociolinguist William Labov of using in his own classic defence of African-American vernacular, 'The logic of non-standard English' (Labov 1972). Here Labov seeks to defend the non-standard vernacular of Harlem adolescents by contrasting the logical and lively utterance of a vernacular speaker with the standard, but on inspection merely verbose and confusing utterance of a middle-class black informant. Right-wing critics have suggested that Labov does not demonstrate the point, he merely presents his data and expects readers to see it for themselves; to the reader whose value judgement differs from his, he has no convincing reply. Marenbon's strategy with respect to standard English is an exactly parallel appeal to the self-evident judgements of 'cultured' English speakers.

From the perspective I adopt throughout this book, the form that Marenbon's argument takes is inevitable and its widespread appeal is no surprise. Once again, it is precisely with value judgements that we are dealing. Facts about standard and non-standard English are not irrele-vant to the argument; points can be scored by showing your opponent is simply wrong, but facts on their own will not settle the question of what value should be given to different varieties of language. Furthermore, to the extent that Marenbon or Honey can air their value judgements openly, whereas their opponents in linguistic science are more constrained by the norm of objectivity, the polemical advantage lies with the conservatives, and the linguists are likely to lose the argument.

The effects of the onslaught against sociolinguists in the debate were, at least initially, more mixed than this last observation might suggest. One one hand, both Kingman and Cox moved away from the liberal pluralism of 'all varieties are equal', by placing much more emphasis on pupils' use of standard English. It is particularly notable that this emphasis applied to speech as well as writing; for whereas no one disputes that standard English is the norm in (almost all) writing, there is more disagreement about norms for speech, which is in any case less codified and more variable (meaning it is more difficult to define, in purely linguistic terms, what counts as 'standard' spoken English). Kingman and Cox justified their insistence on standard English with reference to its status as a *lingua franca*, and also by using Honey's argument about 'entitlement'. On the other hand, they pointedly did not refer to Honey's or Marenbon's argument for the superiority of the standard over other varieties (except in so far as a *lingua franca* has the functional advantage of being more widely understood).

On the question of grammar being 'descriptive not prescriptive', the Kingman and Cox committees also stood by the linguists (linguists were represented on both of these bodies, and also gave evidence to them). The National Curriculum's model of language was to be descriptive in character; variation was to be an appropriate topic for discussion in the classroom; 'knowledge about language' was to be preferred to 'grammar', and decontextualized drills were to be shunned as a way of teaching it.

The reports caused outrage among pro-grammar conservatives, and the great and good who produced them were no longer treated as allies in the campaign. The popular tabloid press was especially emphatic in its denunciations of Cox's proposals: the *Star* was typical in ridiculing the view that while standard English must be used in writing and formal contexts, non-standard grammar was acceptable in casual speech, in a report headlined 'Cor Blimey, would you Adam and Eve it?', which opened:

> It aint 'arf OK for kids not to talk proper. That's the verdict of a shock new report on how Britain's children should be taught. The controversial blue-print by the National Curriculum Council says schools should introduce a new 'three Rs' – reading, 'riting and relaxing the Queen's English.

Actually, the Cox Committee's attitude to linguistic variation would not have struck anyone familiar with prevailing educational opinion as shocking or controversial. But the report brought into the open the gap that existed, not just between Right and Left but between expert opinion and popular common sense. The latter was succinctly summarized by an editorial on the Cox Report that appeared in *Today* newspaper, a slightly less lightweight publication than the *Star*:

> How is a secondary school child supposed to learn anything about how to speak or write in the glorious English language when the advisers cannot lay down any serious rules to guide them? . . . So nervous have Mr Baker's advisers become at being charged with elitism or discrimination by one group or another that they have lost the guts to recommend anything useful at all. . . . Mr Baker must base his curriculum on the recognition that some kinds of English really are more worthwhile than others.

For *Today*, it is axiomatic that all varieties are not equally 'glorious', that children must learn their own language through explicit instruction in its grammatical rules, and that leaving non-standard language uncorrected in any context is the thin end of a permissive wedge that can only lead to universal illiteracy. None of these axioms is supported by the available research evidence on either linguistic variation or children's language development; but popular common sense apprehends the 'new orthodoxy' as nothing more than a gutless refusal to exert authority, lay down rules and acknowledge hierarchies of linguistic worth. What is said to lie behind this loss of nerve is anxiety about 'elitism', along with fear that special interest groups will cry discrimination.

It has traditionally been acknowledged by governments of all ideological persuasions that you cannot make sensible policy on the basis of tabloid common sense, which is why ministers are in the habit of appointing committees to enquire into various subjects, asking them first to consider the evidence impartially and then to make recommendations. Kingman and Cox had taken these terms of reference at face value and come up with models they thought would work in practice. But this was not what the Right had wanted them to do. They had wanted the whole symbolic package: order, tradition, authority, hierarchy and rules (not to mention drills). Any hint of the 'new orthodoxy', however watered down, was perceived as a failure to deliver the goods. The mistake the committees had made was to focus on matters of language and not on the underlying moral symbolism. Without this, grammar (or 'knowledge about language') was worth very little to the conservatives. As we have seen, there is evidence that the advisers who came after Cox were not given the same freedom of enquiry.

This cavalier attitude to expert advisers enabled the pro-grammar conservatives progressively to undermine certain aspects of the 'new orthodoxy'. By the time a review of the English curriculum was announced in 1992, with 'more emphasis on grammar and standard English' among its stated goals, the postulate that 'all varieties are equal' was no longer receiving even lip-service in official statements. David Pascall, Chairman of the National Curriculum Council, felt able to define standard English in terms reminiscent of the tabloid editorials quoted above:

> It's grammatically correct English . . . so that you can be understood clearly, so that you don't speak sloppily, you use tenses and prepositions properly, you don't say 'He done it' and you don't split infinitives. . . . 'He done it' is speaking English incorrectly. That's bad grammar. We think it important that our children speak correctly.
>
> (quoted in *Independent on Sunday*, 13 September 1992)

The revised orders produced under Pascall's direction carried forward this view, but without entirely eliminating all traces of previous policy documents; as a result it contained some rather startling inconsistencies. For example, the new orders defined grammar as 'the correct use of the standard language' (DFE 1993: 9) while remarking on the same page that 'dialects have grammar too', and claiming that to insist on standard English and grammar in no way undermines the integrity of local dialects. This is incoherent to the point of absurdity, since it suggests that when children use the standard language 'incorrectly' they are doing something quite different from using a local dialect; whereas in fact, all the 'incorrect' usages cited are precisely items of non-standard dialect such as 'aint', 'you was' and multiple negation. In this document 'grammar' becomes, by definitional fiat, a laundry list of errors and solecisms that would not disgrace an eighteenth-century guide to polite usage, and whose only discernable purpose is to undermine the integrity of local dialects.

In 1994 when it was reported (wrongly, as it turned out) that there would shortly be a revised document saying that standard English was to be used when circumstances required it rather than all the time, the news called forth a flood of contradictions and qualifications underpinned by the same imaginary distinction between speaking a non-standard dialect of English and speaking English incorrectly. The novelist and peer P.D. James, for example, was quoted as saying that 'we have to make a distinction between dialect and incorrect and ungrammatical English' (*Independent on Sunday*, 13 March 1994). A survey of opinions on literacy and education carried out among members of the Society of Women Writers and Journalists found overwhelming agreement that 'children should learn to speak correct English whatever their dialect' (*Independent*, 11 March 1994).[10]

Preserving local dialects' 'integrity' (which means 'unitary status' or 'wholeness') would require that each dialect be regarded as a system with its own norms of correctness – just as we recognize the integrity of different languages by acknowledging that the norms are not the same in, say, English and Russian. Multiple negation is 'correct' in standard French; it is equally 'correct' in London English. To call it 'ungrammatical English' is to deny that non-standard dialects have either grammar or integrity.

The laundry list approach shows how, by 1993, the other tenet of the 'new orthodoxy', that grammar should be 'descriptive not prescriptive', was also beginning to be undermined. A definition of grammar as 'the correct use of the standard language' is a charter for prescriptive grammar teaching – not 'knowledge about language' but rules for using it correctly. Yet on the question of *how* to teach grammatical prescriptions, even the 1993 proposals shy away from a wholesale return to the practice of the 1950s, stating that 'detailed grammar lessons are not appropriate'.

This shows some continuity with earlier policy. Cox had been forthright about rejecting traditional prescriptive grammar teaching on the grounds that it was too rigid and treated English as a 'branch of Latin'. Right-wing ideologues were less impressed. Their responses made clear how much pro-grammar conservatives had invested not only in the content of traditional grammar but in the pedagogy traditionally associated with it – the method approvingly described by Prince Charles as 'a basic framework and drilling system'. This pedagogy turned out to play an important role in sustaining the symbolic code whereby grammar represents hierarchy, authority and so on; and in the peak phase of the debate, teaching methods assumed much more importance, bringing conflict between conservatives and what they dubbed the 'educational establishment'.

CONSERVATIVES VERSUS THE 'EDUCATIONAL ESTABLISHMENT': THE DEFENCE OF DRILLS AND DESKS

There is a connection between traditional grammar and traditional pedagogy, by which in this instance I mean the use of repetitive exercises ('drills') in parsing, sentence correction and labelling, filling in the blanks, etc., because traditional grammar is not wholly amenable to the independent exercise of either reason or native speaker intuition. It is therefore well-matched with a kind of teaching which emphasizes rote learning and mechanical drilling rather than problem solving, argument or reflection.

English traditional grammar comes down to us from the eighteenth century and is strongly marked in both content and form by the beliefs, values and goals of the age that produced it. These have less to do with current scientific ideas about exhaustive and objective description than with the urgent desire of men of letters 250 years ago to order, improve and 'fix' a language that seemed chaotic, vulgar and liable to degeneration.

Traditional grammar is selective: it does not dwell on what any native speaker intuitively knows (e.g. that the subject precedes the verb in English, or that adjectives go before nouns – foreigners may need to be told these things, but native speakers will get them right without formal instruction). Instead it concentrates on rules that are not intuitively obvious to native speakers because they do not really belong to the core grammar of English, or they are cases of what the Milroys call 'optional variability' (see Chapter 2, this volume), and it is arbitrary in linguistic terms which variant has been deemed 'correct'. Many familiar prohibitions derive from the ungrammaticality of certain features in Latin (e.g. 'split infinitives' – in Latin the infinitive is a single word – and sentences ending with a preposition). It is precisely because they are *not* impossible in English that such constructions have to be proscribed explicitly.

Rules of this type are difficult to explain or justify using rational arguments. The real reason for their existence – the dependence of early codifiers on Latin grammar as a model, and the subsequent reinforcement of that model by educated custom and practice – is not very convincing as a justification for following them, and grammar teachers down the ages have lived in dread of pupils pressing them too closely for a more persuasive rationale. Traditional pedagogy helped to evade the issue. By reducing grammar to a set of arbitrary rules to be memorized and then mechanically applied in repetitive exercises, it upheld the authority of grammatical conventions while ensuring that there would be little time or inclination to discuss the basis for them.

If it was intended either to enhance pupils' actual linguistic performance or to give them a metalinguistic understanding of English structure, traditional grammar teaching was a conspicuous failure. Studies conducted when grammar was still a formal part of the English language syllabus at GCE 'O' level[11] found that instruction in grammatical analysis had no discernable effect on reading comprehension or writing skills, while in addition many examination candidates had failed to master the techniques of grammatical analysis itself, despite many hours of specific instruction (Carter 1990). When Kingman and Cox decreed that 'knowledge about language' should not be taught using the old methods, they were bowing to the weight of research and informed opinion rather than making an ideological stand. From the point of view of pedagogical effectiveness, the Right's continued advocacy of decontextualized drills seemed mindless and perverse.

But here again, the committees had failed to attend to the deeper symbolism of the debate. Conservatives do not advocate teaching grammar for purely instrumental reasons to do with enhancing linguistic knowledge and skill. Their preference for methods that do not work must be seen in the light of the moral significance they accord to grammar. If the lesson is less about language than about order, good behaviour and respect for authority, the value of drilling becomes much clearer. As with military basic training – also held to 'build character' – grammar drills present pupils with an apparently trivial and pointless task which must nevertheless be performed precisely on command. The point is not to teach the task in and for itself, but to teach discipline – obedience and punctiliousness – in all tasks.

The sociologist Mary Evans has argued (Evans 1991) that mindless conformity to pointless rules was the *sine qua non* of the old grammar school system.[12] Her observation is interesting, because throughout the debate we are considering, the issue of grammar was persistently linked to a nostalgic yearning for grammar schools. This became another strand in the discursive web. And the logic of the connection is once again not difficult to see. There is the linguistic coincidence ('grammar'/ 'grammar school'), the historical link (according to popular belief, grammar schools taught grammar whereas secondary modern and comprehensive schools did not), but most of all there is the underlying value system based on order, tradition, authority, hierarchy and rules. Grammar schools embody a lost tradition of selectivity in state education, and therefore come, like grammar itself, to be potent symbols of these cherished conservative values.

In her discussion of the girls' grammar school she attended in the 1950s, Mary Evans pinpoints 'education in the thankless task' as a powerful tool whereby selective schools reproduced in their pupils particular middle-class values. For instance, first-year girls at Evans's school spent a year's domestic science lessons smocking a green gingham domestic science pinafore. Most would never have occasion to wear it, because only the lowest stream continued with domestic science in the second year. Nor was it likely that the girls would find much use for the skill of smocking, even supposing they mastered it. The rationale for the year's work was explicitly a moral one: girls were told they were smocking the pinafore as a way of learning patience and steady application.

Grammar was a similarly 'thankless task'. In fact, Evans's account makes clear it had two meanings for the school. On one level it signified the girls' class status. Dire warnings were issued about the corrupting effects on grammar of American films and English kitchen-sink drama, genres whose linguistic barbarity would render girls' own speech 'common'. But on another level grammar functioned like the pinafore: it taught the virtues of discipline. Evans and her classmates passed their time underlining nouns in red and verbs in green – a procedure which left them with the vague impression that 'grammar is rather like traffic lights' (p. 17).

Except that we ruled columns instead of underlining words, Evans could have been describing my own school grammar lessons twenty years later. During the grammar debate of the 1980s, many similar stories were told both in public and in private. Curiously, though, they were seldom told in the way Evans tells her story, to indict traditional grammar teaching as a stultifying waste of time. On the contrary, most were told in a spirit of nostalgia, mixed with a strange form of self-criticism.

During the furore, in 1990, I wrote a letter to a newspaper on the subject of grammar teaching. I received many replies, and at my place of work (which at the time was a teacher education institute) colleagues who were not linguists sought me out to tell me about their experiences of grammar. When I gave talks on the same subject at other institutions, I encouraged the audience to produce similar accounts of their own schooling. The accounts I received from these sources were both instructive and remarkably consistent.

Most people remembered grammar lessons as scenes of failure and humiliation. 'I could never do it', and 'I never got the hang of it' were recurring comments: while people's memories of exactly what it was they were being asked to do were vague – even vaguer than Evans's memories of underlining nouns and verbs – their emotional memories of feeling totally inadequate were sharp and strong, in some cases forty years on. Yet while some of these people rejected grammar as a result of their experience with it, many did not. Instead, they waxed sentimental about the good old days of order and certainty, often voicing the opinion that they wished they had been better at grammar, since they felt it was very important. One woman wrote to me (exceptionally, I must acknowledge) about her liking for grammar: 'it was the only part of English you could get 100% for.'

These conflicting emotions say something very interesting about the place of English grammar in English middle-class culture. Experiences which ought to have inspired contempt for grammar have apparently given large sections of the middle class an exaggerated respect for it. Believing that dull and difficult tasks are good for you, and that if you fail it must be your own fault, these people are good targets for conservative rhetoric about 'character building' and 'going back to basics'.

This might explain why the conservatives' view of Kingman and Cox as woolly-hatted claptrap, and their equation of traditional grammar teaching with discipline and moral rectitude, was shared by commentators across the political spectrum. It is scarcely astonishing to discover that Conservative MPs and tabloid leader writers hold views like the ones I have quoted in this chapter; it is rather more startling that Des Wilson, a Liberal Democrat known for his radical campaigning stance on various issues from homelessness to pollution, should have drawn applause in 1991 on the BBC's *Any Questions* radio programme when in answer to the question, 'who is to blame for falling standards in education?' he spoke nostalgically of his own school, where pupils 'sat in rows of desks' to be taught 'the basics of grammar' and 'how to read, write and spell'.

This 'sitting in rows of desks' became a touchstone in the debate. It continues the symbolism we have traced throughout this discussion: rows of desks symbolize order physically as grammatical drills symbolize it intellectually. The school described by Mr Wilson represents a perfect marriage of form and content. There was grammar; there were drills; the desks were arranged in rows.

A number of prominent Conservatives, including Mrs Thatcher herself, were the products of grammar schools. Though they preferred private education for their own children, when they turned their reforming zeal to the state educational system it was to the golden age of the grammar school that they looked for models of excellence. This caught the public mood. As Mary Evans argues, in the twenty years since their demise grammar schools have come to be seen as microcosms of a vanished, more stable and happier Britain; as places where bright and well-behaved children prepared to lead useful bourgeois lives. Evans wrote her book as a corrective to this rosy picture, but hers remains a minority view among middle-class people of her generation.

Conservatives traded on the grammar/grammar school connection and the nostalgia grammar schools evoked. They warned that the same pernicious egalitarianism that had tragically destroyed selective education was now resisting grammar in a similar spirit of 'levelling down'. This functioned symbolically as a kind of 'golden age' rhetoric, in which the myth of the late lamented grammar school was contrasted with a less pleasant contemporary image of noisy and disorderly classrooms where rude, illiterate children spoke in rude, barbaric accents.

This classroom dystopia was itself a symbol for the larger unit of the nation. And in time, conservatives began to make that more explicit, shifting the ground of debate to the nation's 'cultural heritage'. It was a theme that had been present throughout the debate, but at the beginning of the 1990s it took on a more apocalyptic tone.

CONSERVATIVES VERSUS PLURALISTS: THE NATIONAL CULTURE

In 1990, Prince Charles made a well-publicized speech ranging over questions of language, literature and cultural heritage. Its most heavily quoted passage sought to exemplify the supposed decline of the English language by using the device George Orwell used with Ecclesiastes: 'if Shakespeare were writing today . . . '. Afflicted by the linguistic malaise of the late twentieth century, the prince suggested, the Bard's immortal soliloquy from *Hamlet* might go as follows:

> Well frankly, the problem as I see it
> At this moment in time is whether I
> Should just lie down under all this hassle
> And let them walk all over me.
> Or, whether I should just say: 'OK,
> I get the message', and do myself in.
> (Quoted in *Manchester Guardian Weekly*, 7 January 1990)

Although this has nothing to do with grammar (like Orwell's own criticism, it is more concerned with jargon and cliché), it gave voice to a feeling that was more and more in the air: a feeling that the very survival of English might be threatened. That feeling was even stronger by 1991, when in her maiden speech to the House of Lords, the newly ennobled detective writer P.D. James chose to appeal for schools to preserve 'the Queen's English'. If they abandoned it, she warned, the nation would 'no longer have a language or a literature worth preserving'.

What lay behind such extreme and melodramatic pronouncements was a more general anxiety about the state of British (or more exactly, English) culture. As Tony Crowley (1989) has noted, the English language has tended to become an issue at times of cultural crisis, when domestic dissent or external threat has undermined the nation's confidence in its identity. The Thatcher era was in some ways a period of unbounded confidence ('Making Britain Great Again', as the post-Falklands war Tory election slogan had it), but it was also a time of considerable anxiety about what it meant to be British. There was polarization of rich and poor, north and south, white and black;

there was the prospect of European integration which many found alarming.

In the midst of these developments, the government threw down a gauntlet by proposing to introduce a National Curriculum for schools in England and Wales. This by definition was an attempt to produce greater cultural homogeneity. To construct a National Curriculum is in essence to identify a common core of things that will be known, experienced and valued by everyone who passes through the system. The proposal was bound to cause confrontation between supporters of a unified cultural tradition and advocates of a broader, more pluralist definition of culture.

The struggle was fought over an extended period, and almost every subject prescribed for the National Curriculum offered suitable terrain. Thus conservatives did not only want grammar: they wanted history to be British and have dates, religious studies to mean Christianity, the arts – literature, music, painting – to be exclusively western European, and so on. Liberals wanted a more multicultural approach in all these areas, and the working parties which made final recommendations were usually somewhere in between.

English, on the face of things, was less contentious than many other areas of the curriculum. No one disputed that English language and literature should have 'core' status. But the fundamental conflict between cultural unity and cultural pluralism was also played out in the debate on English.

At one point, for instance, there was a flurry of concern about whether children of all classes and ethnicities were reading enough Shakespeare. If the nation could rally around no other flag it could apparently be united by respect for our national poet. The question of English language teaching was caught up in a similar sort of anxiety about unifying the nation around a particular view of what matters, and nipping pluralism – which is, for conservatives, a symptom of fragmentation – decisively in the bud.

One form of pluralism against which the English language needed to be protected was multilingualism, and especially the teaching of community languages to minority pupils. This particular threat was addressed in policy documents by a resounding silence: both Kingman and Cox were given terms of reference that necessarily excluded languages other than English from consideration, except in so far as they presented an obstacle to some pupils' acquisition of English; attempts to address bilingualism in the revision of 1994 were deleted by ministers, to the dismay of the advisory panel.[13]

At the level of tabloid commentary, racism was more overt. Around the time that the Kingman Report was published, the press reported a court case in which a Panjabi-speaking man accused of social security fraud outraged the judge by requesting an interpreter, even though he had been in Britain for twenty-three years. The judge made taking English lessons part of his sentence. The *Star* newspaper (6 May 1988) quoted, with incredulity, the reaction of a community worker, who asked: 'where does it say that somebody has to speak English to be a British citizen?' (The correct answer to this question is 'nowhere'.) Even in the case of bilingual British-born children, any tendency for schools to value community languages was presented as a threat to the 'national culture'. The idea of white children learning to count to five in Panjabi could be relied upon to produce outrage in the popular press.

Pluralism in the context of English also means dialect diversity. Here the official line, as represented in the reports of the Kingman and Cox committees, was more explicit: it was to promote standard English as a mark of cultural unity. In the words of the Kingman Report: 'Standard English is a great social bank, on which we all draw and to which we all contribute' (DES 1988a: 14). This much quoted image perpetrates a falsehood. Standard English is and always has been a class variety (its status as a *lingua franca* does not undermine but rather follows from this fact), and most English speakers have been made to 'draw on' it whether they wanted to or not (though the 'bank' metaphor cleverly makes this reading seem perverse: who would refuse a handout?). 'Unity' here thus means everyone subscribing to the values and standards of a particular class: it is they who are the norm for what is referred to as 'the nation'.

The kind of anxiety about linguistic 'deterioration' that we associate with the eighteenth century is alive and well among pro-grammar conservatives: if, as Dr Johnson said, languages are the pedigree of nations, English needs to be protected against mongrelizing tendencies. One of the functions that conservatives allot to grammar teaching specifically is the preservation of a 'pure' and unified standard English variety whose purity is continually threatened just because it is not native to most speakers of English, corrupted as they are by what the 1921 Newbolt report called 'evil habits of speech contracted in home and street'. In other words, many conservatives do not distinguish between teaching standard English in schools and teaching English grammar: they see the latter enterprise as a necessary component of the former.

In this context it becomes more understandable that Prince Charles, in yet another speech on this subject in 1991, should have praised his audience of English teachers in Czechoslovakia for teaching grammar, regretting that the practice had largely been abandoned in Britain. What seemed like mere ignorance, a failure to distinguish between the needs of native and non-native speakers, was actually something more: the Prince went on to warn that unless the flame of grammar were kept burning, English speakers across the globe would eventually be unable to communicate with one another. Local norms and variants would bastardize English and finally destroy it.

This speech recycled an idea that had been around for some time, a sort of 'Decline and Fall' thesis predicated on an analogy between English and Latin. Latin in its time was a 'world language', but as the Roman Empire broke up, its various local dialects diverged and became what are now known as the Romance languages. Eventually these vernaculars were standardized and replaced Latin even in prestige domains such as law, scholarship and religion. Some commentators raised the possibility that the same thing was happening to English, the world language of the late twentieth century. As local standards developed in various parts of the former British Empire there was a danger that the British standard (or perhaps any single standard – for arguably American English is already more important than British) would lose its pre-eminence and thus its lingua franca status.

Global sociolinguistic conditions having changed very markedly since Roman times, it is questionable whether this argument has any merit at all. In taking it up, however, Prince Charles expressed not only the typical verbal hygienist's concern about 'communication' but, more specifically, a British conservative anxiety about the loss of Britain's international status after the fading of imperial power.

If in the educational sphere conservatives looked to the golden age of grammar schools, in the wider cultural sphere they looked to the golden age of empire, when English was carried around the world as a lasting monument to a conquering people. Prince Charles's odd remarks in Czechoslovakia suggested that this monument was under threat, not only in Britain's former dominions but in the heart of England itself. Teachers, with their ideology of pluralism and multiculturalism, were hastening the breakdown of English into a chaos of competing and mutually unintelligible vernaculars. (In her description of her encounter with Tory activists, Marilyn Butler (1993: 11) reports that one questioner insisted that since the 'permissive' 1960s people in Yorkshire and Dorset – that is, the north-east and south-west of England – had become totally unable to understand one another: an absurd proposition from which she was quite unable to budge its supporters.) The dangers of fragmentation could however be averted by a backward-looking and strongly anglocentric curriculum in which the teaching of grammar (and thus standard English) would have a crucial role to play.

CONSERVATIVES VERSUS CONSERVATIVES?

The grammar controversy of the 1980s and early 1990s did not have a single cause; its political roots were deep and tangled. Grammar was made to symbolize various things for its conservative proponents: a commitment to traditional values as a basis for social order, to 'standards' and 'discipline' in the classroom, to moral certainties rather than moral relativism and to cultural homogeneity rather than pluralism. Grammar was able to signify all these things because of its strong metaphorical association with order, tradition, authority, hierarchy and rules.

But it still needs to be asked why the panic occurred at the particular moment it did. Why did this set of symbols – which are well-established in conservative discourse – need to be deployed during what was after all the Conservatives' own moment of political dominance, a period when they had won three consecutive elections (and were soon to win a fourth)? Why did anxieties about national identity, culture and values rise so strongly to the surface under these conditions?

Again there is probably no single answer, but several contributory factors may be suggested. It might be argued that in scapegoating a group of social scientists (linguists) and the so-called 'educational establishment', ideologues of the Right identified two of the few remaining strongholds in Britain for leftist or liberal ideology, and set out to discredit them. In that sense, the panic helped to neutralize a perceived external threat.

But then again, perhaps the threat that conservatives located outside was partly coming from within. Thatcherism was a contested phenomenon within the Conservative party itself, and the shift away from 'one nation' Tory values caused conflict and anxiety. Persistent fears of chaos and fragmentation cannot have been allayed by the social upheavals caused more or less directly by the actions of Conservative governments during the period. Some conservatives responded in ambivalent ways to the very obvious changes in British society – their support for the radical Right was not unmixed with anxiety and nostalgia.

Such feelings demand outlets. But in the new Britain, opportunities to express doubt and criticism were limited. One might argue, then, that anxieties about all kinds of radical change were most conveniently displaced on to symbolic issues to do with language and culture, a relatively peripheral area where old-style Tories and free marketeers could for once unite. Perhaps panics about falling standards and grandiose calls for cultural unity were affordable luxuries of the Thatcher years.

Ironically, though, the force of the argument was often nullified precisely by the imperatives of Conservative economic policy: tub-thumping speeches about 'improving standards' or 'preserving our national heritage' did not move the Treasury. For example, at the same time that Tories up and down the land were raging about the alleged neglect of Shakespeare in schools, the Royal Shakespeare Company was obliged to let its London theatre go dark because of insufficient public subsidy. 'Standards' were insisted on only to the extent that they did not require extra resources: schools plagued by book shortages and water running down classroom walls were told there was no point throwing money at the problem, and urged to throw grammar and spelling at it instead.

It has also been suggested that in the period following Margaret Thatcher's resignation, education became a pawn in what party leaders considered a much more important political game, with European union as the stake. Writing just after the announcement in September 1992 that English teaching was to be reviewed again, Brian Cox propounded what amounts to a conspiracy theory:

> Since the general election [of 1992] a persistent rumour has been going round . . . that the prime minister has agreed to a deal with right wing conservatives. They will go quiet in their opposition to Maastricht [the treaty on European Union] if he will allow them to take control of education. What truth there is in this I do not know, but it certainly fits the situation which has emerged in the last few months.
>
> (*Guardian*, 15 September 1992)

THE MORAL OF THE STORY . . .

To offer this account of the grammar crusade as the outcome of various impulses, some of them ideologically driven, some politically opportunist and others merely muddled does not alter the assessment that right-wing tactics were effective. This requires some comment, if only because there were instances during the same period when comparable attempts at whipping up anxiety met with a much more lukewarm or even hostile public reception. An attempt to scapegoat single mothers for rising crime rates as part of an ill-starred 'back to basics' campaign in 1993–4 was not a great success, for example.[14] But the 'back-to-basics' rhetoric of grammar and standard English undoubtedly commanded popular support. How do we explain the broad appeal of the pro-grammar conservative case?

It is important to recognize that the conservative argument played on widespread fears and desires. Just about every parent wants a better life for their children, and a campaign to persuade parents that trendy left-wing teachers were denying children opportunity by fostering illiteracy and indiscipline had more rather than less resonance in the chilly economic climate most school leavers were facing by the late 1980s.

It could also be argued that the campaign played on that streak of puritan moral authoritarianism that has often been mentioned as a source of Thatcherism's popular appeal. Along with the sugar of promised prosperity, it is said that the English like the pill of reactionary social policies. This rather dubious generalization gained a certain amount of credibility as commentators from the Prince of Wales to the person in the street repeatedly praised the character-building virtues of grammatical drills and spelling tests; and it seemed to be vindicated once again when, in his 1994 New Year message to the nation, John Major explicitly yoked together the fight against crime and the crusade to reinstate proper English in the classroom.

It is interesting, however, that Mr Major's advocacy of 'proper English' got a more enthusiastic reception than the public gave his 'back to basics' agenda overall. This might alert us to the possibility that linguistic authoritarianism has some special appeal of its own; it is more than just the linguistic version of some national tendency to moral authoritarianism. If so, I think there is a reason for this, and it is one that particularly interests me. It serves to illustrate a claim I made in Chapter 1, that in the 'double discourse' of verbal hygiene, linguistic and moral or social considerations are equally important and mutually reinforcing.

The pro-grammar conservative argument about grammar succeeded in appealing to a broad constituency, not only because it symbolically expressed powerful fears and desires to do with moral and social order, but also and importantly because it resonated with common-sense assumptions about *language*. It spoke to the belief almost everyone has that language-using is a normative practice, properly subject to judgements of correctness and value; that in the words of *Today* newspaper, 'some kinds of English really are more worthwhile than others'. People engage in all kinds of everyday practices that confirm this belief: they look up words in dictionaries, they correct others' usage and are corrected themselves, they laugh at the solecisms and mispronunciations that are staples of humour. And this is an important reason why conservatives can so easily manipulate grammar as a political symbol: if the only way of talking about value in language is the one elaborated by right-wing authoritarians, then their prescriptive metalanguage and their moral terms are almost bound to dominate people's thinking on the subject.

Verbal hygiene and social or moral hygiene are interconnected; to argue about language is indirectly to argue about extra-linguistic values. The links which pro-grammar conservatives made between language and moral values were doubtless irrational and mystificatory. But it is just as mystificatory to suppose that issues of language can be stripped of any evaluative dimension. Where linguistic science insists on trying to do this, it diverges from the concerns of most language-users. To be sure, in many areas of linguistic scholarship this will be a matter of indifference: that the ordinary speaker has no interest in complex phonological processes should not preclude scholarly investigation of them, for example. But in socially oriented linguistics – and in the making of public policy about language – it cannot be a matter of indifference.

One of the most depressing features of the grammar debate was that the arguments between linguists and pro-grammar conservatives were aired quite comprehensively, and though the linguists scored the occasional victory in the committee room, in the court of public opinion they were tried and found wanting. It is true their opinions were presented to the public less often, and much less sympathetically, than their opponents'. Nevertheless, the degree to which their arguments utterly failed to register should give us pause. What are we to conclude from it?

My own conclusion is this. The way to intervene in public debates like the one about English grammar is not to deny the importance of standards and values but to focus critically on the particular standards and values being invoked and to propose alternatives – just as the way to change unjust laws is not to abolish all laws but to make more enlightened ones. There is nothing wrong in wanting to set standards of excellence in the use of language. Rather what is wrong is the narrow definition of excellence as mere superficial 'correctness'.

Considered in even the most starkly utilitarian terms, this narrow definition is sadly impoverished. (When employers complain, as they do incessantly, that school leavers and even graduates cannot write well enough, is it really only spelling mistakes and subject-verb agreement they are talking about? In the scale of what can be wrong with a piece of English prose, how much does a misplaced apostrophe weigh?) But the narrowness and triviality of prevailing standards for language use are inescapable consequences of treating (and teaching) grammar as if it were the instrument not of language, but of 'discipline'.

Though it is beyond the scope of this chapter to advance detailed arguments about what alternative standards we might adopt, what I want to emphasize is that the discourse of 'standards' is not only *available* to those who dissent from conservative views about language, it is probably the only discourse in which dissent can gain a hearing. Those who want to question prevailing standards must present their arguments with due consideration for the common-sense perception of language-using as a normative practice – for on this point, common sense has much to recommend it. We may be justifiably critical of certain value judgements, but we must avoid giving the impression that there is no legitimate basis for making judgements on the skill with which language is used.

The idea that there are norms in language need not be a monopoly of political reactionaries. 'Standards' need not always be so narrowly defined, and moral panic might give way to more judicious kinds of concern. Although the attraction between them is magnetic and longstanding, Dr Syntax and Mrs Grundy could still get a divorce.

4 Civility and its discontents
Language and 'political correctness'

THE SPIRIT OF THE AGE

In the early 1990s, a humorous item in the British *Guardian* newspaper reported that the *Fresno Bee*, a Californian newspaper, had been forced to run a curious correction. Inadvertently, the *Bee* had referred to 'a plan for putting Massachusetts back in the African-American'. This, readers were informed, should actually have read 'back in the black'.

The *Guardian* ran this item in a regular weekend column called 'Zeitgeist', meaning 'spirit of the age'. The *Bee's* original blunder and subsequent risible correction had their source in something that has struck innumerable commentators as a worrying manifestation of the 1990s *zeitgeist*, the phenomenon of so-called 'political correctness'. One of the most salient markers of this phenomenon has to do with language use. The so-called 'politically correct' are known for their insistence on replacing usages which they deem insulting and objectionable to various 'minorities'. Thus high school girls become 'women', mankind becomes 'humanity', disabled people become 'physically challenged' and black people in the US become 'African-Americans'.

Before we turn to the details of this particular verbal hygiene practice, we should note that the 'back in the African-American' story manifests the spirit of the age in other ways too. For one thing, it is a story illustrating the modern cliché that 'to err is human; to *really* screw things up takes a computer'. Newspapers which have adopted the preference for *African-American* over *black* as part of their house style can use computerized copy-editing methods to ensure there are no lapses: a stylecheck program or 'search and replace' function can be set up to pick out each instance of *black* in the text of any article and replace it automatically with *African-American*. This, one assumes, is how the *Bee* made its error; it failed to distinguish between uses of *black* to designate a group of people, and other uses of the same word, which do not require replacing. There is a special irony in the paper's having hit on about the only instance in English where *black* is the positive term in a colour metaphor.

Another highly contemporary thing about the 'back in the African-

American' story is its location in the domain of mass media. The story is about the mass media, and it comes to the world's attention through the mass media. As time goes on, moreover, the narrative grows more and more media-bound and self-referential. By the time it moves across the Atlantic to the pages of the *Guardian*, this is a story about a story about a story. The original story, the one in which the mistake occurs, is about something in the 'real world', the Governor of Massachusetts's economic plan. In the subsequent correction, the language of the *Bee*'s original story itself becomes the focus. In the British item, the correction is the main story. (In this analysis, of course, I am taking the whole thing a stage further, by focusing on the *Guardian*'s story about the *Bee*'s correction of the story about the economic plan; and in this parenthesis. . . .)

As we become further and further removed from the first link in the discursive chain, the point where discourse is anchored to anything outside itself, it becomes more and more difficult to know – or for that matter, to care – whether the main 'fact' at issue in the discourse is a fact at all: in other words, whether the *Fresno Bee* ever really did refer to 'a plan for putting Massachusetts back in the African-American'. Even if the *Bee* were to issue a statement saying the story was a fabrication, it would make almost no difference to its accumulated power. By virtue of being repeated many times across a diffuse global communications network, the 'back in the African-American' story has become a kind of urban myth.

One could point to similar examples from other places and other times. In London during the 1980s, socialist local councils were continually accused in the right-wing press of practising ludicrous forms of verbal hygiene. Hackney Council, we were told, had abolished the term *manhole* by order of its Women's Committee; 'Red' Ken Livingstone, the leader of the Greater London Council, had banned references to 'black coffee' in the County Hall cafeteria as racist (his preferred term, allegedly, was 'coffee without milk'); the nursery rhyme 'Baa Baa Black Sheep' had supposedly been forbidden in inner city schools. In these cases, which predated the current furore about 'political correctness', some reporters did try to verify allegations and discovered they were unfounded. Publicizing that fact, however, did not diminish the power of stories like the one about 'black coffee' as symbols of what was wrong with the so-called 'loony Left'. On the contrary, such fabrications have remained in people's consciousness, long after the demise of the radical councils themselves.

The point of mentioning these stories is not simply to accuse conservatives and the gutter press of using smear tactics against socialists, feminists and ethnic radicals. In some cases – the 'black coffee' story is one – that accusation would be warranted; in others, people who repeated a story may sincerely have believed they were reporting something that actually happened;[1] and there are cases where what was reported really did happen. But the question of whether a specific story is true, exaggerated, an honest mistake or a deliberate smear is by no means the central focus of interest here. The interesting question, rather, is why this particular tactic should be effective: why the illiberalism, extremism and general absurdity of radical projects should so frequently be evoked through stories about their verbal hygiene practices.

More generally, how is it that so much passionate political argument has come to be conducted, on all sides, by way of disputes about the proper use of words? When we are surrounded with material problems like war, famine, disease, crime, poverty and violence, why should it be a matter of controversy what expressions we use to describe a beverage or a hole in the road? What conflicting views about language – how it works and how it ought to work – lie behind these wars of words?

There is undoubtedly more at stake in the 'political correctness' debate than words. I do not wish to suggest that this debate is *only* linguistic (verbal hygiene debates are never only about language in any case). In this chapter, though, I intend to focus on the linguistic component in the debate: on 'political correctness', and the resistance it has engendered, as forms of verbal hygiene.

WARS OF WORDS: WHO'S TO BE MASTER?

For some twenty years, speakers of English have been in a position to observe a linguistic guerilla war raging all around them. This war, which most of us have at some time been dragged into, has been fought with cunning and with passion on both sides. Its progressive vanguard was made up of feminists, who captured the high ground in the 1970s with various skirmishes over pronouns and titles. Such figures as 'Ms A., chairperson of B' made their appearance on the public scene. Other embattled groups – ethnic and sexual minorities, older people, people with disabilities – soon opened, or re-opened, similar fronts. Although resistance was stubborn, progress was discernable. Witness 'back in the African-American'.

Few linguists felt called upon to comment on this unfolding drama, and those who did made contradictory and simplistic statements. David Crystal (1984) noted that the feminist campaign against sexist language was among the most successful instances of prescriptivism in living memory; Jenny Cheshire (1984) put the success of non-sexist language down, conversely, to natural linguistic evolution in the face of social change. These extremes – prescriptive conspiracy or quasi-organic evolution effected by the agency of no one at all – are all we have been given by way of explanation on this subject. I believe they gloss over most of what is interesting about it, and certainly much that is of interest to linguists. For while at one level anti-sexist and anti-racist verbal hygiene practices are obviously about non-linguistic matters of political belief or allegiance, they are also about the nature of language itself and about people's conceptualizations of language. This tends to go undiscussed because of the over-simple assumption (discussed in Chapter 1, and see also Cameron 1990) that 'language reflects society'. Thus movements for linguistic change are common-sensically represented as merely parasitic on movements for social change; at the same time they are felt to be a superfluous embarrassment to those movements, since any social change will 'naturally' produce linguistic change.

Common sense on this point is not wholly misguided, in so far as verbal hygiene does not occur in a sociopolitical vacuum; we can also concede that there is such a thing as *unplanned* linguistic change (though it cannot be said too often that language is a form of social practice, and *all* changes in social practice must have agents). We can see, however, that the common-sense account is over-simplified if we pose the question: *why* do so many people so deeply resent campaigns against sexist, racist, ageist and ableist language? Is it because they are dyed-in-the-wool bigots who want language to 'reflect society' by faithfully expressing widespread social prejudices? I think the evidence points in a different direction. As we will see, objections to linguistic reform tend to focus much more on *language* than on the social questions at issue, such as whether women are men's equals. It is 'perverting language' and 'reading things into words' which attract opposition, and which are parodied in such fabrications as the 'black coffee' story.

What many people dislike, specifically, is the politicizing of their words against their will. By calling traditional usage into question, reformers have in effect forced everyone who uses English to declare a position in respect of gender, race or whatever. There is a choice of possible positions: you can say 'Ms A. is the chair(person)' and convey approval of feminism, or you can say 'Miss A. is the chairman' and convey a more conservative attitude. What you cannot do any more is to select either alternative and convey by it nothing more than 'a certain woman holds a particular office'. Choice has altered the value of the terms and removed the option of political neutrality.

It might with justice be objected that the 'neutrality' of terms like *chairman* was always an illusion. But it was not always apprehended as illusory; and it had a number of important functions. It helped, for example, to sustain the even more fundamental illusion that speakers have total control over the meaning of their own discourse – that when we speak, we engage in individual acts of will whose outcome, ideally, is to communicate our own unique intentions (thus if I don't intend to convey a political attitude by my choice of words, anyone who discerns one is making an illegitimate inference). Reformers have called into question this imaginary omnipotence. At the same time they have questioned another cherished illusion: that although my utterances express my own unique intentions, the linguistic code through which those intentions were 'put into words' is unproblematically shared by other speakers of my language. Once again, this implies that someone who fails to recognize what I 'really mean', or who imputes to me intentions I do not in fact have, is not only in error but in breach of universally accepted rules.

One commentator on language who does appear to perceive at least something of what is at stake in current arguments is Geoffrey Nunberg, whose observations in an article titled 'What the usage panel thinks' (Nunberg 1990) I quoted in Chapter 1 (pp. 25–6). It is worth quoting the relevant passage again. Reflecting on how attitudes to English usage have changed over time, Nunberg comments:

> The line of language criticism that stretches from Addison to Fowler was part of the larger critical enterprise of articulating a body of cultural values within a relatively homogeneous public sphere. . . . But the modern view of the importance of language owes more to writers like Orwell, whose language criticism was concerned with maintaining a coherent political discourse in a culturally and ideologically fragmented community.
>
> (Nunberg 1990: 475–6)

Despite the change Nunberg identifies here, his own formulation suggests there is a unifying thread running from Addison to Orwell and beyond: the search for some common language with which a society can conduct its public affairs. The members of a society do not necessarily espouse the same cultural values – this was true even in Addison's time and is more obvious still in contemporary democracies – but for civil exchange to go on, they must agree on terms for the expression of differing views. That is why Orwell, for instance, championed a particular kind of language: plain enough to be intelligible to all, concrete enough not to conceal the reality behind the words, sufficiently free of irrationality, loading or bias to permit propositions couched in it to be challenged and opinions conveyed by means of it to be dissented from. The common language needed for public purposes is portrayed above all as a *neutral* and *universal* language, one that is available to all parties equally and does not predetermine the outcome of their discussions.

One way to read the emergence of so-called 'politically correct' language is as a challenge to the whole idea of a universal and neutral language. It pushes to the limit established beliefs about what a language is, or ideally should be, and therefore it causes considerable anxiety.

What do radical verbal hygienists propose to put in place of commonsense beliefs? This is a complicated matter, because even the practitioners of verbal hygiene do not always take up a unified and coherent theoretical position. Readers of the debate on 'political correctness' will often find themselves in the position of the bewildered Alice trying to pin down Humpty Dumpty's philosophy of language in *Through the Looking Glass*.

Humpty Dumpty first tells Alice that when he uses a word, it means whatever he chooses it to mean. This, as I have noted, reflects a common-sense assumption about the primacy of speaker intentions, but Humpty Dumpty's illustration of it (an absurd claim that *glory* means 'a nice knock-down argument') draws attention to the inherent problem. Accordingly, Alice questions whether meaning can be determined by individual volition; how would we communicate if everyone acted like Humpty Dumpty? There surely must be limits on what words can be made to mean. Humpty Dumpty moves in for the kill. The crucial question, he says, is one of power: 'Who's to be master?'. This remark is usually read as meaning or implying 'Who's to be master, the people or the words? Do we control language or does it control us?' But Alice might also read Humpty Dumpty's words to mean, 'Who's to be master, me or you?'.

Both these versions of the question – and a certain real or strategic confusion between them – recur in discussions of 'politically correct' language. Sometimes the contestants behave like Humpty Dumpty at the start of his exchange with Alice: radicals charge that a certain word is, say, 'racist'; their critics indignantly deny this on the grounds that when they use the word they do not intend to be racist, and accuse the radicals of 'reading things in'. At other times, the critics stress that words *do* have meanings independent of speakers' intentions in using them, and that 'political correctness' precisely perverts those time-honoured meanings. It is therefore an attack on the language, and on the possibility of communication. The radicals respond like Humpty Dumpty at the end of the exchange, by posing the question of power: 'And who has traditionally "owned" this precious language? In whose image have its meanings been made?'

The struggle over 'politically correct' language can certainly be apprehended partly as a straightforward contest about 'who's to be master' in the second, 'you or me?' sense: the issue is to decide which set of values will be affirmed symbolically in the language of public discourse. The proponents of non-sexist and non-racist language are insisting that certain values (feminist and multiculturalist) should prevail; their opponents represent this as an attack on freedom of expression (and sometimes even freedom of thought). Such resistance is in part a sign of adherence to a different set of values, but as I have already suggested, this is not the whole story. Opposition to politically motivated language change is not fuelled only by hostility to feminism or multiculturalism or whatever, but in many cases reflects a second and deeper level of disturbance to people's common-sense notions of language.

The new politically motivated verbal hygiene practices assume that language is not just a medium for ideas but a shaper of ideas; that it is always and inevitably political; and that the 'truth' someone speaks may be relative to the power they hold. This set of assumptions, rather than the mere intention to substitute one set of terms for another, is what makes the question of 'politically correct' language so explosive. In this chapter I propose to argue that the crisis precipitated by recent verbal hygiene developments is not only what it might appear to be, or what it is usually represented as: a crisis of cultural values; it is also a crisis for the common-sense theories of meaning to which most language-users (including some of the reformers) subscribe.

'POLITICAL CORRECTNESS' AND THE POWER OF DEFINITION

One peculiarity of the verbal hygiene debate on 'political correctness' is that the parties to it do not even agree that what they are arguing about is properly labelled 'political correctness'. The contestation of meaning which is the central issue in the debate begins right at the beginning with a contest about the meaning of 'political correctness' itself. Deployment or non-deployment of that term to describe particular verbal hygiene proposals has been an important rhetorical strategy, and the term has thus acquired a rather complicated, not to say controversial, usage-history. That history deserves attention, not only because it helps to explain the intricacies of the 'political correctness' debate but more generally because it provides an excellent example of linguistic politics in action. If anything makes the case that words are powerful and definitions are political – exactly as the so-called 'politically correct' have claimed, and as their critics have ridiculed them for claiming – it is the history of the term 'political correctness' itself.

In the 1980s, a New York feminist friend of mine owned a T-shirt bearing the slogan 'Politically Incorrect'. Recently she threw it out: there was, she explained, only a brief cultural moment when its intended message – something like 'I am committed to leftist/feminist causes, but not humourless or doctrinaire about it' – was likely to be understood. That moment had already passed when in 1991 a now-celebrated article in *New York Magazine* enquired: 'Are You Politically Correct?' (Taylor 1991). The seemingly straightforward yes/no question put people like my friend with the T-shirt in a double-bind. By 1991, to say yes was to claim for yourself a definition constructed by critics for the express purpose of discrediting you; to say no was to place yourself among those critics. Like the example sentence illustrating presupposition in the semantics textbook, 'The King of France is bald', the question 'are you politically correct?' depends on a false or contested proposition (that there is a King of France, or that 'political correctness' refers to a real entity with such-and-such characteristics). To answer it at all is to collude in reinforcing the questioner's presupposition, whether you accept it or not.

The way right-wing commentators have established certain presuppositions about 'political correctness' over the past few years is a triumph – as a sociolinguist I cannot help admiring it – of the politics of definition, of linguistic intervention. 'PC' now has such negative connotations for so many people that the mere invocation of the phrase can move those so labelled to elaborate disclaimers, or reduce them to silence (as another American friend drily observed, nowadays it's a case of 'you say PC when you used to say CP'[2]). There is a certain irony in this, given that among the main charges against the so-called 'politically correct' are on one hand the charge that they abuse language for their own ends, and on the other, the charge that by privileging 'trivial' questions of language they are moving away from real politics into a world where it seems to matter more what you call things than whether you can do anything about them.

The same charges could in fact be levelled against the opposing camp; conservatives have set out to make 'political correctness' a 'snarl term' for their own ends, and they have also put considerable effort into disseminating some of their own nomenclatural variants (including for instance the charming coinage 'feminazi'). But to talk about 'charges', as if attempts to intervene in language were somehow illegitimate, is really to miss the point.

As I hope preceding chapters will have made clear, politically motivated verbal hygiene is not a new phenomenon (it is a particularly irritating feature of the present 'PC' debate that so many people go on as if arguments about nomenclature were a bizarre invention of the last decade). In an era of mass communications, however, of T-shirt slogans and soundbites, the politics of language (more generally, of definition and representation) move from margin to centre. This development seems to baffle practitioners of more traditional politics, both conservative and liberal;[3] but it needs to be borne in mind as we approach the fundamental question: what *is* meant by the term 'political correctness?'

Defining our terms: A brief history of 'political correctness'

If the proverbial Martian anthropologists came down to earth to investigate the phenomenon of 'political correctness' in English-speaking western democracies and began their quest by reading discourse currently in circulation about that phenomenon, they would form the impression that the term 'political correctness' refers to a powerful political movement located on university campuses and in 'alternative' political or cultural institutions – for example, leftist, feminist, anti-racist or green organizations, and public service professions whose ethos reflects these 'alternative' ideologies.

The most general aim of this 'political correctness' movement, the Martians would gather, is to enforce a set of orthodox ('politically correct') views on class, race, gender and other forms of sociocultural diversity. The movement's specific objectives include giving preferential treatment to members of certain social groups (e.g. women, ethnic minorities) in schools and universities; constructing educational curricula in which the traditional ideas of cultural heritage and artistic excellence are replaced with an emphasis on non-western, non-white and female cultural contributions; and prescribing the kind of language that may or may not be used to talk about the differences between humans, especially gender and racial/ethnic differences.

Assuming our Martians exercised proper scholarly caution, however, they would soon notice a rather puzzling anomaly. All this discourse on what 'political correctness' means emanates from sources explicitly opposed to it. The people who are characterized as adherents of the 'political correctness movement' strenuously deny that any such movement exists; they may even deny that the term 'political correctness', as used by their opponents, actually names or refers to any real entity at all. They will grant that certain things do exist: for example, there are affirmative action hiring policies in (some) American universities; there are guidelines for the use of non-sexist and non-racist language in institutional documents in existence on both sides of the Atlantic; there are (and always have been) arguments over what books should be taught in college courses. But those who make no secret of their support for affirmative action, non-discriminatory language and multi-cultural curricula do not refer to these positions collectively as 'political correctness': it is only their opponents who use this expression in that way.

Abraham H. Miller (1993), in an article on 'Political correctness and American higher education' published in a scholarly political science journal, draws attention to one immediate consequence of this dispute as to whether there is a referent for the noun phrase *political correctness*:

> Since denial is frequently the response of those whose philosophy has prominently come to represent what political correctness means, the portrayal and definition of political correctness has been disproportionately yielded to its critics.
>
> (Miller 1993: 22)

Miller goes on to cite several of the definitions offered by 'critics': the implication is that he is justified in uncritically repeating their views because representatives of the 'other side' have declined to give defini-tions of their own. By following their strategy of 'denial' they have 'yielded' the terrain to their opponents, whose definition is therefore the only one a scholar can possibly cite. But in this case, definition is reification – it gives 'political correctness' a fixed and solid existence as the name for a real-world entity, when actually the very point at issue is whether there really is any *thing* that corresponds to the name.

Miller's strategy implicitly requires the people he is talking about to 'yield' to their critics either way; apart from silence (which enables the critics to define 'political correctness' as they please), the only alternative offered to the 'other side' is to accept the critics' characterization of them as representatives of 'political correctness' and then explain what *they* mean by that. Yet it is precisely the idea that what they represent can legitimately be called 'political correctness' that the people in question are trying to contest. It is as though Miller were to say to a group of people, 'We know you are anarchists/terrorists/communists/Nazis, but in the interests of balance, by all means tell us how you define the objectives of anarchism/terrorism/communism/Nazism'. The people so addressed cannot accept his liberal invitation without conceding that the chosen label does apply to them; and they cannot decline it without yielding to others the right not only to label them but to define what the label means.

A variation on the same strategy is observable in the way 'politically correct' terminology is described and defined in newspaper reports, and even in books with scholarly pretensions. Because such quasi-lexicographical efforts depend, like Miller's efforts to define 'political correctness', on sources *opposed* to the alleged 'political correctness move-ment', they have a bizarre tendency to cite not only terms that are or have been in use among gender and race-radicals (such as, say, *woman of color*), but also terms that have been invented as jokes or satires on 'PC' verbal hygiene, such as *vertically challenged*, meaning 'short' (Tisdall 1993 provides one of numerous examples of this confusion being repeated in supposedly 'serious' journalism). The coining of various compounds using *challenged* (*cranially challenged* for 'bald', *sartorially challenged* for 'dressed in bad taste', etc.), is arguably one of the happier results of the controversy, and by now such jokes are as likely to emanate from the Left as from the Right. But for commentators to attribute *vertically challenged* to the 'political correctness movement', and to solemnly explain it as a serious protest against 'heightism' is either incompetence or a smear on a par with the 'black coffee' story.

Thoroughly baffled by now, our hypothetical Martians might attempt to trace the historical origins of the term *political correctness*. Surely its opponents did not simply invent it to give themselves an easy target? They would discover that *politically correct* did, indeed, emerge from the counter-cultural movements of the Left. What it meant and how it was typically used are more difficult questions, however.

Even the most conscientious lexicography never gives more than a partial indication of the range of use of words at any given time because of the inevitable limitations of its source material. Until very recently, the small number of sources sampled for dictionaries was a serious problem:

new technology enables more texts to be sampled overall but there is still a bias to 'mainstream' sources (that is, official and commercially published documents which, as I pointed out in Chapter 2, have been edited in accordance with mainstream linguistic norms), and there is still a bias towards the written language (in the past this bias was absolute). Both these limitations are obviously relevant to the question of determining historical usage among members of counter-cultural movements. All their speech and most of their writing is non-mainstream and to that extent ephemeral; and in addition, the habits of language use that characterized alternative movements were, precisely, 'in-group': there were reasons *not* to expose them to a wider constituency. Terms such as 'politically correct' thus have a hidden history, uncovering which is dependent both on the co-operation and the accurate recollection of those who were there.

Although their accounts must be read with these caveats in mind, some writers have made attempts to pin down the origins and early uses of the terms 'politically correct' and 'politically incorrect' among American New Left activists in the 1960s and 1970s. According to Ruth Perry in a 1992 article entitled 'A short history of the term *politically correct*', the source from which these groups adopted the phrase was probably the English translation of Mao's *Little Red Book*. Alternatively, Barbara Epstein (1992) has suggested a connection with 'correct lineism', a term used in the Communist Party.

The earliest print citation Perry reports for 'politically correct' occurs in a 1970 article by the African-American feminist Toni Cade (later Toni Cade Bambara), which included the statement 'a man cannot be politically correct and a chauvinist too'. Although here the term is used straightforwardly to argue that sexism has no place in radical black politics, Perry points out that this was not the only way it was used, and as time went on it became less and less the dominant way of using it. The most common use of 'politically correct' was *ironic* – to quote Maurice Isserman (1991: 82), 'it was always used in a tone mocking the pieties of our own insular political counterculture, as in "we could stop at McDonald's down the road if you're hungry . . . but it wouldn't be *politically correct*"'. This was also the meaning of the Communist Party's 'correct lineism': a 'correct lineist' was a comrade whose holier-than-thou espousal of party dogma made other comrades want to spit.

Although the exact, pre-New Left origins of the terms 'politically correct' and 'politically incorrect' remain unclear, what does seem clear from various accounts is that once the counter-culture had adopted them, they were used as in-group markers and understood by insiders as a joke at their own expense. They functioned on one hand to differentiate the New Left from the orthodox Marxism it had rejected, and on the other to satirize the group's own tendency towards humourlessness, self-righteousness and rigidly orthodox 'party lines', poking fun at the notion that anyone could be (or would want to be) wholly 'correct'. Thus if someone confessed to, say, finding an epic film about exploited workers in the Kentucky coalfields tedious, or flirting with someone at a party, or reading a trashy romance, the parenthetical evaluation of this behaviour as 'politically incorrect' – either by the person doing the confessing or by someone else – served the purpose of affirming that although group members shared the same high ideals, they also shared the same vulgar weaknesses: 'nobody's perfect'. In other words, the commonest meaning of these terms on the Left was an ironic mirror-image of the one now attributed to them by the Right.

It is, however, that attributed meaning which is the starting point for the current debate on 'political correctness'. It is because of this that I have been alluding to 'so-called' political correctness and putting the term itself in scare-quotes: I mean these conventions to convey a recognition that the use of the term is disputed, and to remind readers that the solidity 'political correctness' has taken on in recent discourse is largely the achievement of its critics.

Discursive drift

Questions about the definition of 'political correctness' have been further complicated as the debate has been taken up in the mass media, and its keywords have undergone a process of 'discursive drift'. For most people who have not been involved in a radical political subculture on either the Left or the Right, 'political correctness' and related terms are neologisms whose meaning must be inferred from context. The media can spread such neologisms more widely and more quickly than either face-to-face communication or elite forms of writing, but the context they provide is insufficient to guarantee an exact transfer of meaning: they do not usually engage in the tedious definition of terms one finds in scholarly journals, and there is no opportunity for the addressee to request further clarification, as happens in face-to-face talk.

People may thus arrive at all kinds of inferences about the meaning of a new term they encounter in the media, and as they start to use it in other contexts themselves, it begins to drift away from its earlier (and usually narrower) sense. In the process, specialist terms can lose their precision, acquire connotations they did not have before, and start to overlap with other terms from which they were once distinguished.

Consider, for instance, the way many English-speakers now use *gender* as a polite synonym for *sex*: you hear people enquiring about the gender of animals, and recently I even heard a geneticist explain on a television programme that there was no reliable genetic test for establishing a person's gender, though it was clear in context he was not trying to make the point that you cannot read social identity from DNA; he was in fact making the more startling claim that you cannot even definitively establish biological maleness or femaleness from it. For the feminists who did most to put the word into circulation, *gender* was a technical term which took its meaning from a *contrast* with *sex*, and the intended contrast was between the biological and the social, not the more and the less polite. There is no point lamenting the inevitable process whereby 'spreading the word' through mass communications also means surrendering control over its fate, but students of language and culture can learn something by paying attention to the workings of this 'drift'.

At the beginning of the present debate on 'political correctness' in the US around 1987, the term was used in connection with a particular set of issues. These had to do with arcane matters of the university curriculum, regulations governing offensive speech on American campuses, and the practice of affirmative action to promote gender and racial equity in the hiring of university professors. The appearance of best-selling books on these issues, along with some newsworthy incidents on campuses, were widely reported on both sides of the Atlantic. This meant that many more people acquired familiarity with the term 'political correctness', but the inferences they made about it were informed not by direct engagement in the unfolding debate, but only by the less richly contextualized reporting of it in the media.

What happens in these circumstances is that meaning starts to drift towards a 'lowest common denominator', the most obvious and general sense it is reasonable for people to extract from a term in the contexts where they encounter it. To judge from current usages of 'political correctness', both in print and in private conversations, many people who encountered the term in media reporting drew the inference that it meant something like 'showing any kind of sympathetic concern about issues of gender or race'.[4]

The term began to emerge with this broad sense in contexts where its use would previously have seemed both odd and unnecessary. For example, the British Methodist Conference of 1992 narrowly defeated a proposal to make 'balanced-gender' liturgy mandatory after the Reverend Roger Ducker made a speech in which he said: 'I very much fear there is a sort of thought police imposing a political correctness' (*Guardian*, 30 June 1992). Arguments about non-sexist language in religious ritual are considerably older than the debate on 'political correctness'; it is only very recently that the term has been invoked by people denouncing feminist interference with language, although the denunciations have been going on for at least twenty years.

It could be asked – indeed, this is a version of a question central to the whole argument – whether talking about old issues such as sexist language in a new terminology of 'political correctness' makes any difference to the way those issues are perceived. I think the answer is 'yes, up to a point'. People like Reverend Ducker see an advantage in appropriating new vocabularies because discursive drift transfers not only the words but also the passions associated with a particular concern to other concerns. Thus anyone who has reservations about 'political correctness' generally must logically have the same reservations about the specific issue that is being defined as an instance of that phenomenon, rather than considering it on its merits (no matter that one might reasonably ask rather different questions about liturgy and the university curriculum, or about images of the deity and epithets used in 'hate-speech'). In addition, as the range of things we are invited to be concerned about grows, the passions themselves intensify. The result of putting more and more activities into the category of 'political correctness' is implicitly to present those activities as parts of a larger picture: things that on their own were once thought fairly innocuous are re-interpreted as signs of a previously unsuspected conspiracy involving an organized and sinister 'thought police'.

It is also possible Reverend Ducker was aware that using the term 'political correctness' to criticize his opponents' proposals would render the criticism instantly newsworthy. The entry of the term into main-stream public discourse has made certain issues topical again, where for years they had been old hat; but at the same time, the 'PC' angle seems to mask the fact that the issues in question are not new ones. In September 1992, for instance, a newspaper report on the annual con-ference of the Trades Unions Congress was headlined 'Suspect words sent to Coventry': the reporter Keith Harper noted that delegates had received a guide suggesting the avoidance of potentially offensive expres-sions such as *blacklist*, *manpower* and *deaf to arguments* (*Guardian*, 8 September 1992). No doubt this was considered worth reporting because it illustrated current concerns about 'political correctness'. What apparently was not worth reporting was the fact that such guide-lines on non-discriminatory language had been commonplace in trades union circles throughout the previous decade.

The issues of language now being debated under the 'PC' banner have all, without exception, been the subject of extended media comment at some time during the last twenty-five years. Does no one remember the row over the allegedly offensive OED definition of *Jew*, the replacement in official parlance of *handicapped* with *disabled* and *old age pensioner* with *senior citizen*, the outraged denunciations of *gay*? These issues attracted media attention well before 'political correctness' had a single newspaper cutting to its credit, and in most cases the proposed innovation is now quite unremarkable.

Current arguments have a particularly obvious precedent in the battles which raged from the mid-1970s onwards over feminist proposals to make English 'non-sexist'. It is worth revisiting the earlier controversy for two reasons. First, the earlier events provide a context for later developments, enabling us to assess how the ideas about language that inform debates of this kind have changed (or stayed the same) over time. Second, it provides a manageable case study with which to approach the question of how politically motivated linguistic reform is accomplished (or not accomplished) in practice.

This is an important question. As I pointed out in Chapter 1, and again at the beginning of this chapter, commentators have tended to attribute the success of feminist linguistic reforms either to the workings of an absolute, authoritarian 'prescriptivism' (a move that has been repeated in the case of 'political correctness'), or else to a mysterious, agentless process of 'natural' linguistic evolution. The truth, I will argue, is considerably messier than either of these alternatives; but it sheds considerably more light on what is really going on when people argue about words.

DÉJÀ VU ALL OVER AGAIN: NON-SEXIST LANGUAGE REVISITED

The controversy over sexism in language predates the 'PC' debate by some years, and it might well seem to those of us who remember the outrage provoked by early skirmishes – by the Sex Discrimination Act of 1975, say, which replaced 'dustmen' with 'refuse collectors', or by Dale Spender's uncompromising title *Man Made Language* in 1980 – that We Have Been Here Before. Faced with Reverend Ducker's description of feminist language reformers as a 'thought police imposing a political correctness', many of us must surely have reacted not with outrage but with a combination of mild surprise and ennui: 'can anyone still be arguing about *that*?'

No one who has been directly involved in a campaign for non-sexist language, or followed one closely, will be astonished to learn that this remains a contentious issue; but it is more surprising, and not a little depressing, to witness the same arguments being rehashed year in and year out as if no one had ever heard them before. I have a collection of newspaper articles about language that appeared during the early 1990s in connection with the 'political correctness' furore. What is striking about most of them, and especially those that deal with gender, is that they could as easily have been written in the early 1980s, or even the mid-1970s. At times I have suspected that some of them were.

Take, for example, an editorial headed 'The Waitron's Knife and Fork' that appeared in the *New York Times* on 28 July 1991, prompted by the appearance of a new *Webster's College Dictionary* containing a brief section on 'Avoiding sexist language'. One might have thought that by 1991 this event would be insufficiently remarkable to merit editorial comment in the *Times*; the earliest non-sexist language guidelines to be issued by a major publisher in the US appeared almost twenty years earlier, in 1973.

But as with the *Guardian* report on the TUC conference, 'political correctness' has made such guidelines newsworthy again, and the *Times* does not hesitate to rehearse the same arguments that greeted them when they were genuinely novel. Having briefly sketched the contents of the new section in the dictionary, it goes on to editorialize:

> Ardent feminists sometimes press verbal causes that risk mocking their own cause. Some of their proposed usages are internally illogical. Should *chairperson*, a corrective for *chairman*, now be re-revised to *chairperdaughter*? Other usages carry a heavy odor of contrivance . . . for instance . . . *waitron*, intended as a neutral alternative for waiter/waitress.
>
> Such jarring usages do not merely strain; they confuse symptom and cause. . . . Words will change, without strain or contrivance, when attitudes change, in the minds of waitrons and patrons alike.

Here we have a virtual anthology of two decades' clichés on this subject. The writer begins with the time-honoured 'I'm telling you this for your own good' strategy: feminists are informed that their concern with language is absurd, trivial and likely to bring their cause into disrepute. Then we have a hoary old joke, whose mechanism is deliberately to confuse gender-marked morphemes (units which are separable and meaningful) like the *-man* suffix of *chairman*, with syllables which are not separate morphemes (and therefore cannot carry gendered meanings), such as the *son* in *person*. Interestingly enough, *The Times* (of London) once published a letter from the Public Orator of Oxford University in which the same joke was stretched out to epic proportions, culminating in the suggestion that the Republic of Oman (whose name, to point out the obvious, is not even English, let alone a compound containing the morpheme *man*) might have to rename itself 'Operson'. This letter was published in April 1975.[5]

On the *Times* goes, objecting to feminist neologisms as 'contrived' (what new coinage is not, quite literally, 'contrived'?), and finishing on a high note with the proposition that, since language merely reflects prevailing attitudes, attempts to reform it confuse the symptom and the cause. As social conditions and attitudes change, words will change of their own accord. (One wonders, in that case, why we are still having exactly the same argument in 1991 as in 1973.)

All the *Times*'s charges have been made against feminists many times before, and all have been repeated in the argument against a more broadly conceived 'political correctness'. ('Back in the African-American' is, perhaps, the racial equivalent of jokes about 'chairperdaughters'.) In due course we must consider whether the more serious objections – that the politics of language are inherently trivial and that those who engage in verbal hygiene confuse symptoms and causes – have any merit. Meanwhile, though, it is worth looking a little more closely at what debates about non-sexist language can tell us about the practical workings of such overtly political verbal hygiene campaigns.

Reform and resistance: non-sexist language guidelines

Verbal hygiene practices operate, and can be examined, on a number of different levels. In my analysis of 'style' in Chapter 2 I distinguished between the gatekeepers who make certain linguistic rules (e.g. the editor of a newspaper or a reference work), the craft professionals who enforce the rules (e.g. copy editors) and the mass of writers – professional and otherwise – who comply with those rules or resist them. The verbal hygiene practice we are concerned with here, that is, the replacement of 'sexist' with 'non-sexist' usages, requires a similar structure to be fully effective: someone has to make the rules, someone has to codify them, and those in receipt of these rules must decide – or be compelled – to follow them.

There are however important differences between the style rules discussed in Chapter 2 and non-sexist language rules. The latter are not a body of traditional lore, but an innovation; and they are likely to be proposed in the first place not by influential gatekeepers but by people (feminists) whose influence is more limited. In this case, therefore, much more attention has to be devoted to *persuading* the gatekeepers to endorse new rules. A further difference is that non-sexist language proposals are overtly political; I have argued that style rules have political implications too, but they do not wear their political heart on their sleeve. The consequence is that non-sexist language guidelines, far more than style books, usage guides and dictionaries, attract controversy and provoke resistance.

This no doubt poses a problem for advocates of non-sexist language, but it offers certain advantages to the researcher. In the case of non-sexist language guidelines, where authority is neither invisible nor automatically deferred to, and change is not seamless evolution, it becomes possible to track the effects of the interplay between persuasion and resistance, and thus to improve on the standard accounts of how and why certain changes happen.

One could study the processes outlined here in various settings which themselves form a hierarchy. For example, I could examine the adoption or rejection of non-sexist norms by such influential linguistic institutions as newspapers and dictionaries. Conversely, I could examine the practices and arguments of people engaging in less formal interchanges, such as those that occur on the electronic nets (where non-sexist and 'politically correct' language are perennial topics). Probably the most instructive setting in which to pursue this sort of research, however, lies between these two poles: a small to medium-sized institution like a commercial company, a governmental agency, a professional association or a university: an institution whose authority and identity are reasonably well-defined, but where at the same time there is a sufficient number of people and enough freedom of exchange to permit debate. With this in mind, I have chosen to look at events surrounding a set of non-sexist language guidelines in my own place of work, the University of Strathclyde in Glasgow.

In 1990, the University of Strathclyde's Programme of Opportunities for Women Committee (POWC) put in hand the drafting of a leaflet on 'gender-free language'.[6] The finished product, entitled 'Gender free language: guidelines for the use of staff and students' was issued to staff in late 1991, and publicized outside the university through a press release. It had been endorsed by the university's governing bodies, Senate and Court, and this information appeared on the leaflet, giving it some status as official policy. In theory, this meant that institutional documents, from the university prospectus to the minutes of committee meetings, should be written in accordance with the guidelines.

In practice, matters were more equivocal. No one was officially responsible for enforcing the rules, but anyone who noticed some lapse in a university document could legitimately draw the new guidelines to the attention of the perpetrator. Conversely, people who wanted to use non-sexist language in official communications no longer had to persuade their superiors that this was not a silly or outlandish ambition; and to the extent that such people felt the need for concrete suggestions about non-sexist usage the leaflet provided guidance.

Overall, the main impact of the document was symbolic – which is not, however, to say it had *no* impact. On the contrary, and despite the lack of enforcement, it provoked a good deal of discussion in the university, both at the planning stage and at the time when it was issued to staff. It also attracted a fair amount of outside interest, with many other universities requesting copies. (Strangely, given the late date, Strathclyde's was one of the first such policies prepared specifically for a university, and it was also very well publicized.) Over time, the convener of POWC built up a sizeable file of correspondence about it.

What is most interesting about this correspondence is that it provides a clear indication of which arguments for linguistic reform are found persuasive and which are unconvincing or likely to inflame hostility. It also indicates which particular linguistic modifications are most and least contentious. In other words, it offers evidence not only about the process of linguistic change, but also about the *reasons* why verbal hygiene succeeds or fails in this kind of institutional setting.

Friendly persuasion: civility, accuracy and fairness

POWC knew that any guidelines they might issue would be essentially voluntary, and they therefore designed the guidelines to be maximally persuasive to their intended audience. The arguments they chose to emphasize have certain characteristics in common. Politically, they are moderate and not radical – their underlying philosophy is a liberal one of equal opportunities, and it is taken for granted that a basic concern to ensure equal treatment of men and women is axiomatic within the institution. Linguistically, the guidelines are more conservative than one might expect, given the association of such initiatives with 'ardent feminists' pressing disreputable 'verbal causes'. A close reading makes clear that far from undermining common-sense beliefs about language, *the beliefs about language to which the guidelines appeal are precisely beliefs that most people can be expected to hold already.*

The first of these beliefs is that public language should be *civil*, i.e. it should not give offence to actual and potential addressees. A recurring theme in the Strathclyde guidelines, therefore, and in the correspondence about them, is the importance of considering whether an expression is likely to give offence to women. For instance, when the POWC initiative was in its infancy, a member of the University Court wrote to the convener urging her to press ahead on the grounds that

> phrases like 'an engineer, the man for the job' are common at university meetings. . . . It is quite obvious that the few women present in such meetings find it embarrassing to make an objection, and it is therefore essentially ill-mannered of senior people to maintain the practice.
> (Memorandum, 7 February 1990)

The concern here is that 'senior people' are unwittingly offending their female colleagues by using non-inclusive phrases such as 'the man for the job'. What makes this objectionable is that the women present – already in a minority – are made to feel excluded.

The guidelines make much of this point: they say, for example, that sexist language may 'alienate' female students, and that non-sexist language is designed 'to include all potential addressees'. They ask lecturers to consider how women in their classes may feel if all the examples are about men and men's experience. To take no account of people who are actually sitting in front of you, the argument goes, is 'essentially ill-mannered', and at an educational institution may place women students in 'an environment which is not conducive to learning'.

This argument seems to have been a persuasive one, but it is not a radically feminist one, and it seems likely that its persuasiveness is directly related to its lack of radical implications. From a 'civility' perspective the point of using non-sexist language is not to challenge androcentric linguistic representations of the world at large, but merely to avoid offending/alienating women in the immediate context. This makes sexism a matter of individual men giving offence to individual women, rather than a systematic social process. Presumably, too, if there were no women present at the meeting or in the class, there would be no offence given and therefore no need to be attentive to sexist language.

'Civility' – also known, especially in the last two years, as 'sensitivity' –

has been a prominent theme in the more recent debate on 'political correctness', where it is invoked in particular by moderates who want to defend a subset of allegedly 'PC' expressions without endorsing linguistic 'excesses'. Writing in the *Observer* in the summer of 1993, Simon Hoggart, a journalist with a record of publicly attacking American 'political correctness', cited with qualified approval the view that 'so-called PC is no more than a way of showing greater sensitivity to people's feelings'. Around the same time, the BBC issued a style book that was suspected of capitulating to pressure for 'political correctness': the section that provoked these charges was entitled 'Sensitivity'. Even Simon Jenkins's *Times English Style and Usage Guide*, whose entry for 'political correctness' calls it 'a new authoritarianism' and warns against 'absurd neologisms' (*The Times* 1992: 116-17) nevertheless recommends paying careful attention to gender and race-related terms on the grounds that 'a story should not cause needless offence' (p. 117).

One sympathizes with Simon Jenkins's desire not to offend his readers, but one also wonders how he can possibly avoid giving offence, whatever he prescribes. The main effect of the 'PC' controversy has been to make every available usage having to do with race or gender politically loaded and thus offensive to somebody. While the argument for treating people with 'civility' or 'sensitivity' is unobjectionable, it is usually produced in a last-ditch attempt to deny that the significance of orthodox linguistic conventions goes beyond the fact that certain groups of people might take exception to them. We will see later on how the civility/sensitivity argument can be used against even the prescriptions made in its own name, and how it tends to break down when faced with more radical challenges.

The second commonplace belief about language on which the Strathclyde guidelines draw for their persuasive power is one we have had occasion to notice elsewhere: a belief that the highest value to which language-users can aspire is accuracy (also known as 'clarity' or 'transparency') in communicating meanings from one person to another. It is therefore pointed out in the leaflet that sexist language can (unintentionally) mislead, and so obscure a speaker's meaning. Citing 'empirical research' on the interpretation of generic masculine pronouns, the guidelines assert: 'there is clearly a disparity between the way generics are intended to be used and the way in which they are commonly understood.' The message is that if speakers and writers do not want at least some people to misunderstand them they should not use generic masculine terms.

An extension of this argument – which does not appear explicitly in these guidelines but is very prominent in more comprehensive documents, for example, Miller and Swift's *A Handbook of Nonsexist Writing*, (1980) – suggests that since the world contains both women and men, a description of the world that is not gender inclusive constitutes a misrepresentation. For example, to talk about 'the recruitment and training of policemen' is simply incorrect, because in reality we know that many police officers are women. Again, this idea has been invoked by moderates to defend some 'PC' usages. Simon Hoggart, for instance, regards the BBC's 'Sensitivity' guidelines as 'mostly . . . common sense. Now that fire brigades are appointing women, "firefighters" isn't PC but is just accurate'.

An appeal to accuracy and 'better communication' is invariably persuasive, but once again it is not particularly radical: it depends on the notion of language as a simple 'mirror of nature', designating things in the world rather than symbolizing values and beliefs (for example, would it be acceptable to use generic masculine pronouns in connection with groups that *are* made up exclusively or almost exclusively of men, e.g. 'the serial killer', 'the airline pilot', 'the Chief Executive'?).

The argument also assumes that when people use generic masculine terms, they *intend* the reference to be generic, and will therefore be receptive to suggestions that they should make that intention explicit. This leaves such utterances as George Bush's classic justification for invading Panama – 'we cannot tolerate attacks on the wife of an American citizen' – unexplained and inexplicable. The problem here is that Bush simply did not think about women in connection with the category 'American citizens', and asking him to be more explicit (desirable as that might have been on other grounds) leaves his particular brand of androcentrism untouched.

A third principle to which the guidelines appeal is fairness or parity – the notion that if you have two groups, they should receive identical or at least parallel treatment. This consideration applies, for instance, to the selection of titles for males and females (why should women but not men have to reveal marital status?); to the use of terms such as *girls* (only acceptable if the equivalent male group would be *boys*) and to the question of feminine suffixes (if two people do the same thing, why call one of them an *author* and the other an *authoress*?).

That an appeal to fairness (meaning identical or parallel treatment) is taken to be persuasive can be observed, paradoxically, in complaints POWC received suggesting that the leaflet treated *men* unfairly. One (anonymous) correspondent drew attention to the sentence 'Sexist language is any item of language which . . . constitutes a male as norm view of society by trivialising, insulting or rendering women invisible'. He or she suggested amending this to 'a male or female as norm view of society' and 'trivialising, insulting or rendering women or men invisible'. This correspondent remarked: 'I found the fact that a document, promoting a type of equality, did not in itself treat subjects equally, quite worrying.'

What this sort of response suggests is that verbal hygienists who live by liberal linguistic common sense may also die by it. The notion that sexism in language weighs equally on men and women, so that every piece of advice on the inclusion/equal treatment of women must be paralleled by advice on the inclusion/equal treatment of men, bypasses the feminist analysis of the *status quo*, defeats the consciousness-raising object of the feminist exercise and renders the guidelines vacuous. On the other hand, more radical innovations, such as the deliberate use of feminine generics to draw attention to women's existence (a strategy that might even get through to George Bush), would clearly be perceived as 'unfair' and thus unacceptable. Those strategies could also be condemned, using the other criteria which are prominent in the guidelines, as 'uncivil' (to men) and 'inaccurate' (since there are men as well as women in the world).

Civility, accuracy and fairness appear from correspondence to have been the most persuasive arguments to recipients of POWC's leaflet; recent media commentary suggests that they remain persuasive as justifications for some measure of so-called 'political correctness'. They are persuasive, first, because they entail an analysis of gender relations that is relatively unthreatening – men and women are equally subject to prejudice and discrimination, and much of this is only a question of individual thoughtlessness – and second, because they resonate with ideas about the use of language which many or most educated people hold dear – for instance, that it should be clear, unbiased and sensitive to the feelings of the addressee.

Each of these persuasive arguments, however, leaves the door open to equally persuasive objections based on the idea that the feminist project ultimately defeats its own purposes. I have already quoted the suggestion one correspondent made that the guidelines, in attempting to be fair to women, ended up being unfair to men. Another point made in correspondence took up the 'accuracy' argument: it was suggested that the elimination of gender distinctions such as those carried by the feminine suffix -*ess* actually made the language *less* accurate by destroying a linguistic distinction. 'To use the same term to speak of or to each of them [a 'host' and 'hostess'] can only lead to confusion' (memorandum, 14 November 1991).

There were also complaints that the idea of civility, while intrinsically worthy, was being taken to absurd and self-defeating extremes. For some correspondents 'sensitivity' was easily recast as *over*-sensitivity or even full-blown paranoia. For example:

> The overall impression that this leaflet gives me is that the female staff and students are sitting there nursing oversized persecution complexes, imagining slights when none are intended. Such folk exist. I have met some of each gender. One can only be sorry for them and perhaps encourage them to seek psychiatric help, for they are a menace to themselves and everyone else.
>
> (Memorandum, 14 November 1991)

This correspondent appeals, just as the guidelines themselves repeatedly do, to speakers' good intentions; he argues that where a 'slight' is unintended, linguistic intervention to prevent it is unwarranted and shows a want of civility towards someone who means no harm. Rather than jump at every imagined offence, those who feel slighted should 'seek psychiatric help'.

Some respondents to the guidelines triumphantly adduced examples where women were *not*, they claimed, offended, alienated or misled by traditional 'sexist' usages. *Glasgow Herald* columnist Jack McLean devoted a column to the guidelines ('Gender-free drivel') in which he referred to 'the kind of feminist trivialisation which the friends of mine who are women, girls, ladies and lassies, actually object to as much, if not more, than I do' (*Glasgow Herald*, 27 December 1991). This invocation of the woman who despises feminists and their verbal hygiene is a common strategy, and feminists who have rested their case on the offence and bewilderment that sexist language causes to women have no very convincing reply to it. The honest reply would be, 'really, we are proposing to change the language for symbolic reasons, because we want people of both sexes to look at the world in a different way, or at least to be forced to question whether the way they have looked at it in the past is "natural".' I know of no practical guidelines which go so far as to say this, however, because it smacks of things the audience finds objectionable and threatening: tampering with language and policing thought.

Since the POWC guidelines first appeared, there have been some changes in the language one hears and reads at Strathclyde University. Generic *he* is rarer in speech (though hardly unknown), and if it occurs in written documents, a memo reminding writers of the guidelines usually elicits a correction. On one occasion when examining boards were given 'chairmen' in a faculty board agenda, there was an objection which received an immediate apology. Subsequent minutes were amended.

It is true that any of these things might have happened – were already happening in some quarters – without the production and dissemination of guidelines, but this in no way undermines the point I mean this discussion to illustrate. The codification of linguistic practice in guidelines, which then provoke an explicit response, simply makes the point easier to document in a specific case. And that point is, it is absolutely untrue that non-sexist language evolves 'naturally' of its own accord, as a simple 'reflection' of (for example) growing numbers of women becoming visible in an institution. Linguistic change is not even an inevitable concomitant of a more general commitment to equal opportunities. It has to be pursued in specific initiatives, whether formal (like guidelines) or informal (like objecting to certain usages at meetings), and these are contentious in their own right.

On the other hand, it would also be inaccurate to suppose that formal acts of prescription backed up by authority have an immediate, overwhelming and consistent impact on people's linguistic practice. Change happens messily in a long drawn-out process of *argument*, in which positions shift only within certain limits; there is resistance (and inertia) as well as compliance; the same arguments that persuade people to make one change can give them principled reasons for refusing to make others. For these reasons, the language practices that result from intervention are extremely variable.

THE POLITICS OF LANGUAGE-CHANGE: TAMPERING AND TRIVIALIZING

Earlier in this chapter I claimed that objections to politically motivated verbal hygiene tend to focus more on questions of *language* than on political questions such as whether sex or race discrimination is a bad thing. Responses to the Strathclyde guidelines offer support for this claim. Critics do not say that sexism is acceptable or inevitable; they 'quibble', as one correspondent expressed it, 'at some of the means to the desired end'. They doubt whether particular usages are in fact biased, insulting or misleading; they deplore any change that results in fewer linguistic distinctions; they shudder at the injury to English grammar and vocabulary done by the use of *they* as a singular (this, in fact, is the single most common specific complaint in the correspondence file), or the use of the suffix *-person*. Overall, when people criticized the contents of the POWC leaflet, it was usually 'the language' whose best interests they claimed to be defending. As columnist Jack McLean put it: 'When you recommend changing the actual language you have got to be challenged' (*Glasgow Herald*, 27 December 1991).

Perhaps the most striking thing of all is the lengths some people went to in their concern to defend the language. Here was a slender leaflet making recommendations for people to follow on an entirely voluntary basis; by no stretch of the imagination could it have been the most urgent, weighty or significant document to cross the desks of university staff in the autumn of 1991. Yet the POWC file contains responses running to several well-polished pages, detailed lists of questions and objections from senior members of the administration, leaflets returned anonymously covered in scrawled emendations that reflect the sender's outrage. A well-known local journalist thought it worth devoting to this leaflet – which the vast majority of his readers would be wholly unaffected by – the kind of vitriolic commentary usually reserved for what he himself argues are far more important concerns.

Here we are confronted with a puzzling contradiction, one that has only become more obvious as the feminist verbal hygiene campaign has given way in public perception to a verbal hygiene campaign on behalf of a larger 'political correctness'. The most common linguistic charges against the so-called 'PC movement' are on one hand that its brand of verbal hygiene abuses language and destroys freedom by perverting the meanings of words, and on the other that it trivializes politics by focusing on language and not reality. One thing that must strike anyone considering these accusations is how contradictory they are. How can intervening in language be both a trivial diversion from politics and a threat to our most fundamental liberties? How can it be at the same time such useless, superficial tinkering that the only possible response is to laugh at it, and on the other, an attack on language and communication so serious it has 'got to be challenged'? The two charges are not compatible; yet as Jack McLean demonstrates, it is not uncommon to find both of them being made by the same person in the space of a few hundred words.

Only words?

The crudest formulations of the idea that demands for language change are trivial can surely be dismissed as *self*-contradictory. The person who levels this charge does not consider it a trivial matter, or why bother to articulate the objection in the first place, let alone in such detailed and/ or vitriolic terms? 'If the point is so trivial', I want to tell this person, 'please humour me by conceding it. If it really doesn't matter what words we use, then let's just do it my way and both of us will be happy'. Of course, this hypothetical conversation calls attention to a hidden dimension in the dispute, which is not just about the content of linguistic rules but also about who will get to make them for whom.

A slightly more thoughtful objection typically comes from liberals or leftists rather than conservatives. Such people are not necessarily opposed to linguistic reform, but they are disturbed by the idea of activists treating language as a priority when 'real' social change should be higher on their agenda. Sometimes, they wonder uneasily if the success of verbal hygiene initiatives might not obscure the fact that, deep down in 'reality', nothing has really changed. In a 1992 essay titled 'The challenge for the Left', Barbara Ehrenreich comments:

> If you outlaw the term 'girl' instead of 'woman' you're not going to do a thing about the sexist attitudes underneath . . . there is a tendency to confuse verbal purification with real social change. . . . Now I'm all for verbal uplift . . . [but] verbal uplift is not the revolution.
>
> (pp. 335–6)

In Robert Hughes's book-length polemic *Culture of Complaint* (even-handedly directed against both the 'political correctness' of the American Left and the 'patriotic correctness' of the American Right, which in true liberal fashion he sees as similar going on identical), Hughes expresses an even more forthright impatience with the pretentions of 'verbal uplift' (1993: 18–19):

We want to create a sort of linguistic Lourdes, where evil and misfortune are dispelled by a dip in the waters of euphemism. Does the cripple rise from his wheelchair, or feel better about being stuck in it, because someone . . . decided that, for official purposes, he was 'physically challenged'?

These remarks beg an obvious question: is there anyone who does believe that 'verbal uplift' on its own is the revolution, or that calling some oppressed group by a different name will magically change the condition of its members? Like the letter to *The Times* about renaming Oman 'Operson', these passages use the rhetorical strategy of crediting your opponents with self-evidently absurd positions which in point of fact none of them have ever subscribed to. Indeed, they have already answered the charges a thousand times.

For example, in the 1970s when non-sexist language policies were a novelty, people who opposed them were fond of saying that modifying language would not get women equal pay. Some of us were equally fond of replying that we never thought it would; but no one was offering a binary choice, *either* equal pay *or* non-sexist language – nothing prevented us from campaigning for both. Nor did anyone that I know of dispute that if you *did* have to make the call, equal pay would win hands down. But the point is, that call was never necessary. Social change is not a finite process or a zero-sum game.

Nevertheless, there is an interesting point here, which takes us back to my earlier remark about the politics of definition and representation moving from margin to centre. It does seem that many radicals of my generation and succeeding generations attach more importance to linguistic and other representations than their predecessors did, so that words and images are treated as useful material with which to work for social change. This is partly a matter of the (poststructuralist and postmodernist) theories about society and power a post-1968 generation of intellectuals has espoused, which place emphasis on the efficacy of language and 'discourse'; but the 'turn to culture' is not confined to intellectuals, nor is it eschewed by arch-conservatives, despite their implacable hostility to trendy postmodern theories. It is a matter of political strategy in a society where our chief agenda-setters are the mass media.

Activists today practise not only the traditional politics of workplace and neighbourhood organizing, but also the mass-media influenced politics of image, spectacle, performance: think of Rock Against Racism, or women dancing on the silos at Greenham Common, or lesbians abseiling into Parliament to protest about Clause 28.[7] On the ultra-Right fringes, too, think how much money is spent on funding cultural intervention via radio and television broadcasts or student newspapers; think of campaigns against 'satanic' rock lyrics, and spectacular blockades of abortion clinics, complete with telegenic images of foetuses. In an article which painstakingly documents the cultural agenda-setting activities of right-wing organizations in the US since the mid-1980s, Ellen Messer-Davidow (1993: 45) quotes from statements made by a right-wing foundation identifying a 'profound political change' and predicting that 'the politics that carry us into the twenty-first century will be based not on economics, but on culture'.

Changing language is a form of cultural intervention, and experience shows it is just as provocative as any other form. One can only agree with Barbara Ehrenreich that the politics of the provocative gesture alone will not bring about lasting social change, but people who believe cultural politics to be inherently 'trivial' have not come to terms with the nature of the societies activists across the political spectrum are working to change at the end of the twentieth century.

Ehrenreich and Hughes both doubt whether changing the words people use by fiat does anything to change the way they think. This is an important issue, and the scientific jury is still out: most linguists and psychologists today are sceptical about the strong version of the Whorfian claim that language *determines* perceptions, but on the weaker claim that it can *influence* perceptions there is conflicting evidence. My own view is that language is a highly variable and radically context-dependent phenomenon which may have effects on perception, but only in conjunction with other factors. Linguistic conventions help to naturalize and reproduce certain beliefs and assumptions, but these are not necessarily dependent on language or 'caused' by it.

For instance, researchers have found in controlled experiments that people do tend to interpret generic masculine terms as referring to men, whereas this tendency is less marked with gender-neutral terms; but even with neutral terminology the tendency to 'think male' is still discernable, and there are many instances of people using neutral terms as if they were masculine (consider George Bush's explanation for the US invasion of Panama, quoted above). Then again, drawing attention to someone's use of language is one way of making previously unremarked assumptions manifest to them; and this can on occasion be the first stage in changing their attitudes.

Yet even if we assume that language has no significant effect on perception, that does not license us to dismiss it as a wholly trivial concern; for speech and writing are not just about representing private mental states; they are also forms of public action, symbolic affirmations of an individual's or a society's values. As Stanley Fish says in his essay 'There's no such thing as freedom of speech and it's a good thing too' (1992: 241), 'words do work in the world of a kind that cannot be confined to a purely cognitive realm of "mere" ideas.'

It seems odd that Barbara Ehrenreich, in a passage that urges us to prefer action over 'mere' words, should place so much emphasis on *attitudes*, arguing that it makes no difference what people say if underneath they are thinking the same old sexist thoughts. Obviously feminists and other radicals would like to change people's attitudes, but from Ehrenreich's own, action-oriented viewpoint it is surely more important to change their behaviour – which is exactly the intention of a rule prescribing 'woman' rather than 'girl'. How someone treats me publicly matters more, in political terms, than how they feel about me privately; the fact that the boss seethes with inward resentment while addressing women staff respectfully is less damaging to the women than if he addressed them disrespectfully in accordance with his true feelings. (Nina Simone puts the point succinctly in her civil rights anthem *Mississippi Goddamn*: 'you don't have to live next door to me/just give me my equality.')

There is nothing trivial about trying to institutionalize a public norm of respect rather than disrespect, and one of the most important ways in which respect is made manifest publicly is through linguistic choices: in the context of addressing or referring to someone, words are deeds (compare 'hey, bitch!' with 'excuse me, madam'). As Trevor Pateman (1980) has observed, even the most cynical compliance with non-sexist norms sets a public example others may take to heart. Changing what counts as acceptable public behaviour is one of the ways you go about changing prevailing attitudes – ask anyone who still smokes cigarettes.

Murky waters: the question of 'euphemism'

This brings us to Robert Hughes's scorn for 'PC' language as 'a linguistic Lourdes where evil and misfortune are dispelled by a dip in the waters of euphemism'. 'Euphemism' has been a keyword in the debate on 'politically correct' language, and it takes its force, predictably, from George Orwell's essay 'Politics and the English language'. It will be recalled that euphemisms are among Orwell's targets because they violate the norm of using plain terms that 'tell it like it is': both circumlocutory and value-laden, they soothe the addressee by wrapping unpleasant truths in a soft cloud of verbal cotton-wool.

As I argued in Chapter 2 in relation to the phrase 'collateral damage', what both Orwell and his latter-day enthusiasts overlook is the difficulty in many cases of finding a neutral term that corresponds to some purported 'euphemism'. Robert Hughes, for instance, appears to be suggesting that whereas *physically challenged* is a ludicrous attempt to gloss over the true condition of the person in the wheelchair, *cripple* would be a perfectly truthful and value-free description. To which one might reply that if the meaning of a word is its use, *cripple* in present-day English is more like a dysphemism. Applying it to someone with a physical disability – as opposed to, say, a playground companion whose clumsiness you wished to deride – was taken to be offensive, or at least tasteless, long before most English speakers had ever heard of 'political correctness'.

Another so-called 'politically correct' term that has been ridiculed as 'euphemistic' is the one this chapter began with, namely *African-American*. Robert Hughes finds this label just about tolerable, but patronizingly adds that 'it seems to have no marked advantages over "black" beyond its length, a quality of language many Americans mistake for dignity' (1993: 23). Actually, I can think of at least three reasons why *African-American* might have marked advantages over *black*, and since each of them embodies an important principle, it is worth unpacking them in a little more detail.

The first reason might be, quite simply, that the people whose name is at issue prefer to be called, and call themselves, *African-American*. Obviously, the point is complicated by differences of opinion and practice that exist within the group; but in general, when someone introduces himself as 'George', it is a bizarre and potentially hostile act to insist on calling him 'Bill'. The usage commentator Geoffrey Nunberg has remarked that the right of any group to choose its own name (unless the choice has 'collateral linguistic effects') is by now 'an accepted principle of usage' (Nunberg 1990: 476). While this formulation is high-handed – Nunberg assumes a gatekeeper's right to grant or withhold approval of other people's names, after due consideration of their 'collateral linguistic effects' – it is still less breathtakingly arrogant than Robert Hughes's apparent belief that what *he* thinks about the relative merits of two names matters more than the opinion of the people whose names they are.

Because of this kind of arrogance on the part of people who typically have no idea what it feels like to be labelled in the relevant ways, the struggle to make others accept the label you choose remains an important component of verbal hygiene practised by subaltern groups. Exactly the same principle is invoked by the women who do not want to be 'ladies' or 'girls', the disabled who do not want to be 'cripples' and the gay men and lesbians who do not want to be 'homosexuals'. Despite the rhetoric of guideline writers, more than mere civility is at stake here. At stake is a power structure in which certain people, often without even being conscious of it, just assume the right to tell other people who they are.

A second reason why *African-American* might have advantages over *black* is that it symbolizes the principle of parity among the various ethnic groups that make up the US population. (This principle has been invoked explicitly by the most influential advocate of *African-American*, the Reverend Jesse Jackson.) The commonest type of ethnic designation in the US is a name that makes reference to the group's place of origin compounded with the word *American*, as in *Mexican-American, Italian-American, Japanese-American, Asian-American*.[8] To rename a particular group *African-American* thus has two symbolic effects. First, it suggests a parallel between this group and other groups, and second, it pointedly appropriates the label *American* for the group. The meaning of such a gesture has to be understood in the context of history: for a group brought to America as slaves and until very recently denied the rights of American citizens, this assertion of identity also represents a claim of the uprooted to historical roots ('African') and of the historically unequal to full equality ('American').

The third reason why *African-American* has advantages over the alternatives takes us to the heart of the 'euphemism' argument, and shows what is wrong with it. The question is the same one I posed in relation to 'collateral damage' in Chapter 2: if *African-American* is a euphemism, what is it a euphemism *for*? The relationship between *African-American* and *black* (or *colored*, or *Negro*) is only comparable to the relationship between, for example, *pass away* and *die*, if you make an assumption I suspect few liberals would want to admit to. If, for the sake of argument, we take the charge of euphemism seriously, and ask what is being 'covered up' in using *African-American* instead of *black, colored* or *Negro*, the only answer that comes to mind is the skin colour of the people in question. If so, is that not precisely the point of the linguistic intervention – to challenge the kind of racist discourse that defines people by skin colour? Someone who claims *African-American* is a euphemism because it 'covers up' the fact that African-Americans are dark-skinned is implicitly asserting that a description of people by skin colour is a value-neutral description, the natural and obvious way to classify them. (In which case one might ask why white ethnic groups in America are rarely classified in this way.)

I concede, by the way, that I have never actually heard or read anyone make such an assertion explicitly. But what else could possibly be implied by calling *African-American* a *euphemism*? Just because an expression is considered more polite than some other expression does not automatically make it a euphemism. Politeness consists in displaying awareness of another's feelings, whereas euphemism consists in the avoidance of a word or idea whose direct expression is taboo. There is some overlap between the two (it can be polite to be euphemistic, and both functions are served by indirectness) but they are not identical: would we say that 'excuse me' is a 'euphemism' for 'get out of my way'? Critics of 'political correctness' are deploying the term *euphemism* in a way St George Orwell would deplore: as a kind of generalized sneer at words they deem somehow inappropriate – too long, too trendy, too new, too 'political'. When they use the word *euphemism*, apparently, it means whatever they choose it to mean.

One point that is often made about successive labels for black people (also old, disabled, mentally ill and gay people) is that they have to keep on changing precisely because verbal hygiene is so ineffectual: the renaming process makes no difference to the underlying prejudice and stigma. Therefore, whatever the 'polite' term is now, in a few years or decades it will have acquired such negative connotations that someone will feel compelled to propose a new one. In this way *Negro* and *colored* yielded to *black*, which has now yielded to *African-American*; *cripple* gave way to *handicapped*, then *disabled* and now (in some quarters) *physically challenged*; *old-age pensioners* became *senior citizens* while *old* itself has gradually been supplanted by *elderly*.

This process no doubt contributes to the perception that new terms are 'euphemisms', but that perception is still inaccurate in most cases. Occasionally one could make the case for an element of euphemism: for instance, it does seem that the main virtue of *colored* was that it enabled people to avoid the then taboo word *black*; *elderly* stands, perhaps, in a similar relationship to *old*. In other cases the old terms have become dysphemisms, so that anyone other than a raving bigot will balk at using them (*cripple*, *lunatic*). In most cases, however, the old and new terms differ in ways that are more complicated than just 'positive' versus 'negative' or more versus less polite.

This, as we have already seen, is the case with the relationship between *black* and *African-American*; another example is *homosexual* and *gay*. *Homosexual* is neither more nor less taboo than *gay*, and most people outside the group regard them both as negative terms, but *homosexual* is a clinical description invented by sexologists, whereas *gay* is by origin an in-group label signifying a social or political identity. Such contrasts may be exploited by group members themselves to signal particular allegiances: there are, for instance, people who refuse to describe themselves as 'gay' because they dislike the politicizing of their sexual preference, and people who refuse to describe others as 'gay' on the grounds that those others are politically reactionary.

Simon Hoggart (1993) almost manages to get to grips with the question of what differentiates variant terms in a discussion of the term *sex worker*, an alternative to *prostitute*. Elsewhere in the piece Hoggart tempers the standard unease about 'euphemisms' with a guarded defence of 'sensitivity'; but his complaint about *sex worker* is precisely that it is *not* just a euphemism: 'it doesn't merely spare feelings but makes a political and moral judgement about prostitution – or rather, pointedly fails to make one, by implying that "the sex industry" is on a par with hairdressing or engineering' (p. 54).

I cannot fault this analysis of *sex worker*, though Hoggart does not follow it to its logical conclusion. In pointing out that it is the conventional plain term, *prostitute*, which 'makes a political and moral judgement', whereas the 'politically correct' alternative 'pointedly fails to make one', Hoggart graphically reveals that in some cases it is considered right and proper for words to express a moral judgement, and objectionable for them not to do so. The problem with *sex worker* is not that it conveys some attitude rather than no attitude; the problem is that it conveys the 'wrong' attitude, which in this case, paradoxically, is moral neutrality itself.

Hoggart's remarks point to the spuriousness of the idea that 'political correctness' either substitutes loaded terms for neutral ones or creates an orthodoxy where none existed before. What is really happening in conflicts over so-called 'politically correct' terminology is the clash of two ideological positions (either of which might in some context warrant the description 'orthodox', though it needs to be said that some orthodoxies are more orthodox – older, more widely believed, accorded more institutional support – than others). Conventional terms imply one evaluation of a given phenomenon; the 'politically correct' alternatives call that evaluation into question not by 'covering up' the phenomenon but by looking at it from a different angle (same-sex preference as a social rather than clinical matter, prostitution as a job description rather than an all-encompassing moral status, race as history rather than genetics, and so on). The words that cause conflict are words that precisely solicit a political or moral judgement from the addressee: substituting 'politically correct' for more traditional labels is an attempt to solicit alternative judgements, or at least problematize the usual ones.

Granted, the attempt does not automatically succeed. New words are not always accepted, and even if they are, old judgements may reattach themselves: the regularity with which particular group labels undergo the process of pejoration does indicate the limits of verbal hygiene's efficacy in getting rid of social stigma. There are two qualifications that need to be made here, however. First, the fact that verbal hygiene is not wholly efficacious does not mean it is completely pointless: notwithstanding the opinions of the *New York Times*, the search for a 'cure' for social ills like sexism and racism does not logically (or morally) preclude interim attempts to deal with their debilitating symptoms. Telling people that their renaming practices are futile and they should therefore stick with existing labels, however unsatisfactory or pejorative these have become, is like saying to someone with a chronic headache, 'what's the point of taking aspirin? You know you'll only have another headache later'.

The other point is that the effects of pejoration are not, in fact, total, and there are verbal hygiene strategies that specifically resist those effects, by 'reclaiming' – i.e. proposing deliberately to ameliorate – taboo words and insults. The movement on behalf of *black* (Black Power, Black is Beautiful) was an early example of this strategy, whose message was essentially, 'we wish to signal that our colour is a source of pride rather than shame'. Even if *black* is now giving way in the US to *African-American*, this does not reflect a widespread perception that *black* is too negative to be used any more. Rather it reflects the belief of people like Jesse Jackson that the time has come to place more emphasis on other aspects of group identity. Terms that are no longer preferred may still have neutral or positive connotations in contexts where they are invested with the dignity of past struggles: it has not been thought necessary to change the name of the National Association for the Advancement of Colored People or the United Negro College Fund.

A more recent example of the amelioration strategy is the reclaiming of *queer* by radical activists, most of whom would until recently have called themselves *gay.* Although *queer* historically had non-pejorative in-group uses, its use outside the community was so associated with hate-speech as to render it intolerable. The strategy of using it publicly – 'We're here, we're queer, get used to it' – is not only an assertion of pride, like 'black is beautiful', but a much rawer, 'in your face' challenge to straight society – the racial analogy is less with *black* than with *nigger,* as used defiantly by, for instance, the performers Niggas With Attitude. This particular act of verbal hygiene is disputed within the group itself. Not all gay men and lesbians find the confrontational stance of queer politics attractive, and for some the word *queer* is too thoroughly tainted to permit amelioration (the same holds for *nigger* among African-Americans).

The effect of the amelioration strategy is to emphasize conflict rather than seeking to resolve it, and thus to place sympathetic people outside the group in a (calculated) double-bind. It is obvious that the use of *nigger* or *queer* means something different in the mouth of a white or straight person than it does when used by Niggas With Attitude or the radicals of Queer Nation. Outside the group, such 'reclaimed' terms have the potential to connote not solidarity but bigotry. Liberals complain that this is unfair – straight white men are damned whatever they say or do, whereas women, blacks and homosexuals can get away with anything. But in a sense, this is exactly the point: to turn the tables in the argument about 'who's to be master', and thus draw attention to the liberals' unexamined (and from the radical perspective untenable) assumptions about language itself.

BREAKING THE LINGUISTIC CONTRACT: 'POLITICAL CORRECTNESS' AND 'NEWSPEAK'

The argument about 'euphemisms' is where two lines of criticism meet: on one hand it is marshalled to support the claim that verbal hygiene is trivial (since using nicer words does not produce a nicer world), while on the other it feeds in, via Orwell, to the contradictory argument that verbal hygiene represents an attack on language whose real-world effects are potentially catastrophic. Robert Hughes exemplifies the resulting confusion. First, he complains that the 'political correctness movement' is tampering with language to no purpose: 'This [changing nomen-clature], as George Orwell pointed out in "Politics and the English Language", destroys language without shifting reality one inch' (1993: 18). A few pages later, however, he is talking about 'the loss of reality by euphemism and lies' during the Reagan and Bush administrations

(p. 27), which suggests that destroying language might mean destroying reality as well.

What do people mean when they speak of attacking, abusing, perverting or indeed destroying language? From a linguist's perspective such talk is strictly speaking nonsensical, like talking about 'an attack on cognition' or 'an abuse of perception' or even 'a perversion of digestion' – phrases no one would ever utter. Terms such as 'cognition' and 'perception' denote a human faculty or the forms of behaviour in which that faculty is made manifest; 'language' belongs in the same category. Short of wiping out the human race you cannot, literally, destroy language. When Robert Hughes says that something 'destroys language', therefore, he is using a figure of speech. The question is, what does it figure?

Words such as *attack*, *pervert* and *abuse* are often applied figuratively to abstractions, as in phrases like 'an attack on freedom', 'a perversion of justice' or 'an abuse of power'. In such expressions, the abstractions *freedom*, *justice* and *power* stand for the institutions and norms of conduct that regulate certain human activities. You attack freedom by, for instance, suspending a constitution; you pervert justice by interfering with the activities of the police or the courts. To think of language as a cultural institution makes more sense than to think of cognition or perception in that way, because language-using is a normative practice. Yet language is a peculiar kind of institution. What would be the linguistic equivalent of the constitution or the courts?[9]

Perhaps there is a clue in the rhetorical link between 'destroying language' and 'loss of reality'. What is felt to be under threat from wanton tampering is not the existence of language *per se*; it is the relationship between language and reality, words and the world, that makes meaningful utterance possible. In the history of linguistic thought, that relationship has sometimes been represented as a 'social contract', like the one that underpins society in liberal political theory. Ferdinand de Saussure, the so-called 'father of modern linguistics', famously claimed that the sign is arbitrary: nothing about the nature or substance of a word ties it indissolubly to a particular meaning. There is no necessary connection between, say, the sound sequence c-a-t and a certain class of animals. This leads to the question: if the sign is arbitrary, how can speakers be sure that when they utter c-a-t they will be understood to mean 'cat'? One answer is that speakers of a language are party to a 'contract' whereby they 'agree' to observe a set of fixed conventions relating words and meanings. This limits the freedom of individual speakers to use words as they please, but it is the price they must pay for a greater social good, namely the possibility of communication.

Taken literally, this idea is obviously absurd: no one in the history of humankind ever had a meeting at which the motion 'that this be called a cat' was proposed and passed unanimously. As in the political fable from which the idea is taken, the linguistic contract and the 'agreement' by which it operates are fictions whose significance is ideological: the 'contract' metaphor suggests that we are ultimately governed in our use of language by consensus rather than coercion. If we defer to authority, we do so by consent. Linguistic norms may restrict our individual freedom, but they are ultimately there for the common good, and the consequences of flouting them are potentially dire for everyone.

If one accepts that the fundamental purpose of language is to communicate, and that communication is only possible if everyone agrees to honour the linguistic contract which prescribes a set of relationships between words and meanings, then certain kinds of verbal hygiene are bound to appear threatening. 'Natural' linguistic change can be passed off (however inaccurately) as reflecting some kind of broad social consensus; verbal hygiene, especially in its overtly politicized forms, is the antithesis of this, reflecting only the sectarian interests of a small minority. If that minority succeeds in influencing the language so that it no longer represents reality in the conventional terms to which speakers have tacitly agreed, we may continue to speak but our speech will lose its agreed meaning and thus its communicative purpose.

This argument explains why the term 'abuse' is so often thought apt in relation to language: to 'abuse' something is to use it wilfully for a purpose contrary to its true or proper purpose. The true and proper purpose of words, according to prevailing common sense, is to correspond exactly to things in the 'real world'. They cannot do this 'naturally' because of the arbitrariness of the sign; they have to do it conventionally, by way of a linguistic contract which speakers are bound to honour. What the alleged abusers of language are abusing, therefore, is the good faith of the other contracting parties; what they are destroying is the consensus about the word-to-world relationships on which linguistic communication depends.

Newspeak

At this point we may return to Robert Hughes's charge that the destruction of language entails a 'loss of reality', a charge that makes sense only if we add a further step to the argument outlined so far. Twentieth-century liberal critics have added just such a step: they have suggested not only that verbal hygiene can destroy the existing relationship between words, meanings and entities in the world, but that it can substitute a new set of relationships by fiat – the difference being that the new code refers to a 'reality' that does not exist. To the extent that speakers agree to use that code, or are compelled to use it, they are likely to lose all sense of what is real or true, and what is an illusion or a lie.

In his dystopic novel *Nineteen Eighty-Four*, George Orwell provided a durable, though fictional, example of the organized substitution of one reality for another in the official language of 'Newspeak'. The main purpose of Newspeak, as a form of communication addressed from the state to its subjects, was to mislead citizens about the true state of affairs in the world; its secondary purpose was to eradicate any language in which those citizens might communicate subversive thoughts to one another, or even just silently to themselves.

Linguistically, Newspeak accomplished its aims in various ways. To begin with, it reduced the overall size of the lexicon by abolishing words; this supposedly made certain real-world phenomena impossible to discuss, certain attitudes more difficult to express, and certain distinctions harder to draw. In addition, Newspeak redefined crucial vocabulary items so that propositions containing them had no truth value or logic. Thus the utterance of contradictions such as 'war is peace' was able to pass unremarked. The language also specialized in circumlocutory abstract formulations that, since they connected with no concrete reality, conveyed no meaning at all. Its speakers not only could engage, but actually had to engage, in a meaningless and nonsensical form of discourse requiring the suspension of rational thought.

Orwell's critique was intended to apply to the language of totalitarian states in general, but after his death the concept of 'Newspeak' came to be associated in particular with the language of communist states, whose official outpourings were often held to have fulfilled the prophecies of *Nineteen Eighty-four* almost to the letter. Rhetorical demonstrations of how Orwell's fiction had become reality were popular among conservatives and liberals alike, providing a dependable formula for anti-Soviet media commentary.

The English right-wing philosopher Roger Scruton, for instance, wrote a column in *The Times* in 1983 entitled 'How Newspeak Leaves Us Naked'. The main part of this piece was devoted to reviewing a dictionary of political terms issued by the Soviet Novosti press, in whose definitions Scruton detected all the hallmarks of Orwellian 'Newspeak'. For example, 'democracy' was defined in such a way as to exclude western democracies based on the principle of universal suffrage and make the Soviet Union itself into a shining example of democracy. Scruton concluded that the Soviet Union was using Orwellian techniques of linguistic manipulation to crush political dissent, not merely by proscribing its public expression but by perverting the Russian language to make anything other than dogma literally ineffable. (He went on to argue that feminists in the West were following the same strategy in their organized attempts to destroy the gender distinctions encoded into languages like English.) Deploring in principle all such wanton interference with words and meanings, Scruton suggested that those who engaged in it were 'mutilating a repository of traditional wisdom'.

Scruton's remarks are worth mentioning for two reasons. First, they provide a particularly clear and explicit statement of the way conservatives conceptualize language, to wit as the 'repository' of our accumulated knowledge about the world. As so often in conservative discourse, traditional wisdom is presented here as both rock solid, in that it embodies the tried-and-tested perceptions of countless generations, and extremely fragile, so that the slightest challenge threatens to destroy it. We are left with a paradox: Scruton is defending a particular order of language because it has stood the test of time, and yet it is precisely the effects of testing it against contemporary perceptions that he feels the need to defend it against.

The second point of interest about Scruton's piece is that ten years after he wrote it, we have reason to believe he was quite wrong about the part played by 'Newspeak' in the former communist world. In 1983 Scruton argued that the citizens of the Soviet Union and eastern Europe were not just *forbidden* to express themselves freely (because they would be censored, coerced into recanting, exiled or put in camps, etc.), but *unable* to express themselves freely (because the necessary meanings had been deliberately destroyed). It has since become clear, however, that although dissent was repressed by a culture of state-sponsored terror, it was never brainwashed out of existence by the language-and-thought police. Even if people prudently kept their subversive thoughts to themselves, they nevertheless continued to be capable of having such thoughts. Far from putting their faith in the contents of publications like the Novosti dictionary, many or most people appear to have regarded them with the same contempt as did Scruton. Charles King (1993: 19) even reports that at the historical institute of the former Soviet republic of Moldova, the interminable volumes of an official history of the Soviet working class are now being used to combat a national shortage of toilet paper.

The Bulgarian linguist Julian Konstantinov has written an account of what he calls 'The breakdown of Newspeak in an Eastern European country' (Konstantinov 1990). Konstantinov takes issue with the idea some westerners had begun to advance in the wake of the anti-Soviet revolutions that 'Newspeak', which he defines as 'the semiotic representation of totalitarianism' (p. 19), had no effect at all; he argues, however, that its effect was less to make people believe in the new order than to make them forget what the old one was:

> We should see totalitarianism not as an efficient stainless steel machine, grinding people into moral pulp, but as a blind and cheerful force which achieves the same goals by substituting traditional stability with chaos, absurdity and general lack of logic.
>
> (p. 2)

As an example of chaos and absurdity, he cites the way the days of the week were moved about to meet the needs of the economy, leading to such bizarre announcements as 'The Lenin Saturday scheduled for Sunday will take place on Monday' (p. 11).

What is most interesting about Konstantinov's paper is the account it gives of the linguistic effects of the ending of totalitarianism in Bulgaria. These were immediate and dramatic, indicating on one hand the *symbolic* importance newly liberated Bulgarians attributed to linguistic change, and on the other the inaccuracy of Roger Scruton's claim that 'Newspeak' had any efficacy *beyond* the symbolic – that it promoted orthodoxy of thought as well as speech.

For example, Konstantinov notes that in Bulgaria (like the Soviet Union itself, but unlike Poland or Hungary), the communist address term *comrade* had completely eclipsed the traditional terms *gospodin*, *gospoza* and *gospozitza* (equivalent to *Mr*, *Mrs* and *Miss*). Nevertheless, when the communists fell from power, *comrade* was promptly and ostentatiously abandoned for purposes of ordinary interaction. At the same time, it acquired a markedly negative connotation when applied to members of the Socialist (formerly Communist) Party, its purpose in this case being to disparage the addressee by emphasizing his or her ties to a now discredited regime.

Another, previously very common usage Konstantinov identifies as 'doomed to disappear' (p. 7) is the attributive *People's*, as in 'Bulgarian People's Army', 'People's Militia', 'Ministry of People's Defence', 'People's Republic of Bulgaria', etc. In communist mythology, this term signified communal 'ownership' of state institutions – the state and the people were supposedly one. The reason it had to change after the revolution, however, was that even as they mouthed it publicly, Bulgarians had inflected it with an exactly opposite meaning to the intended one. *People's* had effectively become a synonym for *State's* or *Party's*: there was no confusion at all about whose interests were actually served by 'People's' militias, armies, ministries and republics.

What these Bulgarian examples suggest is that 'Newspeak' does not work. Even a totalitarian state with a vast array of repressive devices at its disposal cannot control the tendency for words to be inflected with alternative and indeed subversive meanings. It is clear that the 'official' function of both *comrade* and *people's* was a solidary one: they were meant to underscore the sovereignty of the people and the egalitarian relations that supposedly held between them. It is equally clear that no one was fooled. Not only did Bulgarians *not* take the official language of solidarity at face value as a 'true' picture of reality; they used their very different perception of reality to effectively override the official meaning of the language. The words themselves could not, at the time, be rejected outright (one could not, for example, speak in public of 'The Party's

Militia'); but they could be used, and were used, in a way that expressed cynicism and resistance to the established order.

On the other hand, the Bulgarian case also demonstrates that language is not felt to be a mere side issue in situations of rapid social change. In the upheavals that followed the revolution, the newly formed opposition parties and the press devoted time and energy to such linguistic questions as the restoration of Bulgarian placenames and the criticism of usages associated with the old order, such as *comrade, people's* and '*the* party' meaning the Socialist (i.e. the remains of the Communist) Party. (So marked was public hostility to this usage that ungrammatical references began appearing to 'Bulgarian Socialist Party' with no article at all (Konstantinov 1990: 18).) Clearly, those involved in the construction of a new, democratic order felt the need for a public language that would symbolize new values, and mark a decisive break with old ones.

It is interesting in this connection that Bulgarians did not simply return to, for instance, the traditional pre-communist terms of address. Konstantinov reports that people seem uncomfortable with these, so that the result of the demise of *comrade* has been a significant increase in zero address forms and professional titles like *Dr* which are not overburdened with ideological significance. To Konstantinov this uncertainty is indicative of Newspeak's success in destroying the traditional order; but since it cannot be argued that the old titles *gospodin* and *gospoza* have been *forgotten*, perhaps people's discomfort with them indicates something rather different – a feeling that while the social relations of the communist era are now by common consent defunct, the social relations of the post-communist era are yet to be defined, and may not be appropriately symbolized by terms that were current half a century ago.

What is going on when a choice is made between, say, *comrade X* and *Mr X*, or *the Bulgarian People's Army* and *the Bulgarian National Army*? Everyone knows the facts themselves do not change: the army does not magically become an instrument of the people, or of the nation, because it is referred to as a 'People's' or a 'National' army. That is a major reason why Scruton-style attacks on 'Newspeak' are usually so wide of the mark: they assume that words should correspond to facts, that they are taken by right-minded speakers to correspond to facts, and therefore that when the authorities deliberately change certain words, the effect is automatically to mislead speakers about the facts.

Yet in addition to pointing out that speakers are not as passive and credulous as this suggests, one could argue that in any case political discourse is never primarily factual; rather it is *normative*. The implication of announcing 'in future we are going to refer to the army as a "people's" army' is less 'this is how things really are' than 'this is how they ought to be'. One effect of such an announcement is to *constitute* – call into being – an imaginary entity, 'the Bulgarian people'. This construct, as it turned out, strained credulity to the point of being self-defeating; too many Bulgarians thought the rhetoric of 'the people' was a sham, and they were not moved to make a real entity in the image of the imaginary one. The construct which, according to Konstantinov, has replaced 'the Bulgarian people' – to wit, 'the Bulgarian nation' – may arouse more enthusiasm, but it is no less imaginary, no less normative, no less a product of discourse.

The standard critique of 'Newspeak' is wrong in two ways, and in each case for the same reason: it overlooks the power of the creative imagination as a linguistic and political force. On one hand this leads to an exaggeration of the efficacy of verbal hygiene as a technique for brainwashing the masses. 'Newspeak' could only be fully efficacious in that task if people's dealings with words were entirely mechanical. On the other hand, critics of politicized verbal hygiene, from conservative Roger Scruton to liberal Robert Hughes, underestimate the extent to which *all* discourse – and certainly all political discourse – uses the same device of constructing imaginary representations of reality. It is true the aim of doing this may be to spread lies and 'disinformation'. But it may also be to engage the imagination by denaturalizing familiar representations of what is, and constructing representations of what could or should be. Without this discourse of value, how could we have the political debate and dissent whose brutal suppression is universally agreed to have been the most heinous crime of Stalinism?

Facts and values: liberal versus radical verbal hygiene

The point that political discourse has more to do with norms and values than with facts is not always recognized by politically motivated verbal hygienists themselves. Those who engage in the form of political discourse known as 'political correctness' are not united in their underlying conception of the verbal hygiene project. Some advocates of linguistic reform share the assumptions of liberals like Robert Hughes, if not of conservatives like Roger Scruton: as we have seen in the case of the feminists who designed Strathclyde University's 'gender free language' guidelines, they claim (and no doubt believe) that certain changes will have the beneficial effect of making words more true to the world as it really is, and thus of enhancing communication about it. For these reformers language is still a 'fixed code' underwritten by a 'linguistic contract', but – *pace* Scruton – not everything about it merits preservation: it has certain imperfections that both can and should be corrected. This is the same benevolent rationalism that animates such enterprises as spelling reform.

In contrast, there are advocates of linguistic reform – often proposing what appear to be substantially the same changes – whose reasons for practising verbal hygiene are entirely different. For these people, the project is not a modernist attempt to construct a 'perfect' language, but a postmodernist attempt to dramatize the impossibility of such a language. They take it as axiomatic that words can never stand in a simple and direct relationship to 'reality', that their use is contested and their meaning unstable. From this perspective, the object of tampering with linguistic conventions is to make the point that the way of using language which most people consider 'natural' is not natural at all; or, for those who prefer a 'cultural' metaphor, that despite invocations of the common language that serves the common good, some parties to the linguistic contract are actually more equal than others.

An illustration that may make the difference clearer once again concerns the vexed question of gender and English generics. Most feminists reject the traditional generic masculine, as in 'ascertain a client's circumstances before you give him advice'; but on the question of what to replace it with there is a two-way or perhaps even three-way division. One group favours unmarked or *neutral* terms: the sentence above should be recast in the plural ('before you give them advice'), or the passive ('before advice is given'). This solution falls into the first, liberal category of verbal hygiene, stressing accuracy and fairness: 'clients' after all will include both men and women. A slightly more radical variant is to use a disjunct, 'him or her'. Those who prefer this solution usually justify it by arguing that neutral or genderless terms are often covertly interpreted as masculine, so that if your aim is to ensure that women are included you must mention them explicitly.

The third, radical solution, however, is quite different – to use a feminine generic, e.g. 'ascertain a client's circumstances before you give her advice'. Here it is obvious that the aim is not accuracy or fairness. No one believes that all clients are women, and furthermore no one believes that feminine pronouns in English can properly be used as generics. Faced with this sentence, readers must engage in more interpretive work than either the original sentence or the 'neutral' recasting would require. They must begin by asking themselves why the writer has chosen this unusual formulation. They may spend a little time considering the possibility that the sentence is about a service whose clients are, in fact, exclusively women. If the context offers no support for this hypothesis, they must go on to interpret the word 'her' as generic in order to make the sentence make sense. In the process they may find themselves reflecting on such questions as: 'what does it mean that we usually say "him" without a second thought? Why does it bother me if someone says "her" instead?'

There is no doubt that this strategy does not, as the style books would have it, 'enhance communication' by rendering the writer's meaning maximally transparent. On the contrary, it deliberately distracts attention from the content of the message to the form. The use of taboo words like *queer* or *nigger*, or unfamiliar formulations like *differently abled* instead of *disabled*, is intended, similarly, to make people work at extracting a meaning, forcing them to ask for example who is speaking (a white racist or a black militant?), and what assumptions are required to make sense of particular terms.

These questions are actually relevant to every communicative act; what looks like, and is usually apprehended as, automatic decoding really rests on a complicated network of unexamined assumptions about 'reality'. Deliberate departures from conventional usage are meant to bring those assumptions to the surface so they can be noticed, and challenged.[10] What makes radical verbal hygiene radical linguistically is its insistence that words do not simply 'have' fixed, shared meanings. They acquire their meanings only in a context, and a crucial element of that context – one which is usually invisible, but which the radical brand of verbal hygiene is specifically designed to *make* visible – is the power relations operating within it.

Fixed codes and speech codes

The complicated effects of power relations on the use and interpretation of words are relevant to a phenomenon that has attracted particular attention in the 'political correctness' debate: the institution of 'speech codes' on some US campuses which make it a disciplinary offence to use certain expressions deemed racist, sexist, anti-semitic and homophobic. Apart from the general challenge this poses in America to First Amendment guarantees on freedom of speech, it also leads in specific cases to wrangling about what this or that expression 'really means'. This wrangling provides an excellent illustration of the clash between liberal and radical theories of meaning.

For example, one celebrated case concerned a white student at the University of Pennsylvania who was irritated by the noise some black students were making. He told them they were behaving like a 'herd of water buffalo'; their response was to make a formal complaint of racism. Though there was some dispute about whether he had also used an explicitly racist epithet, and the situation was complicated by later events (such as the seizure and burning of copies of a student newspaper), much of the public and private discussion of this case focused in particular on the meaning of 'water buffalo' in this context. To many people it seemed ludicrous to claim that this was a racist insult, as opposed to just an insult directed against people who happened to be black; and outrageous to bring this previously unheard-of expression under the umbrella of an anti-racist speech code. To others, conversely, it seemed obvious that the accusation of racism was warranted.

What this incident pinpoints is the impossibility of addressing problems of this kind by having a simple list of proscribed words. There is no word so pejorative that it might not, in some context, be used without hateful effect (one would hardly want campus police to interrupt a performance by Niggas With Attitude on the grounds that the mere announcement of their name violates the speech code); conversely there are many words, not obviously candidates for proscription, that could in some context reasonably be judged unacceptable.

One solution to the conundrum here would be to argue that the offence lies not in words but in acts; it is not inherent in a particular piece of language, it is constituted by particular, contextualized acts of language *use*, and the actual choice of words may be of varying relevance to it. This solution is particularly unpalatable to liberals, especially in the US, because the notion of 'free speech' and the interpretation of the US First Amendment depend on being able to draw a clear dividing line between speech and action; nevertheless, it merits further examination.

Imagine the decision process the black students in the water buffalo incident might have gone through before making their complaint of racism. To begin with, the one thing they almost certainly did not do was look up the meaning of *water buffalo* in a dictionary; this would have been quite pointless, since what the students had to judge was not the meaning of *water buffalo* itself but the meaning of the white student's action in applying that term to them. Here, they might have begun from the fact that he was white and they were black: this they would interpret as making it more likely that his meaning was a racist one than if he had been black himself, or they had been white. They would also have made judgements on his intentions based on their previous acquaintance with him (if any), the situation, the tone in which he spoke, and so forth: was he just kidding or did he mean to be insulting? If the latter, then was there a specifically racial element in his choice of insult?

Here the black students might ask themselves whether they had ever heard, or could imagine hearing, a group of white people being referred to as 'a herd of water buffalo'. Assuming the answer was no, they might go on to speculate about the connotations of that phrase: they would notice the implication of mindlessness in 'herd' and the fact that 'water buffalo' belongs to a set of terms denoting wild animals. They would be aware that 'mindless', 'wild/savage' and 'animal' are traditional stereotypes in discourse about black people. If the white student did not realize he was deploying a set of well-established and racist metaphors, they might think, then he ought to have known. They would conclude that even though the term *water buffalo* may not be inherently a racial epithet, the act of addressing it to these people in this situation was a racist act.

This outcome is not determined by any one judgement on the students' part, but by the cumulative effect of all of them. It is therefore unique to one context: if any of the situational factors had been different, the students might have reached a different conclusion. (For example, imagine what difference it might have made had they believed their abuser to be a foreigner with a poor command of English, or mentally ill, or under the influence of a hallucinogenic drug.) Meaning is never not affected by considerations like these, and our judgements upon it can therefore never be definitive or absolute. At best we can reconstruct the interpretive process, as I have tried to do above, and show what led to what; but at the end of it we still do not have 'proof' of what the white student's comment 'really meant'. All we have is a set of accounts of how the various parties interpreted it.

This is extremely problematic for administrators whose aim is to have a fair and enforceable code. If virtually any expression can be racist in certain circumstances, if people do not agree on which expressions are racist, and if in addition there is no single criterion that definitively settles the question whether an expression is racist, then we are back in the looking-glass world of Humpty Dumpty – the only question becomes 'who's to be master': the complainant who says something was racist, the defendant who swears it was not, or the administrator who has to adjudicate the case?

If this scenario is disturbing, it is instructive to consider why. After all, it could be a description of any court of law (the prosecution says X did it, the defence says X is innocent, the magistrate or jury adjudicates); why should the meanings of speech-acts be exempt from the same kind of contestation? Furthermore, my hypothetical account of the black students' 'decision procedure' for coming to an interpretation of a particular communicative act could be, in its general outline, a description of what all language-users must do in every speech situation. Our interpretations of other people's speech-acts are based not on simply looking words up in a mental code-book but on a whole constellation of contextual judgements. This is how communication works, though the myth of the 'fixed code' obscures it. Granted, few exchanges cause the kind of overt dispute the water buffalo exchange did, but if a random sample of exchanges were put to the test, it would often be just as difficult to achieve consensus about their 'real' meaning.

What makes the water buffalo case stand out as somehow exceptional is the particular salience of the historical and actual power relations between black and white in polarizing the dispute about meaning. One way in which this polarization is often apprehended can be seen in the disparaging comment that 'black people see racism everywhere'. Just so: but does not everyone, similarly, make sense of the world to a large extent on the basis of personal experiences and cultural beliefs that arise out of collective histories? And if some of those experiences and beliefs come to seem more legitimate guarantors of meaning than others, is that not precisely an effect of power? It is always worth asking why, and from whose point of view, one way of using language seems obvious, natural and neutral, while another seems ludicrous, loaded and perverse.

This, in fact, is the central question the so-called 'politically correct' have posed about language. It is in their answer to it that we will find the real reason for the alarm with which their proposals have been greeted.

If the radical account of language is right, it challenges fundamental assumptions about both language and society.

CULTURAL POLITICS AND THE 'DREAM OF A COMMON LANGUAGE'

Considered in its totality, the debate on 'political correctness' is most obviously a debate about how democracies made up of diverse populations subscribing to a variety of beliefs and customs are to preserve a common culture. A constant theme of critiques of 'political correctness' is the fear, shared by conservatives, liberals and some leftists, that society is disintegrating: 'identity politics' (i.e. political groupings based on race/ethnicity, gender, sexual preference, etc.) is destroying the sense people once had of belonging to a larger polity (Robert Hughes's book *Culture of Complaint* is subtitled, significantly, *The Fraying of America*). For conservatives, this spells the end of tradition; for liberals, the end of civility; and for the Left, the end of effective mass politics.

Whenever culture is at issue, language is also likely to be at issue. It is typical, for example, for anxieties about cultural difference and fragmentation to be paralleled by anxieties about multilingualism as a threat to unity.[11] The possession of a 'common language' is felt to be one of the most salient markers of a 'common culture' (more than this, perhaps, it is thought to have the power to bring such a culture into existence), while the lack of such a language is felt, conversely, to be a sign of fragmentation which may also encourage resistance among alienated minority groups using their own languages as a rallying point.

So-called 'politically correct' language may not be as overt a threat to the project of cultural unity as the existence of militant minority language groups, but the idea that there is some analogy is not without foundation. Endless bickering over what to call things (and people) draws attention to a lack of social consensus; at its most confrontational (the 'water buffalo' incident, for example, or the activities of Queer Nation) it dramatizes the existence of viewpoints that appear not just different but incommensurable. Furthermore, whereas language has traditionally been the privileged symbol of one kind of social identity – ethnicity – the 'PC' phenomenon makes it symbolic of a bewildering range of affiliations: gender, race, sexual preference, region, subculture, generation, (dis)ability, appearance, and so on.

For those whose ideal is a common language in a common culture, this is an unsettling development. Obviously, it alarms conservatives, whose recipe for cultural unity is the assimilation of all groups to a traditional and usually elite norm. But it also disturbs liberals, who espouse a philosophy of tolerance and cultural pluralism. Liberals make much of the idea that differing opinions can be exchanged and debated in a public sphere of free and rational discourse, to produce, if not consensus, then at least a civil compromise. Central to this liberal ideal is the notion that people speaking from widely divergent standpoints can nevertheless find a common language in which to talk to one another.

Some forms of verbal hygiene that are now reviled under the heading of 'political correctness' were acceptable to many liberals at the time they were proposed because they seemed to be in line with this model of language as rational and civil exchange. Feminist proposals to make language gender neutral or gender inclusive are an obvious case in point. The liberal feminist argument stressing civility, accuracy and fairness was sufficiently persuasive to effect real change in many people's usage, because it left their fundamental ideas about what language was, and was for, untouched. It offended only those ultra-conservatives for whom all willed linguistic change was suspect as an attack on 'tradition', or who took the gender conventions of language as the linguistic expression of an immutable natural law.[12]

Now, though, it has become clearer that some verbal hygienists are grounding their claims in a very different kind of argument: far from trying to find a common language with which to bridge the differences between people, they are denying that any such language exists, or ever has existed, or ever could. They are suggesting that what liberals mean when they invoke the idea of a 'common' language is a language based on a massive repression of difference. The intelligibility of this language depends on everyone accepting definitions which are presented as neutral and universal, but which covertly represent the particular standpoint of straight white men from the most privileged social classes. As the postmodernist theorist Donna Haraway has written, the 'dream of a common language . . . is a totalizing and imperialist one' (1991: 173).

This rather cryptic formulation can be elaborated as follows. If people do not all speak from the same position (as must surely be the case in a society whose population is culturally diverse and/or hierarchically organized), any attempt to place their utterances in a 'common' frame of reference is likely to entail making one group's frame – in practice, that of the dominant group – the norm of intelligibility. This is 'totalizing and imperialist' because it casts all experience in the verbal image of the dominant group's experience. From the dominant group's perspective, it is 'obvious', for instance, that *African-American* is a pompous euphemism, that no one should shrink from a good plain word like *cripple*, that *man* includes women, that *water buffalo* is not a racist epithet, that describing prostitutes as *sex workers* is an abdication of our moral responsibility to condemn them, and that homosexuals have no right to compromise a perfectly good English word by calling themselves *gay*. The experiences and analyses that lead others to find these propositions far from obvious are dismissed as absurd, if indeed they are considered at all.

The kind of verbal hygiene I have been calling 'radical' is dedicated to disrupting the complacency with which dominant groups regard their own ways of using language as the only legitimate or intelligible ways of using it. The strategies it employs to that end are various, inventive and mostly confrontational. Some strategies rest implicitly on a turning of the tables: 'we are going to use language as if we, not you, were the centre of the universe: if you don't like it, think how we feel after centuries of having it done to us.' Other strategies deliberately undermine cherished beliefs at the metalinguistic level. For example, as I pointed out before, the 'reclaiming' of terms such as *nigger* and *queer* as markers of in-group solidarity makes it impossible for non-members to observe the norm of 'civility'; whether they adopt the chosen label or avoid it, they risk being guilty of some kind of incivility. And this also undermines the liberal postulate that words have the same value regardless of who speaks them.

Radical verbal hygiene wants to leave speakers with no unpoliticized linguistic corner into which they can retreat. Merely continuing to speak as they have always spoken will not protect them, for the bringing into existence of a different way of speaking makes the old one appear – whether in fact it is or not – as a wilfully conservative or reactionary choice. In this respect, the radicals are iconoclasts, destroying the ideal of a value-free language.

They are also iconoclasts with respect to that sacred object, 'the language' itself. For at least half this century, otherwise intelligent people have been able to get away with any amount of sententious rubbish, simply by uttering this magical phrase. 'The language is under attack! We must ride to the rescue immediately!' Radical verbal hygiene offers a powerful challenge to received wisdom about 'the language'. Explicitly or implicitly, it asks: what language? Whose language? Where does 'the language' reside, if not in the practice of its speakers? And in that case, who can legitimately decide that the practices of certain speakers are 'attacks' on a language that in principle also belongs to the alleged attackers?

The point is not that the accusers have no reply to make (though I suspect in some cases the question might cause them difficulty, since it has never previously occurred to them). The point is that they are finally being challenged to make one. And here they must tread carefully: for many of the most obvious replies will reveal, exactly as the radicals want them to reveal, that the underlying assumption concerns that perennial question, 'who's to be master?'. Defenders of 'the language' regard language as their property.

Whether or not they fully understand the multiple disruptions radical verbal hygiene aims to cause, it is those disruptions, I suggest, rather than specific usages like *African-American* or *physically challenged* that critics find so deeply objectionable about it. They say they do not understand why language, which in their view represents our best hope of bridging our differences, should be turned deliberately into a battleground and used to fragment rather than to unify. They are genuinely bewildered that women or members of minority ethnic groups should persist in reading such bizarre connotations into perfectly innocent words whose meanings should surely be transparent to anyone, since they are simply facts of 'the language'. (To which the women, etc., are likely to retort: 'On the contrary, they are *arte*facts of your historical power to define words for everyone.')

It is always challenging for people to have to justify their assumptions, or even just make them explicit, when those assumptions have previously been taken for granted to the point of evading conscious notice altogether. Those who do not find particular rules irksome may be amazed to discover that there are any rules at all. Stanley Fish (1992) cites the student journalist who complained that a campus speech code would restrict his freedom of expression, since in future when he wrote he would always 'have it in the back of his mind'. Fish remarks that there is always *something* in the back of a writer's mind whether he or she is aware of it or not, and one ought at least to consider the possibility that a speech code might be preferable to whatever was there before.

Free speech, normativity and what's in the back of our minds

The larger point of Fish's essay 'There's no such thing as freedom of speech and it's a good thing too' is similar to the main argument of this book: there is no language without normativity. If there really were no restrictions of any kind on what could be said and how, speech would be inconsequential gibberish, and social interaction at an end. Therefore, Fish argues, it is nonsensical to suppose we could ever have, or for that matter want, absolute freedom of speech. Absolute freedom of speech could only be the utterly trivial freedom to make meaningless noises.

It will not have escaped the reader that this argument could as well be used against so-called 'political correctness' as against fatuous criticisms of it such as the one advanced by the student journalist. One might say that by acting like Humpty Dumpty, as if existing rules and norms did not apply to them and they could substitute new ones unilaterally, the radicals are reducing discourse to a species of meaningless noise. I think, however, that such an objection misses the real force of the argument.

Pointing out that in principle 'there's no such thing as freedom of speech' because language-using is a normative practice is not to argue either for the inevitability of the *status quo* or for the necessity of radical reform. In and of itself, it does not make the case for any particular set of linguistic norms, 'politically correct' or otherwise. (Fish only says we should consider whether a speech code is preferable to something else, not that it is a priori preferable.) The point, rather, is that we cannot avoid arguments about the merits of particular norms. Since the one thing that really is inevitable about our linguistic practices is their normativity, quarrels about language should concern (and in fact, once one has cut through the ideological undergrowth, *do* concern) not whether there ought to be norms but which norms they ought to be.

In order to engage in argument effectively, we need to reject the notion that we have agreed, on pain of forfeiting all ability to communicate, either to the conservatives' traditional 'repository' of meanings, or to the liberal 'linguistic contract'. These imaginary constructs displace on to language itself a set of norms whose real authors can only be other language-*users*; and the aim of this manoeuvre is to mystify these people's authority by identifying their practice with the allegedly immutable laws of 'the language'. Getting rid of this mystification does not magically produce consensus, but it clears the ground for more focused arguments about what (and whose) restrictions on our linguistic practice we are or are not willing to accept.

On this subject there is, unquestionably, plenty left to argue about even after we divest ourselves of irrational and mystifying notions. Just because I agree with Fish that there is always 'something' – i.e. some form of restriction – in the back of a language-user's mind does not mean I think all forms of restriction are equally acceptable. I do not deny there are real and serious grounds for disagreement about whether using certain expressions on a campus should make people liable to disciplinary action, or whether non-sexist language requirements should be added to a list of hyperstandardizing style rules that is arguably far too long already.

On the other hand I do not want to deny that one can legitimately criticize the way somebody else uses language. Many times in this chapter I have myself used this hygienic strategy. I have said, for example, that the way the term *euphemism* is used by critics of 'political correctness' strikes me as imprecise, and I have drawn attention to what I regard as provocative definitions of 'political correctness' itself. Is this inconsistent with the general argument I am advancing? I do not believe so, because my argument is that this kind of normative metalinguistic practice is inevitably part of all language use, the linguistic analyst's included. I am not claiming that the ways of using words which I criticize are 'abuses' or 'perversions'; I am not accusing the people I disagree with of attacking 'the language' or breaking a sacred contract. I am simply reserving the right – which I must also grant to them, and to everyone else – to engage in arguments about how language ought to be used. This is not a relativist, 'to each their own' gesture, akin to announcing that when all's said and done, the meaning or use of words is just a matter of opinion. Rather, the meaning and use of words is a matter of contestation, and I am proposing we engage in the contest openly and with a more explicit notion of what is at stake.

The verbal hygiene movement for so-called 'politically correct' language has the merit of bringing contests that are often submerged to the surface of public discourse. It is no more of a threat to freedom of expression than any other set of linguistic norms (and abandoning all such norms is not an option); nor does it threaten our ability to communicate (even if the tone of the communication may be less civil than ideally we would like). It threatens only our freedom to imagine that our linguistic choices are inconsequential, or to suppose that any one group of people, in the guise of defending 'the language', has an inalienable right to prescribe them.

5 The new Pygmalion
Verbal hygiene for women[1]

FROM RAGS TO RICHES: LANGUAGE, GENDER AND TRANSFORMATION

In his preface to *Pygmalion*, one of the great verbal hygiene stories of modern English literature, George Bernard Shaw remarked: 'it is impossible for an Englishman to open his mouth without making some other Englishman despise him.' To illustrate his thesis, however, Shaw created not an Englishman but an English*woman*, the cockney flower-seller Eliza Doolittle. Eliza plays Galatea to Henry Higgins's Pygmalion: Higgins, a skilled phonetician, makes a bet that he can take the dustman's daughter and in a few months pass her off in London society as a duchess. Higgins, we learn, is a professional specialist in this kind of verbal hygiene. At the beginning of the play he is asked: 'But is there a living in that?' He replies: 'Oh yes. Quite a fat one. This is an age of upstarts' (Shaw 1972: 679).

Pygmalion is conventionally read as a play about class, but it is also quite strikingly a play about gender. It cannot be an accident that Shaw made his working-class 'upstart' a woman, for *Pygmalion* – the title alludes to the classical myth of the creator who falls in love with his own creation – belongs to a narrative genre with certain assumptions about gender built into it. It seems 'natural' (in other words, culturally predictable) that the powerful creator should be male and the malleable creature female, and also that the class hierarchy between the two should re-inforce rather than contradict the gender hierarchy. Nor will it surprise us if the story turns into a romance, with creator and created finally confessing mutual·adoration and falling into each other's arms – a clichéd ending, but one that a great deal of our reading, from childhood fairy-tales onwards, has led us to expect and desire.

Shaw himself took some pains to thwart conventional expectations. The text of his play ends not with a love scene between Eliza and Higgins, but with a note spelling out that Eliza marries the younger, poorer and less powerful Freddy; a note which begins:

> The rest of the story . . . would hardly need telling if our imaginations were not so enfeebled by their lazy dependence on the ready-mades and reach-

me-downs of the rag-shop where Romance keeps its stock of 'happy endings'
to misfit all stories.

(1972: 782)

Shaw was clear that for Eliza, marrying Higgins would not be a happy
ending, for as he noted, 'Galatea never does quite like Pygmalion: his
relation to her is too godlike to be altogether agreeable' (1972: 798).

But later adaptors and audiences thought otherwise. Both the film
Pygmalion and the musical *My Fair Lady* were given the romantic
treatment Shaw had rejected. That this change was deemed necessary
when the stage play was adapted for more popular media might seem to
confirm that many people's imaginations are dependent on the ready-
made formulas of fairy-tales and romance. Yet it is notable that Shaw's
own imagination could conceive of only one ending to the story of a
woman 'upstart': marriage. He spared Eliza the tyrannical Higgins and
gave her the ineffectual Freddy, but the logic of his narrative impelled
him to marry her to somebody. In fiction, when women successfully
transform themselves, whether physically, morally or, as in Eliza's case
linguistically, the love of an eligible man is their traditional reward.

The conventions of fiction in this instance are rooted in the conventions of reality. Why are there so many stories in which a powerful man
remakes a woman in the image he desires and then possesses her – or
alternatively, hands her to another man – and so few where the gender
roles are reversed? Presumably it has something to do with the fact that
for many groups of women in many historical periods, male approval has
been the best guarantee, if not the only one, of economic security and
social respectability. Such women have had good reason to try and
become what men wanted women to be: they have had a powerful
incentive to practise self-improvement. If one consequence of their
situation has been the popularity of fictions based on the rags-to-riches
formula, another, more practical result has been a lengthy tradition of
advice literature specifically addressed to women and dealing with all
aspects of their duties, appearance and behaviour. In this corpus of
literature the question of women's speech has occupied a not
insignificant place.

Although advice for women on speaking is not a recent invention, both
its content and the forms in which it circulates have altered over time.
Today's version of Eliza Doolittle is defined primarily by her gender
rather than her class. It is not her accent but her entire linguistic persona
that needs remodelling, and all kinds of verbal hygiene practices have
sprung up to assist her in this task. If she is especially privileged or
publicly visible she may seek the advice of an image consultant; otherwise she may take a course, or join a group, or sample one of the many
advice books on the market. For women of slender means, similar advice
is offered in women's magazines and on daytime television.

In the past few years practices of this kind have become increasingly noticeable. Towards the end of the 1980s, students taking my courses on language and gender started bringing in more and more material from women's magazines: articles focusing on the alleged problems of women's speech and male–female communication, articles touching on these problems in passing, little tips on verbal self-presentation from various experts, and so on. At the same time, I and other professional women I knew were being deluged with fliers and publicity material advertising packs, videos, training courses, seminars and workshops that promised to make us more powerful speakers and more effective communicators.

My attention was thus drawn to a literature and a set of activities whose existence I had hitherto been only dimly aware of. Partly I had overlooked the phenomenon because it was not always presented as being about language: it often cropped up under more general headings such as 'leadership' or 'management' or 'interpersonal skills'. But when I looked more closely, I had no doubt I was dealing with a species of verbal hygiene. Indeed many of its preoccupations were eerily familiar to me, because they echoed the scholarly literature of my own specialist field, language and gender studies. In 1990 this connection was made explicit when the sociolinguist Deborah Tannen published one of the most successful advice books of recent years (and possibly the bestselling linguistics text of all time), *You Just Don't Understand* (1990) – a book about problems of male–female communication.

The convergence of linguistic scholarship and advice literature is an interesting (if in some ways alarming) phenomenon. As I have emphasized throughout this book, linguistics insists on the absolute distinction between describing and prescribing. Linguists have written popular books in the past, but their message has most commonly been to 'leave your language alone'. True, feminist linguistics – and it is fair to say that most language and gender researchers would identify themselves as feminists – is more equivocal: as with all committed scholarship, Marx's observation that 'the point is to change it' applies. Still, the rapid transformation of feminist research findings about women's speech into prescriptive advice on how women *should* speak sits uneasily with the original, critical aims of feminist linguistics. I therefore decided to investigate this development further, in an effort to understand why it was occurring and what it meant.

Advice aimed at women speakers is not only a particularly visible and topical example of contemporary verbal hygiene, it is also an excellent case study in which to pursue the theoretical argument about identity which I discussed in Chapter 1: the idea that social identities are not merely 'marked' or 'reflected' in verbal and other behaviour; they are performed through the repetition of particular acts, which in turn are subject to normative regulation. Nothing could more aptly illustrate this notion of performance and how it might be applied to linguistic phenomena than the self-help activities described in this chapter. In advice literature of all kinds, we see the norms for what counts as acceptable or unacceptable performance spelled out with especial clarity. And in practices of self-improvement we see people actually being taught how to perform particular identities by consciously replacing their established ways of acting with new and allegedly more desirable ones.

In this case, the identities being performed are (feminine) gender identities. This again makes the example an instructive one, for in contemporary western societies gender remains highly salient but at the same time it is contested and extremely unstable. 'Being a woman' still means a great deal, but the way gender is enacted on the surface through conventions of dress, bodily demeanour and social interaction has altered dramatically over the past twenty years. Such rapid and visible change tends to emphasize the constructed and self-conscious nature of femininity as a performance. Today, advice for women must grapple with the existence of conflicting norms and the possibility of multiple feminine identities.

Contemporary advice on women's speech is at a point of transition between an older type of verbal hygiene that did not have to address conflicts around gender openly, and a new type that is obliged to do so, if only because much of the demand for it is spurred by women's own perceptions of femininity as an uncertain territory which they need expert help to negotiate. This chapter examines the interaction of old and new ideas about language and gender, and focuses on the contradictory quality of current advice about women's speech as a symptom of the contradictions surrounding gender identity itself.

CLEANED UP WOMEN: VERBAL HYGIENE AND FEMININITY

A full history of verbal hygiene for women would be a lengthy and fascinating document, although it is far beyond my scope here. There is much historical and cross-cultural evidence to suggest that the phenomenon is a pervasive one: the norms that regulate gender relations and feminine conduct for any group of people will typically include rules for speaking as well as for the more obvious things such as work, kinship, reproduction, appearance, dress and sexual behaviour.[2] It is important to be aware, however, that the ideal woman speaker has not been defined in exactly the same way in every society or in every age – a point to which we must return below.

It is also important to bear in mind that gender always interacts with other social divisions like ethnicity and class. Though verbal hygienists in modern times have frequently addressed women as if they formed a single constituency (whereas men have more often been addressed according to class or occupation), much advice addressed to 'women' covertly assumes a particular (white and middle-class) model of femininity as the norm. Conversely, many kinds of verbal hygiene that seem to be about something other than gender – social class, most commonly – turn out on inspection to have a hidden gender dimension.

For example, the kind of verbal hygiene Henry Higgins practised on Eliza Doolittle had, and to some extent still has, a gender bias. From Higgins's time to the present day, women have been primary targets for such class-related verbal hygiene practices as speech training and elocution. In Northern Ireland, for example, where speech training continues to feature in the school curriculum, it is still thought more important for girls than for boys to moderate their stigmatized local accents.[3] This is an ingrained prejudice: the coarse accents of flower girls seem always to have struck commentators as more distressing than those of barrow boys.

This recurring emphasis on the importance of 'ladylike' speech manifests not only class prejudice but also a more specifically sexist logic that puts women in a curious double-bind. Tinkering with your speech through such practices as elocution is seen as a 'feminine' activity precisely because it is superficial, merely cosmetic. Yet like other cosmetic practices it is often expected of women and made normative for them.

One consequence of this is that the linguistic norms saying women should 'mind their language' apply to some degree across the social spectrum – 'correctness' is associated with femininity as well as with high social status.[4] It has frequently been pointed out, for instance, that the three most recent British Conservative prime ministers have all had lower middle-class origins, and all have made some accommodation to the speech ways of the traditional ruling class; but the most marked accommodation has been made by Margaret Thatcher.

Mrs Thatcher's case makes clear, though, that there are additional pressures on women's speech that have less to do with the linguistic markers of class and more to do with those of gender *per se*. Thatcher's most celebrated transformation, enacted with the help of those modern analogues of Henry Higgins, image consultants, was to change not her accent (she had done that already) but her overall vocal delivery, making it lower in pitch, less 'swoopy' in range and slower in rate. This collection of deliberate modifications can best be understood as a response to the perceived disadvantages suffered by the unreconstructed female speaker, who is stigmatized as 'shrill' (high pitch), 'emotional' (broad intonational range) and 'lacking in authority'.

Any number of disparaging comments on women's speech in general and Mrs Thatcher's in particular could be quoted in support of this interpretation. Thatcher's biographers, for example, quote the opinion of Gordon Reece, a television producer who advised the Prime Minister on various aspects of her image, including her speech: according to Mr

Reece, 'the selling of Margaret Thatcher had been put back two years by the mass broadcasting of Prime Minister's Question Time as she had to be at her shrillest to be heard over the din' (Wapshott and Brock 1983: 169–70). It was to deal with this 'shrillness' problem that another of Mrs Thatcher's advisers, the playwright Ronald Millar, suggested she adopt the 'steady' delivery (i.e. constant in its rate, pitch and intensity – in lay terms, monotonous) that became her trademark: it would 'eventually drive through, not over or under, the noise' (Wapshott and Brock 1983: 170). That many people found this as irritating as the original 'shrillness' illustrates the double-bind in which women public speakers are caught.

Margaret Thatcher is among the best-known examples of women obliged to transform themselves to meet new and contradictory linguistic demands on their sex. Although few women would go to the lengths Mrs Thatcher did to modify their speech, many face a dilemma not dissimilar to hers. Since *Pygmalion* was written, the status of women has altered. Love and marriage are no longer the only imaginable happy endings for a woman's story, and middle-class women in particular are likely to aspire to career success and personal autonomy as well as better sexual and domestic relationships. As the case of Margaret Thatcher underlines, though, this social change has not dried up the flow of advice. On the contrary, advice aimed at women has expanded and diversified along with the aspirations of its audience. The relationship that women have not just to verbal hygiene advice but to advice in general is an important consideration here, and will bear further comment.

Advice: a genre with a gender?

Even a cursory glance at the bestseller lists confirms that advice literature – also known in the trade as 'self-help', 'personal growth' and 'inspirational' – is a highly profitable sector of contemporary publishing, whose growth in recent years has been marked. There are many reasons for this proliferation of advice, not all of which are directly related to changes in women's social position. It is significant, for example, that there has been a proliferation of media in which to disseminate advice. Although the tradition of advice to women is an old one, late twentieth-century women are faced with a continual barrage of advice, contained in mass-market paperbacks, women's magazines, television talk shows and radio phone-ins.

It may also be significant that urban industrial society has become more mobile and more fragmented since the nineteenth century. Arguably, this creates social insecurity and a need for new sources of guidance on behaviour. Separated from their traditional advisers in the family and community, perhaps facing problems unknown to their parents, both women and men seek out alternative authorities.

That said, women continue to represent an important market for advice literature and, more important still, it can be argued they have a special relationship to it. The message of self-improvement may speak to general modern insecurities, but it also resonates with more traditional feminine anxieties.

Consider, for example, the perennially popular 'makeover' feature in women's magazines. The seductiveness of this formula, in which an ordinary reader is transformed by professional attention to her clothes, hair and make-up, lies in its ability to play both on our desire ('I could look that good') and our guilt ('why don't I look that good?'). It goes to the heart of a powerful fantasy for women in consumerist cultures, namely that such surface alterations as losing weight or cutting your hair will somehow transform your whole life and personality.

This fantasy – perfectly encapsulated in the women's magazine cliché of the 'new you' – is one most men do not seem to share. Men do practise forms of self improvement, but for them it is less a way of life.[5] They may be dissatisfied with aspects of themselves, but they are less subject to that constant surveillance by self and others that fuels women's quest to be all-around perfect. And if the word 'surveillance' most readily evokes the purely physical aspects of femininity, it should be noted that this is only part of the self-improvement story. The same magazines that offer us the 'makeover' also offer articles on how to be a better wife, mother, lover, daughter, friend and employee. The linguistic advice we are concerned with here is just another variation on the same theme.

Verbal hygiene for women: traditional advice

Advice to women on how they should speak is currently enjoying something of a boom. As I have already observed several times, however, it is not a new phenomenon. Its current forms mark the intersection of two different traditions: on one hand the modern self-help movement which is historically an offshoot of American pragmatism, and on the other a much older tradition of 'conduct literature' which can be traced back to medieval Europe. In principle, neither of these traditions set out to address women exclusively, but in practice both acquired over time a strong focus on feminine behaviour.

Although this chapter is primarily concerned with the contemporary forms of self-help, it is also of interest to examine the older tradition of conduct literature, which is part of self-help's inheritance. In their introduction to a fascinating collection of essays on conduct literature, *The Ideology of Conduct*,[6] Nancy Armstrong and Leonard Tennenhouse (1987: 5) explain that from the middle ages onwards there existed a genre of writing whose aim was 'to refine a woman's judgement, taste, demeanor, speech and dress'. Among the forms this kind of writing took between the fifteenth and twentieth centuries, Armstrong and

Tennenhouse list devotional manuals for daughters of the aristocracy, courtesy books for would-be ladies-in-waiting at the royal courts, politeness texts for women of the gentry and mercantile class, domestic economies for women managing households, pamphlets on marriage and domestic life, and texts on etiquette, beauty and 'glamour'. All these subgenres included material about appropriate feminine speech.

According to another contributor to *The Ideology of Conduct*, Ann Rosalind Jones, prescriptions about women's behaviour, including their verbal behaviour, played a crucial part in the ideological struggle that took place in early modern Europe between the aristocracy and the bourgeoisie. Jones argues that the stereotypical norms of linguistic femininity with which we are familiar today (such as silence, deference and unassertiveness) are not as ancient or as unchanging as has sometimes been implied, but are specifically modern and bourgeois in origin.

The great change that took place, Jones explains, was that 'the court lady was required to speak; the bourgeois wife was enjoined to silence' (1987: 40). A lady-in-waiting at a European royal court was expected to engage in witty, public talk, often in mixed company and often on the sexually-charged subject of love. Well-known texts on courtly conduct, such as Castiglione's *Book of the Courtier* and Guazza's *Civil Conversation*, make clear that female speech and wit were valued by the aristocratic elite, but they also make clear that there was a double standard: court ladies had to take special precautions to protect their sexual reputations, for too frank a wit might be taken as a sign of loose morals. In time, the 'immodesty' of the witty court lady became a theme in an anti-aristocratic discourse that held up bourgeois morals as superior to aristocratic ones, and bourgeois women as superior models of femininity.

One important marker of her superior femininity was the bourgeois woman's *silence*, contrasting with, on one hand, the promiscuous talk of the court lady, and on the other, the free speech of the bourgeois man. This is illustrated with particular clarity in a 1614 text on marriage and domestic life by John Dod and Robert Cleaver, called 'A Godly Forme of Householde Gouernment', which laid out the respective duties of a husband and a wife in two columns:

Husband	*Wife*
Deal with many men	Talk with few
Be 'entertaining'	Be solitary and withdrawn
Be skillfull in talk	Boast of silence

(Quoted in Armstrong and Tennenhouse 1987: 8)

The advice in the 'Husband' column, addressed here to bourgeois men, is parallel to the advice court writers gave to ladies-in-waiting, who were expected to be as 'entertaining' and 'skillful in talk' as male courtiers. But middle-class and puritan texts like Dod and Cleaver's equated proper femininity with silence, and banished women's legitimate speech to the sphere of the private household, where women were also urged to show deference in speaking to their menfolk.

Within a hundred years or so, this silent and domesticated woman became the dominant ideal of linguistic femininity for society as a whole. Even now it is proving difficult to shake off the legacy of a tradition in which, as Armstrong and Tennenhouse observe,

> Conduct books for women, though written by people of different regions, sects, factions and genders, rather singlemindedly represented the social world as one divided into public and private, economic and domestic, labor and leisure, according to a principle of gender that placed the household and sexual relations under female authority.
>
> (1987: 12)

The effects of the historic shift in attitudes to women's speech can be discerned clearly in later verbal hygiene advice. In the year of the American bicentennial, 1976, Connie Eble published a study of nineteenth-century American conduct books (Eble 1976). Around the same time, Cheris Kramarae performed a similar analysis of later etiquette books (cited in Kramarae 1981). They found the themes of verbal hygiene for women during this period (from about the eighteenth century to the 1950s) consistent with the bourgeois ideal of Dod and Cleaver.

To begin with, the private domestic sphere was marked as the only appropriate domain for women speakers. Public speaking was ill-advised and unfeminine, and women were in any case incompetent at it. (In a separate investigation of early broadcasting practice, Kramarae (1988) found the equation of women with domesticity carried over into the ambiguous public/private sphere of radio talk. According to early BBC announcers' handbooks, women lacked the authority for a convincing news broadcast, but might have just the right tone for an item on domestic appliances. On BBC television this prejudice against women presenting news persisted into the 1970s.)

On the other hand, women conversing in private were routinely warned to shun domestic topics along with 'gossip' and trivia. Although competent hostesses would have a supply of innocuous remarks for breaking the ice at parties, these should be tailored to the concerns of their guests – always imagined as men – and not to their own presumed interests as housewives and mothers. Women were urged to 'draw out' their interlocutors by asking questions; they were advised to listen rather than speak whenever possible, and to leave erudition and wit to their husbands. One of the most popular American etiquette books, Emily Post's *Etiquette: The Blue Book of Social Usage*, which sold almost a million copies between its publication in 1922 and the end of the Second World War, sums up the prevailing idea: 'The cleverest woman is she who, in talking to a man, makes *him* seem clever.' Among Post's specific suggestions for accomplishing this feat of 'cleverness' is, ironically, the following (Post 1922: 51, emphasis added):

> Another helpful thing, if you are a woman talking to a man, is *to ask advice.* 'We want to motor through the South. Do you know about the roads?' Or, 'I'm thinking of buying a radio. Which make do you think is best?' In fact, it is sage to ask his opinion on almost anything.

The ideal female conversationalist who emerges from the pages of advice books is obviously a stereotype. It is important to bear in mind that we cannot know whether women actually followed the advice they were given: conduct literature offers us only an indication of the norms that were in circulation at a particular time, and its endless repetition of particular norms (e.g. silence) may even suggest that many real women stubbornly refused to comply (just as old elocution manuals telling people how not to speak can be used as indirect evidence of how they actually did speak).

Interestingly, though, it seems that the shade of Emily Post's ideal woman lingers on; even now she is still a familiar enough figure to be invoked by contemporary writers celebrating 'how far we've come'. British *Cosmopolitan*, for example, marked its twentieth anniversary in March 1992 with an article on just this theme, written by a man. It opens as follows:

> It used to be so simple. Men paid, drove and made the first move. Women dressed up, pretended they liked the restaurant, got the bubbles up their nose and said 'Really – how interesting!' a lot. . . . Dinner was never spoilt by women saying, as you hit the foyer, 'well damn me, but that was the worst bit of cinematography I've seen in a long time'. Women didn't say that. Women said, 'What did you think of the film?'
>
> (Bywater 1992)

Two things are striking here. One is the use the writer makes specifically of *language* to symbolize women's past oppression and present liberation. We are expected to read off female subordination from the use of questions soliciting a man's opinion ('What did you think of the film?') and hearer-support tokens ('Really – how interesting!'). Conversely, we are expected to interpret features like swearing ('damn me') and the forceful expression of a woman's own opinions ('the worst bit of cinematography I've seen in a long time') as connoting a new feminist confidence.

The other striking thing is the location of the shift from oppression to liberation in historical time. Eble and Kramarae, writing in the 1970s, presented the subordinate and deferential woman speaker as a figure from the unenlightened past – anything from the 1700s to the 1950s. The *Cosmopolitan* article, written to celebrate the magazine's twentieth anniversary in 1992, presents this same woman as belonging to the 1970s. If we juxtapose these two accounts, and add to them more recent empirical findings which show women still using high levels of question forms and support tokens (e.g. Fishman 1983; Coates 1989), we may begin to wonder if the alleged shift from deference to assertiveness ever took place at all.

Caution is certainly needed when we interpret material of this kind. Once again, even recent advice literature and popular texts like the *Cosmopolitan* article are not a reliable guide to trends in people's actual behaviour: they are a better indicator of changing norms and attitudes (how these relate to people's behaviour is a complex question). Bearing this caveat in mind, the *Cosmopolitan* piece does seem to point to a shift in attitudes about feminine speech. It presents the stereotypically un-assertive woman of previous advice literature not as a role model but as a problem, even a joke; furthermore, it suggests that this attitude is no longer confined to a feminist vanguard, as it was in the 1970s, but has entered the mainstream, where it is assumed to be part of *Cosmopolitan* readers' mental furniture. The question then arises: how and why were the old norms supplanted by new ones? What exactly are the new norms, and in what verbal hygiene practices are they embodied?

Feminism and verbal hygiene: the case of 'assertiveness'

To answer these questions we must go back to the 1970s and to the distinctive political practices of Anglo-American feminism. Even without benefit of advice from experts and scholars, many feminists had reached the conclusion that their socially conditioned speech habits might be a problem. Women's subordinate status seemed to be confirmed each time they opened their mouths, with consequences both symbolic (the display of deference) and practical (the inability to get what you wanted out of verbal exchanges). The work of early feminist linguistic scholars such as Robin Lakoff, whose *Language and Woman's Place* (1975) was widely read, especially in the US, helped to popularize the idea that women were suffering from oppressive expectations about 'feminine' or 'ladylike' speech. Another source of ideas that influenced feminists in the 1970s was popular psychology. Many women chose to address their perceived linguistic problems by participating in a verbal hygiene practice developed by psychologists and known as 'assertiveness training', or in its early forms 'assertive training'.

While assertiveness may seem to be a mental attitude rather than a linguistic practice, assertiveness training (AT) focuses on particular strategies for communicating verbally: its ideal is, to quote a statement of purpose made by one leading British organization, 'clear, honest and direct communication'. Trainees practise, for example, making 'I' statements (e.g. 'I feel unhappy when I have to do all the housework' rather than 'you never do any housework'); putting speech-acts such as complaining, refusing and requesting in a direct form; and repeating a point until it is heard (the so-called 'cracked record' technique).

AT did not originate as a feminist practice or one specifically for women. Richard Rakos, author of a recent survey of the field, traces its origins as far back as 1949 (Rakos 1991: 3). In the 1950s and 1960s it was used by psychotherapists in clinical practice, where its purpose, in the rather jargonistic language of one influential practitioner, was the 'deconditioning of unadaptive anxiety habits of response to people with whom the patient interacts' (Wolpe 1973: 80). As the reference to (de)conditioning suggests, AT is associated with behaviourist psychology, and specifically with social learning theory, which holds that dysfunctional behaviour is learned and can be replaced with functional behaviour, given appropriate encouragement and practice in the form of, for example, role-play exercises.

Feminists who think of it mainly in connection with the Women's Liberation Movement of the 1970s might well be surprised to discover the range of 'unadaptive' and antisocial behaviours AT has been used to treat clinically. These include not only anxiety, depression and the lack of social skills associated with psychotic illnesses such as schizophrenia, but also substance abuse, sexual 'deviations' like exhibitionism, and even violence against women, which from a clinical standpoint may be seen as stemming from a man's inability to express his anger or his sexual desires 'appropriately'.

The reasons why AT has been such an all-purpose therapy are to a large extent ideological. Rakos suggests that although it has been diffused to many parts of the world, AT is quintessentially American in character, not only in the emphasis it places on the rational and pragmatic (altering people's dysfunctional behaviour rather than looking for its deeper causes as psychoanalysis would do) but more particularly because it represents 'America's enduring allegiance to individual freedom' (Rakos 1991: 13). Thus AT's status as a panacea reflects a sort of secular morality, based on a model in which social competence is defined and happiness maximized by striking a balance between asserting your own rights as a free individual and respecting the rights of other free individuals.

Within this model, assertive behaviour is idealized as a 'golden mean': it is the mid-point on a continuum that stretches from passive behaviour (abdicating your own rights) to aggressive behaviour (disregarding the rights of others). AT is therefore indicated for both passive and aggressive patients. Obviously it is a highly normative practice, explicitly based on, and intended to bring its recipients into conformity with, what are described by practitioners as 'mainstream societal values' – which really means, as some commentators now acknowledge, the highly individualistic and goal-oriented value system of white male middle-class middle America.[7]

On the question of gender bias, Richard Rakos remarks that 'the AT movement was prompted by behavioral definitions of social competence whose criteria were derived from male perspectives' (1991: 191). AT might therefore seem an unlikely paradigm for feminists to have adopted, and latterly, feminist psychologists have been prominent among those professionals who have expressed dissatisfaction with it. But in the early stages of any liberation movement that emerges within a basically democratic society, the appeal to every individual's rights is a powerful one, precisely because the mainstream culture's general enthusiasm for rights makes it difficult to dismiss the claims of individuals from excluded groups that they should have rights too. American feminism – or at least, important strands within it – followed the black civil rights movement in deploying this argument. Although there were other reasons for its subsequent popularity, it was in this context that AT became attractive to many feminists.

AT was taken up for explicitly feminist purposes in America around the mid-1970s. It was noted that female socialization tended to discourage such assertive traits as directness, willingness to challenge others and to express your own needs and feelings, while on the other hand it encouraged women to resort to unassertive, indirect and manipulative strategies. Thus many women, though socially competent by prevailing cultural standards, might benefit from modifying their habitual behaviour through AT. And while this kind of AT for women retained many of the tenets and techniques elaborated by clinicians, its connection with an active political movement meant that the context for it was often more like a collectively organized feminist support group than a session between a therapist and a group of patients.

In March 1975, for example, the US feminist magazine *Ms* carried a feature on AT which began by relating the experiences of women involved in what they described as 'the first [course] of its kind in Seattle', sponsored by a women's organization and led by 'a young assistant professor':

> We are 10 women who find it difficult to say No or to express an opinion at all. Education, experience and feminism may make us *feel* equal. But learning how to speak up for ourselves and what we believe in is something else again. That is why we have signed up for a course in verbal self-assertion.
>
> (Withers 1975: 106)

The feature refers to the kinds of problems women have in speaking up for themselves: it mentions a woman whose husband interrupts her, a student unable to speak in class, a community worker who dreads public speaking and a secretary who is exploited at work but feels unable to refuse unreasonable requests. The piece also includes a glossary and sample dialogue illustrating assertive behaviour in situations like these. The author Jean Withers is described as having organized an 'Assertive

Rap Group' and edited a brochure on AT, available to *Ms* readers for US$1.50. The implication is that, armed with some basic information, women can set up AT groups for themselves; it is not necessary to be a qualified 'expert'. Classified advertisements in feminist publications of the period attest that women responded to the invitation to set up AT groups of their own, so that more 'professional' forms of AT coexisted with informal 'grassroots' (and strongly feminist) ones.

If the feminist practice of assertiveness looks a lot like a variant of self-help that should not surprise us, for post-1968 feminism has always had an important self-help element. This is not, however, an uncritical transfer into women's politics of the traditional link between femininity and self-improvement. Rather it is a consequence of the founding axiom, 'the personal is political'. The distinctive contribution of the Women's Liberation Movement is to have recognized, more explicitly than most other radical political movements, that social change must work at the level *both* of institutional structures *and* of individual consciousness. Feminist small group practices, most obviously consciousness-raising (CR) but also some forms of AT, placed personal experience in a wider political context and subjected the minutiae of women's behaviour and their feelings to the same critical scrutiny that was accorded to such institutions as the law.

'The personal is political' has many virtues, but it also has at least one disadvantage, the danger that it will simply collapse into its opposite, replacing collective politics with an individualized quest for 'personal growth'. Many activists would agree that this did happen to some extent as feminism became more mainstream. During the 1980s it became commonplace to hear feminists expressing anxiety about the waning of CR and the growth in feminist therapies and (in the US especially) 'twelve-step programs' modelled on Alcoholics Anonymous.

A shift of this kind occurs relatively easily, precisely because there is some continuity between the practices. For instance, therapy retains one of CR's goals (self-knowledge) while discarding the other (collective struggle), and introducing a hierarchy between therapist and client(s). The twelve-step programme, while it retains the group process of a feminist support group, imports a set of procedures from a non-feminist practice, procedures that impose both a structure and an ideology. The shift thus involves both an institutionalization and a depoliticization of the original feminist practice, turning grassroots self-help into top-down advice-giving.

Assertiveness training is a more complicated case, because AT always did have its roots in a therapeutic rather than a political movement, and its ideology of individualism was always problematic for the more radical US feminists (a point made by some of them even in the 1970s: see, for example, Henley 1978). The fact that it does not go beyond the most consensual of democratic values – the idea that people have rights – has probably been a major reason for AT's broad and long-lived appeal. As Richard Rakos drily remarks, though it rose to prominence in an era of radical counter-cultural movements, AT has turned out to be 'equally well suited for the societal shift toward conservative philosophies, centred on material gain and personal self-improvement, that was prompted by the social and political climate in the West in the 80s' (1991: 6).

Even the particular form of AT that was done by and for women with an overt feminist agenda has been mainstreamed, codified, professionalized and institutionalized. Cheris Kramarae notes that this tendency encountered more resistance in Britain than in the US. She reports finding few texts on assertiveness in British feminist bookshops as late as 1978, and notes that those she did find were American imports: she refers approvingly to British feminists' suspicion of 'apolitical' self-improvement literature (1981: 149). Yet even as Kramarae remarked on this, AT in Britain, like AT in the US, was rapidly becoming an institutional, as opposed to grassroots political, practice: this time not in clinical institutions but in education, training and commercial self-help publishing.

One could analyse institutionalization as a two-stage process. The first stage is *codification*, defining the aims and methods of AT in a written form to which potential trainers and trainees have access. Before codification there is scope for variation and fluidity in the activities people undertake under the heading of 'assertiveness', and in their understanding of what they are doing. But once AT is codified, once there are standard texts defining it and telling you how to do it, fluidity gives way to fixity, and the second stage, institutionalization proper, can occur. Codification turns AT into a tangible, well-defined and much more uniform 'product', a familiar quantity which organizations can 'buy'.

In the US, popular texts on assertiveness for women began to appear in the mid-1970s (see for example Bloom *et al.*'s *The New Assertive Woman*, first published in 1975). In Britain, the key moment of codification came rather later, in 1982, when Anne Dickson's *A Woman in Your Own Right* was first published (it has since been reprinted seventeen times). Dickson claims credit for introducing AT for women into Britain following her own discovery of it on a visit to the US in the 1970s, and her book remains extremely influential: many informants for this chapter reported that they used it in an AT course, or were recommended to read it in conjunction with one, or read it later and realized the course had been largely based on it.

There are striking differences between Dickson's book and early American texts like *The New Assertive Woman* which I think have less to do with the cultural distance across the Atlantic than with the political distance between the 1970s and the 1980s. Although the earlier text is open to criticism for its heavy reliance on psychologistic theories that most feminists have now repudiated (e.g. Matina Horner's 'fear of success' thesis), and more generally for its therapeutic approach to social and political issues, a reader nevertheless gets the feeling that the authors regard their brand of AT as an integral part of the Women's Liberation Movement, and that the claims they are making for it, while they may be naive or exaggerated, are intended to be explicitly political. For example: '*as an active force, assertive training goes beyond the process of consciousness-raising, by preparing women to act on what they recognize as problems*' (Bloom *et al.* 1975: 26, emphasis in original).

By contrast, the various reprints of *A Woman In Your Own Right* provide a clear demonstration of AT's increasing institutionalization and depoliticization. Right from the start, Dickson seems to vacillate between invoking feminist political aims and denying them, as when she gives the following rationale for addressing AT specifically to women (Dickson 1982: xvi):

> Given our prevailing culture, women are, with obvious exceptions, in less powerful positions than men. This can be made into an overtly political issue – but that is not the purpose of this book. It is designed to help individual women in their own particular setting to live more assertively and powerfully. It provides simple, effective tools to accomplish this, and in some small measure, potentially to change the overall status of women in our society.

These remarks draw on two contradictory ideas: on one hand, that there is some connection between showing individual women how to live more assertively and changing the overall status of women collectively ('the personal is political') and on the other hand that there is no such connection: women's generally subordinate status 'can be made into an overtly political issue', but it does not have to be, and moreover, 'that is not the purpose of this book' – rather its purpose is to provide 'tools' which by implication are politically neutral. In this curious passage Dickson apparently cannot decide whether to present herself as a dispassionate expert doing therapy, or a committed feminist doing politics. Or perhaps she is deliberately trying to be all things to all women.

In an afterword headed 'Five Years On' that seems to have been added in later editions, Dickson remarks approvingly on the growing institutionalization of her work in adult education and workplace training, and seems to repudiate her earlier suggestion that women have a particularly pressing need for AT. Men, she says, can benefit just as much, but unfortunately they are more resistant to this kind of training. Dickson specifically reassures her readers that AT is 'not just a feminist tool'; it seems then that she has resolved the question raised in her preface by further detaching the practice of 'assertiveness' from the politics of feminism.

One result of this process is that AT has moved decisively into the mainstream, and most women who encounter it for the first time today do so not under the auspices of an autonomous feminist group, but in the context of adult education (e.g. courses for women 'returners') or work-place training. The principles and techniques of AT may also be encountered in programmes of training that are not specifically addressed to women at all. Graddol and Swann (1989) follow Anne Dickson in remarking on the inclusion of AT in many management and 'leadership' courses, and we may also recall Norman Fairclough's (1992) point about the shift towards service industries where employees are required to interact with the public, which leads to a corresponding growth in workplace communication training, often including an AT component. Outside the workplace one could also point to programmes designed to combat social problems such as drug-taking and teenage sex, in which assertiveness is taught on the grounds that it enables people to resist peer pressure (well known examples of this include the US 'Sex Respect' and 'Just Say No' programmes).

In cases such as these, AT returns to its clinical roots even though it is being done outside the clinic, and it loses its political edge even though it retains (and sometimes deliberately trades on) the 'feminist' connotations it acquired at an earlier point in history. It is not seen as the solution to a particular political problem (women's socially constructed unassertive-ness) but as something from which almost everyone can benefit. Nor does it have to have feminist objectives. 'Saying no', for example, took on a particular meaning in feminist AT, reflecting a feminist analysis of women's socialization to meet other people's needs at the expense of their own; but in the 'Sex Respect' programme the message is a pro-family conservative one of abstinence for traditional moral reasons. In corporate programmes, saying no may be not just an assertion of the individual employee's right not to be exploited, but part of a lesson about maximizing efficiency by 'prioritizing' and 'delegating'.

The training, consultancy and publishing activities that make up the new AT for women do have some continuities with its feminist pre-decessors, just as feminist AT had continuities with earlier clinical theory and practice. Many of the same techniques are used, and the rhetoric of 'empowering women' remains. Nevertheless, the new institu-tional structures make a crucial difference to the overall meaning of the practice. The new AT is provided by expert professionals who are paid, either by employers or by trainees themselves. It is concerned less with collective empowerment than with individual career enhancement. And most importantly, the training aims are often determined by the sponsoring organization.

These aims are variable. At worst, employers may sponsor AT for women workers as an easy way of being seen to do something about equal opportunities (cheaper than a nursery, less provocative than affirmative action on hiring and promotion). Only a little less cyni-cally, AT may be provided in the hope of making staff happier and therefore more productive. For example, I know of a local health authority which brought in AT experts on the grounds that learning more assertive behaviour would reduce levels of stress among (mainly female) health workers. Where AT is provided for all staff, men as well as women, it is often because the communicational norms that define 'assertiveness', such as being clear, honest, direct, firm but not aggressive, etc., are also those which are thought to serve the goals of the organization: harmony, efficiency, productivity, and by implication therefore profitability.

If these motivations underlying many current AT programmes are problematic, it is not necessarily because people receive no benefit from the training: there often is a pay-off for the worker as well as the organization. Even where they felt patronized, or where the techniques they learned struck them as mechanical and unhelpful, most of my informants told me they (or their trainees, if they were trainers) benefited from the opportunity to talk to other women about shared concerns. Some trainers I spoke to also reported subverting the official agenda of an AT course by turning it into an occasion for discussions about institutional sexism or union rights.

In practice, therefore, institutionalized AT is far from uniform in its effects. The problem with it, though, is the underlying paternalism: how empowering can it be to be made more assertive 'for your own good'? And anyway, it is not only for trainees' own good but for the perceived good of their organizations that there is so much AT on offer nowadays; and the interests of such organizations are frequently in conflict with more radical political interests. The institutionalizing of AT means that radical ideologies of gender are increasingly being co-opted or made marginal in the process of redefining what counts as desirable speech for women.

WHY CAN'T A WOMAN BE MORE LIKE A MAN?

In *My Fair Lady*, the musical version of Shaw's *Pygmalion*, Professor Higgins at one point muses: 'why can't a woman be more like a man?' The authors of traditional advice on women's speech were not detained by this question, since they took it as axiomatic that women couldn't, shouldn't and didn't want to be like men. But present-day advice literature exists within a context where traditional definitions of gender have been called into question. It is therefore concerned – indeed obsessed – with the problem of gender difference: how much and what kind of differentiation is desirable?

As we shall see, the advice pundits have produced two completely different answers to this question. One is mainly associated with career-oriented advice, the other mainly with relationship-oriented advice. Since most women in the target (middle-class) audience have both careers and relationships, the result is likely to be a degree of incoherence. We may pursue the point by examining each advice genre in turn.

Careers advice for women: 'talk like a man'

In corporate versions of AT, and the literature associated with them (such as training manuals and texts on 'leadership skills'), we may discern a shift in the norms that define the ideal female speaker, not only away from traditional advice but also from classical notions of 'assertiveness'. Feminist AT rejected the old stereotypes of acceptable femininity, but it retained a critique of the opposite 'masculine' values – hierarchy, competition, aggressiveness, toughness and impersonality, for instance. Deep in the heart of corporate capitalism, the new verbal hygiene takes a more equivocal view.

Career-oriented advice on women's speech is the bastard offspring of feminist 'assertiveness' and corporate 'leadership'. It is dedicated to the proposition that women should be more like men in certain ways. If they wish to succeed, they should take their cue from the successful men whose values and behaviour command respect in the workplace.

This is by no means an obvious proposition: it carries the risk of trapping women in the familiar double-bind. Insufficiently 'feminine' women may be labelled deviant, and powerful women are almost by definition threatening. On the other hand, a display of femininity can be used as a justification for not taking women seriously. The problem for ambitious women – and for the advice literature addressed to them – is how to resolve this real contradiction.

In many texts, the (rather unconvincing) solution is to associate preferred linguistic strategies not with a gender (men) but with a domain or sphere of activity (business). Certain values and strategies are 'appropriate' in this sphere, and it is a merely contingent historical fact that those values and strategies are also considered 'masculine'. Men are 'better' speakers in the public sphere of industry, politics, the professions and education simply because they have had such a long head start. Now that women have entered the race, they must accept the need to compete on terms historically established by men. They can minimize their handicap by adopting the verbal equivalent of power-dressing.

What is the linguistic analogue of the corporate woman's uniform, as worn by – among others – Margaret Thatcher? An explicit and comprehensive answer may be found in an American training manual entitled *Leadership Skills for Women: Achieving Impact as a Manager* (Manning and Haddock 1989). This text repeatedly urges women to emulate the behaviour of male colleagues, even when it is not clear that behaviour has any intrinsic virtue. For example: 'Men typically use less body language than women. Watch their body language to see how they do it' (p. 7).

The claim that men 'use less body language' is a strange and dubious one in any case. But what is striking (and typical) is the absence of comment on why 'less' would in principle be preferable to 'more' body language. As usual, the verbal hygienist's mantra that such-and-such a usage is 'appropriate' or 'conventional' is designed to prevent anyone asking why things have to be done like this and not like that.

There is a reason, of course, and again the rhetoric of 'appropriateness' is used to obscure it. Using 'less' body language is preferable to using 'more' because masculine behaviours are automatically preferred to feminine ones. What is 'wrong' with women's body language is that it marks them out as being women. Were this to be acknowledged explicitly, however, the result would be to undermine the careful equation of appropriateness with domain rather than gender, and to draw attention to a glaring fault in the self-improvement project. Women are still women whatever modifications they make to their verbal and non-verbal behaviour. If the secret of men's success is not their more appropriate behaviour but simply their gender, advice to women to 'talk like a man' is ultimately self-defeating. It is therefore important for the advice writer not to broach the subject of power and prejudice.

Accordingly, when the authors of *Leadership Skills for Women* are not exhorting readers to act like men, they are blaming them for not standing up to men.

> Speak directly to men and stand firm when you are interrupted. Statistics show that women allow themselves to be interrupted up to 50 per cent more often than men. Don't contribute to those statistics!
>
> (p. 15)

Once again, the authors give no explanation of why 'speaking directly' is preferred to the alternatives. On the other hand, they do provide an account of why women get interrupted: women 'allow themselves to be interrupted'. Such an interpretation would astonish the researchers on whose findings it is based (e.g. Zimmerman and West 1975; West 1984; Woods 1989). But within the logic of self-help it is virtually unavoidable. Self-help rests on the axiom that we are each responsible for our own destiny: we can change ourselves, but not other people. Manning and Haddock's approach to interruptions is an excellent illustration of the problems such an axiom raises in relation to gender inequalities.

The injunction to 'speak directly' has become something of a touchstone in career-oriented advice to women. In February 1992, British *Options* magazine included, as number nine of the 'Ten Classic Career Mistakes All Women Make', the following observation on 'tentative language':

> How many times have you heard someone say things like 'I'm not really sure if I'm right, but perhaps . . . '. With that kind of talk, who is going to believe we are confident in what we are saying? . . . Too often we make statements as if they were questions, such as, 'we'll bring the deadline forward, OK?'

The general emphasis on directness has important antecedents in assertiveness training, but readers familiar with the scholarly literature on language and gender will have no difficulty recognizing a more specific source for this particular piece of advice, namely Robin Lakoff's *Language and Woman's Place* (1975). The examples given illustrate several of the features Lakoff claimed as typical of 'women's language' and characterized as 'weak', 'tentative' and 'lacking in authority': hedging (I'm not *really* sure . . .), the use of tags (*OK?*) and interrogative intonation on declaratives (making statements as if they were questions). Virtually all the career-oriented advice literature I have surveyed makes heavy unacknowledged use of Lakoff's work, constantly presenting readers with a laundry list of Things To Be Avoided that for anyone unacquainted with Lakoff must appear completely arbitrary. Lakoff's argument that women who use these features sound insecure and childish is also presented without acknowledgement or explanation. In February 1990, US *Cosmopolitan* went so far as to entitle a piece on the theme of women's language 'Why Not Talk Like a Grown-Up?'

That Lakoff is never actually cited suggests that her views, first aired in the early 1970s, have simply passed into the annals of received wisdom. This is galling, because both her anecdotal description of women's speech and her interpretation of it are disputed by most present-day researchers. Not all criticisms of Lakoff bear directly on the issues addressed in advice literature, but one at least is crucial: what does indirectness *mean*?

Advice writers often seem to work with a naive model of language that drastically underestimates what the average speaker is capable of doing with it. Attitudes to indirectness are a good case in point. A speaker who says, 'We'll bring the deadline forward, OK?' may not, in context, be heard as indirect at all. Alternatively, she may be using indirectness for a particular purpose: for instance, because although she is confident that what she says goes, she wants her subordinates to assent to her wishes. That way they are accountable if they fail to meet the new, earlier deadline.

Another, even more common reason for using indirect speech styles is to mark concern for another speaker's 'face' – in plain language, to be polite. The message of 'OK?' in the utterance under discussion might be less 'I am insecure and unconfident in what I say' than 'I know what I think, but since I respect you I am signalling the fact that I value your opinion too'.

It is an oft-repeated principle of AT that assertive behaviour is not the same as aggressive, rude or inconsiderate behaviour, but enthusiasts of assertiveness and directness show remarkably little understanding of the linguistic workings of politeness. In their pursuit of directness and clarity, therapists and advice writers often appear to be recommending a degree of rudeness that most speakers of English, regardless of gender, would never remotely approach, and which would probably backfire on them if they did.

For instance, in a section about what she calls 'padding', or in more technical linguistic terms 'hedging', Anne Dickson (1982: 23) criticizes utterances like 'I'm terribly sorry to trouble you, but I'd like you to change this for a clean cup'. She suggests a version without the padding: 'I'd like you to change this for a clean cup.' Actually, this stops short of eliminating all 'padding': to be consistent, Dickson ought to have recommended 'change this for a clean cup', but evidently she recognizes how blatantly rude and overbearing that would sound. For most speakers of English, however, even the slightly padded version is odd, for a very good reason. Asking someone to do something for you is what politeness theorists call a 'face-threatening act'. The speaker risks refusal and the addressee risks being imposed upon (in this case the utterance also implies the addressee is at fault for not providing a clean cup in the first place). To mitigate these threats, even if only by displaying aware-ness of their existence, it is usual to make requests indirectly, rather than baldly. A trivial request like 'pass the salt' does not need much mitigation, but one which makes significant demands (e.g. 'get this work done two days earlier than we agreed') or implies prior negligence by the addressee ('get me a clean cup') requires considerable 'padding' if it is not to be downright offensive.

The general point here is that speakers routinely exploit the fact that messages can be conveyed more or less directly to construct (not just reflect) different kinds of social relationships. Hearers are expected to understand the rules of this game.[8] Thus competent users of my variety of English, approached in the street by someone who asks, 'Have you got the time?' will reply 'half past three', not 'yes' or 'stop beating around the bush'!

If there is any 'scientific' basis for the fetish of directness in advice literature for women, I suspect it is a study by O'Barr and Atkins (1980) which investigated the credibility of courtroom testimony given in different styles. The researchers scripted two pieces of testimony, one 'powerful' (containing few of the indirectness features associated by Lakoff with 'women's language') and one 'powerless' (containing many such indirectness features). Informants judged the 'powerless' testimony less credible whether it was delivered by a woman or by a man. O'Barr and Atkins concluded that there was something intrinsically 'powerless' about certain verbal strategies. They noted that these strategies were associated with women speakers, but this was because women were more likely to occupy low-status positions: high-status women avoided the strategies, and low-status men used them.

In assessing this argument, though, it is crucial to take the context into account. The courtroom makes specific demands, and someone who hedges under cross-examination ('I'm not really sure if it was Tuesday

I saw him, but perhaps . . . ') can only be judged as uncertain of their facts. Since establishing facts is the purpose of a courtroom, this does undermine credibility. But in the context of, say, a marketing meeting, a similar degree of hedging may be interpreted very differently. Suppose someone says, 'That's great Mike, but I think perhaps it might be a good idea to do X.' This could convey reluctance to criticize a colleague's suggestion, and might therefore enhance rather than diminish the speaker's credibility as a team member. The direct utterance that is credible in court – 'Yes, it was Tuesday' – becomes boorish in a different context ('No, we'll do it this way').

Telling speakers to 'be direct' in every conceivable situation ignores the significance of the interpersonal as opposed to the informational function of language. In most face-to-face contexts the former is at least as important as the latter; not surprisingly, then, there is evidence that real speakers respond less than enthusiastically to the direct style of speech advice writers recommend.

In a review of the research literature on the evaluation of assertive behaviour (that is, experiments in which lay judges watch videotapes or read transcripts of people behaving in 'assertive' or 'unassertive' ways and then fill in questionnaires rating the people on such qualities as 'competence', 'aggression', 'likeability', and so forth), the psychologists Amy Gervasio and Mary Crawford (1989) conclude that 'assertive' speech is often judged rude and aggressive. They attribute this in part to the sociolinguistic bizarreness of strategies like endlessly repeating the same point, or baldly stating your own needs while eschewing any reference to the feelings of the addressee.

The other main finding of Gervasio and Crawford's review casts further doubt on the wisdom of advising women to 'talk like a man'. As I have pointed out already, such advice is predicated on the idea that particular speech styles are inherently powerful or powerless; Gervasio and Crawford's survey of relevant research however confirms that it makes a significant difference who is speaking. Negative reactions to assertive speech are consistently more marked where the speaker is a woman. Gervasio and Crawford suggest that assertive women arouse particular hostility because they defy conventional expectations about feminine verbal behaviour. 'Speaking directly' might therefore be a high-risk strategy for women.

The finding that assertive women provoke more negative reactions than assertive men illustrates once again the double-bind in which women are caught. On one hand, being assertive and direct carries an extra risk for women because it is seen as 'unfeminine' behaviour; on the other hand, would we therefore want to recommend that women should stick to acting out traditional stereotypes?

Recently, clinical practitioners of AT have begun to grapple with problems of the kind Gervasio and Crawford raise. Many clinicians now recommend so-called 'empathic assertion', which reduces the baldness and the exclusive 'I'-focus of standard assertion, and is to that extent less sociolinguistically bizarre. Rather more dubiously, the question of AT's differential appropriateness and/or degree of risk for particular social groups has been addressed by teaching assertiveness selectively, to suit varying cultural norms.

Commenting on this trend, Richard Rakos alludes to the problem of designing AT courses for women from cultures that prescribe extreme deference from wives to husbands, or young people from cultures where challenging parents and other elders is taboo. He cites a programme in which Puerto Rican women were encouraged to express their feelings and make more direct requests to their husbands, but discouraged from saying no to their husbands.[9] 'To be effective with Hispanic women', Rakos explains, 'AT programs must teach assertive strategies that are consistent with [the] relatively intransigent cultural norm [of "machismo"]' (1991: 82).

There is a glaring contradiction in this approach. The values on which AT is based are certainly ethnocentric, in the sense that they are not cultural universals; but this ethnocentrism cannot be eliminated without making the whole enterprise incoherent. Assertiveness by definition cannot be made consistent with a norm of unquestioning submission to the will of another person. Even if we can set aside the ethical dilemmas posed by the particular example (which, taken to its logical conclusion, would imply that Puerto Rican women should submit to rape out of respect for their cultural heritage), cultural relativism makes nonsense of AT's founding axiom that everyone has the same rights and obligations. If similar criteria had been applied to white American women in the 1970s, the AT-for-women industry would never have got off the ground, since it too was predicated on getting trainees to claim rights that were not routinely granted by the culture at the time, even to the economically and racially privileged.[10]

As muddled as most of it is, the current debate on the 'social validity' of AT does bring into focus the determining effects on interaction of the social arrangements and power structures within which people interact. This is as relevant for corporate women as it is for Puerto Rican women; one of the 'relatively intransigent cultural norms' that prevails in the corporate world as elsewhere is that women must be careful not to alienate men. In practice, this consideration tempers all advice to women: the overt message (be direct, be assertive, be more like your male colleagues) is only the beginning of a complex process whereby women try to negotiate conflicting norms and pressures. Within this contradictory framework it is possible to 'fail' either by not taking the experts' advice or by taking it too literally.

The entire edifice of career-oriented verbal hygiene is ultimately based on the kind of circular and sexist reasoning that will brand women inadequate whatever they do. The fetish of 'speaking directly' exemplifies this circularity: research findings suggesting that women use more indirect speech strategies than men[11] have been combined with the stereotype of women as less effective speakers in public contexts to yield the (illogical) conclusion that indirectness is itself a mark of ineffectual communication. This is the same kind of sexist thinking that informs Manning and Haddock's strictures on body language: it simply defines whatever men do as appropriate and whatever women do as problematic – a classic case of double standards.

Far from enhancing women's authority in the workplace, career advice may contribute to undermining it by harping on women's supposed linguistic deficiencies. If indirectness is not the universally dysfunctional strategy advice literature suggests, then at best, advice to avoid it is irrelevant; at worst, it may *create* a problem by priming both women and men to read women's use of indirectness as insecure, weak and tentative.

Of course, if you are in the business of marketing a cure, it pays to discover a disease. The new forms of training and the texts they have spawned are profit-driven: with their eyes fixed firmly on the bottom line, the enterprising purveyors of verbal hygiene for women have every reason to exaggerate both the scale of the 'problem' and the effectiveness of the solution they are selling.

The techniques used to market training programmes for professional women are illustrated in an eight-page 1992 brochure advertising the wares of SkillPath, Inc, a US training and consultancy firm. Tastefully designed in shades of pink, purple, peach and red (an interesting balance between femininity and power), the brochure describes a one-day seminar entitled 'Power-packed communication skills for women', and the cover-line urges readers to 'Get Ready for the most EMPOWERING day of your life!'. Inside, this positive message is balanced by an appeal to familiar anxieties, as we learn that 'unconscious credibility-robbing speech habits and mannerisms can all work against you': the more detailed description of the seminar's contents includes such headings as 'how to use "I language" to connote power, confidence and authority'; 'how to avoid the 14 common language mistakes that can sabotage your credibility', and 'how to eliminate power-robbing speech habits, words and gestures that say "I'm a lightweight!"'. For readers familiar with current career-oriented verbal hygiene for women it is not difficult to guess just which habits will be presented as 'power-robbing' and 'lightweight'.

The brochure gives no reason for its exclusive address to women (the course is for women only), but the thinking behind it is by now so familiar it hardly needs restating: women at work have particular problems with power, authority, credibility and confidence. Such a claim is not incompatible with feminism; but SkillPath, Inc is not a feminist organization; it is part of the self-improvement industry.

Training time will not be spent analysing the social roots of women's communication problems, nor indeed explaining why their speech habits should be treated as problems. The emphasis is on identifying 'bad' habits and replacing them with 'good' ones; 'empowerment' for women is synonymous with individual women getting ahead.

On this point, perhaps the most suggestive piece of information in the brochure is the cost of participating in a seminar: US$49. In the world of professional training seminars, US$49 is a rock-bottom price. It suggests that SkillPath, Inc has identified its target woman client as someone in a fairly junior position, earning a rather unimpressive salary. The testimonials it reproduces from satisfied participants confirm this: the job titles given are 'administrative assistant', 'management intern' (i.e. trainee) and 'sales consultant'. Of course, one might argue that the time to learn 'power-packed communication skills' is when you are still at the bottom of the ladder. Or perhaps SkillPath is on to a commercial winner with women-only courses precisely because so many women are concentrated at the bottom of the corporate heap, and know they are likely to remain there indefinitely unless they create their own ladder by way of self-improvement activities. Even then, one wonders how much faith women should place in 'power-packed communication skills' as a means to career advancement.

Career-oriented advice to women on their speech depends on a simple and negative stereotype of women as communicators lacking authority and credibility. The good news is that by adopting different strategies women can make themselves as promotable as their male colleagues. The linguistic quick-fix joins wardrobe management and courses on self-esteem as a miracle cure for professional women's problems; as firms like SkillPath, Inc can attest, it is an attractive and profitable idea.

Here, as elsewhere within the capitalist system, however, product diversification and consumer choice are the order of the day. As I noted earlier, success in the workplace has not replaced success in personal relationships as a cherished female ambition. Rather the two have been grafted together in the new fantasy of 'having it all'. And just as the market provides specialist advice for the ambitious corporate woman, so it offers specialist advice for her other, private and relationship-oriented self.

These two genres are in conflict with one another. The fundamental question is still Professor Higgins's: 'why can't a woman be more like a man?' But whereas the proponents of 'leadership' tell women they can and should be more like men, relationship advice is concerned to explain to women how and why they are destined to be different.

Relationship advice for women: 'it's different for girls'

The 'you and your relationship' genre of advice to women is primarily a textual genre, located in easily identifiable categories used by the publishing trade. It is also prominent in women's magazines, particularly those aimed at a middle-class readership. Where a magazine like *Cosmopolitan* typically carries relatively few and brief careers features, it devotes much more space to relationship features. There is in fact considerable overlap between the book and magazine sectors. One of the best ways to publicize a new book is to get an excerpt or spin-off feature into one (or several) of the women's glossy magazines, while to judge from their copy, the people who write relationship features for women's magazines are among the most avid consumers of self-help titles: even those that have long gone out of print are liberally quoted, with a recommendation to readers to seek them out in a library.

This, then, is the lucrative world of bestselling books with titles like *The Cinderella Complex* (Dowling 1981) and *Women Who Love Too Much* (Norwood 1985), written by women with prominently displayed academic credentials ('Dr Jane Smith'; 'Mary Brown Ph.D'). Both the snappy title and the doctoral degree are generic conventions, part of a formula that extends also to the style of presentation. This is quite different from a training manual such as *Leadership Skills for Women* (Manning 1990). Instead of barking orders at the hapless reader ('Don't contribute to those statistics!'), or puncturing her self-esteem with a single, searching question ('Does Your Voice Let You Down?' or 'Why Not Talk Like a Grown-up?'), relationship literature gently leads her on a journey of a thousand anecdotes ('Anne, 38, discovered her husband Derek had been having an affair . . . ') in which a source of misery and misunderstanding is identified, labelled, dissected and finally transcended.

The problems and parables that structure this genre are drawn from a familiar discursive territory where men and women have such difficulty communicating with each other that they might as well be living on different planets. (One recent advice book on cross-gender communication is actually entitled *Men Are From Mars, Women Are From Venus* (Gray 1992).) The landmarks are ancient clichés like 'My wife doesn't understand me'; 'Men!'; 'What *do* they find to talk about?'; 'What do women want?'. This idea of an unbridgeable communication gap between the sexes has been endlessly recycled, often in more or less misogynistic terms – Shaw's Henry Higgins remarked more than seventy years ago that 'Women upset everything. When you let them into your life, you find that the woman is driving at one thing and you're driving at another' (1972: 701) – but custom does not seem to stale its infinite variety. It has long been fertile ground for popular psychology, and it is now being dug over by exponents of a related discipline, popular linguistics.

Popular linguistics begins with a series of observations familiar to readers of popular psychology. Relationships most often become dysfunctional because of a 'breakdown in communication' between the partners. Whether or not a couple can 'talk things through' is a sign of the health of their marriage. But the distinctive and original role proposed for linguistics, with its detailed understanding of how inter- action works, is to explain *why* 'lack of communication' between the sexes is such a common problem. The explanation reveals that a large part of the problem is, in a sense, technical: whereas some communicational breakdowns are the proper concern of psychologists and counsellors, stemming as they do from deeply-rooted psychological conflicts, many more arise from quite superficial differences in the speech styles typically used by men and women.

The most spectacular success-story in the popular linguistics of gender is *You Just Don't Understand*, the work of the respected American socio- linguist Deborah Tannen (Tannen 1990).[12] This book, which spent over three years on the *New York Times* non-fiction bestseller list, draws on an approach to language and gender that has recently become influential in academic linguistics, superseding earlier work like that of Robin Lakoff – the so-called 'difference' or 'subcultural' approach.

Before I outline Tannen's work, it is important to understand that linguists who work in the 'difference' paradigm conceive of gendered speech styles in a way that diverges from earlier models. Whereas Lakoff and many of the researchers who followed her used the 'powerful/ powerless' contrast as their main organizing principle for talking about male and female styles, 'difference' researchers like Tannen work with an entirely different opposition, one that is most conveniently defined as 'competitive/co-operative'. Although these terms can be value-laden (many feminists who use them make no secret of their moral and political preference for co-operation), they do not have to be value- laden to the same degree as 'powerful/powerless'. (For example, one could in principle advocate a balance of competition and co-operation, but hardly a balance of power and powerlessness.) Thus the shift from power to (quasi-cultural) 'difference' is also a shift towards relativism. Advice based on the idea that women's speech embodies different values from men's will be unlike advice based on the idea that women's speech is 'powerless'.

According to the 'difference' approach, women and men find difficulty in communicating because they have different interactional goals and styles, learned early in life on the Planet Peer Group. Tannen argues that men talk to gain or maintain status (hence their liking for such competi- tive speech genres as boasting, ritual insults, joke-telling and exchanging sports statistics), whereas women talk to promote intimacy and connec- tion (hence they prefer gossip and try to minimize conflict). This differ- ence arises in the first place because the sexes are segregated in the formative years of childhood and adolescence: they choose to play, hang out with and form primary relationships with others of the same sex. Doing different things and having different values, boys' groups and girls' groups develop different strategies for talking.

In itself, proponents of the theory argue, this is no more problematic than the existence of differing speech norms among, say, African-, Jewish- and Japanese-Americans. We would not want to rank ethnic styles as 'better' or 'worse' than one another, and the same should go for gendered styles. What *is* problematic is most people's unawareness of the differences. If a Japanese-American marries a Jewish-American, each may be baffled by aspects of the other's behaviour, but at least this couple will be expecting issues of cultural difference to arise. When a man marries a woman – and this of course is the norm rather than the exception – he is far less prepared for the misunderstandings that plague their interaction. Instead of thinking 'What does my wife mean by X?' he just assumes she means what he would mean, and grows ever more puzzled and resentful at her peculiar, apparently insensitive responses. This is a recipe for marital disaster.

The solution proposed by Tannen is not to change people's speech habits – after all, like ethnic styles, male and female verbal strategies are 'equally valid' and part of people's identities – but to change their responses to the habits of the opposite sex. It is a question of understanding the differences and learning to be more tolerant of them. This takes the heat out of simple misunderstandings; if each sex becomes passively bilingual in the other's language it may even avert misunderstanding altogether.

The metaphor of bilingualism is echoed in the way Tannen's book has been received. Many reviewers have used the image of the phrase book: 'A fine Berlitz guide', says one of the testimonials on the back cover of the US paperback edition; or in the words of US *Cosmopolitan*, which ran a long excerpt, 'Here, the secrets of Mantalk – and how to decode it'. *Elle* magazine in March 1993 posed the question: 'Are men and women doomed to speak different languages?' and then immediately answered it: 'Experts say there's hope – and you don't even need Berlitz.' Tannen is the first and most important 'expert' that the article cites.

This sort of response underlines that we are in fact dealing with a work of popular advice literature – something Tannen herself has tended to deny. Not only does it conform to the generic conventions mentioned above, it is clearly being read as a practical guide to better male–female communication. Another prominently placed eulogy on the American paperback begins: 'People are telling Tannen the book is saving their marriages.'

I would be prepared to bet that these 'people' are actually women. If it is legitimate to judge books by their covers, then *You Just Don't Understand* is not only popular advice literature, it belongs to the 'you and your relationship' genre which is marketed specifically to women. (The UK rights were bought by the women's press Virago.) Tannen avoids addressing her audience as women, but her own thesis that relationships are of more concern to women than to men would predict a female readership.

There is no point pretending that the literature of 'you and your relationship' appeals equally to men.

But this places Tannen's message in a rather different light. Preaching mutual gender tolerance to an audience composed overwhelmingly of women means in essence telling women to adjust to male behaviour, to accept a *status quo* in which their own needs for intimacy and connection will continue to go unmet by male partners.[13] Interestingly enough, this point is made quite openly in an earlier book by two men, Steven Naifeh and Gregory White Smith, *Why Can't Men Open Up?*. Their chapter 'How to talk to a man: techniques for better communication' notes:

> In an ideal world it would be different, but in the world as it is today, it's not very likely that a man will go out on his own and learn the female code of expression. A woman's going to have to come to him.
>
> (Naifeh and Smith 1985: 115)

One of Tannen's own magazine articles, written for *McCall's* in 1991, is entitled 'How to talk so men will listen'. Possibly Tannen did not choose this title herself, but it does not misrepresent her piece.

Tannen obviously hopes that women who read her book will no longer feel oppressed by men's apparent crassness, manifested in such quirks as their obdurate refusal to ask for directions, their tendency to lecture when all you wanted was a word of reassurance, and so on. The lifting of oppression will however be achieved not by changing men's behaviour but by changing women's evaluation of it as crass ('a woman's going to have to come to him'). Once again we notice here the peculiar self-help ethos in which anyone can change the world by a private act of will.

Although this kinder, gentler form of self-help may avoid the worst excesses of victim-blaming to be found in the career-oriented advice genre, it is actually doing similar things in subtler ways. Tannen, after all, wants women to understand that their feelings about men's behaviour are often 'wrong'; that is, based on a mistaken interpretation of the behaviour. This sense of the word 'wrong' is arguably distinct from its other meaning, 'morally culpable', but there is an unavoidable slippage between them. If your feelings of irritation persist even after you have recognized they are based on misunderstanding, not only are you in error, you are also being intolerant: your intellectual failing is compounded by a moral one. Tannen does not, she says, believe in prescribing to her readers; but the step from diagnosis to prescription is a small one, and women readers with years of experience in the self-improvement game are quite capable of taking it alone.

Women's magazines are, as usual, there to help them. In recycling Tannen's arguments, many magazine features have explicitly recommended that women adjust their behaviour to men's expectations, and have given them checklists of handy hints on how to do it. *She* magazine explains, for example, that 'Men and women use language differently. It may be that your husband, partner or boss (if male) will react better if you use the traditionally male "I think" approach' (Sampson 1993: 89). This, incidentally, is puzzling advice from a linguistic point of view, since although 'I think' is here labelled masculine by contrast with 'I feel', both expressions actually exemplify hedging, the classic hallmark of the dreaded women's language.

Another example comes from *Glamour* magazine, which glosses Deborah Tannen's remarks on the directness/indirectness question in the following piece of advice: 'Make requests directly to male subordinates. Women tend to shy away from giving a blatant order, but men find the indirect approach manipulative and confusing.' *Glamour* here shows no signs of eschewing either prescription or loaded moral terminology (e.g. 'manipulative'). Clearly, the magazine does not understand Tannen's professional distaste for prescribing; what it does understand, much better than Tannen, is that when parties to a conflict are unequal it will be the less powerful party that does the adjusting.

This point might seem to be undermined by the focus on 'male subordinates'. I will leave aside the question of how many women workers have male subordinates: women's magazines exist in a social world that contains many elements of pure fantasy, and it is well known that their implied readers (addressed as managers and other professionals) are of a higher social status than their real ones (many of whom are probably clerks and secretaries). Yet it is significant that even within the fantasy of women bosses making requests to male subordinates, it is women who are advised to alter their customary behaviour. If the men are subordinate, why is it not incumbent on them to do things the way the boss prefers? The answer must be that in a certain important sense men cannot be subordinate to women. Individual status positions notwithstanding, 'masculine' behaviour remains the norm, not (as Manning and Haddock might claim) for such specialized domains as 'business', but for persons in authority in any domain.

It is also significant that *Glamour* puts Tannen's work into a 'careers' rather than a 'relationships' context. Career-oriented advice is more brutally realist: it has no truck with liberal wittering about styles being 'equally valid'. And perhaps there is some virtue in this resistance, for relationship-oriented advice exists in another kind of fantasy world, one from which ordinary everyday sexism has mysteriously vanished.

Deborah Tannen has been criticized by a number of reviewers (see especially Troemel-Ploetz 1991) for neglecting the issue of sexism. As her critics note, if men and women do have the differing communicational goals and styles she claims, this is hardly a random fact arising from arbitrary differences in children's peer groups. Rather it is a consequence of the sexual and sexist division of labour in which men are destined to inhabit the public sphere with its dominant values of status and competition, while women specialize in domestic nurturing, both in the family and in jobs that are seen as extensions of it (like childcare, teaching, nursing and social work). Children do not construct their peer group norms from nothing. The codes and social relations of gender are facts of life with which even very young children have first-hand acquaintance. The question for feminists is whether these codes can be changed.

Divisions of labour: evaluating 'difference'

In their book *The Ideology of Conduct*, Nancy Armstrong and Leonard Tennenhouse (1987: 12) make the point that bourgeois conduct literature in the early modern period was based on a division of the social world into 'public and private, economic and domestic, labor and leisure, according to a principle of gender that placed the household and sexual relations under female authority'. (The unstated corollary here is that other spheres were placed under male authority.) Exactly the same assumption about the division of labour between men and women pervades the new verbal hygiene for women: particularly marked in texts that adopt the 'difference' approach, it is also present in a more general sense in the way the genre is split between career and relationship advice.

In this 'separate spheres' model, women appear to be the losers both in men's traditional sphere of authority and, more unexpectedly, in their own. Career advice defines the public sphere of work as a masculine domain, and tells women who wish to enter that they must therefore adopt masculine norms to succeed: importing the values of the other sphere is one of the 'classic career mistakes all women make'. Relationship advice grants women authority over domestic life and (hetero)sexual relationships, but all women seem to be authorized to do within their allotted sphere is to ensure things run smoothly, without conflict and misunderstanding – which entails once again that they adjust to masculine norms. Heads you win, tails I lose.

What lies behind this Catch-22 is a structural asymmetry: the male and female spheres are not equal, the obligations they impose are not reciprocal and the kinds of authority men and women have in their respective spheres are not parallel. Ultimately it is men who have power (in public and private life) whereas women have only responsibility. But in a genre that is *itself* divided between public (career advice) and private (relationship advice), it is virtually impossible to address this asymmetry, or to discuss the connections between a group's position in one sphere and its position in the other (for example, the connections between women's domestic responsibilities, their economic dependence or lesser earning power, and the way men's wishes tend to prevail even in the homes women supposedly rule).

Deborah Tannen has been accused of anti-feminism, but it would be more accurate to say she represents a current in feminism that asks, essentially, 'why *should* a woman be more like a man?'. At times this line of argument can pose a genuinely radical challenge to conventional judgements of worth. (Why should a doctor be worth more than a nurse? Why is fashion trivial if football is important?) It insists that the problem is not what women do, but how society values it. Women should be able to be different from men without being unequal to them.

On the other hand it is not by accident that 'different but equal' has acquired such dubious connotations. A persistent difficulty with it is its tendency to essentialize, taking for granted that men and women just *are* different and forestalling any questions about the origins of difference in systemic social inequality. To say that only sexist prejudice prevents us valuing the skills of nurses as highly as those of doctors may be reasonable as far as it goes, but the question it fails to ask is why the two professions are so markedly gendered in the first place. The same point holds for the arrangements in children's peer groups: why – that is, to what purpose – are boys and girls not just different, but different in these particular ways?

Tannen gives us a reason (separation in the formative years), but she refuses to speculate on a purpose. Consequently her analysis is superficial: as Dean MacCannell and Juliet Flower MacCannell aptly remark (1987: 208), 'institutional separation and segregation of the sexes is not the cause of gender disorders, but only a part of the system, its maintenance equipment.' Tannen focuses on the maintenance equipment to the exclusion of the system it maintains.

This is why the analogy between gender differences and ethnic or national ones is so misleading; for whereas Japanese and American executives with their differing cultural norms have not been designed to exist in a system that prescribes a particular, complementary (but unequal) relationship between them, males and females in one society are specifically socialized for just such a system. Gender differences service a whole social, economic and moral order.[14] Feminism is not about celebrating the skills required of women by our present arrangements, but about changing those arrangements root and branch. Feminism must question sexual divisions of labour in every sphere of life.

Because it cannot or will not see gender relations in their totality, verbal hygiene based on the 'difference' model is a good deal less radical than its exponents imagine. It may question the value accorded to this activity and this kind of language over that, but the association of one set of activities with men and another with women remains unchallenged and indeed unexplained.

The same difficulty arises with what looks on the surface like an even more radical shift. Very recently, the 'feminine' speech style characterized by researchers as co-operative and dedicated to avoiding conflict has begun to be praised in some unexpected quarters, and even to be institutionalized in some forms of education and training. What is happening, at least in theory, is a shift in the culture of Anglo-American corporate capitalism away from traditional (aggressive, competitive and individualistic) interactional norms and towards a new management style stressing flexibility, teamwork and collaborative problem-solving, which is thought to be better suited to changing global economic conditions. Some companies attempting to promote the new values have begun to practise linguistic intervention aimed at 'feminizing' the interactional styles of *male* employees (Graddol and Swann 1989); while in women's magazines there has been a vogue for features celebrating 'female management styles' as an idea whose time has come.

The novelty here is not the idea that women are more 'sensitive' interactors, but the suggestion that men should start to emulate them. The growing acceptability of this proposal is dramatically demonstrated in a recent (1994) television advertising campaign for British Telecom: fronted by the actor Bob Hoskins under the general slogan 'It's good to talk', the campaign includes one advertisement suggesting that men should spend more time talking to friends and relatives on the phone. Brief vignettes contrast men's brusqueness with women's tender regard for the feelings of others ('it's just nicer, innit?', observes Hoskins, the (male) voice of authority). A number of media commentators have remarked on the shock of seeing men rather than women being patronized; but in truth, the BT campaign patronizes both sexes, for it depends on, and recycles, grossly stereotypical notions about 'masculine' and 'feminine' behaviour.

A debate on the value of different styles is also taking place in the arena of education. Questions of gender and speech style have taken on new importance in the context of assessing school pupils' oral skills (a recent innovation in England, Wales and Scotland). Developing assessment criteria has proved problematic, since there is considerable potential for gender bias. While some analysts have found criteria working to the advantage of dominant (competitive) speakers, others argue that there is a definite shift towards valuing co-operation. This in turn has provoked mixed responses. Many teachers welcome the emphasis on co-operative discussion, but some complain about cases where a 'leader' who makes substantive comments and shows skill in arguing – usually a boy – gets less credit than a supportive listener who 'acknowledges the contributions of others' – usually a girl.

There are two issues at stake here: one is about gender bias in assessment, the other about the value that would ideally be placed on different interactional skills. In practice, however, they are difficult to separate. Early research results (Jenkins and Cheshire 1990; Cheshire and Jenkins 1991) suggest that 'feminine' styles *are* acquiring more value in the classroom, but this, paradoxically, is working to boys' advantage: boys are rewarded for showing 'feminine' interpersonal skills, whereas girls' (superior) skills in this area are not always rewarded precisely because they are interpreted as 'natural'. The moral of this story would seem to be that you can revalue 'feminine' qualities without conferring any advantage on actual female individuals.

Contemporary verbal hygiene for women struggles to reconcile beliefs about language and gender that are ultimately incompatible. On one hand it champions a kind of equal opportunities model according to which, once prejudice and historic disadvantage are overcome, anyone should be able to do anything, and everything anyone does should be accorded the same value. On the other hand, all the advice it offers as a means to this laudable end is permeated by assumptions about the irreducibly gendered nature of particular domains and behaviours. It remains unclear why individuals can change but the structures of the social world must remain forever the same.

In the light of this, perhaps it is not surprising that overall, advice to women on how they should speak is incoherent. There is advice telling women they can be more like men; conversely there is advice explaining to them the deep-seated reasons why they cannot, and reassuring them that there is nothing wrong with being, and wanting to be, different. In both the public and private domains, 'feminine' speech styles can be valued negatively or positively; women may be counselled either as men's partners or as their colleagues to embrace 'feminine' speech (it is equally valid; it embodies the values of 'caring' or 'teamwork') or to avoid it (it is 'powerless'; it is an obstacle to communication with men).

In this whole contradictory discourse, the most important common factor is simply the idea of an eternal opposition between 'masculine' and 'feminine' styles. And this is the basic problem: any kind of verbal hygiene advice based on the a priori acceptance of an all-pervading gender duality will end up being co-opted to reactionary ends, because the starting assumption is itself reactionary.

This is an argument I will take up again later in this chapter. Meanwhile, we may note a second assumption that is common to the various kinds of advice I have examined: the assumption that gender differences in speech styles present some kind of problem. In the light of the general incoherence of the literature, the question surely arises: what is the problem? Is there a 'real' problem at all?

THE PROBLEM OF WOMEN'S SPEECH: FACT, FANTASY OR FIGURE?

The answer, I think, is 'yes and no'. It would certainly be naive to suppose that an outbreak of advice on any subject necessarily signals a pre-existing demand. The self-improvement industry thrives by discovering problems it can package, from cellulite to the Cinderella complex; if recently there has been a vogue for 'the problem of women's speech', that need not reflect any upsurge of concern in the world outside. One might even say that advice literature, like press scares and advertisements, has the function of creating problems that did not exist before. Consumer capitalism is littered with examples of the solution that creates a problem: 'feminine freshness' and 'the understains' come to mind (who on earth had defined a category of 'understains' before a detergent advertisement claimed to be able to tackle them?). Similarly, a rash of articles on the problem of women's speech might lead people who had never noticed it was a problem to become anxious about it.

The question of women's alleged 'indirectness' is a classic example of a non-problem turned into a crisis by constant reference to it in advice texts. There is little evidence that it exists in the relevant contexts, and no convincing argument it would constitute a serious problem if it did; yet forests have been felled and hours of training time expended on the project of getting women to be more direct.

That said, though, it would also be naive to deny that the literature on 'the problem of women's speech' is at some level addressing real, as opposed to merely manufactured, concerns. As with the types of verbal hygiene we have considered in earlier chapters, the question is what kind of anxieties are being mobilized and given sharper focus in the creation of this particular 'problem'.

First, I think there is plenty of evidence that cross-sex interaction, both in public and in private, is regarded by many women as an area of genuine conflict. The 'private' problem has long been a rich seam mined in women's conversation with each other; the popular linguistics of Deborah Tannen *et al.* gives readers access to a metalanguage with which to interpret familiar phenomena. The 'public' problem is also one which women have become increasingly willing and able to notice. Again, the popularization of research findings plays a part in this, as women become aware that their personal experience of being 'silenced' (interrupted, ignored, not called on to speak, not confident enough to speak) is replicated in other public arenas.

It is this question of getting access to the floor, and more specifically the phenomenon of 'silencing', that women have tended to comment on when I have asked them, individually or in groups, what linguistic problems they encounter in public domains. It is clearly something women are consciously aware of; it is always the first thing they mention, and often it is the only thing.

It is interesting, therefore, that advice literature rarely mentions this problem (it is certainly less prominent than women's 'indirectness'), and is unable to propose a single solution of any consequence ('Don't contribute to those statistics!'). Questions about speaking rights cannot be contained within the framework of self-help, where individual speech styles are the only object of concern. The social contexts and relationships within which people are speaking are a much more important determinant in this crucial area of how the floor is apportioned and managed, but self-help is ill-equipped to deal with structural inequalities in social relations. It is thus of limited use to women in addressing the one problem whose existence they appear to acknowledge unequivocally.

We might say, then, that verbal hygiene advice to women picks up on their experiential sense that there is a problem, but focuses their discontent on to various concerns that are not, in fact, the problem. How, though, can self-improvement texts get away with this sort of displacement?

My answer would be that neither the advice itself nor the anxiety it mobilizes is entirely, or even mainly, about speech. I argued earlier that this form of verbal hygiene must be addressing real concerns 'at some level', but those concerns may be deeply buried. It could be that 'the problem of women's speech' is a figure for the problem of femininity in a world where gender identities seem to be increasingly unstable. This returns us to the point I made earlier: that the trouble with verbal hygiene for women is its unquestioning acceptance of femininity and masculinity as opposed and quasi-natural states from which particular ways of being and speaking are inseparable.

This may seem an unwarranted criticism, in so far as much of the advice we have surveyed seems to be premised on the contingency and plasticity of gendered behaviour: as Ann Rosalind Jones points out (1987: 41), advice literature assumes that 'men and women are *produced*. They are malleable, capable of being trained for changing roles; proper instruction can fashion them into successful participants in new social settings and the etiquettes belonging to them.' The very existence of such a literature underlines Judith Butler's point about the 'performativity' of gender (see Chapter 1, page 16).

Yet it does seem that there are limits on how malleable we want men and women to be. Certainly we seem to want there to go on *being* men and women, and however they remake themselves they must continue to be defined in relation to one another. It is striking that popular discourse on gender, though seemingly prompted by the increasing complexity and fuzziness of gender boundaries, continues to be organized around a simple binary opposition. The new verbal hygiene for women may be training us for changing roles, but it remains deeply wedded to the masculine/feminine dichotomy as an organizing principle for thinking about the world. When advice writers cast about for alternatives to 'speaking like a woman', the only one that occurs to them is 'speaking like a man': these two alternatives exhaust all the possibilities.

Such binary thinking is symptomatic of much broader tendencies in cultural products aimed at a female audience. Anyone who regularly reads self-help books for women or women's magazines must be struck by how obsessed such publications are with differences between men and women. Whatever their ostensible subject matter, from substance abuse to childcare and from achieving promotion to achieving orgasm, the deeper subject is gender difference itself. How do men and women differ, and what meaning does the difference have in women's lives? The mere fact of these questions being brought to our attention so relentlessly tells us how much anxiety and conflict must surround them.

It may seem strange that language, of all things, should become a key focus for anxieties about gender difference, but arguably the use of language as a figure for difference has a certain logic. Language is inextricably connected with identity, both individual and social – it is something that contributes to people's sense of who they are, and conveys messages about who they are to others. Because of this, the hidden workings of language have been accorded an important place in the popular advice tradition. Talking is, to use Eric Berne's familiar phrase, one of 'the games people play'; one purpose of many self-help books is to give readers an advantage in the game by spelling out its rules, enabling those 'in the know' both to control the messages they convey through words or gestures and to decode the 'real' meaning of others' behaviour. The new verbal hygiene for women puts together the interest in decoding hidden messages and the fascination with male–female difference. One might therefore locate its appeal in a combination of two fantasies: one about language and one about gender.

The linguistic fantasy is one we have already encountered many times in this book: that perfect communication can be achieved by following certain rules. In this case, the trick is to be aware that there are two sets of rules rather than one, and to design your interactions accordingly. By enabling men and women to read one another like the proverbial books, this minor adjustment is supposed magically to dissolve conflict and bring the sexes into perfect harmony: not love but telementation conquers all.

The 'two codes' model is especially appealing because it suggests a way of eliminating certain troublesome consequences of gender difference without taking what to most people would be the unacceptably radical step of dismantling the entire edifice of gender. This is the second fantasy that underpins the new verbal hygiene: that women and men could be made less damagingly alien to one another without undermining the concepts of masculinity and femininity. By learning to interpret and manipulate the gendered codes of language we can resolve the problems associated with difference while leaving difference itself intact.

In relationship advice this is simply a matter of understanding linguistic differences and performing the necessary translation between, in John Gray's terms, women's 'Venusian' and men's 'Martian'. Careers advice proposes a more active bilingualism: women must not only understand the male code but be able to use it where necessary. This remains, however, what you might call 'Martian for specific purposes'. A woman's ability to slip into the language when on Mars does not have to threaten her core identity as a Venusian.

The notion of gender as core identity is crucial to the new verbal hygiene, and in that sense it is a conservative phenomenon. Importantly, however, its conservatism is not traditional anti-feminism, which most of its audience would find as unpalatable as gender radicalism. What advice literature wants desperately to conserve is not traditional gender roles, but simply the sense that gender is a fixed and fundamental component of each person's essential self. Men may cultivate sensitivity and women assertiveness – indeed, advice texts routinely encourage them to do so. But at least it can still be taken for granted that there are and always will be two types of people: women and men.

Like a lot of current popular discourse on gender, the new verbal hygiene for women is about accommodating and even celebrating change while at the same time reassuring us that change has its limits. In my view it is neither a panacea for gender troubles, nor a sinister expression of the anti-feminist 'backlash', but an ambiguous and often contradictory discourse which leaves considerable scope for interpretation. In the concluding section of this chapter I will consider what is reactionary and what is potentially subversive in women's self-help practices, paying particular attention to the matter of how verbal hygiene advice is interpreted by its women addressees.

READING SELF-HELP: NORMALITY AND NORMATIVITY

A feminist poster that was popular some years ago read: 'If being a woman is natural, stop telling me how to do it.' Feminism proceeds from the axiom that femininity (like masculinity) is a construct rather than a natural given. This gives rise to overt questioning of the processes whereby it is constructed; it also reminds us that even in periods when no one is questioning the nature and meaning of gender, it still has to be constructed and negotiated. To paraphrase Simone de Beauvoir in the style of a woman's magazine: 'One is not born a woman, rather one has to work at it.'

But one of the resources that twentieth-century western women bring to the work of becoming and remaining women is a body of knowledge that does on the whole treat gender as a natural given: science. It is science that provides our most privileged information about what men and women are like, and because we take that information as objective fact, what passes for a description of *normal* gendered behaviour very soon becomes a blueprint for *normative* gendered behaviour. Scientific discourse might seem to be telling us who we are, but its authority is such that it also has the function of telling us who to be. The desire to be 'normal' is a powerful one, and nowhere more powerful than in relation to gender.

Self-help trades on this conflation of the normal and the normative. In the popular self-help texts and practices that mediate science for a mass audience, it is more obvious that the experts are telling us who to be, though they carefully ground their prescriptions in generalizations about who we are (in the case of verbal hygiene advice these generalizations are drawn from scholarly work in linguistics and psychology, and it is to give force to such generalizations that publishers put their authors' Ph.Ds on the covers of their books). But if self-help is more overtly prescriptive than science proper, it is also more reassuring. It tells people, first, that it is normal to have problems being normal; and second, that those problems can be solved. With the right attitude and the appropriate expert guidance, all of us can measure up to the highest standards.

One common criticism of self-help is that behind the twin façades of scientific knowledge and human concern, it sets out to create anxiety and encourage low self-esteem in order to sell people quack remedies for non-existent or trivial complaints. Feminists have argued that by playing on existing insecurities and indeed creating new ones, self-help contributes to the very devaluation of women that impels so many of them to turn to self-help in the first place. There are certainly criticisms to be made along these lines of the new verbal hygiene for women. For example, one possible detrimental effect on women of reading endless books and articles about 'the problem of women's speech', or of undergoing AT and other forms of communication training, might be to make them anxious about things they had never previously worried about, so that they become as self-conscious about the way they talk as many already are about the way they look.

The recent hyping of 'the problem of women's speech' and 'the problem of male–female communication' may also have ill-effects that go beyond making individual women anxious and self-conscious. As these 'problems' enter the repertoire of public discourse about gender, they provide one more pseudo-explanation for women's 'under-achievement', one more excuse for the raw deal women get, and one more ingenious strategy for not tackling the root causes of women's subordinate status.

This, in fact, is what worries me most, particularly about the way the new verbal hygiene is being used in workplaces. Now that most institutions feel obliged to pay lip-service to the principle of equal opportunities, their best defence against actually doing anything to advance gender equality is the kind of deficit model that treats inequality as the consequence of women's own inadequate behaviour. The idea that women's speech 'lacks authority' is manna from heaven for employers who think in this way. Instead of addressing institutional sexism, they can send women on courses to bring their communication skills up to scratch. The culture of the workplace and the behaviour of men within it can stay exactly as they are; and if the women still don't get promoted after receiving exclusive training opportunities at company expense, then we can only conclude they are not up to the job – exactly as the sexists have been telling us all along.

It is impossible to believe that systemic problems of low wages, restricted job opportunities and poor promotion prospects could either be caused by the way women speak and act, or cured by a few hours of assertiveness training. Far more salient influences on women's career opportunities include sex discrimination, heavy domestic responsibilities and lack of childcare provision, sexist corporate cultures and sexual harassment. The 'problem of women's speech' is not just less significant than these other causes of inequality; one could argue that it is largely an invention whose main function is precisely to obscure them. If so, the identification of this 'problem' does women a considerable disservice.

The fact remains, however, that many women respond positively to self-help literature and such activities as AT. Very few of those I interviewed were willing to dismiss AT as useless, for example, though some did feel their employers placed too much emphasis on it. They certainly did not see it as an objectionable attempt at social control. How is this response to be explained?

Reading between the lines

Students of popular culture have pointed out that any text or practice can support a variety of differing interpretations. Meaning does not reside only in words or images, or in the mind of whoever created them; finally it has to be produced by the person reading the text. And what that person 'sees' will depend not only on what is there for them to see, but also on what they are looking for, and what assumptions or attitudes they bring to the search. Thus if you want to know what its consumers make of self-help, and why they find it useful and/or pleasurable, there is much to be said for asking them. Their answers may not be the ones your own reading has led you to expect.

The sociologist Wendy Simonds set out to investigate the appeal of self-help literature by conducting in-depth interviews with thirty women who regularly read self-help books. Her findings are published in *Women and Self-Help Culture: Reading Between the Lines* (Simonds 1992). The subtitle is apt, because Simonds found her informants to be rather selective recipients of the self-improvement message. Most strikingly, the advice component of self-help texts seemed relatively unimportant to these readers. What they liked was the way books identified and labelled problems (prompting the reader to recognize herself as a 'woman who loves too much', or a sufferer from the 'Cinderella complex'). This, they claimed, provided both insight and reassurance. As one woman explained, 'If I understand things, I feel a little bit better about them;

I don't feel so overwhelmed and so helpless' (Simonds 1992: 36). If that seems naive, it is worth remembering that even the most prestigious and expensive forms of psychotherapy are wary of making any larger claim.

There is, however, a difference. Psychotherapy (like feminist consciousness raising) is supposed to give participants insight into uncomfortable truths that have been repressed and denied. Self-help literature appears to have the rather different function of making readers feel better by reaffirming their existing interpretations of experience. As Simonds's informants told her on a number of occasions, reading self-help is less a process of discovery than a process of recognition. Paul Lichterman, another sociologist who conducted interviews with self-help readers, similarly came to the conclusion that the point of the genre for most of his informants was not to change anything, but to validate existing perceptions by recasting them in a more authoritative, 'scientific' register: '[Readers] are seeking not so much a perfect self as a new language for personal life' (Lichterman 1992: 443). Some of my own informants made a comparable point about AT, saying that role-play exercises in which they adopted different personae had not caused them to alter their customary behaviour, but rather gave them the confidence simply to 'be themselves'.

A specific function of self-help books about any aspect of male–female relationships is to clarify and codify readers' pre-existing sense of the differences between men and women. Far from destabilizing common-sense ideas about gender, books on this subject seem to cater to an insatiable demand for 'proof' that the sexes really are profoundly different, just as readers had always known. In the self-help universe it is axiomatic that differences between men and women are the source of a good deal of misery; yet many women apparently derive satisfaction from having their beliefs about who they are and who men are triumphantly vindicated, and seeing their own folk knowledge given the official stamp of science by a person with a Ph.D.

I found support for this analysis in various conversations I had with women about Deborah Tannen's *You Just Don't Understand*, which at the time of my research was at the height of its popularity. I had not set out to do a reader study – in most cases I was interviewing women about their participation in forms of linguistic training – but many of my informants had read Tannen, they saw a connection with the subject of the interview and they were eager to tell me what they thought of the book.

What I found most remarkable in these discussions was that no one ever cited Tannen's overall thesis about gender difference as a reason for liking or disliking *You Just Don't Understand*. Instead, they dwelt on the book's many anecdotes purporting to describe instances of male–female misunderstanding. Over and over again, those who liked the book praised the *accuracy* of these vignettes, particularly in relation to the portrayal of men; 'that's exactly how my husband/boyfriend/father behaves.' Conversely, the few who disliked the book also fastened on the anecdotes to explain why, saying they were 'unconvincing' or 'overgeneralized'.

The appeal of *You Just Don't Understand* for my informants had little to do with either Tannen's explanation of cross-sex misunderstandings or her proposals for dealing with them. The reading pleasure lay in the familiarity, the banality even, of the scenarios presented in the book. Contrary to the claims made on the cover, it seems that the secret of *You Just Don't Understand*'s success does not lie in its potential to bring about change, either in individual couples' lives or in society at large, but in the reassurance it offers to readers that their experience is widely shared: in short, that they are normal.

Not only are women readers learning that they are normal, they may also implicitly be getting support for the idea that in the 'battle of the sexes', they are the ones who have right on their side. Advice literature offers them a covert message that however much they may be suffering, they are actually *superior* to men. Those among my interviewees who praised the accuracy of Deborah Tannen's portrayal of men were nevertheless in little doubt that it was a negative portrayal. Tannen appeared to them to be validating another well-known gender stereotype, the one that says men (poor things) are just no good at expressing their feelings and conducting their relationships.

One could of course dismiss such a reading as both essentialist and reactionary, a fantasy with which women compensate for real-world powerlessness. Personally I have little sympathy for the view that women are interactionally superior to men, just as I have little sympathy for the opposite view as peddled in some workplace training programmes. Still, the interesting (and marginally encouraging) point about the 'poor useless men' response is that it seems to undercut Tannen's own evaluation of male and female styles as 'equally valid'. The message she is trying to convey evidently has not been accepted without question by all her readers. Although in this case the alternative interpretation is stereotypical and reactionary, the fact that readers can produce an interpretation at odds with Tannen's own intentions must raise the whole question of reader *resistance*. Those critics who regard self-help as a fundamentally pernicious form of social control may not be giving enough weight to the idea that any attempt at control runs the risk of engendering resistance – a critical response that might not otherwise have been articulated.

The potential for either control or resistance is obviously dependent on the context in which a practice occurs and the purpose for which it is undertaken. I do not wish to play down the sexism of many verbal hygiene practices examined in this chapter, for it is clear that their ill-effects can range from wasting women's time to undermining their self-confidence, not to speak of giving sexists new stereotypes with which to trivialize women and discriminate against them.

On the other hand, in the course of this research I met not only women who 'read between the lines' of *You Just Don't Understand*, but women who had used workplace training programmes for purposes quite at odds with the 'official' purpose, such as discussing women's collective employment rights, and one woman who had resigned from a job in a Scottish hotel when the new American management required workers to say 'have a nice day' to departing guests, which she felt was 'demeaning to me as a Scot'. Not only does verbal hygiene not always 'work' in the way it is supposed to; occasionally it can alert people to the existence of more general power structures and move them to articulate their criticism or protest.

Leaving your job may be a fairly ineffectual form of political protest, but for the Scottish hotel worker it reflected an important political insight: that verbal hygiene is more than just a trivial manipulation of unimportant linguistic details. In adopting particular norms of speech we are constructing particular identities for ourselves – and in submitting to other people's linguistic prescriptions we are also submitting to their ideas about who we are, or should be. The positive side of verbal hygiene – seldom realized, admittedly, but not to be ruled out in principle – is that by drawing attention to the way identity is created in everyday linguistic practice, it enables us to reflect on the identities we currently perform, and beyond that, to imagine alternatives.

Empowering fictions? Feminism and self-help

The notion that there *are* alternatives to our current ways of enacting gender, and that we could make a principled decision to do things differently, is at least as central to feminism as it is to self-help literature. That is not to say that linguistic and other forms of self-help are by definition feminist: I hope this chapter has shown that they are not. Yet those feminists who argue that the transforming impulse behind self-help is pernicious in itself seem to be missing an important point. In order to have any political purchase, feminism too must mobilize women's dissatisfaction with the way things are and convince them that they can change things for the better by their own efforts. Even the victim-blaming message 'it's all your own fault' also implies 'it's yours to control'; and while at a literal, absolute level this is obviously a delusion, since we do not control every aspect of our destinies and some of us have far less control than others, at some level 'it's yours to control' is a necessary empowering fiction for anyone committed to change.

Increased control over their lives is, I believe, among the benefits women seek, and to some extent find, in the various self-help practices

I have examined in this chapter. These practices may justifiably be criticized for their gender conservatism, individualism and victim-blaming; but that is not all there is to say about them. Self-help is powerful *both* as a tool of oppressive 'regimes of truth' that tell women who to be, *and*, potentially, as a stimulus to the imagination, an arena in which women can experiment with alternative possibilities.

If that seems an overly positive assessment, I should add an important qualification. Whatever empowering or subversive potential is latent in self-help can only 'come out' under certain conditions. Specifically, how radical or progressive any 'experiments with alternative possibilities' will be depends on whether they have social and ideological supports of the kind made available by an active social movement.

It could be argued that self-help now fulfils what were once prime functions of feminist politics: it takes women's experience seriously, it gives voice to aspects of that experience that make many women unhappy, and it says that something can be done.[15] What it does not provide, however, is a coherent political analysis of the present, a clear alternative vision for the future, or a self-consciously oppositional community in which proposals for change can be put into practice, and alternative values can become collective norms. As Paul Lichterman argues, self-help as it is most commonly practised – that is, through reading self-help texts – is a 'thin culture'. 'I name this culture "thin"', he explains, 'because it does not support a deep commitment from readers' (1992: 427). Reading self-help is typically accommodated within individuals' existing lifestyles rather than incorporating people into new collectivities that might foster a deeper commitment. (This is why, as some of my own informants commented, an AT *group* is more likely to be 'subversive' or to deserve the epithet 'political' than a day seminar or a training video.)

In the absence of collective supports it is unlikely that discontent with the *status quo* will be translated into radically different values and practices. Instead it will result in the sort of thing I have been criticizing in this chapter: a kind of discourse that airs women's discontent without analysing its systemic causes, confirms rather than challenging received ideas about gender, and makes proposals about language use that are curiously remote from the problems and complexities of social interaction as women actually experience it ('speak directly'/'don't contribute to those statistics'/ 'it's just a misunderstanding').

There are many things wrong with the new verbal hygiene for women, and feminists should not forbear to point them out. But we need to be clear about what it is we criticize: not the idea of self-transformation *per se*, but the banal and stereotypical images in which the pundits and experts of the self-help industry would like us to be transformed. These images can and should be challenged, just as they themselves challenged, and eventually supplanted, earlier stereotypes. Let Eliza Doolittle turn her back on Henry Higgins – and on Henrietta Higgins Ph.D. – and make herself over in a different style, unfettered by their restrictive norms of linguistic femininity.

6 On the state of the state of the language

STORIES OF LANGUAGE

In the preface to this book I remarked on the sheer volume of print and broadcast material aimed at a broad general audience and dealing with linguistic subjects. One of the abiding preoccupations of this genre is to assess what it often calls 'the state of the language' – a difficult and somewhat paradoxical undertaking. Popular as well as scholarly discussions emphasize that language is not static but constantly in flux; and where English is concerned, great stress is typically also laid on its heterogeneity and diversity. Commentators thus appear to acknowledge that there is no (fixed) state and no (one) language to discuss under the heading of 'the state of the language'. And yet their attempts to delineate such a state, to provide an overview that will tell us where we are, continue unabated.

The 'state of the language' is a discursive construct: not an objective description of certain linguistic phenomena, but the product of certain ways of talking about them. My aim in this book has been to examine these ways of talking, and in particular to pinpoint the conventions and assumptions in virtue of which some ways of talking about language make more sense to us than others.

This may sound simple, but it should not be over-simplified. Metalinguistic discourse is itself diverse and fragmentary, and its concerns do not stand still. Even while I have been writing this book, it has been business as usual for verbal hygienists all over the world. For example:

An upper-class Englishwoman freed after serving a prison sentence told reporters that the worst part of her ordeal was hearing fellow inmates 'mangling the English language'. Following heated arguments among academicians from Spain and Latin America, the Spanish alphabet lost two of its letters (<ch> and <ll>). In France the Minister of Culture introduced legislation (the '*loi Toubon*') compelling goods and services to be described in French; vocal opponents of this measure included a French advertising executive who declared that 'words, just like products, have to be competitive', and a British Conservative member of Parliament who drafted a French Words (Prohibition) Bill outlawing the use by British businesses of words like *café*, *guillotine* and *lingerie*.[1]

Controversy raged around a new Roman Catholic catechism, whose English language version pointedly eschewed gender-inclusive terms; and conversely, around a new version of the official dictionary for Scrabble players, which outlawed a number of 'offensive' but previously legal words and was therefore suspected of 'political correctness'. While in the US psychiatrists and psychologists redefined the inability to produce coherent sentences and paragraphs as a pathological condition ('Disorder of Written Expression'), meriting inclusion in the latest edition of the *Diagnostic and Statistical Manual of Mental Disorders*, in Britain the Plain English Campaign published an anthology of incoherent utterances forthrightly entitled *A Decade of Drivel*.[2]

A row broke out over a clergyman's refusal to permit the inscription of *Dad* or *Grandad* on a gravestone in his churchyard. The Church of England's consistory court confirmed that such familiar terms were not acceptable, and confidently asserted that 'the use of father/grand-father does not indicate cool or unaffectionate feelings'. (The family concerned, unable to agree, expressed a desire to have Dad's body exhumed.) Meanwhile, across the Atlantic there was a rift among scholars engaged in the unlikely task of translating the Bible into 'Klingon' – the invented language of a fictional race of aliens familiar to viewers of the television series *Star Trek*. One 'literalist' faction proposed to render the words into Klingon directly, while the other preferred to recast the text using concepts more meaningful to Klingons.[3]

What, in general, can be said about this ill-assorted ragbag of examples? One could note that collectively they illustrate the vast range of human concerns, from commerce to religion and from international politics to games, that have (or can be given) a linguistic dimension. Or one could make something of the simple fact that they were all reported in the press, which suggests that in spite of their diversity they satisfy certain cultural criteria of intelligibility and noteworthiness. (Indeed, most solicit stock responses from our repertoire: 'amazing!' 'ludicrous!' 'shouldn't be allowed!'.) They belong, in other words, to a genre with whose conventions and underlying assumptions we are expected to be familiar.

One of the characteristics of this genre is precisely its elasticity, the way it can comfortably accommodate diverse and even contradictory propositions. Readers of the stories I have cited are unlikely to notice or be troubled by the fact that they imply rather different attitudes to language, or that many or most of them run counter to certain overarching narratives about its nature and state.

They do not sit comfortably, for instance, with the idea of language as a 'great natural force' rendering human intervention irrelevant or futile. How could such questions as the legality of a word in Scrabble, or the ordering of names in the Spanish telephone directory, possibly be decided by 'the language itself'? These are matters of convention, not nature, though in time they will be naturalized: it will be taken for granted, for instance, that Spanish 'has' *n* letters, not *n*+2. A significant proportion of our everyday linguistic practice has similarly non-natural antecedents; and this bears witness to the fact that verbal hygiene is not altogether futile; nor, assuming we wish to do more with our languages than just form syllables and sentences, is it altogether unnecessary.

A variation on the 'natural' story about language is the teleological narrative of evolutionary progress, in which languages are constantly evolving to meet the changing needs of their speakers as they strive towards the ultimate goal of efficient communication; verbal hygiene can be justified if it gives language a push in the right direction. However, the picture we get when we contemplate examples like the ones given at the beginning of this discussion is hardly one of orderly linear advance towards a predetermined goal. If the alphabetic reform of Spanish represents a standardizing impulse, and thus appears to fit in with the logic of 'efficiency', the French *loi Toubon* is an attempt to turn back the tide of Anglo-American linguistic hegemony in the spirit of '*vive la différence*'. The authorities who watch over Scrabble are clearly moving in the opposite direction from the Pope, and in neither case is 'communication' the issue. Linguistic interventions are usually goal-oriented, but the search for any single goal that will somehow explain them all is doomed to fail.

Nor is it easy to detect in our examples much support for the narrative favoured by various prophets of doom, according to which language is in terminal decline and/or constantly threatened by sinister forces intent on controlling our innermost thoughts. What is striking in the above-mentioned instances is not the decline of linguistic practices but their vitality; not people's apathy in the face of linguistic tampering, but their vigilance and resistance. These verbal hygiene initiatives have not gone unchallenged, however weighty the authority behind them. Each pronouncement has been met with approval from some quarters and vociferous disapproval from others.

Our commonplace narratives about language are themselves a kind of verbal hygiene: they are bits of discourse whose function is to tidy up the messiness of linguistic phenomena and package them neatly in forms that make sense; they do not have to be consistent with one another to fulfil this function. I do not doubt that we need stories about language, just as we need creation myths and botanic classification systems and theories about the dimensions of the universe or the causes of disease, to give us a better grasp of the world we inhabit. But I do think that in the case of language we are especially tenacious in clinging to stories that distort and mystify far more than they explain.

AGAINST NATURE

Stories which represent language as solely or primarily a 'natural' phenomenon are problematic, whether they are written in the scientific jargon of experts or the vernacular of popular cliché.[4] What they distort and mystify is our relationship to language and the extent of our responsibility for shaping it. Natural forces operate irrespective of what humans say, do or believe about them (the apple fell before Newton; the rain comes or doesn't come whether you take readings from a satellite or pray to the gods), but social practices, even at their most habitual and unreflective, do not work in the same mechanical way. Language-using is a social practice: what people think language is, or should be, makes a difference to the way they use it, and therefore to what it becomes.

We may pay lip-service to the idea of language as a 'living thing', impervious to our efforts to exert control over it, but I hope the preceding chapters have made clear how much of our behaviour belies this rhetoric. The notion of linguistic 'naturalness' is one people deploy strategically, to suit the needs of the moment. If they dislike a particular change, such as the loss of the apostrophe or the spread of the glottal stop, they will conveniently forget that change is meant to be 'natural', and demand that it be halted; conversely, if the object of disapproval is clearly not a 'natural' development – if it is, say, a feminist demand for 'non-sexist language' – its opponents will criticize it as unwarranted interference with nature.

The fact is that we are constantly intervening in language, whether in support of what we perceive as the *status quo* or in pursuit of something different. We are convinced that, to paraphrase the newspaper editorial I quoted in Chapter 3, 'some kinds of language really are more worthwhile than others', and we regularly act on that conviction. We think and argue about the words we use; we correct the speech and writing of our children (and our students); we look things up in usage guides and dictionaries; some of us increase our word power with the *Reader's Digest*, while others take courses in Elocution or Neurolinguistic Programming, or join societies devoted to such linguistic causes as spelling reform, Esperanto and even Klingon. Activities like these are difficult to square with an account according to which language-using is as unreflective as digestion, and language change as natural as the phases of the moon.

To the extent that we can identify a 'state of the language', therefore, we should acknowledge that it is not simply a phenomenon of nature, at which we marvel from a distance: our own actions have played a part in producing it, and they will also play a part in maintaining or changing it. It must also be acknowledged, however, that these actions do not only reflect our concerns and beliefs about *language*: other motivations influence the things we do, or would like to do, with words.

THE SOCIAL FUNCTIONS OF VERBAL HYGIENE

I argued in Chapter 1 that verbal hygiene arises out of the normative character of language-using as a human social activity. Our propensity to make reflexive critical judgements on language use has an obvious utility in the process of communication – enabling us, for instance, to judge when something is amiss in interaction and perform what discourse analysts call 'repair', to recognize and interpret metaphor and irony, and in general to make, in the phrase familiar to linguists, 'infinite use of finite means'. At the same time it is evident that the practices I have focused on in this book deploy our critical metalinguistic abilities for purposes that are not necessarily or primarily to do with the workings of language.

One function of verbal hygiene is quite simply to entertain. Interest and delight in language for its own sake is a common motivation, and in some cases the main one. The Klingon phenomenon is an obvious case in point, one which belongs with the weird and wonderful obsessions of the 'anoraks' described in the preface. The *Wall Street Journal* reporter Carrie Dolan (1994) notes the existence of 'Klingon newsletters, Klingon Internet conversation groups and audio cassettes with titles like "Conversational Klingon" and "Power Klingon"', and quotes a spokesman for the Klingon Language Foundation defending people's enthusiasm for such things as 'no more bizarre than sports trivia, or knowing the details of engines of cars that haven't been manufactured in 20 years'.

Even this strangest of instances, though, hints at additional and perhaps 'deeper' motivations. If splitting into factions over a Klingon Bible looks as absurd on the face of things as the dispute between the Big- and Little-endians in *Gulliver's Travels*, it may nevertheless be observed that the actual point at issue in the argument – essentially a question about the commensurability of different world-views – is part of a long-running debate which has non-trivial applications back on Planet Earth. It has frequently been pointed out that space fictions like *Star Trek* are in part moral and political allegories. The Klingon project, similarly, offers a way to explore contentious issues imaginatively and thus 'safely'.

There is an analogy here, perhaps, with the debates on grammar and 'political correctness' that I examined in Chapters 3 and 4: in both cases, arguments about language provided a symbolic way of addressing conflicts about race, class, culture and gender. It is true that this symbolic deployment of language tends to obscure the true sources of disagreement and discomfort. I am not defending it, but simply pointing out that one common function of arguments about language is to stand in for arguments on subjects people are reluctant to broach more directly.

The Klingon project has a further social function: if there is no Klingon speech community in the conventional sense, the proliferation of discourse on Klingon has nevertheless brought into existence another kind of community, one in which some people may find a supportive social network, or at least a sense of belonging to some collectivity. This creation of community is a function of many apparently pointless pastimes, with their social apparatus of newsletters, conventions, swap-meets, and so forth; and it is no small matter in societies where more traditional forms of community can be hard to sustain. Several of the verbal hygiene practices examined in previous chapters – the more active among the self-help practices in Chapter 5, for example, and the professional craft practices discussed in Chapter 2 – are partly about creating communities and networks where individuals can bond together through their engagement in a shared project.

The notion of belonging to a community or collectivity has its obverse (not converse: they are two sides of one coin) in the notion of individual identity, and this is also important in understanding verbal hygiene. Take the upper-class woman prisoner who complained about other prisoners 'mangling the English language'. She wanted her audience to believe that she had borne without complaint the loss of her liberty, the humiliation of being labelled a common criminal, the lack of privacy and of luxury, the separation from loved ones; but that having to hear the other women's glottal stops and split infinitives (her own illustrative examples, not mine) had driven her to distraction. What are we to make of such a claim?

The most obvious non-literal interpretation of the woman's remark is that the story is 'really' about social class. Prison inmates are over-whelmingly poor people (that is what made the story of the upper-class prisoner newsworthy in the first place): thus the tale of a gentlewoman distressed by bad grammar and sloppy diction is actually about her distress at being forced to associate with her social inferiors, at being treated as if she were no different from them. It is possible that she really did apprehend the loss of her class status as the ultimate humiliation (though it is also possible that she was deliberately playing to a stereotype of upper-class women as plucky eccentrics for the benefit of the press). Yet it is significant that the woman fastened on *language* as the mark of class distinction. Had she deplored the way her cellmates smelled instead of the way they talked, she would have appeared as no more than a crashing snob. But in this context there is more mileage to be had from verbal hygiene than from personal hygiene, because language is symbolically inflected with a rich set of meanings, and resists reduction to any one of them.

The woman's concern about glottal stops and split infinitives need not be read solely as a matter of class. It is also a concern about preserving the orderliness of the world and the integrity of the self against the forces of disorder and fragmentation. The woman's determination to keep up linguistic standards functions in this prison story much as a daily routine of exercising or bible study might function in the account of a different kind of prisoner; as something people do in extreme and adverse circumstances to recapture a semblance of the dignity and self-respect they valued in their previous, 'normal' lives. The discourse of verbal hygiene offered the upper-class woman a way to articulate contradictory responses: on one level she could use it to figure her real distress at the assault on her sense of self that imprisonment represented, while on another level it could signify her difference from the other inmates and her consequent ability to rise above the 'real' humiliations of prison life.

Verbal hygiene in the prison story signified the maintenance of order and meaning in one individual's life; but as we have seen, it can also address analogous concerns at the level of the wider society. The style rules in Chapter 2, the grammatical rules in Chapter 3, the conventions of 'politically correct' language in Chapter 4 and the norms of 'assertive' or 'effective' communication in Chapter 5 all function (among other things) to tidy up messy or troublesome realities. The rules affirm basic distinctions like true/false, good/bad, correct/incorrect, and they insist that those distinctions are categorical absolutes, not matters of opinion or arbitrary convention, and not contingent judgements that could vary with the context. Thus some expressions are neutral, others biased; some are correct and others incorrect. Either *water buffalo* is always a racist epithet or it is never a racist epithet. If directness or transparency is a virtue in one context, then it must be a virtue in all contexts. Messiness, fuzziness, uncertainty and relativism may be part of life, but if we try we can banish them from the more tractable sphere of language. In the words of Professor Grammar, a tiresome character who used to address foreign learners of English on the BBC World Service, 'there's a rule for everything'. If there isn't, we can make one.

The most fundamental desire to which verbal hygiene appeals is this desire for order, and the most fundamental fear it is used to ward off is the corresponding fear of disorder. The rhetoric of pro-grammar conservatives, examined in Chapter 3, renders this conjunction of desire and fear in an astonishingly literal form: despairing of the lawlessness of working-class youth, the bewildered, frightened and vindictive people encountered by Marilyn Butler really had pinned their hopes on the discipline of grammar – on linguistic law and order as a surrogate for the real thing.

The desire for order and the fear of chaos are at their most spectacular in the grammar example, but are also discernable elsewhere: in hyper-standardization as practised by stylistic authorities, for instance, where orderliness takes the form of an endless quest to make the rules exhaustive and absolute, dotting every i and crossing every t (it is interesting that we use this metaphor, specifically an image of *writing*, to signify an obsession with order more generally). The fear of chaos is often manifested in resistance to certain kinds of language change, so-called 'politically correct' language being a notable case in point. In this case, what is feared in particular is the disintegration of shared norms for using language, which raises the spectre of communicative breakdown.

Taken literally, this is an unfounded fear. Humans have always managed to communicate to their mutual satisfaction for various purposes in the absence of a shared language, and the differences which provoke most anxiety on this score are in any case too trivial linguistically to pose any serious threat to meaningful interaction. But the underlying fear is not the literal fear of being unable to make yourself understood. It is the fear that the meanings which anchor your own view of the world are not, after all, shared by everyone; which in turn expresses a more general fear of difference, otherness, relativity.

AGAINST MAGICAL THINKING

In Chapter 1 I asked why intervening in language should so often become a kind of surrogate for dealing with more general social conflicts. One answer might be that there is a symbolic connection which is deeply embedded in human culture between exerting control over language and exerting control over things and events in the world. It is, to take an obvious example, a fundamental assumption of religion and of magic that the utterance of certain linguistic formulae will have predictable and powerful effects – casting out spirits, calling genies from bottles, turning bread and wine into flesh and blood. Such reverence for the word is apt to strike more secular people as mere superstition, but in fact it also has secular manifestations. It survives, for instance, in attitudes to swearing that are not held only by religious believers. It also survives in our attachment to certain verbal hygiene discourses, the ones which warn (or promise) that language can be used to control people's thoughts.

Some of the most bizarre cases of verbal hygiene motivated by what amounts to a belief in word magic come not from the rituals of so-called 'exotic' peoples but from the 'scientific' practices of late twentieth-century capitalism. Some years ago, I had a student in one of my classes who did casual work for a telemarketing company. Like most organizations whose business is calling up complete strangers on the telephone and attempting to sell them products, this company provided its employees with a script for use in exchanges with customers. The script was very detailed (though of course one-sided; you could never be sure customers would keep up their end of the conversation): it specified not just what the salesperson must say, but also what words to emphasize, where to pause and what tone of voice to use. Supervisors listened in to calls at random to check that employees were not departing from the script. Equally rigid prescriptions governed employees' interactions with one another. There were 'inspirational' formulae they were obliged to utter in chorus at the start of their shift, and if anyone made a sale there was a script for announcing it to co-workers, as well as a script for the co-workers to signal their appreciation. Again, the supervisor had to be vigilant in ensuring these scripts were followed, and in preventing as far as possible any additional, unscripted interactions.

Eventually the student enquired of his supervisor what the point of all this was meant to be. She said that the various scripts had been 'scientifically' designed to maximize sales and thus the company's profits. They accomplished this by putting the salespeople in what science had ascertained to be the correct frame of mind for successful selling. However an employee might be feeling on a given day – tired, unenthusiastic, ill, bored – the utterance of particular formulae was supposed magically to imbue them with the positive attitude and persuasive power required to make a sale. Scripted exchanges with colleagues were supposed to keep the mood going throughout the shift; departures from the script or interactions not provided for by a script were frowned on because they might disrupt the mindset that had been so carefully created and nurtured.

At the time the student told me this, I found it astonishing; now I know there are many verbal hygiene practices whose premise is that by using language in particular ways one can actually reprogramme one's mind, or even one's brain. (For example, so far as one can judge without actually paying to be initiated into its mysteries, this is the idea behind Neurolinguistic Programming.) Practices of this type might seem a long way from the ritual chanting of priests, but they are based on ideas about the function and power of language that are not entirely dissimilar. And anyone who finds George Orwell's vision of Newspeak convincing is being somewhat inconsistent if they dismiss Neurolinguistic Programming and its ilk as absurd; for Newspeak is NP's dystopian inverse, in which the power of language over the mind is used for ill instead of good.

This degree of faith in the power of language is as irrational as the belief in spells which it resembles. My objection to it is not so much that linguistic manipulation does not work at all, as that it cannot work in the totalizing way that both self-help gurus and Orwellians would like us to believe; and here I would like to pursue this objection in a little more detail.

In one sense, it is undeniable that the design of a linguistic act is meant to have an effect on the thoughts of the recipient. When columnist Anthony Everitt warns us (apropos, needless to say, of 'political correctness') that 'control of language covers an intention to manage thought' (*Guardian*, 9 May 1994), the obvious retort is 'well of course it does'. When I choose some words in preference to others I am axiomatically hoping to influence the thinking of the person or persons to whom my words are addressed, if only by getting them to focus on the topic at hand. But far from being a sinister threat to human communication, this 'intention to manage thought' is necessary by definition to the communicative enterprise. As sociolinguists and philosophers long ago pointed out, a speaker who uttered sentences at random, without the intention to direct the thoughts of an addressee to her meaning or purpose in uttering them, would be communicatively incompetent.

However – and this is a crucial qualification – the relationship between what I say and the effect I obtain is far from straightforward; neither my intentions nor my words can determine it absolutely. The relationship that holds between medium and message is inevitably subject to inferencing on the part of the audience. There is thus no automatic, cause-and-effect relationship between, for example, saying 'collateral damage' and blocking the concept 'death' from the hearer's mind, or between speaking directly in 'I' language and magically gaining, or persuading others to attribute to you, particular qualities like competence and authority.

Unlike the pragmatically-challenged dimwits who populate usage guides and sales manuals, real language-users automatically probe for the meaning beneath the surface. They are quite capable of forming some assessment of the speaker's intentions: they know when someone is trying to sell them something, be it a set of replacement windows or an economical version of the truth. Over and over again we find that obvious attempts at manipulation – Mrs Thatcher's 'makeover', the renaming of an accident-prone nuclear plant, the use of bland military terms which in essence mean 'killing people' – backfire, not only because no one is fooled, but also because people resent being taken for fools.

This does not mean that there is nothing to worry about. On the contrary, one danger of overblown 'thought control' rhetoric is that it encourages us to worry about the wrong things. For instance, the workers at the telemarketing company may not be being brainwashed by the scripts and slogans they are compelled to recite, but arguably they are still being depersonalized, deskilled and demeaned. Managers cannot control employees' thoughts, and are probably not interested in doing so, but they are very interested in controlling their *behaviour*, in creating a climate of fear and compliance through various regimes of surveillance and discipline. Their brand of verbal hygiene serves this purpose very well, by creating new criteria on which to find workers' performance wanting and new pretexts for supervisors to snoop on workers' activities.

Just because this falls short of 'thought control' does not make it inconsequential.

Conversely, there are kinds of language, such as 'plain English' and 'assertive communication', which might be said to manipulate by harping on their uniquely *un*manipulative qualities. Again, there is no law of nature which says this strategy must succeed; if it does succeed, it is because we too often fail to remind ourselves that disclaiming all pretentions to rhetoric is the oldest trick in the rhetorical book.

LANGUAGE MATTERS

In Chapter 1 I posed the question: 'why do so many forms of verbal hygiene work so well?' Here I will make explicit the answer that has been implicit in this chapter so far, and to some extent throughout the book: where verbal hygiene 'works', it works not by controlling our thoughts, but by mobilizing our desires and our fears (its other main mechanism, which is not to be underestimated, is sheer inertia). Admittedly there is rational calculation at work in many verbal hygiene practices: editors want work, Conservative politicians want votes, self-help pundits want money. But their lines would not 'sell' if they did not appeal to more widespread and less rational impulses, ranging from the fear and loathing exhibited by pro-grammar conservatives to the more benign (but still irrational) desire of liberals and self-help pundits to believe that we live in a basically just world, where if only everyone could communicate better, no one need suffer social disadvantage or personal misery.

It is because of this element of irrationality that linguistic science sets its face against most popular forms of verbal hygiene, while making an exception (as I pointed out in Chapter 1) for technocratic forms of language management ('language planning') based on rational scientific principles. But this attitude, arguably, is misguided. For one thing, anyone who sets out to influence, explain or even just to describe some aspect of human behaviour, must recognize that it is not governed entirely by rational principles. The question therefore cannot be, 'how do we get rid of verbal hygiene, and of the irrational impulses that lie behind it?': for I do not think we can get rid of them; at most we can try to become more critically aware of them and, if we think it desirable, to change the social conditions that give rise to or intensify certain kinds of desire (I am thinking, for instance, of the conditions and the desires which have permitted dubious self-help practices to flourish).

But in any case, there is a real and serious question as to whether it is inherently irrational to care about the way language is used. I agree that the forms in which some verbal hygienists express their concerns about language are unreasonable, and I do not accept all of their concerns as legitimate ones; but from this it does not necessarily follow that there is no more reasonable alternative, or that the only legitimate stance to adopt would be a stance of total *unconcern* about language use – the relativist 'anything goes' position that is popularly attributed to linguists. It is precisely because I believe that the way we use language does matter, and that some of the functional, aesthetic and moral concerns that preoccupy verbal hygienists are indeed legitimate things to care about, that I am critical of so much current verbal hygiene discourse: for if something matters, it also matters how we talk about it.

Of course, not everything matters equally or in the same way. If a controversy breaks out among scholars about the dating of the Great Vowel Shift, or among Klingonists about the correct translation of 'loaves and fishes', the effect on most people's lives is negligible. The public at large has little or no stake in such debates, or in the way they are conducted. But there are some issues in which members of a society do have a stake – questions that are neither trivial nor merely technical. It seems to me reasonable, for instance, that people should be concerned about how language is taught in schools; about adult illiteracy; about provision for people who speak minority languages; about prejudice and bias in institutional language, and about 'hate speech'; about the comprehensibility of official and legal documents; about standards of accuracy, impartiality and taste in the language of mass media. In fact, it is not only reasonable that these issues should generate public debate, in a democracy it is highly desirable that they should. Yet it is also desirable that the debate should be worthy of its subject matter. Too often, as I hope I have demonstrated in the foregoing chapters, what passes for debate on linguistic issues falls short of the standards we demand in other spheres.

The question that remains is whether we can envision any more constructive way to address questions of language and value. I would like to think there is something between the apocalyptic discourse of those verbal hygienists who seem to believe that language is both the cause and the solution for every social ill, and the Panglossian complacency of the 'leave your language alone' approach. What, though, might that something be?

Not a manifesto

This question might be taken as a preface to some kind of manifesto for a 'better' verbal hygiene. The desire for me to put my own hygienic preferences on record recurred, in fact, in comments made by friends and colleagues on drafts of this book: in the words of one reader, 'I look forward to hearing what values and standards *you* would support' – or more brusquely, 'right then: what are you going to do about it?'

I cannot really complain about this. After all, I have criticized the value judgements that are commonly invoked in linguistic debates, but I have also criticized the argument according to which we should not make value judgements at all. I have confessed to agreeing, as in practice I suggest we all do, with the proposition that 'some kinds of language really are more worthwhile than others' (a proposition that might serve as the motto for all verbal hygiene). If I strongly *dis*agree with someone about which kinds of language these are, it is up to me to argue for my own definition of 'worthwhile'. People who ask me, 'well then, what norms and values do you support?' are not so much taking issue with me on the time-honoured basis that 'it's easy enough to criticize' as showing they have taken my argument seriously.

I accept, then, that someone who believes that the real question is not 'should there be norms?' but 'which norms?', has a responsibility to put forward alternatives to the value systems of which he or she is critical. The trouble is, I have little desire to do this in isolation from a wider debate. I do want to argue about what kinds of linguistic practice have value, but I fear such arguments are fruitless unless we have some principled means of conducting them – shared criteria for evaluating assertions about language as more or less valid, relevant and convincing. So with apologies to anyone who would prefer me to launch a manifesto, I propose at this point to offer instead a few general principles which might usefully be brought to bear when we deliberate on issues of verbal hygiene, and particularly the kinds of issues that I have mentioned above as matters of broad public concern.

1 Language and values

Useful discussion of the kinds of issues that have figured in this book depends, at the most basic level, on the recognition of two connected points. The first is that one *can* legitimately make value judgements on the use of language. Such judgements are not inherently impossible or nonsensical or unwarranted. Furthermore, while value judgements are not, by definition, objective truths, they do not have to be completely subjective outpourings of personal opinion or prejudice. This brings me to the second point: it needs to be recognized that not all judgements are equally valid. An acceptable public discourse of language and value must be accountable to certain norms which we demand of other public discourses – reasoned argument, logic, the marshalling of evidence, the making of relevant distinctions and so on.

If linguists have a tendency to underestimate the first point, popular verbal hygienists have a symmetrical tendency to underestimate the second, and the result is a kind of discourse without dialogue in which either nothing can be said about values and standards at all, or else anything, however fatuous or outrageous, can be said with impunity. This situation is not inevitable; it strikingly does not obtain in other contexts where argument centres on values rather than just facts. In ethical discussions we manage to get beyond polarized and dogmatic statements like 'X is just wrong' versus 'everything is relative'. Critical discourse about literature, architecture or painting (or for that matter football) aspires to say more than just 'this is what's good', or 'I know what I like' or 'it's just a matter of opinion'. Such familiar platitudes may be part of public discourse, but they are not the beginning and end of it; and they certainly do not pass for intelligent debate.

In these cases there are criteria for conducting arguments about what is right or good. True, the criteria themselves are vigorously contested. It is a feature of moral and aesthetic debates that the parties must argue not just for the validity of their judgements, but for the validity of the criteria on which those judgements were made. But no one supposes there are no criteria, or that any old criteria – no matter how obscure, illogical or ill-defined – will do.

2 Rules and reasons

In Chapter 1 I noted that rules for language use are typically followed automatically and without question; it is seldom if ever asked what explains or justifies such hallowed principles of English usage as 'the comma goes inside/outside the quotation marks', 'avoid the pronoun "I"', 'prefer Anglo-Saxon to Latinate words', 'never split an infinitive', '"consensus" is an odious word', 'a good writer never uses clichés', etc., etc. My second principle is that we should seek to know on what basis such rules have been promulgated, going on to judge each rule by the cogency of the argument advanced for it.

Here it should be admitted that people may reasonably differ on what arguments *are* cogent. For example, the statement 'we do X because we've always done X' – an appeal to continuity and tradition – is persuasive for some people, while others find it feeble. If a rule turns out to rest on either political or aesthetic criteria – as for instance with the question of whether to use disjuncts like *he* or *she*, which are often recommended as 'gender neutral' (a political value) but are also frequently criticized as 'clumsy' (an aesthetic value) – then here again it is likely that people will disagree, because they have different political and aesthetic values, or differ on whether politics or aesthetics should weigh heavier in the balance.

The principle 'demand reasons for rules' does not have to imply that language-users *must* in conscience stop following any rule that turns out to be unreasonable. There is nothing wrong with idiosyncratic prefer- ences which have no rational justification, so long as we acknowledge that this is what they are. I do not expect to be criticized for my 'irrational' habit of preferring black ink over blue, but equally I do not expect this preference to be elevated to the status of a universal norm. Similarly, I am happy to grant that William Rees-Mogg regards the word *consensus* as 'odious', but if he wants me either to join him in regarding it as odious or to observe a prohibition that is based on its being odious, he is going to have to marshal an argument that it *is* odious (not to mention defining what he means by 'odious') – which may or may not convince me he is right.

The point of the 'demand reasons' principle is, first, to prevent the enshrinement and mystification of personal linguistic preferences as Great Linguistic Truths; and second, in cases where people's disagreements are of some social consequence – the questions of nomenclature discussed in Chapter 4 might be one example – to provide a basis for weighing different criteria against each other. For example, someone might privately share Robert Hughes's view that *African-American* is an unnecessarily long and pompous term, but decide to give precedence to the need to signal in public their support for the political stance associated with using the expression.

If we cannot actually *resolve* disagreements of this kind, it need not be disastrous. The point is less to produce consensus on what rules to follow than to reduce the mystification that surrounds the question of *why* we are attached to certain rules. Even if people do not change their linguistic practice, by enquiring into the basis for it they have 'owned' their choices, instead of allowing them to be dictated by some arbitrary authority.

3 Hidden agendas and vested interests

Most of the verbal hygiene practices discussed in detail in this book are not finally about language at all, and therefore enquiring into the reasons for particular rules will not always take you to the heart of the matter. Accordingly I propose a third principle: 'look for the hidden agenda'. When evaluating any act or practice of verbal hygiene, we should ask ourselves what and whose interests it serves.

The question of interests is one I have considered at some length in the case study chapters. In Chapter 2, I suggested that style rules served the interests of craft professionals, and were particularly important in the construction of an ideological position for journalists. In Chapter 3, I identified the Great Grammar Crusade as an expression of certain right-wing political interests, and suggested that their true aim was less to improve the nation's English than to whip up the kind of anxiety that would legitimize a more general shift towards educational and cultural authoritarianism. The 'political correctness' debate discussed in Chapter 4 also serves political interests: in the case of the so-called 'politically correct' themselves these interests are out in the open; for their opponents, more covertly, the debate has functioned as a remarkably effective smear campaign against those engaged in the new 'identity politics' of gender, race/ethnicity, sexual practice or (dis)ability. And the kind of linguistic self-help practices described in Chapter 5 can also be linked to a wider movement, of the kind Norman Fairclough has called 'technologizing of language' – a matter of 'experts' regulating speech communication as a way of exerting social control, particularly in the workplace.

It will be noticed that all these interests belong to groups of *people*. We must treat with the gravest suspicion all claims to the effect that a certain linguistic practice should be supported, or opposed, in the interests of 'language itself'; for languages cannot have interests (any more, to paraphrase James Milroy, than swimming or birdsong can have interests). It is we, the human inheritors and agents of language, who have interests. To base arguments on an appeal to the interests of 'the language' – a move made, for instance, by some of the opponents of 'political correctness' – can only be an obstacle to the kind of open, explicit discussion of conflicting interests which is desirable in public debate.

4 Having regard to the facts

Although I am not uncritical of the claims of linguistic science, I am enough of a scientific rationalist to find one proposition uncontroversial: there is no point conducting an argument in ignorance or defiance of the relevant facts. Another principle I suggest, therefore, is to bear in mind that disputes about language may turn on matters of fact as well as value, and that the arguments should be informed by an awareness of the facts. It may seem astonishing, not to mention depressing, that such an elementary point requires any spelling out; but in a lot of discourse on language (expert discourse included) there seems to be remarkable difficulty in disentangling the different kinds of statements (e.g. facts, principles, hypotheses, opinions) that can figure in an argument, and deciding what value to accord them.

Linguists, as I commented in relation to the standard English controversy, are apt to suppose that facts about language would, in any rational argument, speak for themselves. This supposition is false, both in theory and in practice. That something is factually true does not automatically render it desirable; we cannot simply induce what we should do by accurately observing what is currently being done, any more than we can induce the facts from the way we think things ought to be.

When we argue about what *is* desirable and why, however, it is surely incumbent upon us to acknowledge that the facts of a given matter must affect what arguments we can legitimately advance about it. They may also affect what can be done about it in practice. Today, we think it pointless to debate whether it is better for a language to be 'fixed' while still imperfect than for it to go on changing continually; nearly three centuries ago this was an issue of some moment to verbal hygienists, but since it is now generally accepted that we cannot stop language changing, it scarcely matters whether or not we think it desirable to do so.

The principle 'acknowledge the facts' has application everywhere, but it seems to me especially important in the sphere of public policy. We have reason to be alarmed when those who govern us feel able to disregard fact and design crucial policies on the basis of fantasy. By all means let us grant that facts can be disputed; that even when they are not in dispute, their meaning or significance can be contested; and that some at least can be altered. We expect politicians to use all these strategies, for politics after all is ideological. But it is one thing to ascertain the facts, decide you do not like them and, in the light of that decision, take action to change them. It is something else again to disregard the facts entirely: to accept popular beliefs, or the views of narrow interest groups, without feeling any need to look for supporting evidence, or to consider counter-evidence presented to you (a tendency that was displayed, for example, by Conservative politicians planning the national curriculum).

If pundits and politicians can get away with cavalier pronouncements on the subject of language, where on other subjects they would encounter more resistance, it is because the audience they are addressing too often responds to statements on linguistic matters in a particularly credulous and uncritical way. No doubt a lot of credulous and uncritical talk goes on in relation to other topics of public concern (crime, drugs, sex, race, genetic engineering, etc.). But in the case of language, I am always struck by how far credulity extends. Influential opinion-formers who are quite capable of mounting a serious and carefully researched argument about the utility of legalizing drugs or the ethics of bio-technology – the kind of argument that takes on prevailing common sense in an effort to make people think again – will speak and write about language in a way that simply parrots the received wisdom of the saloon bar, accepting common sense (or nonsense) at face value, and attacking as if by reflex anyone who presumes to dissent from it.

In all the principles I have proposed here, there is an underlying plea for less credulity and more critical engagement on the part of language-users, from philosophers speaking on radio programmes to ordinary parents faced with a tabloid scare story about 'falling standards' of grammar and spelling. This is the single most important precondition for developing a better and more constructive kind of public discourse on language. But there is a second condition, almost as important: reducing the damaging polarization of lay language-users and linguists. Whatever its shortcomings, linguistics has produced valuable knowledge that bears on questions of wider concern. If public discourse is to be informed, it cannot go on in total isolation from linguistics.

LINGUISTICS AND VERBAL HYGIENE

As I noted above, the issues with which I am mainly concerned in this discussion are those in which there is a legitimate public interest. The role of experts in debating issues of this kind is a delicate one: while there are excellent reasons to make use of specialist expertise for the benefit of all, there are also pressing reasons why experts should not be given *carte blanche* to set the agenda, dominate the discussion or determine the outcome. In democracies, the power or influence of unelected experts in the public arena can legitimately be exercised only by persuasion and by consent.

Ferdinand de Saussure was presumably alluding to the danger of an expert monopoly when he remarked that language was too broad a subject and too important for society as a whole to be left entirely to linguists.[5] Yet almost a century later, this warning strikes a somewhat ironic note. Far from producing a dictatorship of experts, linguistic science in the course of its short history has produced a state of mutual distrust between experts reluctant to speak to lay concerns and lay speakers with no interest in listening to linguists.

This lack of interest is certainly not because people do not care about language, nor is it because they reject all forms of authority in relation to it. It is specifically the authority of linguistics they reject. The ideas about language that have captured hearts and minds in the twentieth century are many and varied, but they have had only the most tenuous connection with the science of language that is arguably among the century's great intellectual achievements.

One of the questions I wanted to address in this book was how far linguists themselves might be responsible for this dismal state of affairs – and I call it 'dismal' because although I may be critical of my own discipline, I have sufficient respect for its achievements to be dismayed by the public indifference or antipathy that is often shown towards them. I want to end by asking how linguists might respond to the challenge of verbal hygiene. Can we make any useful contribution to the discourse of language and value without compromising our own essential values?

Beyond 'anything goes'

Why does the language-maven in the street (or the senior common-room, or the bar at the Groucho Club[6]) have such a low opinion of linguists? Because, to repeat a point I made in the preface, the popular image of linguists is one of people who believe, for reasons totally obscure to most outsiders, that in the use of language, 'anything goes'. Linguists do not give a hoot about maintaining standards, checking abuses, following rules or honouring traditions. As insensitive aesthetically as they are irresponsible morally, they refuse to distinguish the good, the bad and the ugly in usage, and there is no language too debased, no expression too vile, to be defended by a linguist on the grounds that it is 'acceptable' to someone or 'appropriate' in some context.

This view of linguists is regularly aired in public. Here, for instance, are some remarks made by the journalist Catherine Bennett in conclusion to an interview with Professor Jean Aitchison, the holder of a chair in language and communication which the media magnate Rupert Murdoch endowed at Oxford University:

> Perhaps only a linguistics scholar could study the media without reflecting uncharitably on Murdoch's own publications, and thus appeal to both News International executives and the Oxford English faculty's increasingly pluralistic dons. . . . From Aitchison's [point of view] the Sun is as 'interesting' as the Times because there is only 'appropriate' language – no such thing as right or wrong.
>
> (Bennett 1994)

This piece is both an example of and a comment on the lay/linguist 'gulf' I discussed in the preface. Bennett mentions that Rupert Murdoch included among his reasons for endowing the Murdoch Chair a desire to improve linguistic standards in the media. This suggests that, like the man in the Conway Hall, Mr Murdoch is sadly misinformed about linguistics. Or else, and this is what Bennett is implying, that giving such a remit to a professor of linguistics was a prudent (not to say cynical) precaution. Linguists alone can be relied on not to criticize Murdoch for his outstanding contribution to debasing linguistic standards through the medium of the *Sun*; for unlike everyone else, linguists believe that in language there is 'no such thing as right or wrong'.

The charge of relativism refers back to an earlier section of the interview, about the infamous *Sun* headline announcing the sinking of the Argentinian ship Belgrano during the Falklands War, which read simply 'GOTCHA!'. Aitchison says that while privately she found the sinking of the Belgrano appalling, nevertheless she would judge 'GOTCHA!' 'a very good headline, linguistically', adding that 'whether you agree with [the] message is entirely irrelevant, professionally'. Bennett comments: 'Where does this stop? Der Sturmer? Pravda?'

I am going to argue that – for reasons that are understandable, but potentially also remediable – Bennett is doing less than justice to Aitchison and to linguistics. First, though, we should clarify the substance of her criticism. In relation to a morally objectionable text like 'GOTCHA!', *Der Stürmer* or *Pravda* (and for the sake of argument let us assume that there is indeed something objectionable about these items), how can the analyst justify a neutral, 'anything goes' stance? Is this shying away from moral judgement not itself in effect immoral? And what can it mean that Aitchison is willing to characterize 'GOTCHA!' as 'very good' *linguistically*, but at the same time adamant that the message of 'GOTCHA!' is 'entirely irrelevant'? For Bennett, it means that linguistics itself is irrelevant: it cannot or will not address the only issue that really matters about 'GOTCHA!'.

I think Bennett is partly right and partly wrong. Where she is wrong is in the assumption she seems to make that describing something in the 'objective' language of science automatically confers moral legitimacy on it. In other contexts this might seem a curious notion. Epidemiologists are not thought to be in favour of disease, and criminologists by and large are not considered propagandists for crime. On the contrary, their investigations of these undesirable phenomena are usually undertaken with a view to preventing or ameliorating them. Nevertheless, the contribution we expect from them is to describe and analyse things rather than simply rant about them. As we shall see, linguistics can fulfil an analogous function, putting the 'neutral' tools of description and analysis in the service of a less neutral and more critical purpose.

Where Bennett has a point, by contrast, is in finding the way Jean Aitchison tries to explain her position puzzling, inconsistent or contradictory. Bennett has come up against the problem that linguists use a language of value which is either not explicitly acknowledged as such, or whose criteria are not stated, or both. Linguists are familiar with the conventions of this language, but outsiders may interpret it rather differently.

It is difficult, for instance, to blame Catherine Bennett for hearing such typical linguists' expressions as 'appropriate' and 'effective' as straightforward (if rather mealy-mouthed) expressions of approval. But this is not quite how linguists mean them. Rather the judgement that something is 'appropriate' (or for that matter 'very good linguistically', which looks even more like uncritical endorsement) is made in relation to the goals of the speaker and the norms of the context. Quoted in full, what Aitchison says about 'GOTCHA!' is this:

> If you view it [the war] as they [the *Sun*] obviously did, as a sick game, when you're trying to win, then Gotcha! is a very good headline, linguistically. You could argue that what a newspaper has to do is get people's attention, and get across their message. Whether you agree with their message is entirely irrelevant, professionally.

Mesmerized by what appear to her to be positive value judgements, and possibly also by her stereotype of what a linguist is bound to think or say, Catherine Bennett skates over a crucial point that is certainly 'there' in the text if you are looking for it. This point is that Aitchison's apparently favourable judgement of 'GOTCHA!' is qualified by an *if* clause. *If* you have certain views, and if your goal is to get your audience to acknowledge and perhaps share these views, *then* the choice of a particular linguistic formula may be assessed on how well it meets the goal by conveying (or enabling the audience to infer) the intended message.

What makes this particular headline 'good' (for the newspaper's purpose of 'getting across its message') is the way it directs readers to retrieve an underlying schema in which war is represented metaphorically as a game where the only thing that matters is who wins. 'GOTCHA!' is the victor's cry of triumph, the sort of thing that might be uttered by a child playing tag or a teenager blasting aliens on a computer screen. In order to interpret the headline, we have to entertain the hypothesis that there is some similarity between these scenarios and the sinking of the Belgrano, and to suspend, for the moment, alternative ways of thinking about that event. When we make the required connection (whether or not we go on to question the validity of the comparison), the message has 'got across'.

Aitchison's insistence that 'whether you agree with their message is entirely irrelevant *professionally*' should probably be interpreted as meaning that the analyst's opinion of the message is irrelevant to the analysis of how it 'gets across'. Once made, however, the analysis may offer support for conclusions that are morally non-neutral. Far from being a blanket endorsement of the language and morality of the *Sun*, Aitchison's observations suggest that the impact of 'GOTCHA!' depends on our entertaining a set of assumptions remarkable for their puerility and callousness (Aitchison herself calls them 'sick'): that war is good fun, that killing a large number of Argentinians is something to rejoice and even gloat about, and so on.

There is a strand within linguistics (sometimes labelled 'critical discourse analysis' or 'critical linguistics') for whose adherents the point of analysing texts like those appearing in the *Sun* is to bring to the surface hidden ideological presuppositions (in this case, admittedly, they are not very deeply buried, but more interesting and sophisticated examples could be adduced) *precisely so they can more easily be subjected to critical scrutiny*. In a piece she wrote for *The Journalist's Handbook* (quoted in Whitehorn 1994), Jean Aitchison makes clear she has some sympathy with this approach. She suggests that there *are* 'abuses of language' in the media, and identifies the problem as lying in usages that convey false implications: for instance, the implication of terms like 'surgical strike' and 'precision bombing' that in a certain kind of warfare only inanimate targets and not people are damaged.

This position on the 'abuse of language' is not uncommon among linguists, even those who do not identify themselves explicitly with the 'critical' current. The general professional intolerance of popular alarm about linguistic 'abuses' is sometimes qualified, in other words, by a distinction between 'real' abuses, defined in terms reminiscent of Orwell as those which mislead or falsify, and trivial or imaginary abuses such as confusing *less* and *fewer* or misplacing the apostrophe. (A similar distinction is made by Milroy and Milroy (1985) in their discussion of the 'complaint tradition', and by Robin Lakoff in *Talking Power* (1990), whose argument I discussed in Chapter 1.)

For all kinds of reasons, this is not quite the position I would want to take myself (one pertinent criticism might be that it does not license objections to something like 'GOTCHA!', which is hardly *misleading*, though it is certainly crass). But while it is possible to disagree with Aitchison's analysis or her examples (compare, for instance, my own remarks on 'collateral damage' in Chapter 2), it is inaccurate to describe her position with the sweeping statement that for her there is 'no such thing as right or wrong'.

Even if we believe fervently in right and wrong, detailed linguistic analysis has its uses. It can help us to do what Catherine Bennett notably fails to do: show, as opposed to just tell, what it is that one might find objectionable in a given text. We do not need the linguist to tell us that certain propositions are objectionable; what we may need her for is to demonstrate that these propositions are covertly embedded in a piece of discourse, and to explain how certain linguistic strategies and choices may induce us to entertain such objectionable propositions.

It may be, as Bennett says, that some texts deserve unequivocal condemnation; even so, it is dishonest as well as unenlightening to deny that repugnant texts can also be seductive. Much as moralists might wish that worthless or objectionable sentiments could only be expressed in ugly, ill-judged words (a view largely endorsed by George Orwell with his contempt for 'verbal refuse'[7]), this patently is not the case. It takes a good ear and eye for language, as well as sensitivity to the semantic nuances and metaphorical associations of words, to produce catchy soundbites, memorable advertising slogans, striking tabloid headlines and stirring political oratory. But recognizing this, as Jean Aitchison does in the case of the *Sun*, is not the same as saying that 'anything goes'.

The last few paragraphs are intended to clarify what I meant when I said that Catherine Bennett had not been entirely fair. I also said, however, that Jean Aitchison had not been entirely perspicuous in her remarks, and that Bennett had some warrant for the conclusions she drew. The conclusion I draw from this is that if linguists are to engage more productively with non-linguists, we need to think seriously about our own use of evaluative terms: both about the fact that we do actually use them, in spite of protestations to the contrary, and also about which terms we use and how.

If linguists want to deflect the 'anything goes' interpretation of such terms as 'acceptable', 'appropriate', 'effective' and the like, we need to specify more clearly the norms in relation to which an utterance is being described as 'acceptable', 'appropriate' or 'effective'. This, of course, would mean acknowledging that norms are relevant in the first place. The real core of the problem is the tendency of linguists to deny that their terms have any evaluative content or normative intent, when in reality they have both.

Consider, for example, a term that peppers linguists' public pronouncements: the word *appropriate.* Many linguists seem to imagine that some great victory would be won over the forces of ignorance and prejudice if only people would stop fetishizing what is *correct* and pay more attention to what is *appropriate.* Thus Jean Aitchison tells Catherine Bennett, 'I don't think there is a correct English . . . I use the word "appropriate" . . . much more readily'; while a point much harped on by the pro-linguistics faction in the grammar and standard English debate was that children should be required to speak 'appropriately' rather than 'correctly'.

Yet if this substitution of terms is made without further elaboration, what we get is a distinction without a difference. As with *correct, appropriate* is nothing if not normative. In everyday English it is virtually synonymous with etiquette book uses of *correct* (cf. 'what is the ———— way to dress for a funeral/address a Bishop/eat an artichoke?'). The claim that it means something totally different in linguistics does not really bear examination: an injunction to speak 'appropriately', as opposed to 'correctly', still carries the meaning, 'observe certain norms for using language'. In practice, the difference boils down to the idea that correctness is fixed whereas appropriateness varies with the situation, so that, for instance, non-standard forms that are popularly labelled 'incorrect' may not always be 'inappropriate'.

Good intentions notwithstanding, this use of the term *appropriate* is mystificatory, because it seems to rest on functional criteria when really the criteria can only be normative. It misleadingly suggests that certain ways of speaking just *are* more appropriate, that they simply 'work better' than the alternatives in a given situation, and this glosses over the crucial question, what *makes* a way of speaking appropriate?

Why, for example, is it appropriate to use standard rather than non-standard English in a job interview? (This is an oversimplification, but since it is a *locus classicus* in discussions of 'appropriateness' let us pursue it for the sake of argument.) A common answer makes use of ostensibly functional criteria: it is appropriate to use standard English in a job interview because in an interview your goal is to impress, and standard English is more impressive than non-standard English. And why is standard English more impressive than non-standard English? Research on attitudes has shown it is associated with such qualities as competence, intelligence and prestige, which are (understandably) more impressive than their opposites. Fine, and why do people associate standard English with just these qualities? Yes, you guessed it, because they believe standard English is synonymous with 'correct' English, and this belief in turn derives from the fact that standard English is the dialect of a certain class of people. Thus the judgement of standard English as 'appropriate' turns out to rest on the same linguistically arbitrary basis as the judgement of it as 'correct'. It is, in effect, the exact same judgement dressed up in functional terms which lend it a spurious air of objectivity.

Appropriate is supposed to be less prescriptive as well as more objective than *correct*, but the effect of substituting it, ironically, is less to suggest that 'anything goes' than to reify the norms we currently happen to have, however illogical or unjust they may be. Most linguists believe, for instance, that the characterization of non-standard English as 'incorrect' or 'bad' English is arbitrary and mistaken, and that prescriptions or judgements based on this characterization are therefore illogical and unjust. Yet once we have recast such judgements in the language of 'appropriateness' they become much more difficult to contest. If it is hard to convince people of the proposition that standard English is not in fact better linguistically than non-standard, it is impossible to convince them of the proposition that it is not more appropriate at a job interview; for the latter proposition is simply untrue.

Yet it is also untrue that there is anything inevitable about the particular norms that currently define what is 'appropriate' in a given context. In the past, it would have been equally accurate to make such statements as 'Welsh is not an appropriate language for use in the classroom' and 'it is not appropriate for women to speak in mixed company'. Today these propositions have the status, not of truths, but of old-fashioned prejudices held by a marginal minority.

I have no wish to suggest that linguists do not *recognize* the contingent and temporary nature of social norms for language use, nor am I saying that if we find such norms objectionable we should simply refuse to notice their existence. I am suggesting rather that the way we use the language of 'appropriateness' has the effect of treating norms as facts, of obscuring their contingency and thus of blunting critical responses to them. The alternative is to make clear that while norms materially affect people's behaviour (giving rise in the process to certain observable facts about that behaviour, e.g. that people do on the whole try to use standard English at job interviews), these norms are open to challenge and to change. Though it will never be true that 'anything goes' (that is, there will always be *some* norms in operation) language-users themselves can and do take issue with prevailing orthodoxy about what 'goes' and what does not.

It is clear that many linguists, too, would like to take issue with prevailing orthodoxy on various points. If we wish to make progress toward this goal, however, we cannot stand aside from the popular discourse of value. Attitudes cannot be changed by fiat, but only by persuasion; and persuading people to any point of view or course of action depends not only on telling them what is true to the best of your knowledge, but also on engaging their sense of what is right.

Very many language-users hold passionate convictions about what is right in language, and conversely about what is wrong with it. Unfortunately, the strength of passion with which verbal hygienists express their views and pursue their goals is not often matched by the strength of their arguments. If this is to change, and if linguistics is to make any contribution to changing it, we must acknowledge people's genuine concerns about language, understand the desires and fears that lie behind their concerns, and try to work with them, not against them.

Notes

PREFACE

1 'No hobbies or interests' (*Independent on Sunday*, 13 March 1994).
2 All of these pastimes are cited in the newspaper report. Most are self-explanatory, if odd; but readers unfamiliar with the traditional British pastime of 'trainspotting' may find a brief explanation helpful. A reference work detailing all the locomotives operating in Britain appears each year: the object of trainspotting is to 'collect' sightings of as many different trains as possible. This usually involves travelling to a major railway terminus, standing there all day and recording the serial numbers of the trains you observe. (The question 'why?' is more difficult to answer satisfactorily.)
3 More precisely, 'verbal hygiene' describes the set of normative metalinguistic *practices* that arise from this urge to meddle. For a full discussion of what I mean by the term, see Chapter 1.
4 Quoted in *Time Out*, 29 June–6 July 1994. By August 1994 Bryson's book, *Made in America*, was at the top of the London bestseller lists.
5 I have in fact profited throughout the writing of this book from regular forays into cyberspace; people are very unguarded about expressing their views there, and I take those views as a useful indication of current concerns and the range of opinions they support – always with the proviso that net-users represent a fairly narrow social stratum. Because of the unguarded quality of many posted messages, however, and in the absence of a consensus on questions of privacy/intellectual property, I will not reproduce any material from this source.
6 This is the first in a long series of generalizations about linguists, and the usual, all-generalizations-are-false-including-this-one conditions apply: I accept that not all linguists hold the views I attribute to 'linguists' (though in later chapters I will argue that certain views are orthodox within the profession, and it is also significant in my argument that linguists are *perceived* by non-linguists as collectively holding these views). The various exceptions and qualifications which need to be made will be discussed in more detail later, particularly in the conclusion.
7 For an account of Prodicus' life and his beliefs about language, see Guthrie (1969: 275–80).

1 ON VERBAL HYGIENE

1 This chapter extends the argument of an earlier essay, 'Demystifying Sociolinguistics' (Cameron 1990), and I am grateful to the editors of the

volume in which that piece appeared, John Joseph and Talbot Taylor, for their comments and encouragement. I also thank the Society of Women in Philosophy and the Social Anthropology research seminar at Manchester University for giving me useful feedback on versions of the extended argument.

2 This last example is discussed in the preface. See Bourland and Johnstone (1991).

3 The theoretical perspective that informs the present study is one in which the term 'natural' will be approached with the utmost caution. Therefore, to clarify one possible confusion: the term 'natural' applied by linguists to linguistic change can mean either, loosely, that change itself is natural, or more technically it can refer to particular kinds of change that are explained in terms of systemic tendencies within languages. Conversely, there are kinds of change that are less 'natural' (in this technical sense) because they violate what seem to be inherent constraints. However, as Milroy points out, to specify a class of 'natural' changes is not to explain any particular instance of change. Natural changes are always waiting to happen, as it were, but they only actually happen sometimes, when *social* conditions are favourable.

4 While I welcome Milroy's statement here, I am dubious about his concept of a 'consensus norm', agreed on in a kind of social contract to which all speakers in a community are party. Milroy insists that the social formation overall is characterized by conflict, but he seems to feel there is consensus at the micro-level of the (homogeneous) community. No doubt some communities are more consensual in their values than others, but an a priori assumption of consensus can mask the coercive workings of power and authority (which is not always institutional, of course). A high level of conformity need not mean everyone assents to the relevant norms: it could mean rather that they live within social relations that make deviance and resistance particularly difficult.

5 I am indebted to Roy Harris (personal communication) for making me appreciate the full force of this point. Citing Saussure and Bloomfield, Harris also notes that '[a] prescriptive role was never at any point in the history of modern linguistics rejected by the leading theorists'.

6 This in spite of the fact that the same examples are routinely used in textbooks to illustrate both: the work of the language academies is a notable case in point.

7 It should be said here that this idea about performance is not original to Judith Butler, or to those 'postmodernist' theorists who locate themselves in opposition to 'Enlightenment' notions of subjectivity and identity. Quite similar points are made, for example, albeit in a different kind of language and from a different theoretical standpoint, in the work of the sociologist Erving Goffman and his followers (cf. Goffman 1979).

8 Soon afterwards, as it happened, the LAGB elected a woman (Ruth Kempson) as chairman, upon which her title mysteriously, quietly – and, no doubt, 'naturally' – 'evolved' into *president*. As far as I know there is still no official LAGB policy mandating non-sexist language. The Linguistic Society of America (LSA), by contrast, has a set of guidelines (much disliked by some of its members) which extend to prescribing acceptable usage in the example sentences linguists make up to exemplify syntactic points. (They are published as Linguistic Society of America 1992 and I thank Janine Scancarelli for drawing my attention to them.)

9 J.V. Neustupný, 'History of language planning: retrospect and future

prospects', keynote address to the tenth AILA World Congress, Amsterdam, 13 August 1993.

2 RESTRICTIVE PRACTICES: THE POLITICS OF STYLE

1 This chapter draws on a number of conversations with copy editors, sub-editors and journalists about their style practices. I thank Meryl Altman, Mary Dearborn, Simon Frith, Simon Jenkins, Dominic Lutyens, Jennifer MacKay, Pete May and Sarah Pearsall. I am also grateful to Colleen Kennedy, from whom I learned how to teach freshman composition and through whose good offices I became familiar with the genre of the college writing handbook; to Keith Nightenhelser for introducing me to the *Editor* program; and to Clare Lees for explaining to me that scribes had house styles too.

2 Throughout this chapter, *The Times* means the Times of London; where another paper, e.g. the *New York Times* is intended it will be specified. References hereafter to *Times* style guides will be made thus: *The Times* 1913; *The Times* 1992.

3 A rather cosy relationship has developed over time among the three authorities just mentioned. When Fowler's *Modern English Usage* was revised in 1965, the task was undertaken by Sir Ernest Gowers, author of *Plain Words*. A further revision of Fowler is due in 1995, and the person responsible is Robert Burchfield, formerly editor of the *OED*. To the extent there is consensus among modern authorities, one reason for it may be that a few individuals have played a disproportionate part in compiling the texts.

4 There is a distinction between copy editors – people who do word by word checking of a text – and other kinds of editors, e.g. commissioning editors, production editors and (on newspapers and periodicals) sub-editors and the editors who oversee particular departments (art, news, features, etc.), though these editors too may on occasion check and amend copy. In this chapter the word 'editor' will normally refer to someone who edits copy, whether as part or the whole of their professional function, unless context makes clear that some other meaning is intended (e.g. 'the editor of *The Times*').

5 I am grateful to Sarah Pearsall of Routledge for discussing style policy and practice with me.

6 A nice point for any copy editor reading this: current American usage has 'copyeditor' as one word, whereas British usage still has 'copy editor' as two. Here I quote Elsie Myers Stainton exactly, but the reader will note my accuracy comes at the price of making this chapter's overall usage inconsistent. I draw attention to this point because it is an example of exactly the sort of dilemma that confronts editors all the time.

7 Subsequently I consulted correspondence retained in the archive (see below). I did not find any complaints about inconsistency, though admittedly that could be because *The Times*'s procedures for preventing it actually work. In fairness, I should also add that some comments on drafts of this chapter have strongly endorsed the editor's opinion that readers care about consistency, and this need not be because they are pedants. One friend remarked: 'it has something...to do with courtesy, the idea that people have taken trouble to get something "right" for you, the consumer.' Nevertheless, I suspect that many inconsistencies that would pain a professional copy editor go unnoticed by the average reader.

8 Although I have been unable to ascertain the exact date of publication, it is clear that Joad was writing in the 1930s, after Fowler and before Gowers: the

date of accession listed in the British Museum Catalogue is 1939. Thanks to Christopher Stray for this information.

9 An interesting, if anecdotal postscript: in August 1994 the Evening Standard challenged five *published writers* (two academics, two novelists and the Prime Minister's brother, a small businessman whose memoirs had just appeared) to spell six words, rather harder than the ones in the ALBSU's survey (*withhold, corroborate, supersede, harass, desiccated* and *peccadillo*). The highest score was three out of six; the lowest was one. It would be difficult to argue that any of the five participants was 'illiterate', and it is noticeable that those with most formal education were on the whole the lowest scorers ('So, you think you can spell?' *Evening Standard*, 15 August 1994).

10 Professionals I interviewed for this chapter were sceptical about this. Editors working for academic publishers found it a particularly dubious idea, claiming that authors had not become any more accurate or consistent as a result of the shift to computerized methods of text production; many authors had received no training in the use of their software and therefore were unable to exploit its novel capabilities (even straightforward ones such as spell-checking, word-counting or search and replace functions). I take this point, but my response would be that it is early days. There is no reason to think that a new generation of writers who grew up with computers will be as inept as their elders.

11 The intended publisher was HarperCollins, an imprint owned, like *The Times* itself, by Rupert Murdoch. The book subsequently appeared as Jenkins 1992.

12 These are hypothetical examples: for the record, *The Times* recommends the traditional that/which rule (1992:145), it permits *Ms* only in reference to US stories and where an individual woman has asked to be called *Ms X* (p.16), and it uses the designation *American Indian* (p.72).

13 I am grateful to Simon Jenkins for telling me about the archive on which this section is based, to the archivist Melanie Aspey for her assistance in locating the relevant files, and to her successor Eamon Dyas for helping me sort out permissions.

14 The memo originally read 'could you please make certain that no four-letter word gets into the paper...'. The word 'obscene' had been carefully typed in above the line.

15 This is a strong theme in the style policy of the British quality press generally, and the arrogance with which it is trumpeted is frequently quite breathtaking. My favourite example comes from *The Economist Pocket Style Book* (1986: 7): 'Above all, remember that many Americans read *The Economist* because they like to read good English. They do not want to read prose loaded with Americanisms.' *The Times* for many years made a distinction between 'English' (what British people speak) and 'American' (another language entirely), explaining for example that the phrase 'ranking officer' is 'American for an officer who is senior to another' and has 'no meaning in English' (*Times* 1953: 128).

16 This is the view of Simon Jenkins (personal communication). He regards the newspaper as less given to 'pomposity' than it was in the past.

3 DR SYNTAX AND MRS GRUNDY: THE GREAT GRAMMAR CRUSADE

1 The arguments developed in this chapter owe much to work I have done in dialogue and collaboration with others, among whom I particularly wish to

thank the London Linguistics and Politics group 1986-8 (the late Roger Andersen, Maria Black, Jill Bourne, Shula Chiat, Ben Rampton, Euan Reid and Michael Stubbs), and the staff and students of the English, Media and Drama Department at London University Institute of Education. I am also indebted for additional information to Sabrina Broadbent, Rebecca Bunting, Anne Turvey, the London Association for the Teaching of English, and the Hudson Institute in Indianapolis.

2 According to *Brewer's Dictionary of Phrase and Fable,* Dr Syntax, the protagonist of Combe's *Three Tours of Dr Syntax,* verse narratives published between 1812 and 1821, was a 'pious, henpecked clergyman, very simple-minded, but of excellent taste and scholarship'. Mrs Grundy is slightly older: an archetype of moral censoriousness, she first appeared as a straitlaced neighbour in Morton's play *Speed the Plough* (1798).

3 A 'state school' in Britain is equivalent to a 'public school' in the US; a 'public school' in Britain is an elite private school. The 1988 Act does not apply to private schools, though many have in fact adopted its prescriptions on the curriculum. It also does not apply to schools in Scotland or Northern Ireland (therefore the terms *Britain/British* will be used with caution in this chapter), nor to schooling after the minimum school-leaving age, which in England and Wales is 16.

4 US conservatives proposed this for university and college courses as well as for schools (cf. Cheney 1989), and in fact the 'curriculum wars' at under-graduate level have been a more salient public issue than analogous debates about schooling up to the age of 18. Since British universities do not have the US tradition of broad-based undergraduate 'liberal arts' education, the idea of a university core curriculum was less relevant in Britain. Nor is there a British equivalent of the notion of 'cultural literacy' (cf. Hirsch 1987).

5 The most important difference in the salient issues reflects the greater ethnic diversity of the US, and the much greater political significance this is accorded by Americans. So on one hand the debate in America was marked by more overt right-wing hostility to bilingual education and 'multicultural' or non-Eurocentric curricula; on the other hand, the school core curriculum actually proposed by Reagan's education secretary William Bennett (1987; 1988) is noticeably more multicultural in its content than the corresponding proposals for England and Wales. For further discussion of the differences in institutional framework, see below.

6 Here it might also be noted that the size and diversity of the US population makes central control over educational provision as unappealing logistically as it is politically; and, even more important, centralization would create insuperable problems of resourcing. In the US, economic disparities not merely between states but between individual school districts are frequently immense, and there is no way for the centre to enforce redistribution. In these circumstances it is hardly feasible for all schools to teach the same things and meet the same standards – a point which radical leftist commentators believe is far more important than respect for local prerogatives in understanding why US conservatives back away from British-style legislation.

7 For example, in 1993 teaching unions voted to boycott planned tests: they were challenged in the courts, but the courts ruled this was a legitimate trade dispute. The government retaliated by considering proposals to outlaw industrial action if it was 'designed to frustrate the will of Parliament' (cf. *The Guardian,* 23 April 1993). This was a striking example of the Conservative government's willingness to resort to coercion where they could not secure consent. By January 1994, on the other hand, the government was welcoming

a report whose proposals to streamline the curriculum and the associated tests were in line with the views of the teaching unions.

8 The government had split up the Department of Education and Science and renamed the education half the Department for Education: hence the change of acronym.

9 I am indebted to the classicist Keith Nightenhelser and the art historian Mitch Merback for pointing this out to me and showing me some examples.

10 The writers were asked to rank ten statements about the acquisition of literacy in order of importance. Their top priority, stressed by 97 per cent, was that 'parents should read to their children often'. The next set of statements, each of which received over 85 per cent agreement, concerned the teaching of spelling, punctuation, spoken standard English, written standard English and phonics. The only aspect of Conservative policy with which most of the writers surveyed disagreed was the insistence on children learning by heart from a canon of great literary works. It is absolutely typical that the opinions of these writers, whose own linguistic skills are exceptional but whose views on how children learn to read and write are not, were given far more weight in the press and by the Secretary of State for Education than opinions expressed by teachers, educationists or linguists.

11 GCE O [i.e. General Certificate of Education Ordinary] level was a nationally recognized public examination taken by pupils in the upper ability range at the age of 16. It has been replaced in England and Wales by the 'General Certificate of Secondary Education' or GCSE, intended for a wider range of pupils.

12 Again, this terminology may confuse non-British readers. A 'grammar school' was a secondary school (11–18) for which entrants were selected by means of an exam known as the 'eleven plus', usually an IQ or verbal reasoning test. Grammar schools took approximately the top 20 per cent of candidates, the rest going to less academic 'secondary modern' schools. This system was largely abandoned by the mid-1970s in favour of 'comprehensive' (that is, non-selective) secondary education.

13 An exception was made here for Wales, where Welsh was given legitimacy alongside English. Otherwise, official attitudes were aptly summed up in the Secretary of State for Education's *Notes of Supplementary Guidance* to the Cox Committee (DES 1988b), which enjoined members to bear in mind the 'cardinal point that English should be the first language and medium of instruction for all pupils in England' (para 13). For more detailed analysis of this issue in relation to the National Curriculum, see Cameron and Bourne 1989.

14 It was ill-starred because its announcement was immediately followed by a number of damaging revelations about the sexual and financial misconduct of several Conservative politicians, some of them government ministers. 'Back to basics' thus exposed the conservatives to charges of hypocrisy, and to a certain amount of ridicule.

4 CIVILITY AND ITS DISCONTENTS: LANGUAGE AND 'POLITICAL CORRECTNESS'

1 For instance, in 1992 I participated in a BBC radio discussion of 'political correctness' in which my co-panellist alleged that at one British higher educational institution it was a disciplinary offence to use the word *charwoman*. Since she named the institution, I later tried and was unable

to verify this allegation. I do not however believe that my co-panellist was deliberately lying. Rather I think she was credulous in simply accepting rumours without checking the facts.

2 I take this line from a satirical lyric written and performed by Bill Defotis. It goes to the tune of *You Say Tomato*.

3 Throughout this chapter I will try to be scrupulous in distinguishing between conservative and liberal critics of 'political correctness' (and to keep in mind that it also has leftist, that is, socialist as opposed to liberal, critics). The evidence is overwhelming (for an overview, see Messer-Davidow 1993) that the main source of opposition to 'PC', which was also the constituency responsible for instigating the debate during the 1980s, is an organized group of self-proclaimed 'cultural conservatives' in the US. It is nevertheless true that in the 1990s some very high-profile critics have been liberals, not conservatives; and that these two groups of critics have differing anxieties as well as different theoretical presuppositions concerning language.

4 Very recently there has been a further broadening of the term: people can now be defined as 'politically correct' not because of their *views* on race/ gender/sexuality but inherently, because they belong to a minority group. For example, the film *Bhaji on the Beach* was labelled 'politically correct' by reviewers simply because it was made by and about British Asian women. As *Independent on Sunday* columnist Nick Hornby enquired (13 March 1994), what are minority artists supposed to do if they wish to avoid the stigma of 'political correctness': get white men to make their films for them?

5 Though not, sadly, on 1 April. The occasion for it was the passage of the Sex Discrimination Act, which among other things outlawed the generic use of *-man* compounds in job advertisements. The letter is reprinted in Gregory 1989: 196.

6 'Gender-free language' here refers to what is more usually called 'non-sexist' language. The person mainly responsible for the drafting of the guidelines was Sara Mills. I am grateful to Janet Brand, formerly convener of POWC, for making available her file of memos, correspondence and press cuttings. Quotations from the correspondence will not be attributed.

7 Clause 28: a statutory provision restraining local authorities in England and Wales from 'promoting homosexuality'. 'Abseiling': a mountaineering man-oeuvre which in the US is called 'rappelling'.

8 The two major exceptions are the historically dominant Anglo-Saxon descent group and the historically subjugated indigenous peoples, who are sometimes called 'Native Americans' but often prefer more specific terms (*Cherokee, Navajo*) that acknowledge they (a) are not a homogeneous mass and (b) had already named themselves long before the conquest of the Americas.

9 Simon Frith (personal communication) plausibly suggests that one answer to this question is 'the education system'. That is why the most passionate arguments about linguistic standards are conducted in the context of what kind of language is taught in schools (see Chapter 3).

10 It follows that the linguistic strategies designed to do this have to keep changing; if they become so familiar as to permit automatic decoding then their power to jar or shock is lost. The continual invention of new terms and new strategies is another thing that baffles and irritates critics of radical verbal hygiene, since for them it is axiomatic that for the sake of communication we should seek to maximize the stability of the system.

11 In the US over the last decade these anxieties have been expressed in the

emergence of organizations like 'US English', which has campaigned with some success to outlaw the use of languages other than English in public domains. In Britain, as I noted in Chapter 3, similar anxieties have given rise to a strong emphasis on standard English – and only English – in the national school curriculum. And in the former Soviet republics, whose national languages were often suppressed, downgraded and deliberately Russified, major battles are now going on to force Russian-speaking minorities to prove their proficiency in the now-restored tongues, or lose their citizens' rights (King 1993; 1994).

12 Roger Scruton exemplifies both these points of view. The 1983 article quoted earlier in the chapter (see pages 151–2) accuses feminists of going against nature by promoting the principle that men and women are 'morally indistinguishable'.

5 THE NEW PYGMALION: VERBAL HYGIENE FOR WOMEN

1 The sixteen women who talked to me about their experiences of assertiveness/communication skills training for this chapter were in no sense a representative sample: in most cases they were either acquaintances or they volunteered after hearing me present a talk on verbal hygiene texts for women. Four of the women were or had been trainers, the others trainees. Most (though not all) were either students or academics at the time of the research, but their experiences of training were much more varied, including management and professional programmes provided by non-university employers, courses taken within adult/community education, seminars run by commercial consultancy firms and sessions sponsored by voluntary organizations and women's groups. Only one student and one academic had participated in AT through a university. Overall, informants spanned a large age range, came from many different parts of Britain and had varying occupational backgrounds, but all were white and highly educated and most were middle class. That probably makes them not untypical of AT's clientele, but it excludes the experience of working-class and less educated women who encounter training either through their work or through courses for women 'returners' which are now quite common. (One of the trainers I spoke to had worked on such a course, while two more had worked with women and men in non-elite public sector occupations.)

Interviews were informal and unstructured, sometimes involving a small group of two or three, though more often one-to-one: I usually asked people to describe their experiences of the kinds of training I was interested in, and say what they felt they (or their trainees) had got out of it. The topic of self-help books was also introduced by some of the interviewees, and also by various people I met in other circumstances (this research was done at the peak of Deborah Tannen's popularity). I am grateful to all those who shared their experiences and opinions with me, and/or supplied written information I have used in this chapter; I also extend my warmest thanks to Mary Crawford and Liz Hampson, whose knowledge of and research on AT I have drawn on throughout this chapter.

2 A good overview and discussion of gender differences and gender norms across cultures is Joel Sherzer's 'A diversity of voices: women's and men's speech in ethnographic perspective' (Sherzer 1987). Sherzer gives examples of verbal hygiene practices among the Kuna and Araucarian peoples of South America, and makes the important point that while the actual content of gender norms for speaking is extremely variable

cross-culturally, it is common to find that prescriptions for women's and men's speech are taken by a society as symbolic expressions of what women and men are like; e.g. a rule specifying deferential or modest speech for women is taken to reflect the 'fact' that women are by nature deferential or modest. This is as true of Anglophone societies as it is of indigenous American peoples.

3 I owe this information to Sharon Millar.

4 This is one of the reasons why sociolinguists report persistent gender differences in the use of standard and non-standard variants. Women are often (though not always) more standard speakers than men of the same class, and some studies also find them over-reporting their use of standard variants in self-evaluation tests, which might suggest they have more negative attitudes than their male peers to non-standard speech (Trudgill 1972). There are some material (economic) factors in play, in that sex-segregated labour markets reinforce the need for working-class women to be 'better spoken' than men of the same class (cf. Nichols 1983). But this does not entirely explain why the same kind of gender differentiation is found across classes.

5 In fairness, it must be acknowledged here that market research carried out on the demographics of self-help reading (Wood 1988) reveals that men and women are equally likely to buy self-help books; and that men buy texts from the genre devoted to personal relationships as well as from the more traditional 'how to succeed in business' genre. Though I admit to finding this information somewhat surprising, I do not feel it undermines the analysis offered here: even if the market survey made clear (which it does not) that men and women read the same books with the same enthusiasm, it remains true that they do not read them from the same position – their histories and the social contexts in which they read place the two genders in a different relation to the self-improvement project.

6 I am grateful to Beverley Skeggs for drawing this book to my attention.

7 This may be why, as Mary Crawford (1995) points out, AT has in practice been targeted overwhelmingly at women rather than men, and at modifying passive behaviour, a stereotypically female problem, rather than aggressive behaviour, stereotypically a male one – even though *in theory* these behaviours are equally deviations from the ideal assertive mean. (I would add here that to the extent AT is a 'for profit' enterprise it will obviously target groups it suspects are willing to invest in self-improvement; middle-class women, as I suggested earlier in this chapter, are probably the single largest such group.)

8 The game actually has different rules in different speech communities: culturally patterned variation in the conventional meanings of direct and indirect speech styles are a source of interethnic and cross-cultural miscommunication, as when Americans find British people 'stand offish' and Britons find Americans 'pushy'. Male–female miscommunication has also been explained as an instance of cultural difference (by Tannen 1990; see also Maltz and Borker 1982): but to my mind, less convincingly (I will say why later on in this chapter).

9 A similar procedure is often resorted to with abused women of all ethnicities, on the grounds that encouraging assertion towards violent men can be so risky as to constitute unethical behaviour. This makes an ironic contrast with the treatment of abusers themselves, who are often seen as good candidates for AT.

10 That no such argument has ever been made in relation to women of the

majority ethnic group might well suggest that the treatment of Puerto Rican women in this case is racist as well as sexist, multiculturalist rhetoric notwithstanding. 'We' are individuals whose culture encompasses a range of opinions and practices, not to mention internal conflicts of interest; 'they' are a lumpen undifferentiated mass, uniformly in thrall to the ideology of 'machismo'.

11 It is worth pointing out here that these research findings are rarely if ever directly relevant to the specific case of English-speaking corporate women; on the question of whether their speech strategies differ significantly from those of male colleagues, there is, so far as I know, little evidence one way or the other. The idea that women are more indirect than men is extrapolated from research on female friends talking casually or women in 'caring' professions such as medicine, where one would expect a high degree of sensitivity to addressees' face. If it is accepted that context strongly influences speech style, then generalizations about the 'indirect' behaviour of women executives may well turn out to be misleading.

12 Although I will focus here on Tannen's book, there are plenty of other self-help texts wholly or partly in the same vein (whether some at least were directly inspired by Tannen's runaway success I do not know). They include Berkowitz and Gittines's *What Men Won't Tell You But Women Need to Know* (1991), voice coach Lillian Glass's *He Says, She Says: Closing the Communication Gap between the Sexes* (1992), John Gray's *Men Are From Mars, Women Are From Venus* (1992), and Naifeh and Smith's *Why Can't Men Open Up?* (1985).

13 I accidentally came across a piece of evidence that men who do read Tannen's book may understand its message very differently. In June 1992 *Good Housekeeping* magazine ran a feature on four women who left their husbands at home with the children while they went away together for a weekend in the country (Buchanan 1992). The writer interviewed the men about their attitudes to this (apparently extraordinary) event. One said that he understood that women had needs he could not meet, and must therefore be allowed the company of other women from time to time. As his authority he cited 'a book on male–female relations' that explained why 'women love to talk endlessly about nothing, to no purpose or conclusion'. Given the timing and description, I feel fairly sure the book in question is *You Just Don't Understand*, and it does not seem to have increased this male reader's tolerance for differing gender styles.

14 It should of course be acknowledged that in certain circumstances this can be just as true of racial and ethnic differences (e.g. under slavery or colonialism) and of class differences. The ethnic analogies used by 'difference' theorists are themselves rather selective and politically naive about racism.

15 I owe this argument to Meryl Altman, who expressed it with customary elegance: 'the self didn't die, it just moved to another shelf in the feminist bookstore.'

6 ON THE STATE OF THE STATE OF THE LANGUAGE

1 All examples are taken from press reports. A brief postscript to the French example: the *loi Toubon* has now been significantly watered down (at the time of writing it looks as if it will apply only to public bodies, not private businesses). The British MP's Bill was, of course, a publicity stunt rather than a serious piece of legislation. Britain has a parliamentary procedure (the 'ten-minute rule') expressly so MPs can vent their feelings in this way.

2 Information on 'Disorder of written expression' comes from an op-ed piece that appeared in the *New York Times* headlined 'Is Bad Writing a Mental Disorder?' (Kirk and Kutchins 1994). The piece is worth citing as an interesting and cogent critique of the D.S.M-IV in general.

3 Connoisseurs of this kind of material will appreciate a full citation for the Klingon story: Carrie Dolan, 'Translating the Bible into Suitable Klingon Stirs Cosmic Debate', *Wall Street Journal*, 13 June 1994. My thanks to the indefatigable Keith Nightenhelser for furnishing me with this reference, which I would otherwise almost certainly have overlooked.

4 This should not be taken as a denial of the proposition that language has a biological basis (though a great deal remains to be discovered about what exactly is meant by that). The error I am criticizing lies in supposing either that language is itself an organism (as opposed to a faculty of certain organisms), or that because some things about the shape of human languages are biologically determined, everything about language and language use must be explained in similar terms.

5 Saussure's words appear as an epigraph to all books in the Politics of Language series.

6 An establishment patronized by media folk in London (provided the club will have them as members).

7 The phrase 'verbal refuse' (which was, incidentally, one inspiration for my own 'verbal hygiene') appears in the much quoted last sentence of 'Politics and the English language', which advocates putting 'verbal refuse into the dustbin where it belongs'. Throughout 'Politics and the English language' Orwell continually remarks on the fact that his examples of misleading or morally reprehensible statements are also prime examples of ugly prose. He has little to say, at least in this essay (and to my mind it is a weakness), about the problems posed by, say, fascist political oratory or advertising, where linguistic skill, force, persuasiveness and sometimes even elegance and wit may be deployed to reprehensible effect. (You wonder what he would have said about the *Sun*, with its unswerving commitment to clarity, Anglo-Saxon vocabulary and calling a spade a spade.)

References

Note: *Not all items cited in the main text appear in these references. Full references are given for press columns and features carrying a byline, but not for anonymous news reports and editorials, or for broadcast items. In these cases the name and date of the newspaper or broadcasting network is given in the main text where a piece is first cited. Where public speeches have been cited or quoted, reference is made to the publication or broadcast network which reported them. Information regarding academic papers delivered orally and for which there is no published or unpublished text available is given in the notes.*

Armstrong, N. and Tennenhouse, L. (eds) (1987) *The Ideology of Conduct: Essays on Literature and the History of Sexuality*, New York: Methuen.

Aronoff, R. (1992) 'Review of *Gender*, by Greville Corbett', *Language* 68.3, pp. 605–10.

Aufderheide, P. (ed.) (1992) *Beyond PC: Toward A Politics of Understanding*, St Paul, MN: Graywolf Press.

Baker, G. and Hacker, P. (1984) *Language, Sense and Nonsense*, Oxford: Blackwell.

Baker, N. (1993) 'Survival of the fittest': review of *Pause and Effect: an Introduction to the History of Punctuation in the West* by M.B. Parkes, *New York Review of Books*, 4 November.

Bakhtin, M. (1981) *The Dialogic Imagination: Four Essays*, ed. M. Holquist, trans. C. Emerson and M. Holquist, Austin: University of Texas Press.

Baron, D. (1980) *Grammar and Good Taste*, New Haven: Yale University Press.

Bennett, C. (1994) 'Gotcha, you wimpy words', *The Guardian*, 4 July.

Bennett, W. (1987) *James Madison High School: A Curriculum for American Students*, Washington DC: US Department of Education.

——— (1988) *James Madison Elementary School: A Curriculum for American Students*, Washington DC: US Department of Education.

Berkowitz, B. with Gittines, R. (1991) *What Men Won't Tell You But Women Need To Know*, New York: Avon Books.

Berman, P. (ed.) (1992) *Debating PC: The Controversy Over Political Correctness on College Campuses*, New York: Laurel.

Berne, E. (1966) *The Games People Play: The Psychology of Human Relationships*, London: Deutsch.

Billig, M. (1991) *Ideology and Opinions*, London: Sage.

Bloom, L.Z., Coburn, K. and Pearlman, J. (1975) *The New Assertive Woman*, New York: Dell Books.

Bodine, A. (1990) 'Androcentrism in prescriptive grammar', in *The Feminist Critique of Language*, ed. D. Cameron, London: Routledge.

Bourland, D. and Johnstone, P. (1991) *To Be Or Not: An E-Prime Anthology*, San Francisco: International Society for General Semantics.

Brailsford, K. (1993) 'The sexes: a dialogue of the deaf', *Elle* [US] March 1993, pp. 120–2.

Brown, P. (1980) 'How and why are women more polite?' in *Women and Language in Literature and Society*, ed. S. McConell-Ginet, N. Furman and R. Borker, New York: Praeger.

Buchanan, C. (1992) 'Why £75 saved these women's sanity', *Good Housekeeping* [UK] June 1992, pp. 82–4.

Burling, R. (1993) 'Review of *Lunatic Lovers of Language*, by Marina Yaguello', *Language* 69.1, pp. 168–70.

Butler, J. (1990) *Gender Trouble: Feminism and the Subversion of Identity*, New York: Routledge.

Butler, M. (1993) 'Ambush: the politics of National Curriculum English, 1990–3', *Critical Quarterly* 35.4, Winter, pp. 8–12.

Bywater, M. (1992) 'Move over darlings', *Cosmopolitan* [UK] March 1992, pp. 88–93.

Cameron, D. (1990) 'Demystifying sociolinguistics: or, why language does not reflect society', in Joseph and Taylor.

—————— (1994) 'Words, words, words', in *The War of the Words: The Political Correctness Debate*, ed. S. Dunant, London: Virago Press.

—————— (1994) 'Verbal hygiene for women: linguistics misapplied?', *Applied Linguistics* 15.4.

Cameron, D. and Bourne, J. (1989) 'No common ground: Kingman, grammar and the nation', *Language and Education* 2.3, pp. 147–60.

Carroll, L. (1971) *Alice's Adventures in Wonderland, and Through the Looking Glass, and What Alice Found There*, London: Oxford University Press.

Carter, R. (1990) 'The new grammar teaching', in *Knowledge About Language and the Curriculum*, ed. R. Carter, London: Hodder & Stoughton.

Cheney, L.V. (1989) *50 Hours: A Core Curriculum for College Students*, Washington DC: National Endowment for the Humanities.

Cherreson, A. (1993) 'The voice of reason', *New Woman* February 1993, pp. 160–2.

Cheshire, J. (1984) 'The relationship of language and sex in English', in *Applied Sociolinguistics*, ed. P. Trudgill, Oxford: Oxford University Press.

Cheshire, J. and Jenkins, N. (1991) 'Gender issues in the GCSE oral English examination, Part II', *Language and Education* 5.1, pp.19–40.

Chicago Manual of Style: For Authors, Editors and Copywriters (1982) 13th edn, revised and extended, Chicago: Chicago University Press.

Coates, J. (ed.) (1985) *Language and Sex*, Committee for Linguistics in Education (CLIE) Booklets.

—————— (1989) 'Gossip revisited', in *Women in their Speech Communities*, ed. J. Coates and D. Cameron, London: Longman.

Cochrane, R. (1993) 'Niggles in a haystack', *Verbatim* 20.2, Autumn, p. 20.

Cohen, S. (1987) *Folk Devils and Moral Panics: the Creation of Mods and Rockers* (new edn), Oxford: Basil Blackwell.

Cox, B. (1990) 'Editorial', *Critical Quarterly* 32.4, Winter, pp. 1–6.

Crawford, M. (1995) *Talking Difference*, London: Sage.

Crowley, T. (1989) *The Politics of Discourse*, London: Macmillan.

—————— (ed.) (1991) *Proper English? Readings in Language, History and Cultural Identity*, London: Routledge.

Crystal, D. (1984) *Who Cares About English Usage?*, Harmondsworth: Penguin.

DES (1975) *A Language for Life* [the Bullock Report], London: HMSO.

—— (1988a) Report of the Committee of Inquiry into the teaching of the English language [the Kingman Report], London: HMSO.

—— (1988b) *National Curriculum English Working Group: Terms of Reference and Notes of Supplementary Guidance*, London: DES.

—— (1989) *English for Ages 5–16* [the Report of the National Curriculum English Working Group chaired by Professor Brian Cox], London: DES.

DFE (1993) *English for Ages 5–16, 1993: Proposals of the Secretary of State for Education and the Secretary of State for Wales*, London: HMSO.

Dickson, A. (1982) *A Woman In Your Own Right: Assertiveness and You* (revised edn), London: Quartet Books.

Dolan, C. (1994) 'Translating the Bible' into suitable Klingon stirs cosmic debate', *Wall Street Journal*, 13 June.

Dowling, C. (1981) *The Cinderella Complex: Women's Hidden Fear of Independence*, New York: Summit.

Eble, C. (1976) 'Etiquette books as linguistic authority', in *LACUS Forum II*, ed. P. Reich, Columbia, SC: Hornbeam Press.

The Economist (1986) *The Economist Pocket Style Book*, London: Economist Publications Ltd.

Ehrenreich, B. (1992) 'The challenge for the Left', in Berman.

Eisenstein, E.L. (1979) *The Printing Press as an Agent of Change: Communications and Cultural Transformations in Early-Modern Europe*, New York: Cambridge University Press.

Epstein, B. (1992) 'Political correctness and identity politics', in Aufderheide.

Evans, M. (1991) *A Good School: Life at a Girls' Grammar School in the 1950s*, London: Women's Press.

Fairclough, N. (1992) 'Introduction', *Critical Language Awareness*, ed. N. Fairclough, London: Longman.

Fish, S. (1992) 'There's no such thing as free speech and it's a good thing too', in Berman.

Fishman, P. (1983) 'Interaction: the work women do', in *Language, Gender and Society*, ed. B. Thorne, C. Kramarae and N. Henley, Rowley, MA: Newbury House.

Fowler, H.W. (1926) *Modern English Usage*, Oxford: Oxford University Press.

—— (1968) *Modern English Usage* (2nd edition revised by Sir Ernest Gowers), Oxford: Oxford University Press.

Fromkin, V. and Rodman, R. (1983) *An Introduction To Language* (3rd edn), New York: Holt Rinehart Winston.

Gervasio, A. and Crawford, M. (1989) 'Social evaluations of assertiveness: a critique and speech act reformulation', *Psychology of Women Quarterly* 13, pp. 1–25.

Glass, L. (1992) *He Says, She Says: Closing the Communication Gap Between the Sexes*, London: Piatkus.

Goffman, E. (1979) *Gender Advertisements*, New York: Harper & Row.

Gowers, E. (1948) *Plain Words*, London: HMSO.

—— (1954) *The Complete Plain Words*, London: HMSO.

—— (1973) *The Complete Plain Words* (revised by Sir Bruce Fraser), London: HMSO.

Graddol, D. and Swann, J. (1989) *Gender Voices*, Oxford: Blackwell.

Gray, J. (1992) *Men Are From Mars, Women Are From Venus: A Practical Guide for Improving Communication and Getting What You Want In Your Relationships*, New York: HarperCollins.

Gregory, K. (1989) *The Last Cuckoo: The Very Best Letters To The Times Since 1900*, London: Unwin Hyman.

Guthrie, W.K.C. (1969) *A History of Greek Philosophy Vol.III: The Fifth Century Enlightenment*, Cambridge: Cambridge University Press.

Hajdu, D. (1990) 'Why not talk like a grown-up?', *Cosmopolitan* [US] February 1990, pp. 129–31.

Hall, R. (1960) *Linguistics and Your Language* (2nd revised edn of *Leave Your Language Alone*), Garden City, NJ: Anchor.

Hall, S., Critcher, C., Jefferson, T., Clarke, J. and Roberts, B. (1978) *Policing The Crisis: Mugging, the State and Law and Order*, London: Macmillan.

Harper, K. (1992) 'Suspect words sent to Coventry', *Guardian*, 8 September.

Haraway, D. (1991) 'A cyborg manifesto', *Simians, Cyborgs and Women: the Reinvention of Nature*, New York: Routledge.

Harris, R. (1980) *The Language Makers*, London: Duckworth.

——— (1981) *The Language Myth*, London: Duckworth.

——— (1983) 'All my eye and Betty Martin', *London Review of Books*, 1–21 December.

——— (1987) *The Language Machine*, London: Duckworth.

Harris, R. and Taylor, T. (1989) *Landmarks in Linguistic Thought*, London: Routledge.

Hattersley, R. (1993) 'Spelling out correctly one's inadequacies', *Guardian*, 11 January.

Haugen, E. (1972) 'Dialect, language, nation', in *Sociolinguistics*, ed. J. Pride and J. Holmes, Harmondsworth: Penguin.

Henley, N. (1978) 'Changing the body power structure', *Women: A Journal of Liberation* 6.1, pp. 34–8.

Hirsch, E.D. (1987) *Cultural Literacy: What Every American Needs to Know*, Boston: Houghton Mifflin.

Hoggart, S. (1993) 'Silly shibboleth of the sex workers', *Observer*, 11 July.

Honey, J. (1983) *The Language Trap: Race, Class and the Standard English Issue in British Schools*, Middlesex: National Council for Educational Standards.

Hornby, N. (1994) 'Why I'm a bleeding-heart drippy pinko pansy', *Independent on Sunday*, 13 March.

Hughes, R. (1993) *Culture of Complaint: The Fraying of America*, New York: Oxford University Press.

Isserman, M. (1991) 'Travels with Dinesh', *Tikkun* 6.5.

Jenkins, N. and Cheshire, J. (1990) 'Gender issues in the GCSE oral English examination, Part I', *Language and Education* 4.4, pp. 261–91.

Jenkins, S. (1988) 'Dr Syntax to wed Mrs Grundy shock', *Sunday Times*, 20 November.

——— (1990) 'A change of style to suit *The Times*', *The Times*, 12 June.

——— (ed.) (1992) *The Times Guide to English Style and Usage*, London: Times Books.

Joad, C.E.M. (n.d.) *How To Write, Think and Speak Correctly*, London: Odhams.

Jones, A. (1992) 'Ten classic career mistakes all women make', *Options*, February, pp. 110–12.

Jones, A.R. (1987) 'Nets and bridles: early modern conduct books and sixteenth century women's lyrics', in Armstrong and Tennenhouse.

Joseph, J. (1987) *Eloquence and Power: the Rise of Language Standards and Standard Languages*, London: Frances Pinter.

Joseph, J. and Taylor, T. (eds) (1990) *Ideologies of Language*, London: Routledge.

Kanfer, S. (1972) 'Sispeak: a misguided attempt to change herstory', *Time*, 23 October.

King, C. (1993) 'The new Bessarabian question: politics, ethnicity and the two

Romanian states', paper delivered to the American Political Science Association.
———— (1994) 'Soviet policy in the annexed East European borderlands: language, politics and ethnicity in Moldova', in *The Soviet Union in Eastern Europe 1945–1989*, ed. O.A. Westad, S. Holtsmark and I. Neumann, London: Macmillan.
Kirk, S.A. and Kutchins, H. (1994) 'Is bad writing a mental disorder?', *New York Times*, 20 June.
Konstantinov, J. (1990) 'The breakdown of Newspeak in an Eastern European country', unpublished paper delivered at Roehampton Institute.
Kramarae, C. (1981) *Women and Men Speaking: Frameworks for Analysis*, Rowley, MA: Newbury House.
———— (1988) 'Censorship of women's voices on radio', in *Gender and Discourse: The Power of Talk*, ed. A. Todd and S. Fisher, Norwood, NJ: Ablex Publishing Corp.
Labov, W. (1972) 'The logic of nonstandard English', *Language in the Inner City*, Philadelphia: Pennsylvania University Press.
Lakoff, R. (1975) *Language and Woman's Place*, New York: Harper & Row.
———— (1990) *Talking Power: The Politics of Language*, New York: Basic Books.
Lang, B. (1991) *Writing and the Moral Self*, New York: Routledge.
Leith, D. (1983) *A Social History of English*, London: Routledge.
Lichterman, P. (1992) 'Self-help reading as a thin culture', *Media, Culture and Society* 14, pp. 421–47.
Linguistic Society of America Guidelines for Nonsexist Usage (1992) *LSA Bulletin* no.135, pp. 8–9.
Locke, J. (1975) *An Essay concerning Human Understanding* (1690), ed. P.H. Nidditch, Oxford: Clarendon Press.
MacCabe, C. (1990) 'Language, literature, identity: reflections on the Cox Report', *Critical Quarterly* 32.4, Winter, pp. 7–15.
MacCannell, D. and MacCannell, J.F. (1987) 'The beauty system', in Armstrong and Tennenhouse.
Maltz, D. and Borker, R. (1982) 'A cultural approach to male–female misunderstanding', in *Language and Social Identity*, ed. J. Gumperz, Cambridge: Cambridge University Press.
Manning, P. and Haddock, M. (1989) *Leadership Skills for Women: Achieving Impact as a Manager*, California: Crisp Publications.
Marenbon, J. (1987) *English Our English: The New Orthodoxy Examined*, London: Centre for Policy Studies.
Messer-Davidow, E. (1993) 'Manufacturing the attack on liberalized Higher Education', *Social Text* 36, pp. 40–80.
Miller, A.H. (1993) 'Political correctness and American higher education', *Politics* 13.1, pp. 22–8.
Miller, C. and Swift, K. (1976) *Words and Women: New Language in New Times*, Harmondsworth: Penguin Books.
———— (1980) *A Handbook of Nonsexist Writing*, London: Women's Press.
Milroy, J. (1992) *Language Variation and Change*, Oxford: Blackwell.
Milroy, J. and Milroy, L. (1985) *Authority in Language*, Oxford: Blackwell.
Naifeh, S. and Smith, G.W. (1985) *Why Can't Men Open Up? Overcoming Men's Fear of Intimacy*, London: Frederick Muller.
Naughton, J. (1993) 'Cuddling the crocodile', *Observer*, 5 September.
Nichols, P. (1983) 'Linguistic options and choices for women in the rural South', in *Language, Gender and Society*, ed. B. Thorne, C. Kramarae and N. Henley, Rowley, MA: Newbury House.

Norwood, R. (1985) *Women Who Love Too Much*, London: Arrow.

Nunberg, G. (1990) 'What the usage panel thinks', in Ricks and Michaels.

O'Barr, W. and Atkins, B. (1980) '"Women's language" or "powerless language"?', in *Women and Language in Literature and Society*, ed. S. McConnell-Ginet, N. Furman and R. Borker, New York: Praeger.

Orwell, G. (1946) 'Politics and the English language', in *The Collected Essays, Journalism and Letters of George Orwell, Vol. 4, In Front of Your Nose, 1945–50*, (1968), ed. S. Orwell and I. Angus, Harmondsworth: Penguin.

—— (1949) *Nineteen Eighty-Four*, London: Secker & Warburg.

Oxford Dictionary for Writers and Editors, Oxford: Oxford University Press.

Pateman, T. (1980) *Language, Truth and Politics*, Lewes, Sussex: Jean Stroud.

Perry, R. (1992) 'A short history of the term *politically correct*', in Aufderheide.

Post, E. (1922) *Etiquette: The Blue Book of Social Usage*, New York: Funk and Wagnell.

Quirk, R., Greenbaum, S., Leech, G, and Svartvik, J. (1985) *A Comprehensive Grammar of English*, London: Longman.

Rae, J. (1982) 'The decline and fall of English grammar', *Observer*, 7 February.

Rakos, R.F. (1991) *Assertive Behavior: Theory, Research and Training*. International Series on Communication Skills, London: Routledge.

Ricks, C. and Michaels, L. (eds) (1990) *The State of the Language*, London: Faber.

Ross, A.S.C. (1954) 'Linguistic class indicators in present-day English', *Neuephilologische Mitteilungen*, 55, extract reprinted in Crowley 1991.

Sampson, V. (1993) 'All you need is clout', *She*, November, pp. 88–93.

Scragg, D.G. (1974) *A History of English Spelling*, Mont Follick Series vol.3, Manchester: Manchester University Press.

Scruton, R. (1983) 'How Newspeak leaves us naked', *The Times*, 1 February.

Shaw, G.B. (1913) *Pygmalion*, in *The Bodley Head Bernard Shaw: Collected Plays with their Prefaces* vol. 4 (1972), London: Bodley Head.

Sherzer, J. (1987) 'A diversity of voices: women's and men's speech in ethnographic perspective', in *Language, Sex and Gender in Cross-cultural Perspective*, ed. S.U. Phillips, C. Tanz and S. Steele, New York: Oxford University Press.

Shorter Oxford Dictionary (1993) Oxford: Oxford University Press.

Simonds, W. (1992) *Women and Self-Help Culture: Reading Between The Lines*, New Brunswick, NJ: Rutgers University Press.

Spender, D. (1980) *Man Made Language*, London: Routledge & Kegan Paul.

Stainton, E.M. (1991) *The Fine Art of Copyediting*, New York: Columbia University Press.

Strunk, W. and White, E.B. (1979) *The Elements of Style*, 3rd edn, New York: Macmillan.

Tannen, D. (1990) *You Just Don't Understand: Women and Men in Conversation*, New York: Ballantine.

—— (1991) 'How to talk so men will listen', *McCall's*, May 1991, pp. 66–70.

Taylor, J. (1991) 'Are you politically correct?', *New York Magazine*, 21 January.

Taylor, T. (1990) 'Who's to be master? The institutionalization of authority in the science of language', in Joseph and Taylor.

Thiesmeyer, E.C. and Thiesmeyer, J.E. (1990) *Editor: A System for Checking Usage, Mechanics, Vocabulary and Structure, Version 4.0. MLA Software for Students and Scholars*, New York: Modern Language Association.

The Times (1913) *Style Book and The Spelling of Words Adopted by The Times*, London [revised 1928, 1936, 1939].

—— (1939) *English in The Times*, London [revised 1945].

—— (1953) *The Times Style Book*, London [revised 1960, 1970, 1981].

——— (1992) *The Times English Style and Usage Guide*, London: Times Newspapers.

Tisdall, P. (1993) 'A row that looks like America', *Guardian*, 5 June.

Today (1985) *Style Book*, London.

Trahern, J.B. Jr. (ed.) (1988) *Standardizing English: Essays in the History of Language Change*, Knoxville, Tenn: University of Tennessee Press.

Troemel-Ploetz, S. (1991) 'Selling the apolitical', *Discourse and Society* 2.4, pp. 489–502.

Trudgill, P. (1972) 'Sex, covert prestige and linguistic change in the urban British English of Norwich', *Language in Society* 1, pp. 179–95.

——— (1978) 'Sociolinguistics and sociolinguistics', in *Sociolinguistic Patterns in British English*, P. Trudgill (ed.), London: Edward Arnold.

University of Strathclyde (1991) 'Gender free language: guidelines for staff and students', Glasgow: University of Strathclyde Programme of Opportunities for Women.

Wainwright, M. (1992) 'Methodists embrace concept of God without sexual bias', *Guardian*, 30 June.

Wapshott, N. and Brock, G. (1983) *Thatcher*, London: Futura.

Waterhouse, K. (1981) *Daily Mirror Style*, London: Mirror.

Weiner, E.S.C. (1983) *The Oxford Miniguide to English Usage*, Oxford: OUP.

West, C. (1984) 'When the doctor is a "lady"', *Symbolic Interaction* 7.1, pp. 87–106.

Whitehorn, K. (1994) 'In other words, keep up to date', *Observer*, 7 August.

Winn, D. (1992) 'Does your voice let you down?', *She*, May, pp. 70–3.

Withers, J. (1975) 'Don't talk while I'm interrupting', *Ms*, March, pp. 106–9.

Wittgenstein, L. (1953) *Philosophical Investigations*, trans. and ed. G.E.M. Anscombe, Oxford: Blackwell.

Wolpe, J. (1973) *The Practice of Behavior Therapy* (2nd edn), New York: Pergamon Press.

Wood, L. (1988) 'Self-help buying trends', *Publishers Weekly*, 14 October, p. 33.

Woods, N. (1989) 'Talking shop: sex and status as determinants of floor-apportionment in a work setting', in *Women in their Speech Communities*, ed. J. Coates and D. Cameron, London: Longman.

Yaguello, M. (1991) *Lunatic Lovers of Language* [*Les fous du langage*], trans. C. Slater, Cranbury, NJ: Fairleigh Dickinson University Press.

Zimmerman, D. and West, C. (1975) 'Sex roles, interruptions and silences in conversation', in *Language and Sex: Difference and Dominance*, ed. B. Thorne and N. Henley, Rowley, MA: Newbury House.

Name index

Subject index